NO EASY FIX

No Easy Fix

Global Responses to Internal Wars and Crimes against Humanity

PATRICIA MARCHAK

McGill-Queen's University Press

Montreal & Kingston · London · Ithaca

© McGill-Queen's University Press 2008
ISBN 978-0-7735-3368-4

Legal deposit second quarter 2008
Bibliothèque nationale du Québec

Printed in Canada on acid-free paper that is 100% ancient forest free
(100% post-consumer recycled), processed chlorine free.

This book has been published with the help of a grant from the Canadian
Federation for the Humanities and Social Sciences, through the Aid to
Scholarly Publications Programme, using funds provided by the Social
Sciences and Humanities Research Council of Canada.

McGill-Queen's University Press acknowledges the support of the Canada
Council for the Arts for our publishing program. We also acknowledge the
financial support of the Government of Canada through the Book Publishing
Industry Development Program (BPIDP) for our publishing activities.

Library and Archives Canada Cataloguing in Publication

Marchak, M. Patricia, 1936–
    No easy fix: global responses to internal wars and crimes against
    humanity / Patricia Marchak.

    Includes bibliographical references and index.
    ISBN 978-0-7735-3368-4

    1. Humanitarian intervention. 2. Civil war. 3. Crimes against humanity.
    4. Humanitarian intervention – Case studies. 5. Civil war – Case studies.
    6. Crimes against humanity – Case studies. I. Title.

    KZ6368.M355 2008   341.5'84   C2007-906358-6

This book was typeset by Interscript in 10.5/13 Baskerville.

Contents

Contents

Maps and Photographs

Acronyms

AI	Amnesty International
AR	African Rights
ASEAN	Association of Southeast Asian Nations
ASF	Avocats sans Frontières
BiH	Bosnia and Hercegovina
CCHR	Cambodian Centre for Human Rights
CPP	Cambodian People's Party
CPP/SOC	Cambodian People's Party/State of Cambodia
DCC	Documentation Centre of Cambodia
DOS	Democratic Opposition of Serbia
DK	Democratic Kampuchea
DRC	Democratic Republic of the Congo
DS	Democratic Serbia
DSS	Democratic Party of Serbia
EC	European Community
ECCC	Extraordinary Chambers in the Courts of Cambodia
EU	European Union
FAR	Forces Armées Rwandaises
FBiH	Federation of Bosnia and Hercogovina
FRY	Federal Republic of Yugoslavia
FUNCINPEC	Front Uni National pour un Cambodge Indépendant, Neutre, Pacifique et Coopératif
GII	Global Intervention Institute
HRW	Human Rights Watch
ICC	International Criminal Court
ICG	International Crisis Group
ICISS	International Commission on in International Intervention and State Sovereignty

ICJ	International Court of Justice (World Court)
ICRC	International Committee of the Red Cross
ICTR	International Criminal Tribunal for Rwanda
ICTY	International Criminal Tribunal for Yugoslavia
IDP	internally displaced person
IMF	International Monetory Fund
ISG	Institute for the Study of Genocide
JNA	Jugoslovenska Narodna Armija
KLA	Kosovo Liberation Army
KR	Khmer Rouge
LICADHO	Cambodian League for the Promotion and Defence of Human Rights
LIPRODHOR	Ligue Rwandaise pour la promotion et la défense des droits de l'homme
MSF	Médecins sans Frontières
MDR	Mouvement Démocratique Républicain
NAFTA	North American Free Trade Association
NATO	North Atlantic Treaty Organization
NGO	non-governmental organization
OHR	Office of the High Representative
OPEC	Organization of the Petroleum Exporting Countries
OSCE	Organization for Security and Cooperation in Europe
PDK	Party of Democratic Kampuchea
PDR-Ubyanja	Party for Democratic Renewal-Ubyanja (Rwanda)
PKO	Peacekeeping Operation
PRK	People's Republic of Kampuchea
PRPK	People's Revolutionary Party of Kampuchea
PRK/SOC	People's Republic of Kampuchea/State of Cambodia
RPA	Rwandan Patriotic Army
RPF	Rwandan Patriotic Front
RS	Republika Srpska
RSK	Republika Srpska Krajina
SAO	Srpska autonomna oblast
SDF	Social Democratic Forum (Serbia)
SDP	Serbian Democratic Party
SFOR	Stabilization Force (former Yugoslavia)
UN	United Nations
UNAMIR	United Nations Assistance Mission for Rwanda
UNESCO	United Nations Educational, Scientific and Cultural Organization

UNDP	United Nations Development Program
UNHCR	United Nations High Commissioner for Refugees
UNICEF	United Nations International Children's Emergency Fund
UNCRO	Unconfidence Restoration Operation in Croatia
UNMBiH	United Nations Mission in Bosnia and Hercegovina
UNPA	Unprotected Area
UNPROFOR	United Nations Protection Force
UNTAC	United Nations Transitional Authority in Cambodia
US	United States
USSR	Union of Soviet Socialist Republics
WB	World Bank
WCC	War Crimes Chamber (Bosnia)

Notes on Spelling

"Hercegovina" and "Herzegovina" are simply alternative spellings. Both spellings are used inside the country as well as by outsiders. I tossed a coin and chose the "c" spelling – no political symbolism intended. Where others who are quoted or where maps use the "z" form, their original spelling is preserved. The country is called Bosnia and Hercegovina, sometimes just Bosnia, other times BiH.

The current term for the Muslim population of Bosnia is "Bosniak." Inhabitants of Bosnia, whether Bosniaks, Serbs, Croats, Jews, or others, are all Bosnians; however, since the war, they are often distinguished from their former compatriots in Serbia and Croatia as "Bosnian Serbs" or "Bosnian Croats."

The Croatian Nazi Party is generally spelled in English as "Ustashe." That is the spelling throughout this text.

All placenames in Cambodia and Rwanda are given in English translation.

The terms "Tutsi" and "Tutsis," "Hutu" and "Hutus" are all used as plural designations of Rwandan populations in the standard literature, and I have followed this usage here.

Acknowledgments

This research was funded in part by the Social Science and Humanities Research Council of Canada.

I wish to thank the following individuals for lengthy interviews and for permission to quote them by name:
Cambodia: Dr Youk Chhang; Dr Helen Jarvis; Dr Kek Galabru
Rwanda: Professor Simon Gasiberege;
Bosnia: General Jovan Divjak; Dr Amor Masović; and Dr Zilka Vejzagić.
I also wish to thank many others in these locations and in Serbia and Croatia for interviews and other contributions to this research. They are not quoted by name, but I learned much from them.

Interviews were conducted with representatives of numerous organizations. Speakers are not identified in the text, but I wish to thank them and the organizations for their time and thoughtful comments, and for the work they have put into research contributions and publications. In particular, I am grateful to African Rights, Amnesty International, the Documentation Center of Cambodia, Human Rights Watch, the Organization for Security and Cooperation in Europe, the United Nations Development Program, and the World Bank. Beyond these, I am indebted to national organizations concerned with human and legal rights, government policies on a wide range of issues, women's organizations (particularly in Rwanda), and local newspapers and periodicals.

I wish to acknowledge the following sources for quotations used in this book:
Jaime Malamud-Goti, "Transitional Governments in the Breach: Why Punish State Criminals?" *Human Rights Quarterly* 12, 1 (1990):

1–16. Reprinted with permission of the Johns Hopkins University Press.

Frederick H. Fleitz, Jr., *Peacekeeping Fiascoes of the 1990s* (Greenwood Westport, CT: Greenwood Publishing Group, 2002). Reproduced with permission of Greenwood Westport.

Elizabeth M. Cousens and Charles K. Cater, *Toward Peace in Bosnia: Implementing the Dayton Accords* (Boulder, CO: Lynne Reiner and International Peace Academy, 2001). Reproduced with permission of Lynne Reiner and International Peace Academy.

Other quotations did not require specific permission, but I thank the publishers for allowing me to cite them. They are appropriately referenced.

Map 4.1, drawn by *Brian Ally*, is based on original by Kenneth Cramer of Canby Publications, Cambodia.

Map 4.2 was prepared by Taylor Owen and originally published in "Bombs over Cambodia" with Ben Kiernan, in *The Walrus*, October 2006, 62–9, with Owen's permission.

Map 6.1, drawn by Brian Ally, is based on web reproduction by the University of Texas Libraries.

Map 8.1 is reproduced from Tim Judah, *The Serbs*, 2nd ed., Yale University Press, 2000, with permission of the publisher.

Map 9.1 was prepared by Brian Ally.

The text was examined in detail by the copy-editor assigned by McGill-Queen's University Press, Dr Joanne Richardson, whose conscientious attention is appreciated.

Coordinating editor Joan McGilvray has given steady support and I thank her most sincerely.

Finally, I wish to express my deep appreciation to my husband, William, for his many kindnesses and patience while I wrote this book.

Preface

I walked along Sisowath Quay in Phnom Penh, tentative because there were so many legless beggars there whose accidental meeting with landmines is all too common a fate, and also because there were many undernourished children and my meagre purse could not satisfy their needs. I did not fear for my own safety: Phnom Penh is not a violent city for outsiders. I have travelled it on the back of a motorcycle and vehicles I cannot describe – all called taxis – so that even at night and alone I did not fear the walk along the riverside road. I find myself caring a great deal about Cambodia and other global pieces like this, small fragments caught up in global conditions over which most people have so little control. Treated like flotsam on the Tonle Sap, they did not deserve their fate, and I keep hoping that somehow, some way, the international community – however we imagine that entity – can reduce the pain. But I am not convinced that a hybrid trial with a mixture of Cambodian and international judges trying five old men who once ruled the Khmer Rouge is the best way. I'm willing to be proven wrong.

My objective in this research was to consider how the international community – a phrase that obscures as much as it reveals – is involved in the affairs of countries that experience serious crimes within the borders of a single state. These crimes include genocide, crimes against humanity, and war crimes. I have already written about some of these societies, but my questions in earlier works were about the immediate preconditions to the mass murders that are characteristic of these crimes. This elicited a concern for what happens to them after the battles. Initially, my interest was in how these societies coped with violent histories and began their reconstruction. But with time I became equally concerned with how their situations were affected by outsiders before, during, and after the violent period.

I chose to focus on three societies – Cambodia, Rwanda, and two parts of the former Yugoslavia, Bosnia and Hercegovina, and Serbia and Montenegro – that have recently experienced what are now called "serious crimes." The questions were about interventions, internal accommodation of former enemies, and approaches to accountability, justice, and reconciliation. The three societies differ in many ways, but the most pertinent to this examination is their differing situations following their respective violent periods. In Cambodia, many people are implicated in the crimes of the Khmer Rouge, so a trial restricted to five elderly surviving leaders will not provide adequate information or explanation for the enormous crimes of their many accomplices. In Rwanda, there is an unambiguous victor, and this victor is determined to make the losers fully accountable for the genocide. In the phase of the wars in Yugoslavia that were fought on Bosnian territory there were no victors, all were losers, ultimately even the interveners whose good intentions were lost amidst the horrors of Srebrenica. Outsiders took over the task of trying to achieve a just conclusion.

While I was writing the earlier book (Marchak 2003), an international commission was appointed by the Canadian prime minister of the time, Jean Chrétien, to consider the appropriate responses by the outside world when societies descend into that particular form of hell. The International Commission on Intervention and State Sovereignty submitted its report, *The Responsibility to Protect*, in 2001. Its primary recommendation was that the world has a "responsibility to protect" people at risk. In particular, it said that "state sovereignty implies responsibility, and the primary responsibility for the protection of its people." It declared that "where a population is suffering serious harm, as a result of internal war, insurgency, repression or state failure, and the state in question is unwilling or unable to halt or avert it, the principle of non-intervention yields to the international responsibility to protect." The recommendations were later adopted by the United Nations.

These were noble sentiments, and I, along with many others, hoped that this was the beginning of a new phase in international relations. At last, we thought, state sovereignty will no longer be permitted to shield state-sponsored terrorism and murder. By then, as well, the International Criminal Court (ICC) was finally established. It would gradually take over from the two earlier Tribunals – the International Criminal Tribunal for Yugoslavia (ICTY) and the International Criminal Tribunal for Rwanda (ICTR). International criminal law would finally be a vital source of deterrence, justice, truth, and reconciliation for all of the world's populations. These two thrusts, then, humanitarian intervention and the establishment of international criminal courts, promised beneficial changes for how humanity would respond to serious crimes in its component states.

No Easy Fix under a more benign title grew out of that optimism, but by the time I had completed it I had become much more skeptical of the possibilities for humanitarian intervention and for the capacities of courts (international or national) to elicit truth and to bring about reconciliation. Justice, at least of the variety the Western world has adopted, may be served, and that is no small achievement, but the notion that the courts would enable people to eschew violence in their relationships within states was probably naïve.

Notions of humanitarian intervention were not widespread in the 1970s, while Cambodia endured a civil war and then the rule of the Khmer Rouge. Though the United Nations was well established, its operations were strongly linked to the Cold War concerns of its members and, more generally, to interstate rather than intrastate wars. Peacekeeping missions were established within that context. Cambodia's internal repression was not a priority for international action.

After Vietnam invaded Cambodia and established a government under its tutelage, other powers became concerned because Vietnam at that time was closely linked with the USSR. The decision within the UN to allow the Khmer Rouge to retain Cambodia's seat came about by virtue of a temporary confluence of interests between China, Thailand, and the United States. Later, with the removal of USSR interests in the region, the UN finally intervened by setting up the Paris Peace Talks to end the fighting and to establish democratic elections. This intervention did not succeed in fully ending the war, though the UN did introduce and oversee elections. But the formal actions of the UN were not the more important external influences on Cambodia. The history of French colonialism and of US bombing preceded the Khmer Rouge period, and the Vietnamese invasion influenced politics and government long after Vietnam withdrew.

Cambodia as it exists today is a tragic society, showing all the signs of widespread trauma, continuing rural poverty, failure to establish a working economy, and corruption in every pore. It is within this context of external forces and internal war that we deliberate on whether a hybrid court is the most appropriate way of helping Cambodians today, thirty years after the beginning of the Khmer Rouge period. The court is supposed to be a mixture of Cambodian and international criminal law, yet the judiciary in Cambodia is still weak: most observers deem it to be corrupt as well.

In Rwanda, Belgian colonialism had a deep impact on its people's versions of who they were – versions that carried over to the genocide of 1994. Just before that slaughter, a small contingent of soldiers under UN auspices was sent there to engage in peacekeeping. These people were not equipped to intervene militarily, and the UN, the US, Canada, and others chose not to intervene with more troops or other military force. The soldiers who stayed in Rwanda during that horrific attack on resident Tutsis and moderate Hutus witnessed the slaughter but were unable to stop it. Towards the conclusion of the massacre, with an invading army poised to take over the capital, France suddenly decided to send a 2,500–strong well-equipped force, ostensibly for humanitarian reasons. Humanitarian relief may have been its impetus, but the problem was that the force was not neutral in its attitude towards the two protagonists. The rest of the world belatedly became active following the genocide by providing aid and establishing the ICTR.

Intervention in Yugoslavia's internal wars took many forms. Initially, it consisted of trying to prevent arms reaching Croatia and Bosnia, unintentionally leaving Serbia fully armed. Various commissions were established to try to sort out the issues and create a ceasefire arrangement: they failed. UN interventions helped to feed the cut-off population of Sarajevo and keep the airport open, but other UN actions, including the establishment of "safe zones" that it couldn't sustain, were catastrophic. Srebrenica was one of these. That war was finally ended by NATO bombing and forced negotiations between the leaders of former republics under US auspices. Interventions in the Balkans continue in the first decade of the twenty-first century, including the ICTY and, more recently, the International Court of Justice (ICJ, often called the World Court).

NOTE ON RESEARCH

I conducted field research in Cambodia, Rwanda, Bosnia, and Serbia between 2000 and 2006. Many of these interviews had to be confidential to ensure the privacy of interviewees. There are still dangers for many people in speaking frankly, so identities of interviewees are provided here only if they have given explicit permission. The field research was intended to provide information on the perspectives of different groups in each society. The more general research depended on books and articles authored by others, documents, and publicly available news services reports. These are extensively referenced in case readers wish to go further with the inquiry.

Doing field research in broken societies is challenging. Much of the infrastructure one takes for granted elsewhere is sparse or nonexistent – including, for example, accurate maps, telephone books, organized associations, and standard and fully operational public and private institutions. Mass questionnaires, as are used in public opinion research, are often not possible or, if conducted, are flawed either because one can't identify the potential universe from which to sample or people simply are not accessible by house-visits or telephones. However, where they have been conducted by credible institutions or survey firms, I cite them.

There are always particular issues, such as: who controls military force? Are there valuable resources on or under the land that continue to attract competing exploiters? Has organized crime infiltrated business and government? How brutal was the war? Is there a rural-urban division? Is the sex ratio following the war unbalanced so that there are many more women than men, and were women frequently raped during the war? How many orphans are left without care? Some of these questions are addressed in data on governance, political stability, corruption, rule of law, accountability, and other indices published by the World Bank and other centres, institutes, and associations. Human rights organizations also provide data on these societies.

ORGANIZATION OF THIS BOOK

In light of these interventions, humanitarian and otherwise, and the development of international criminal courts, *No Easy Fix* expanded beyond its original focus on how afflicted societies cope with their violent histories.

Part 1 is an introduction to the issues, and it consists of three chapters: chapter 1 offers an overview of general issues; chapter 2 offers a discussion of the notion of state sovereignty, peacekeeping, the role of the United Nations, and interventions in recent history; and chapter 3 offers a discussion of the growth of international criminal law and courts. These provide a basis for the chapters to follow.

Part 2 consists of chapters on Cambodia, Rwanda, and the former Yugoslavia, the latter in the new forms of Bosnia and Serbia, with emphasis on interventions and how these societies are dealing with persons accused of participating in the serious crimes of their immediate past. Beginning with Cambodia, chapter 4 discusses the global context of the Khmer Rouge period and the UN Peace Conference. Chapter 5 considers Cambodian society from 1993 to 2006. The next two chapters are about Rwanda. Chapter 6 focuses on the links between Belgian colonial practices and the 1994 massacre and includes a section on the UN and French interventions. In chapter 7, I concentrate on the massive attention to accountability and the three levels of justice in Rwanda. UN, European, and American interventions in the 1992–95 crisis in Bosnia are the subject of a lengthy chapter 8. Chapter 9 offers a brief description of contemporary Bosnia, and chapter 10 offers a similar description of contemporary Serbia. I chose not to add another chapter on Croatia because it would not have added further understanding to what occurred in the former Yugoslavia or to the development of international criminal justice.

Part 3, consisting of two chapters, returns to the themes of humanitarian intervention and the issues related to international and domestic courts. In the first and last sections of the book, the examples include discussion of the three societies examined in the central section but range beyond them to other societies where similar issues emerge. Although criminal courts are important to my discussion, I propose to approach these and other issues from a sociological rather than a legal perspective.

END DATE

The research was supposed to stop in 2006, but the proposed trials in Cambodia and an important trial at the ICJ were too interesting to leave alone. I stop at last in April 2007. At this moment it is still uncertain that court cases will go ahead in Cambodia.

FOR WHOM THIS IS WRITTEN

I hope that the book, written in a straightforward style and provided with sub-headings throughout every chapter, will be of use to senior undergraduate and graduate students in International Relations, Political Science, Sociology, Human Geography, History, and Law, as well as to their teachers and a more general reading public interested in these global issues. The book should be of particular interest to those who are studying or working in the fields of human rights, international criminal law, conflict management, or development. Other students in such areas as Asian Studies, African Studies, and European Studies may be interested in the chapters on Cambodia, Rwanda, and the former Yugoslavia. However, these are not intended as new information on these societies but rather as case studies that raise relevant issues regarding the relevant influence of outsiders and the capacities of insiders to establish new societies on the broken pieces of old ones.

The missed journalistic and academic style of the text, with the author occasionally writing in the first person, is intended to convey the understanding the author is not here acting as the all-knowing expert but is instead inviting readers to share in a discussion of these issues.

PART ONE

Global Context for Broken Societies

Cambodia Stilt-houses near Tonle Sap River

1

Introduction to the Issues

This book addresses three questions. First, should non-involved states mount humanitarian intervention in other states' internal wars, acts of genocide, and crimes against humanity? Second, when the warring parties or the aggressors have stopped fighting, what conditions influence how the society deals with its past? Third, are international criminal courts the most efficacious ways of dealing with perpetrators of heinous crimes?

Although throughout this book many societies are briefly discussed, the focus is on Cambodia, Rwanda, and the former Yugoslavia in its present state forms of Bosnia and Hercegovina, and Serbia and Montenegro. In Cambodia, the estimated death toll from the Khmer Rouge period (forty-four months between 1975 and 1979) was between 1.8 million and 2.5 million persons. In Rwanda, the estimated death toll in a four-month period in 1994 was about 800,000; in Bosnia, one of the theatres of the Yugoslav civil war between 1992 and 1995, the estimated death toll was 100,000, with 1.8 million displaced persons.[1] I do not deal in depth with the wars in Croatia or Kosovo during and following the break-up of Yugoslavia because, though both were replete with human rights crimes, further detail was unnecessary for dealing with the issues of concern in this book.

In each case these societies had a prior history of muffled conflict, but the episodes of extreme violence dealt with here broke out at specific times: they were not merely incidents in a much larger struggle. No warlords were involved in the sense that they were in Afghanistan, Somalia, and the Democratic Republic of the Congo. The societies resided in recognized territories with borders; the populations were not nomadic, and there were no complicated land conflicts between pastoralists and subsistence farmers as in Sudan and Ethiopia. Prior to the wars, the international community recognized these countries as states. They were on three different continents, thus their problems were not due to particular conditions in one region. None of them was blessed or cursed with oil or other extremely valuable resources, thus their wars were of less pecuniary interest to external powers than were those in the Middle East, Sudan, or Nigeria.

These three countries are different in many respects, but there is one particular difference that is especially important for this study: how their respective populations identify the perpetrators and the victims of the crimes. In Cambodia, the perpetrators are identified as the Khmer Rouge, the victims as the rest of the population. This is problematic because the Khmer Rouge included a large number of people, some of whom are now in leadership positions throughout the country. Thus, the perpetrators were "us" as well as "them."

In Rwanda, Tutsis see the perpetrators as Hutu and, along with the international community, see the crucial events as a genocide with themselves as the victims. Hutu still in the country, many of them in jail, continue to argue that Tutsis also killed Hutus, and they see the events of 1994 as the final stages of a civil war. But Tutsis are in charge now, and their claim takes priority: the perpetrators were "them," a subordinate population.

The populations of Bosnia, Croatia, and Serbia are no longer members of the same political union. What started as an internal battle concluded with the breakup of Yugoslavia. In Bosnia, a society that included then and still includes all three ethnic groups, the population recognizes as aggressors not only Croatians and Serbs but also, and this is touchy, Bosnian Croats and Bosnian Serbs. Thus the perpetrators are both "them" and "us." In Croatia, the enemies are viewed as Serbs. Their version is the least complicated, though it does not explain for them their own armed interventions in Bosnia. In Serbia, the enemies are Croats, Muslims, and Slovenians who, in Serb understandings of the wars, destroyed Yugoslavia. Many people in Serbia regard themselves as the victims of the breakup of Yugoslavia. Others, Europeans and Americans, are also seen by many Serbs as part of the enemy camp.

These perceptions lead to different approaches to accountability and, because of that, to different notions of how the society might be recreated and what would be required to move towards reconciliation. When everyone is implicated in the crimes, who should be held accountable? And who can hold them accountable if the current leaders are among the complicit? That is the dilemma for Cambodians. By contrast, Rwanda is governed by victors who consider themselves innocent and morally superior to those whom they now govern. All Hutu are presumed guilty until proven innocent. In the former Yugoslavia, the principal agents of justice since the wars have been international courts because none of the new states could claim innocence, though all blamed others for their present unhappy situations.

When these societies erupted in violence, the international community – as it is called, and as I will call it for the time being – acted or failed to act according to its members' national interests. The only one of the three societies that elicited what might be termed "humanitarian intervention" during the battles was Yugoslavia. Intervention in Cambodia included a range of disastrous impacts involving France, Japan, and the United States prior to the emergence of the Khmer Rouge, Chinese mentoring and aid to the Khmer Rouge during their period of control, an invasion by Vietnam, and an unsuccessful UN peace initiative afterwards. Intervention in Rwanda consisted of arms sales and other commercial operations prior to the outbreak of violence, a small peacekeeping force that was not supported when it became clear that there was no peace to keep, and a strange French force sent as the war wound down, apparently to help one of the two contending groups.

After the wars, the international community established international criminal tribunals for Yugoslavia and Rwanda. These are scheduled to wind down by 2008, at which time internal war criminal courts will take over the prosecutions. The Rwandan government also established national courts and, later, neighbourhood courts known as "gacaca" to try the thousands of Hutu captured and jailed. In Rwanda everyone is involved, voluntarily or not, in a process of justice that consumes the country.

International criminal proceedings were not undertaken in Cambodia, despite prolonged and often acrimonious negotiations between the United Nations and Cambodian government teams over the course of two and a half decades. This fraught path is discussed further on. Finally, in 2007, negotiators announced that they would prosecute cases against five surviving leaders.

This book is concerned with issues attached to humanitarian intervention both at a general level and vis-à-vis these three extremely

different societies. Implied in the discussion is that a blanket statement about the moral necessity of intervention may speak well of
good intentions, but action may be ineffective if the differences between societies is not understood. This is discussed below. It is also
concerned with the role of the international community after the
wars. Are international criminal courts the most effective instruments
for ensuring accountability, deterring others from committing similar
acts, demonstrating justice, revealing truth, and providing the basis
for reconciliation? Indeed, is it possible for any method for bringing
criminals to account capable of performing such a wide range of benefits as is claimed for international criminal courts?

Finally, this book is concerned with how each society deals with its
situation following the wars. Can a society in which many people are
complicit in previous crimes succeed in moving ahead, putting the
past behind it? Can a society in which victors impose a superabun-
dance of accountability on the vanquished succeed in creating a new
society where victors and vanquished can coexist and move towards
reconciliation? Can new states born in battle with their neighbours
develop new institutions to enable peaceful relations between them?
These questions are asked in this almost "soap opera" fashion by way
of making it clear that reconstruction and reconciliation are not abstract terms. Outsiders may talk about aid, transitional justice, institution building, state building, and the like – there is a large vocabulary
shared by numerous international NGOs and states engaged in the reconstruction and development business – but what matters is whether
any of these prescriptive measures apply across the board to societies
as different from one another as these three.

INTERNATIONAL HUMANITARIAN INTERVENTION

In 2001, the International Commission on Intervention and State
Sovereignty recommended that, when states fail to protect their
people, the rest of the world has a responsibility to intervene and to
provide that protection. Commission members argued that the obligation of states to look after their own populations is what gave
them their legitimacy; thus, when they did not do this, they lost the
right to claim sovereignty. The commission laid out a number of
ways in which external powers could intervene short of military
force, but the threat of force still had to be in the wings and was to
be used if no diplomacy or other peaceful methods did the trick.

Through the UN and, on a couple of occasions, the North Atlantic Treaty Organization (NATO), the notion of international humanitarian intervention has had some currency over the last three to four decades. However, Cold War concerns were dominant until the 1990s, and the extent of humanitarian action was necessarily limited within those parameters. Peacekeeping was possible under certain circumstances, and the UN engaged in it. Since the disintegration of the USSR, the debate on the respective rights of sovereign nations and the international community has heated up, the commission recommendations being the culmination of humanitarian efforts. These recommendations were put before the UN General Assembly and approved, but no implementation motions accompanied them. No country volunteered to provide the troops to back up humanitarian intervention as a general principle. So UN intervention is still but a noble intention; if a particular event raises such ire that member states are prepared to provide the muscle, then the UN may intervene militarily in intrastate violence.

NATO has intervened on a few occasions, most particularly in the first Iraq war and in the Serb province of Kosovo. Whether either of these interventions had humanitarian origins is debatable. While the UN in such instances might be the respectable organization making the decision to send in military force, in fact it has no military capacity of its own. It must depend on member states and on the member states of NATO, or, alternatively, on the United States (because the US has more military capacity than any other, or combination of other, states).

The next chapter provides a history of intervention including those undertaken by NATO. It addresses the issues associated with humanitarian forms of intervention, and its current status vis-à-vis such troubling places as Sudan, Somalia, and the Democratic Republic of the Congo. A few of the issues are noted here by way of introduction.

Objectives of Humanitarian Intervention

First, would-be interveners have to ask themselves, what exactly is the objective? Is it to stop violence in the internal affairs of a country other than their own? If so, are they prepared to withdraw as soon as the contending parties have reached a peaceful modus vivendi? Or, even more problematic, are they prepared to stay if the contending parties are unable to coexist in peace? And if they stay, what are they prepared to do? Who will foot the bill?

Some interventions have been undertaken as attempts to impose democracy on undemocratic states. Then the question is, is it reasonable to try to recreate the world in our own image (whoever "we" are)? Will the goal be attained if the country in which we have intervened agrees to hold elections? What happens if elections are held yet the rule of law is nowhere in sight? What happens if all the organs of the state and society's institutions are corrupt to the core: will elections solve the problems? And suppose the population does not want to have a democratic outcome?

Among the difficulties facing would-be interveners is the problem of identifying which groups are predators and which groups are victims in civil wars. Had outsiders intervened in Cambodia during the 1970s, how would they have distinguished between Cambodians who were supporters of the Khmer Rouge and Cambodians who were not? Had they intervened in a much stronger way in Rwanda, how would they have known who were resident Tutsi and who were Hutu; moreover, how would they have known what the dynamics in that situation were while the genocide was happening? Even in European Yugoslavia the intervening Europeans and Americans were unable to distinguish between Serbs and Croats, Serbs and Muslims, let alone between Bosnian Serbs, Bosnian Croats, and Bosnian Muslims. Perhaps most critical is the difficulty of ensuring that interventions actually are humanitarian. States have intervened in the affairs of neighbours for all the years that states and their predecessor political formations have been in existence. They have not generally had to legitimate themselves in terms of humanitarian objectives. There is now much more pressure to do so, but that simply ratchets up the rhetoric. The US and allied intervention in Iraq, beginning in 2003, was called a humanitarian military action once it became clear that there were no weapons of mass destruction in that country. The intervention in Kosovo in 1999 was called a humanitarian exercise. Were either of these humanitarian in intent? Experts and ordinary observers will no doubt argue about these for many years, and perhaps historians will have the final say, but the point is that an invading power can almost always find a way of labelling what it is doing as humanitarian.

How many of our interventions over the past half century were designed to help other populations in contrast to helping ourselves secure our own or allied national interests? If we are serious about humanitarian interventions, how would we ensure that we eliminate the particular interests of potential intervening states before moving in? And, perhaps even more seriously, how would we ensure that we know what we're doing? As the example in Bosnia and Hercegovina will indicate, our noble intentions are sometimes encased in ignorance about the cultures, societies, and states in which we propose to intervene and are carried out by a global institution that itself is desperately in need of remediation.

United Nations and NATO

At the present time, and in the time of the societies upon which we focus here, the only organizations capable of putting together an international effort to provide humanitarian intervention are the UN and NATO. The UN has the moral power to organize a humanitarian intervention of disinterested parties, but it lacks the political will, the funding, and the military capacity to do much beyond peacekeeping: and the day of peacekeeping is largely past. Its deficiencies are caused by its deeply flawed organization and charter (see chapter 2). Briefly, it is hampered by an organization that gives a handful of countries veto power over decisions and a charter that guarantees the sovereignty of states. Further, it has no military capacity of its own and is thus absolutely dependent on individual funding by member states and/or has to rely on NATO forces to do its work. NATO is the only international organization with serious military power, but it is effectively run by one country, the United States, in the sense that, unless the US agrees with intervention, NATO will not be mobilized.

So if we – the international community – want to go beyond rhetoric to action, based on not-so-humble beliefs about our superiority, we are either going to have to reconstruct the UN or create a new organization devoted entirely to intervention. Such an organization would have to have an ensured military capacity so that it need not rely on votes by member states of the UN on a per-instance basis. It would have to employ, on a permanent or secondment basis (secondment might be preferable for all concerned), cultural specialists with language proficiency in regions in which wars are anticipated or in progress; science specialists who might find ways of enabling populations to subsist together where resources or land are scarce and populations are dense; and, alternatively (because both scarcity and richness of resource endowments can cause internal wars), investors and business specialists who can help people turn natural resources into investments rather than wage wars over their ownership.

Objections to Intervention

Some observers of internal wars in far-off countries, especially wars in countries unlike the comfortable West, might shrug and say, "Let them kill each other, why should we get involved?" The defect of that stance (besides its lack of compassion) is that such wars tend to spill over, produce refugees, and create such terrible conditions where they occur that both the warring country and its neighbours suffer not just for a little while but for generations. Rwanda's war contributed significantly to the destabilization of the entire African Great Lakes region. The Balkan wars had less devastating impacts throughout their region, though there was much fear of a widening of the conflict.

As well, most Western nations today are multicultural, and they have large diasporic extensions. These extended populations tend to pressure their politicians and businesses to become involved. At the commercial level, all this international activity is not unrelated to the process of increasing globalization. Small societies have very little bargaining power compared to their larger and richer neighbours, but they sometimes have resources, sometimes a skilled labour force, sometimes a little purchasing capacity, or simply a strategic geopolitical location. It is when they have nothing except poor rural people that they have most trouble getting the world to bother about their internal wars.

It is rare for other states to intervene on purely humanitarian grounds prior to the onset of the conditions that lead to crimes against humanity, even when informed observers know that the society is moving in that direction. They do not generally intervene when they see no national interest or international acclaim associated with committing troops or funds to save populations beyond their own borders. Abiding by the UN Charter, which forbids interference in the internal affairs of other states, state actors are often reluctant to move against a government, such as that in Sudan, that expressly demands respect for its sovereignty.

Non-Military Forms of Intervention

Less direct interventions include economic sanctions, cessation of armaments sales from legal sources, arms inspections (as in Iraq prior to 2003), and, occasionally, being ostracized from international sports (as happened to South Africa under apartheid). These are useful when the chief victim is an errant state (from the perspective of other states) but not when the real victims are innocent citizens – the very people the other states want to help.

THE AFTERMATH OF WARS

Within states, the external context interacts with internal events. Today, there are no societies that exist entirely outside the framework of the state system or the influence of dominant states and markets. Before its civil war, Cambodia was deeply influenced by French colonialism, regional anti-colonial wars, the Vietnam War, and American bombs; then came the advent of the Khmer Rouge. To explain what happened we must recognize the context and not treat the Khmer Rouge as an independent anomaly. Rwanda, also deeply influenced by its colonial history and, especially, by its immersion in Belgian colonial practices, cannot be understood without that context. Yugoslavia was influenced by generations that grew up under three different empires with their different religions; by the Second World War, which brought with it the Nazi Ustashe Party in Croatia and the conflict between two liberation movements; and by the Cold War, during which the country's geopolitical situation was crucial to its relations with both the USSR and the Western nations.

Recognizing the external context is necessary if we want to understand either the onset of an internal war or its aftermath. But it is never sufficient because each society has particular characteristics that influenced its entry onto the battlefield in the first place and that afterwards affect its capacity to move on. In our eagerness to solve the world's problems we have developed institutions to provide development aid and theories about how to help people get back on their feet. Some of us talk about "the transition to democracy" and "rebuilding the state" or "establishing social capital." These are all noble intentions, but the problems of postwar societies are numerous and not easily addressed by outsiders. There is no simple solution that fits all cases. Among the many hurdles is the fact that societies might adopt the trappings of democracy in order to obtain external funding but that these democracies might well lack substance.

Why They Went to War

Civil wars are not fought because people are bored with peace. Some are fought because of disputes over division of territory or resource wealth. In other instances, there are serious dysfunctions, inequalities, brutalities, or abuses that cause people to organize resistance to a government or other authorities. There are generally underlying reasons that may be apparent to perceptive outsiders but that, for insiders, are cloaked by prejudices and ideology. Overpopulation relative to the carrying capacity of the land, an example particularly apt for Rwanda, may, as in that instance, be transformed into ethnic hatreds. Societies with a healthy physical and social infrastructure are probably less prone to lapse into madness when they bump into adversities, but even those that appear to outsiders to be fairly buoyant – Yugoslavia in the 1970s, for example – might be seething with angers beneath the surface.

Though we cannot come up with a list of solutions for a society following an internal war, we can consider some of the variables that might influence its capacity to reconstruct itself. As suggested above, the most critical of these is citizens' perceptions regarding who the perpetrators were and who the victims, and what each did during the conflict. This is crucial for arriving at explanations of different attitudes towards accountability and reconciliation.

Other variables include the physical and social infrastructure and what is called human capital. They also include the rights and capacities of displaced persons to return and be accepted; remediation of the inequalities that characterized prewar society; general security; and the pervasiveness of corruption and organized crime at the end of the wars. Without suggesting a theoretical framework for the many variables likely to have an impact on these societies, in what follows I offer a brief discussion of some of them.

Institutional Infrastructure or Social Capital[2]

Such institutional sectors as hospitals and health clinics, schools and universities that provide services for all groups in the population, functioning (and not corrupt) police and armed forces, independent mass media, businesses and other units independent of governments, public events, and, overall, a nurtured sense of inclusion and belonging for all parts of the population appear to be crucial to revival. It is possible for these services and organizations to develop even without a democracy or rule of law; indeed, they might be the necessary platform upon which democracy is erected.

Among the variables is the presence/absence of human capital – individuals who have the necessary skills to get the social and physical institutions working. If survivors include few teachers, scarcely anyone knowledgeable about the law or medicine or able to manage a corner store; if neither government nor private enterprise has sufficient trained staff to begin the process of reconstruction – as was and in many ways still is the situation in Cambodia – then clearly that society is in a worse position than is one that is wounded but still able to recharge its institutional infrastructure. As well, when the society is extremely poor, the few who do have skills are the ones most likely to have opportunities to emigrate.

Another obvious component of a reviving society are physical structures within which people can make a living and work together. A modern state requires roads and/or railways, airstrips, vehicles for travelling by water (if that is important to the physical landscape), and public and private buildings whose purpose is to maintain economic and social activities. Following a civil war, many of these physical conditions are in disrepair or absolutely demolished, so the rejuvenation of the society may depend on repairs or new construction. Mined farm land or forests are physical impediments to reconstruction. Such mines are still maiming and killing people in Cambodia and Bosnia.

Inequality

Whatever the issues before the war, persistent inequality remains an issue after it. It is not so much poverty per se that is the problem as its distribution and the opportunities to alter it. When we consider Cambodia, we discover the same massive inequalities between the urban elite (many of whose members are returnees from elsewhere and still holding citizenship elsewhere) and the rural peasantry. There is more wealth than there was a decade ago, but its distribution is scarcely more equitable than it was before the civil war of the 1970s.

Infrastructure and distribution of goods and services are fairly obvious variables to any observer, and, of them all, one might say, "Yes, of course, but how to get there from here?" It is the getting from the end of wars to reconstruction that gives rise to such a proliferation of advisers and helpers. While trying to build the infrastructure and find ways of overcoming the inequality, anyone who contemplates these broken societies soon realizes that there are many other and complex variables that are less tractable and that may be much less easily addressed. Some of the variables are well recognized, such as the extent of trauma throughout the society. Others may be harder to understand, and it may be more difficult to determine what would be the appropriate stance with respect to them. But they matter, and they may even determine – certainly they influence – the chances of making genuine infrastructural changes.

Control of Military Force

Control of military force is one of the defining characteristics of states, but of course it has its downside: states with overwhelming military capacities are often the very institutions that either instigated the wars or were the object of revolutions. Still, if several groups have sufficient military or guerrilla force to challenge any other groups who seek the same power, the war will continue until one or all sides are exhausted or defeated. If there are external forces in play and they stop the fighting, the military war might be put on hold, but it will not be dissipated until a government gains unilateral control of the legitimate use of force. In the case of Cambodia, for example, the installation of a new government by the Vietnamese did not stop the fighting. The final skirmishes in northern regions under Khmer Rouge control continued for years after peace was more or less installed in the capital.

Armed conflict continued in some regions of Rwanda as well, but the incoming army (the Rwandan Patriotic Front) was capable of taking over government in the capital while continuing to engage in battles at the borders. The war moved into neighbouring countries (of which more in the chapter on Rwanda), but, unlike what happened in Cambodia, in Rwanda the continuing skirmishes did not threaten to destabilize the new government. In the former Yugoslavia, one of the republics had control of the main Yugoslavian armed forces, but other republics gained military capacities through various means (including the illegal arms market), and so the strongest power could not unilaterally impose its version of Yugoslavia on all groups within the territory by the concluding months of the war.

Land, Resources, and Property Rights

Greed for land is an age-old reason for wars between populations; greed for other resources, such as oil, valuable gems, timber, or heroin poppy farms, is also of long duration but, at any given time, is contingent on world markets for such goods. Where property rights are well established and supported by solid legal instruments the transfer of such resources is more likely to be controlled by investors and markets; where ownership is a slippery concept contingent on who occupies the land and its resources, wars become more common. Wars often redistribute property, and peace at their conclusion requires some agreement on who owns what.

Berdal and Malone (2000, 5) and a group of researchers and theorists who looked at the economic incentives behind civil wars came to the conclusion that "much of the violence with which bodies such as the UN have been concerned in the post-Cold War era has been driven not by a Clausewitzian logic of forwarding a set of political aims, but rather by powerful economic motives and agendas." They claim that, "Between 1993 and 1997, many Khmer Rouge commanders, Cambodian government officials, and Thai army officers were more concerned about enriching themselves through illegal logging activity and trading in gems than they were about bringing war to an end" (ibid.). For our quest here, it is the reluctance to bring the war to an end or to seriously engage in the creation of peace that matters. If there are more economic advantages to continuing with war, a peace imposed from the outside – or even one accepted by leaders on the inside – might not be welcomed and might not last.

In the former Bosnia, land ownership has been a major stumbling block to peace because Bosnian Serb forces took over nearly half of what had been a multi-ethnic republic, and wartime leaders of the neighbouring republics of Serbia and Croatia openly discussed carving up Bosnian territory between them. Further, under the concept of "ethnic cleansing," Bosnian Serb and Serb forces took over territory formerly belonging to individual Croats and Muslims in Bosnia, and using the same economic logic Croats took over Serb properties in Croatia. The peace at the end was imposed by external powers, but the resulting land distribution continues to be a barrier to resumption of collegial relationships between Serbs, Croats, and Muslims inside and outside Bosnia.

War as a Cover for Genocide

Economic motives aside, civil war provides a cover for activity that in peacetime would land people in jail. As this is being written, the Turkish government is yet again insisting that the 1915–16 assault on Armenians was not genocide. Between 800,000 and 1.5 million Armenians died, some (primarily young men) were shot, most others died from starvation during a forced trek. Turkey argues that the deaths were caused by civil strife, famine, and diseases during the First World War.[3] Another frequent explanation from Turks is that the Armenians were causing disruption by consorting with Europeans who wanted to carve up the Ottoman Empire, thus the so-called genocide was merely a defensive measure.[4] These arguments are about motives for genocide. Genocide, however, is defined not in terms of why perpetrators committed it but in terms of whether they could or should have known what would be the consequences for any portion of the population (the UN Convention on the Prevention and Punishment of Genocide is discussed in chapter 3). I have not found any non-Turk scholar who has agreed with the position of the Turks on this issue, even where they acknowledge that Turks had a legitimate grievance against Christian Armenians. This is one of the events in which war is used as a cover for genocide.

With respect to the countries I study here, similar rationales for war might be elicited. The Khmer Rouge were disinterested in governing a Western-style state, so taking over the state was not their primary objective except insofar as it was necessary to disarm and disband the state army. In Rwanda, Hutus acted in fear, and war was a lashing out process more than a strategy for winning a conflict. The wars in the former Yugoslavia had a lot to do with economic reasons, but they also provided the cover for attacks against other groups for which people had long held contempt that, hitherto, they had been unable to express. They also provided opportunities to do things that were unacceptable in civil society, such as engage in gang rape and torture. Paul Collier writes persuasively about greed as a prime motivator for civil wars, and David Keen argues that grievances and greed tend to interact (Collier 2000; Keen

2000). In our cases, the interaction thesis seems to fit, but it is important not to lose sight of the greed that often begins wars and undermines attempts to gain a peaceful resolution.

Organized Crime

Societies afflicted with state institutions that are weak, corrupt, and lacking the legitimacy provided by approval of the population are ripe for the influx of criminal activities. According to Williams and Picarelli (2005, 124) in their study of organized crime, "it is no coincidence that the era of the qualified state – in which more and more states are weak, fragmented, decaying, collapsing or imploding – is also the era of transnational organized crime, which is exploiting weaknesses in state structures as well as the new opportunities provided by globalization." The former Yugoslav states and Cambodia are among the host regions for organized crime. Organized crime, as its moniker suggests, involves people who are organized and systematically engaged in criminal acts for profit, but it may have two different objectives: one being simply to gain profit as an end in itself, with no ideological or political dimension; the other being to gain funds for political purposes.

Williams and Picarelli warn that there are numerous hybrid forms in which an organization might include both ideological and mercenary interests. This may be especially true where those in control of the state – the political elite more generally – are engaged in corruption and rent seeking. The corruption undermines state legitimacy and reduces resources being put to uses that enable the society to move ahead. Tom Naylor (1993, 23), in a study of guerrilla operations and black markets, argues that "any insurgency using the international black market to finance its activities inevitably forms mutually profitable and likely quite durable relations with international criminal groups."

Williams and Picarelli also note that governments use criminal activities to stay in power, and they single out as an example Serbia under Milošević. They argue that Milošević's Socialist Party of Serbia and the United Yugoslav Party of the Left (headed by Milošević's wife, Mirjana Marković) set up businesses and individuals who, between them, held a tight rein on power. Further, "Other key members of the ruling elites were able to exploit their official positions and benefit from Milošević's tendency to reward political supporters with government monopolies. In effect, key figures in the regime had taken over the business of organized crime – they were not only its beneficiaries but also its leaders and organizers" (Williams and Picarelli 2005, 133).

The legacy of what some observers call "the international mafia" has continued to influence the successor states. Corruption at every level of society in Bosnia-Hercegovina and Serbia impedes their capacities to move beyond their impoverished states. The international arms trade, the drug trade, trade in human captives for purposes of prostitution, and illicit exploitation and trade in resources of all kinds find niches in societies that have experienced wars. Often the trades began before and during the wars, sometimes even aided or used by international peacekeepers. As well, in wars of this kind, there are usually thugs, sometimes released convicts known to have violent tendencies, powerful local hitmen, or latter-day warlords who get their funding and their power through these illicit trades and who become important figures in nasty wars. Demagogues and dictators who lead their people into wars know how to use the Arkans and rabid radio voices of their world.

The General Framework Agreement for Peace in Bosnia and Hercegovina (the Dayton Agreement) added to the corruption in the former Yugoslavia. It created a governing structure so porous that criminal groups were able to move between Bosnia and Hercegovina, Republika Srpska, and Serbia without penalty. Though peacekeeping forces were being trained and put on patrol, they did not have the capacities to prevent criminal activity. In the view of Williams and Picarelli (2005, 135), "the introduction of peacekeeping forces as well as a large presence of the international donor community created a large market for commercial sex – and the trafficking of women through and to Bosnia has increased enormously since the end of hostilities." One consequence of these relationships is that those in control of state machinery have an incentive to reject changes that might threaten criminal activity. Specific and coordinated strategies would be required to reduce the influence of those engaged in it, and these would need the support of the international community through global policing, peace missions, law enforcement units, focused attacks on criminal gangs, and reform of the judiciary.

Brutality: Comparisons between Chile and Others

Civil wars are mean and brutal events, but some are more brutal than others, and it makes a great difference to what happens afterwards. The theoretical literature does not, in general, make these distinctions.

Take a war such as that in Chile from 1973 to 1989. It was nasty and prolonged, there were thugs, torturers, and tragic victims, but it differed in significant ways from the kind of wars that occurred in Cambodia, Rwanda, and Bosnia. The Chilean war was waged by a professional military force representing the state against not the whole of the population but that portion deemed by the military to be subversives. Occasional bystanders were killed, some people were shot because they happened to be in the wrong place at a critical moment or because their names were in the address books of suspected dissidents. But most of the targeted victims were chosen for political reasons: they were trade unionists, liberals or leftists, human rights advocates, writers, social workers, and members of the former government. True, General Pinochet created a paramilitary group that tortured and committed the more sickening deeds, but it had to report to him, and, eventually, he was obliged to get rid of it. The toll was about three thousand people in a population of some 12 million.

By contrast, in the first part of the civil war in Cambodia, an inept professional military force was defeated by a poorly trained and largely illiterate peasant army, and in the second part the peasant army shot, starved, or worked to death over 2 million civilians in a population of about 8 million. In Rwanda, a combined state army and teenage militia slaughtered 800,000 civilians, often hacking them to death with machetes. Some victims were imprisoned in the churches to which they had fled and were burned to death when the militia torched them. The common fate of women in the targeted population was rape, including gang rape. Neighbours killed their friends, and sometimes men killed their own wives and children. In the war zones of Yugoslavia from 1992 to 1995, the death toll was much lower, but the modus operandi was, again, slaughter of civilians, including rape, torture, arson, concentration camps, starvation, and bestiality. Again, as well, trained armies were flanked by armed gangs who performed many of the atrocities. In short, the Chilean case was politicide; the others, genocide or gross crimes against humanity.

Chileans were traumatized by the Pinochet regime, but within a decade of its conclusion they had rebuilt political parties, the institutions of the state were functioning reasonably well, schools and universities were in full operation, other institutions were alive and well, and the economy was flourishing. Although Cambodia, Rwanda, Bosnia, and Serbia are officially democratic, political conditions are not supportive of pluralist democracy, educational institutions are weak, non-state institutions (apart from foreign-funded NGOS) are sparse, and the economies are not healthy. Ordinary citizens are poor in material terms and often still suffering from trauma. I detail the problems in each of these societies in later chapters.

It seems reasonable to infer that some of the differences in recovery are related to differences in degree, extent, and origins of brutality. Important differences include whether the aggressors were state armies or neighbourhood thugs; whether one group was any more aggressive or brutal than the other or others; whether the brutality included torture and rape; whether the instruments of death were small arms or machetes and similar instruments; and whether the victims were targeted by virtue of ascribed variables such as religion, ethnicity, and nationality; by regional location along the rural-urban dimension; by political and ideological positions; or by random variables and sheer accident of location.

Refugee Reabsorption

Societies that have experienced civil wars typically lose an important part of their population, usually the most talented and best educated components because these can most readily obtain visas and immigration papers to other locations. As well, there are always refugees whose capacity to move to foreign countries is restricted but who end up in camps near borders or in nearby states, waiting for the opportunity to return to their homeland. These people have to be accommodated by whichever group has gained governing capacities after a war or they remain a serious obstacle to reconstruction. We see the problem in its starkest form in the successor states of the former Yugoslavia, where ethnic cleansing has left many refugees and emigrants unable to relocate in their former homes or neighbourhoods for fear of a renewal of ethnic tensions.

Death of Males and Rape of Females

Although civil wars may not be carried out between armies of men, and although civilians – women, children, the elderly, along with fighting-age men – are targeted, even so, more males than females are generally killed. Men kill males of the target group first, thereby ridding the target group of their strongest members and the ones best equipped for retaliation. As well, in patriarchal societies, they kill men to reduce the capacity of the group to reproduce; women are more often raped so that any offspring would be blood-related to the aggressors and so that the women would be disgraced, unable to mate again. The society that emerges from such frenzied killing has severe shortages of men and boys. Women, often still traumatized and suffering from rape, sometimes also caring for the unwanted offspring and the children of their dead kin and elderly relatives, are the survivors who must carry the load for their families. Where rape is prevalent so is AIDS: and this disease threatens to orphan the children.

Societies with such demographic imbalances and trauma are less able to sustain themselves than are societies with a fairly equal distribution by sex and age – a distribution that ensures sufficient numbers in the middle ranks to carry the workload and to create and maintain the institutions needed for general reconstruction. Intervention in order to enable female survivors to provide food and shelter while raising children and caring for the elderly may be essential. For the generation that went through the war, recovery may be impossible, but aid in rearing the next generation could result in the recreation of a viable society. If this line of reasoning is valid, then nurturing and education should be primary concerns for external funders and internal leaders. As well, female survivors in patriarchal societies need legal help to obtain property rights.

Continuing Ideological Rationales

Hating the "others" is, it seems, a universal problem. Whomever the others are, they are different from oneself even if they happen to be, as is usually the case, the next door neighbours. Demagogues use these emotions to whip up collective energies against any groups that are considered to be unlike our own. These hatreds become the cover for actions that are otherwise the outcome of sheer greed for land and resources or political and economic power. The question is, do the ideologies continue, perhaps covertly, after the battles are done? How long does it take to dissolve beliefs that have enabled their owners to build a history of inhumanity?

JUSTICE AND TRUTH

Theories and Realities

The process of obliging those who engaged in or directed criminal activities during civil wars is generally understood to be essential for the return of mental health and the beginning of social development. Knowing what happened to loved ones who "disappeared" is supposed to provide a certain degree of comfort, of closure. Catching and obliging the perpetrators of heinous crimes to account for themselves and pay for their crimes is supposed to give a sense of justice. When at last the full truth is known and justice meted out, the theory is that survivors should find it possible to accept the past and to move on with some hope for the future, perhaps even to become reconciled with those who supported leaders with criminal intent.

As well as enabling survivors and descendents to know what happened and to be comforted by judicial processes that oblige criminals to take responsibility for their actions, justice systems also have social advantages. At a most elemental level, catching and trying alleged criminals takes them out of action and removes their power to contaminate others. Another benefit is that judicial processes inform would-be criminals that they, too, could be caught and forced to pay the price. Yet further, they inform citizens that they have rights and that, if they choose to live according to the law, they will be protected. Of course, all of these benefits have to be understood as what we want to happen: reality, as usual, is less sweet.

Wars are not simple affairs in which the victors are always right and the losers wrong and evil. In internal wars there are aggressors, but it is not always clear, either while the war is in progress or afterwards, which groups are the primary aggressors and which the most frequent victims. Usually, every group has its feet in both camps. When the war is over, it is seldom so fully over that the primary aggressors (if they can be identified) are rendered impotent even if outsiders end the war by force. If they are a state army, they may still have a good deal of potential power to threaten the peace unless they get the amnesties and other conditions they want in return for cessation of hostilities. If they are several gangs, they are even less likely to be reined in by peace agreements, as was the case in the former Yugoslavia. Their leaders generally cannot force them to obey, and they may so infiltrate the society that their personal identities are hidden by like-minded citizens. Even more problematic are societies in which many people were involved in the horror show. This is the case in Cambodia. The past is too much with everyone, and people are afraid that either they will be discovered or that others who know who they are will reveal what was done under the duress and fear of those terrible years.

So it is that truth may be earnestly desired by some people and feared by others. The victorious Tutsis in Rwanda might anticipate benefits if the truth is revealed and widely disseminated. The Cambodian government and many leaders in the society, however, might fear too many revelations. Serbs have been deeply shocked by what two international courts have revealed about the activities of their kith and kin. Though many knew already, and those who wanted to know had no difficulty learning about the genocidal events, what happened was not discussed by most people, and state governments had no desire to publicly declare the truth. Bosnians are divided in their responses to revelations by international courts, their divergent ethnic roots having become more prominent during and since the war than they ever were before it.

Justice, however, does not always rest on truth, particularly when it is dispensed by adversarial courts. The task of lawyers is to present that version of truth that favours their clients, and so between the prosecution and the defence partial truths may be revealed, and the affected population may not learn the whole story from the courts. A modern court case, such as those undertaken by the International Criminal Tribunal for Yugoslavia (ICTY) and the International Criminal Tribunal for Rwanda (ICTR) involves the use of witnesses and documents. Witnesses inform the Court of what they believe they saw or heard, but people are influenced, consciously or otherwise, by what they believed before they saw or heard anything, by their relationship to the accused, and by the trial outcome they want. Documents, likewise, can be selective in their information. Further, either the prosecution or the defence might create restrictions on the use of certain documents or the calling of certain witnesses. In the review of the case of Bosnia and Hercegovina versus Serbia and Montenegro, heard in the International Court of Justice in 2007 (chapter 3), these limitations are evident.

Judging Collective Crimes

Among the problems that we have to deal with when considering the crimes of war and of genocide are the differences between individual and collective crimes and, thus, the differences between individual and collective responsibility. This is not straightforward.

The Western judicial system is undoubtedly a remarkable development in human history, with its focus on individual responsibility for the commission of crimes. However, when we examine the breakdown of societies, one of the features that appears is the commission of "collective crimes." Murder is a crime committed by one or a few individuals for personal purposes. Genocide, war crimes, and crimes against humanity, however, are collective crimes. Whether or not they are initiated as state crimes, they require organization, planning, a division of labour, and a shared ideology; and, in the initial stages, they are generally carried out by an army or a militia, though often aided and abetted by civilians who share their objectives. The targets are civilians who either have or are believed to have a different persuasion, religion, ethnic origin, or class membership. The purpose may be the eradication of a population, as in genocide; or the dispersal of a population with the intent of obtaining its property; or persecution of others who have the "wrong" ethnicity, religion, political ideology, or other group attributes. Power may be an end in itself, or the group members might share a view of utopia that obliges them to get rid of all those who are less pure than themselves. Terrorism, rape, mass killings, and bestiality are the deliberate means to this end, and they are not incidental to it. Indeed, sometimes they are the purpose, and war is merely the context. However these actions begin, as they proceed they become wars of armed people in groups against either other and similar groups or, more often, unarmed people.

When we observe group crimes in other societies it might be helpful to keep in mind the fact that Europeans engaged in such crimes during religious wars between Roman Catholics and Protestants during the sixteenth and seventeenth centuries. Europeans who settled South and North America and Australia and New Zealand killed native groups, and settlers in North, Central and South America enslaved Africans who arrived in vessels owned and outfitted for the slave trade by British companies. Collectivities were engaged in both of the European wars of the twentieth century, rallying to nationalist causes. The 1940s Holocaust in Nazi Germany is also very much a part of European history. That Europeans and some of their descendents on other continents are currently able to live with one another and non-Europeans may be (as supporters of the European Union argue) a testament to the human capacity to learn from experience. It may also be due to opportunities that came their way under changed economic and political conditions, but let us hope that learning is indeed part of the process.

Group Identification

Groups define themselves in a variety of ways. In relatively poor regions, clans, lineages, tribes, and ethnic groups are among the most common types of groups. Nationalism is a more recent phenomenon. When one is raised within the embrace of a group fundamental to the survival of one's family, there is little room for thinking about alternatives. It is not simply wilful meanness or the mindless following of leaders that explains why members of a cohesive group would take up arms against neighbours who are not also members. The brutality that goes with these wars is not surprising if the protagonists are convinced that their enemies have done them much harm or that their group is in danger of extinction if they fail to destroy the others. So it is that interveners who come in with nice theories of educating people not to demean others, of mutual tolerance and acceptance of pluralism, often meet up with blank stares. The behaviour they advocate is fine – if the opportunities for survival are as good as they are in the home countries of the interveners.

By way of example: what we note in the case of Rwanda is that, during the colonial period, Belgian teachers actively taught both Hutu and Tutsi populations to see one another as different ethnic groups. The minority group, the Tutsi, were told that they were superior, and they were educated, sent to external universities, and provided with civil service positions and relative wealth; the majority group, the Hutu, were told that they were inferior and good only for subsistence farming. Whether in fact there was any real racial difference between the two (and many ethnographers and historians dispute that), over time there certainly came to be a class divergence that festered in the hearts of the "inferior" Hutu. When population density exceeded land capacities and no alternatives to herding and farming were available – and when, coincidentally, the Belgian yoke was removed so that the majority could establish its own agenda through the mechanisms of what was called democracy – the hostilities erupted. It took several decades of forced emigration of Tutsis, rebellions, and small rounds of force, but finally the anger erupted in the Hutu genocide of the remaining Tutsis and armed invasion by émigré Tutsis.

The Groupthink Thesis

By way of a very different example, but one that falls within European and offshoot cultures, researchers in social psychology have argued that very intelligent people in government, corporations, and other large organizations engage in what Irving L. Janis (1982) calls "Groupthink."[5] The groups included in Janis's original study were American foreign policy decision makers who agreed to launch the "Bay of Pigs" invasion of Cuba, the Korean War, and the escalation of the Vietnam War. Janis argues that, in each case, the decision makers had enough information to signal the probable disaster, but their collective understandings – one might call them group ideologies – did not allow them to acknowledge the signals and to reconsider the decisions. He identified the causes as highly cohesive groups, group isolation from outside experts, and strong leadership. He also identified eight symptoms of groupthink: (1) a sense of invulnerability that gives rise to optimism and risk-taking behaviour; (2) the discounting of warnings; (3) a belief in the group's moral goodness; (4) a stereotyped view of enemies; (5) pressure to conform; (6) a tendency to prevent the expression of deviant opinions within the group; (7) the illusion of unanimity; and (8) members who act as prefects to shield the group from internal dissent.

A later study involved the launching of the *Challenger* space shuttle, which exploded after liftoff in 1986. Diane Vaughan (1996) argues a case similar to those presented by Janis, while P. Hart (1994) provides a case study pertaining to the Iran-Contra scandal. The groupthink thesis is not without its critics: it is virtually impossible to test the argument in experimental settings, and any "live" discussion is subject to the writer's interpretation and to the information available to her/him at the time of the events.[6]

The groupthink thesis has been applied primarily to government and public agency decisions in the US. But much of what Janis was looking at is applicable to groups in very different settings, including those that mount vicious wars against their neighbours. These may not be led by people with great knowledge, like the decision makers at NASA, but they are led by people who, at the time and place, have what amounts to essential knowledge before deciding to engage in battle. Like their American counterparts, they were members of cohesive groups that were excessively optimistic about their potential success and were convinced that what they intended to do was moral. Pressure to conform was certainly present: accounts given by young people rounded up to become killers in Rwanda are documented. Deviance was out of the question, and deviant ideas or dissonant judgments were blocked. Leaders were persuasive.

Browning's Study of German Reservists, 1942

In an intensive study of members of a German reserve police battalion that had been obliged to round up and kill Jews in Poland in 1942, Christopher R. Browning observes that these ordinary working-class men from Hamburg, all too old for regular army service, were not rabid Nazis and that many did not even share minimal sentiments with Nazi leaders. Put in a situation in which they were required to kill, most of them did as they were told not because they were afraid of superior officers but because they didn't want to let down the other men in their group. They became progressively brutalized after their initial murders, but they did not act "out of frenzy, bitterness, and frustration but with calculation" (Browning 1998, 161). The calculation was of a technical nature: how best to get the job done.

In Browning's estimation, between 10 percent and 20 percent of the men refused to comply with the orders to kill. In this particular setting, the officer in charge was himself averse to the orders. Those who refused were given other duties. No one was ever punished by superior officers for their dissent. Most of those who refused cited "sheer physical revulsion" rather than ethical or political reasons. Browning concludes that the explanation for conformity had more to do with peer pressure than with authority, but he has no explanation for the few who refused to conform.

Decline of Social Movement: Cambodia

In the Cambodian case, we see the whole movement falling apart towards the end, turning inward and killing its own cadres. We need more studies of this phenomenon, but it, like groupthink studies and social movements more generally, is not open to examination in laboratories. The Khmer Rouge movement displayed intense group solidarity and unquestioned belief in the morality of its mission during the early months of the revolution, but its gradual downfall has yet to be explained in theoretical terms (the history is well documented and discussed in the chapters on Cambodia). By contrast, the tenacity of groupthink among Serbs and Bosnian Serbs who were led by Slobodan Milošević, Radovan Karadžić, and Ratko Mladić, even after 1995, suggests that adversity is not automatically translated into cognitive changes.

Cognitive Dissonance Theories

In fact, there is another literature documenting the phenomenon of group-centred beliefs discounting contrary evidence. One famous study in the 1950s examines a group whose religious belief in a particular end date for human existence was contradicted by continued life; even with such a disconfirmation, the group was able to keep going for some time afterwards. The general argument for its continued hold on members was that they had invested so much in that belief system, they would have experienced painful cognitive dissonance by abandoning the faith (Festinger, Riecken, and Schachter 1956). There are qualifications to this generalization, particularly with regard to self-images and their relationship to beliefs. However, the basic idea still has currency in the social psychology literature.[7] The point here is that groups have an existence independent of individual members, though that existence is played out by them. Groups have enormous influence over how individual members behave, what they believe, what decisions they make, and how they deal with discordant events afterwards.

Relevance to Dispensation of Justice

This discussion of group actions is relevant not only to explaining why people kill and rape others during these violent episodes but also to how justice might be dispensed and to the process of reconciliation. The international tribunals have handled this carefully, stating in their judgments that the accused, "acting alone or with others," committed specific crimes. Each of the group members is put through the same process. If the Court determines that one of these was the ringleader, that individual might be given a stiffer sentence; if another is found to have been guilty more of stupidity than of a crime, he or she might receive a lesser penalty. The argument in favour of this approach is that, by individualizing group crimes, those who committed them are obliged to accept responsibility for their own actions and contributions to the group.

The defect of this approach is that it doesn't penetrate the nature of the groups. As I note in the chapters on Rwanda and Serbia, those who committed heinous crimes were often acting not only on orders from above or out of fear but also with absolute conviction that what they did was necessary and morally acceptable. They lived in communities that encouraged them and in cultures that provided them with impunity. These communities and cultures did not spring into being at the beginning of these episodes of violence. They were fully formed before that, and the killers or rapists were raised in the culture and cheered on by the community they represented. Court cases disable the criminals, but they do not seem to dissolve the communities or cultures. Indeed, the courts themselves become the "enemy" unfairly harming the community's children; and the culture may be reinforced by the penalties meted out to those children. These sentiments become impediments to reconciliation.

ALTERNATIVES TO WESTERN COURTS

Truth Commissions

The point of truth commissions, such as those mounted in Argentina after the military repression in 1984 and in Chile after the Pinochet period in 1991, is to document what happened, to whom it happened, when, how, and with what consequences. Truth commissions may determine who or which groups were the perpetrators, or even why the events occurred, but they are not legal instruments and are not designed to impose penalties on perpetrators (Argentina, Comisión Nacional sobre la Desaparición de Personas, 1985; Chile, La Comisión Nacional de Verdad y Reconciliación, 1991). The Argentine commission was staffed by human rights activists and was the basis for subsequent court cases. All cases were investigated and were published in the final report, *Nunca Más*, only when the commission had strong support for the claims of those who came forward. Proceedings were public and were televised. Thus people learned what had happened and who were the perpetrators. The Chilean commission was conducted by equal numbers of representatives of the political right and left, but it did not name perpetrators. Its objective was to achieve reconciliation. Both commissions operated in difficult circumstances, with the former military juntas waiting in the wings and threatening to return, so, in both cases, the respective society was vulnerable. However, in both cases the publication of the reports of these commissions considerably lessened tensions, and the armed forces gradually backed off.

South African Truth and Reconciliation Commission

In the South African Truth and Reconciliation Commission hearings, perpetrators were obliged to meet surviving victims and to acknowledge their crimes if they wanted immunity thereafter. They were not required to repent, but if their accounts turned out to be less than accurate they could still be sent to trial. The South African format is possibly inappropriate or even impossible elsewhere since apartheid was not a form of genocide, even if it was a form of cultural denigration and racism. Even when there were tragic murders, in general those in charge of the apartheid regime were not trying to eradicate black South Africans: it was in their own interests to keep them alive and in servitude. So it was a different cultural context than, say, that in which war crimes were committed during the breakup of Yugoslavia, genocide was committed in Rwanda, or the cultural revolutions took place in Cambodia and China. On the other hand apartheid is listed as a Crime Against Humanity, and that is no less serious a crime under international law than genocide.

While the South African model may not be appropriate for other societies, it had the merit of revealing the group nature of the crimes without shifting the responsibility off the shoulders of those who committed them. The apartheid system was, by implication, on trial when groups of people confessed that, between them, they had done things that caused the deaths of innocent people or that they had acted together to maim or silence informers; indeed, by implication, those who had done none of these deeds were even so shamed because they had accepted the benefits of cheap servants and a racist society.

Some of the perpetrators had acted in the genuine belief that what they did was acceptable not only under the law of the land but also under the moral law of the Dutch Reformed Church. The manner of bringing them to account has been much criticized by human rights groups because it allowed the guilty to go free – also because the format did not ensure that everybody's rights as defined in Western law were protected. But, unlike many other societies faced with tragic histories, guilt, and trauma, South Africa has been able to carry on without a civil war. The Truth and Reconciliation Commission provided an escape from war that still ensured the revelation of facts. (South Africa has yet to find a way to reduce the enormous economic inequalities between ethnic groups in consequence of its history, but that is a story for another telling.)

Acknowledging the collective nature of these crimes, we may want to rethink the zeal with which we commit criminals to Western legal chambers. The International Criminal Court, the ICTR, and the ICTY are appropriate locations for leaders who formed the intention to eradicate, murder, torture, rape or evict and displace a human population. If the objective is revenge, the international courts may be appropriate; however, if the objective is to reveal the truth and to enable the society to get on with reconciliation, truth commissions may be superior when it comes to dealing with the foot soldiers.

Lustration, Neighbourhood, and Gacaca Courts

Methods other than court cases or truth commissions have been tried elsewhere. Lustration was used in Eastern Europe after the breakdown of the USSR. This prevents collaborators and snitches in earlier regimes (as discovered in records and sometimes through public hearings) from holding jobs or other positions in the civil service, schools, hospitals, and universities. It is a punitive measure, much more concerned with blaming the generation that was complicit in the crimes than with finding a modus for reconciliation, but it has the merit of shaming people without going through lengthy court trials.[8]

Neighbourhood trials sponsored by people who claim to share a residential area were used for collaborators in Czechoslovakia and several other Eastern European countries after the Nazi period. They have the merit of getting the job done immediately and without legal niceties, but they provide an easy opening for revenge and petty personal vendettas. They may disintegrate into vigilante justice, as discussion in chapter 3 demonstrates.

The gacaca courts in Rwanda provide a more complex and formal process for neighbourhoods to deal with the culprits in their midst, and I describe them in chapter 7. A variation on such courts operates in northern British Columbia, Canada, where First Nations peoples have recreated an ancient form of justice, whereby elders determine the guilt of individuals and establish penalties, including ostracism for stipulated periods. When the time is past, and provided the individual expresses regrets and promises to reform, he or she is welcomed back and helped to become reintegrated into society. Similar judicial forms were used throughout Africa before colonial powers destroyed indigenous cultures. The common theme in these village and neighbourhood forms of justice is the notion that the perpetrator needs to take responsibility but also that the society has to be prepared to treat him or her as a member of the group after a period of isolation or ostracism. This is more problematic when the perpetrator is a group engaging in groupthink and gang action.

Apart from determining individual responsibility for crimes, there is a different approach altogether: to address the nature of the groups that commit them. In our own society we expect social workers and police to deal with gangs of thieves, juvenile gangs, or gangs engaged in more sinister operations, such as illicit trade in arms or dangerous drugs, or kidnapping or prostitution rings. Where these gangs cross borders, we have international police operations and sometimes armies to deal with them. We might deal with crimes against humanity more appropriately if we treated them, as we do gang rapes in peaceful society, as crimes committed by groups against representatives of other groups rather than as individual criminal acts. This need not efface the crimes of individuals but, rather, also connect them to groups, all of whose members share in the guilt. Another possibility is to treat such crimes as we treat corporate crimes, where an entire economic organization is implicated as well as its executive officers. The claims made against Talisman Energy in Sudan (see below) are indicative of such possibilities, though a law to sue companies for indirect support for genocide in the form of resource rents is not (and may never be) established.

THE GLOBAL CONTEXT

Large global actors organize the world around their own interests. The little pieces are rarely important to the project, but they do have to conform to the global rules that surround them. Those rules have become more numerous over the past half century. As economies became more closely intertwined, international laws, including criminal law, expanded to deal with international relations.

Decline in Number of Interstate Wars

Since 1945, interstate wars have diminished in both frequency and the number of deaths attributable to them. There are two chief reasons for the peace between the dominant states of the post-Second World War era: (1) direct hegemonic clashes between them were rendered unlikely by the development of nuclear weapons, and (2) since about the 1970s, territorial aggression has become less rewarding than high technology and human capital as a path to power. However, these considerations have less meaning for small pieces in the global mix – pieces that are not in the race for technological supremacy and that are, in a sense, stuck with rural agricultural conditions, where land remains the primary economic good.

Decline in Number of Civil Wars

On a broad canvas there is reason to believe that the global institutions are beneficial even though there are still wars and even though imperialism in new guises has not disappeared from our world. Internal wars are fewer, and, despite the viciousness of some of them, such as those in Cambodia, Rwanda, and Yugoslavia, they, too, have diminished in frequency. In the post-Cold War period, trends towards peaceful resolution of conflicts, fewer deaths directly attributable to wars, and substantial growth in the number of democratic states and in the rule of law have been documented (Gurr and Marshall 2005; Human Security Centre 2005), though two decades may not constitute a long enough period for judgment.

We should note that there are contrary views, and comparative statistics on violence and war deaths are notoriously poor and often not comparable. Even with that caveat, however, there are changes that should lead to greater peace. Old-style colonialism is now but a memory, so wars of liberation are no longer high on the agenda, and the termination of the Cold War means that proxy wars in Third World countries may be less likely to be supported by the big powers (subject, however, to the way Western countries deal with the perceived threat of Islamic powers). Vetoes by members of the United Nations Security Council are no longer automatic, though reform of the UN itself is still blocked by one interest group or another. The development of international law, courts, and global institutions has contributed considerably to a more peaceful world and to an emerging normative order that puts world peace at the centre of global affairs where it used to be on the periphery.

Armed aggression at this stage of history may be foregone in favour of investments by foreign countries or corporations. This may be benign, but examples suggest that, where there is contention over who controls the resource rents, investments may absolve the investors while providing fuel for war against resident populations. China's investment in oil extraction in southern Sudan and a pipeline to transport oil to a port on the Red Sea from which it can be shipped to China is an example. China is not one of the combatants in southern Sudan, but the war that has raged there for two decades involves internal groups, one in control of government, competing to obtain resource rents. Critics have labelled the war as genocidal; at the least, it includes war crimes.

A Canadian company, Talisman, also operated in Sudan while the war was in progress. From 1998 until 2003, Talisman Energy was a major participant in the Sudanese oil industry. NGOs and churches undertook public campaigns against Talisman for providing resource rents that enabled Sudanese officials to harm local populations. The Ontario Teachers' Pension Plan threatened to sell its shares if the company retained its holdings in Sudan. In the course of this conflict, a Christian church in Sudan attempted to sue Talisman in an American court for genocide. The case was eventually dropped but not before publicity had persuaded Talisman to withdraw from Sudan.[9]

Darfur: Desertification and Discoveries

The war against peasant farmers in the Darfur region of Sudan may be another example of external interests in resources being paramount, but the existence of oil has not been publicly proven. A militia, composed of herders (known as the Janjaweed, a term apparently meaning "bandits") who have long contended with local farmers for the land, has been encouraged (presumably paid) by the government to kill and disperse the population, and this does seem suspicious. However, there is another explanation as well: droughts have frequently gripped the region since the 1980s, and a 2007 UN report argues that desertification, land degradation, and population explosion are the chief underlying causes of the conflict. In July 2007, American researchers claimed that a vast underground lake the size of Lake Erie had been discovered in the region. If this claim is accurate then the discovery could turn out to be either a boon or a curse depending on how the government and its exterior supporters govern the new resource (Polgreen 2007).

Somalia

Land in Africa and, until now, the sparse resources in Cambodia, Bosnia, and Serbia have not attracted much external interest. This constitutes a reason for international indifference or, at best, action for the purpose of preventing escalation of the conflicts. However, non-economic kinds of external power interests and ideological concerns can sometimes come into play: US backing of Ethiopian troops in Somalia during late 2006 and early 2007 would be a case in point.

Somalia is an anarchic region run by a variety of warlords and child soldiers. It was given state status by colonial powers, but its population never accepted central rule by any one of its many ethnic groups, clans, and factions. For a brief four months at the end of 2006, the capital, Mogadishu, was controlled by a group calling itself the Union of Islamic Courts, which managed to maintain the peace there and further south. Neighbouring Ethiopia, with a Christian majority, was concerned that Islamism would spill over the border. The US administration supported an invasion of Ethiopian troops with both sea and air power to rout the Islamists whom it considered to be a terrorist threat.[10] The point is that external participation is generally contingent on there being, if not resources or geopolitical advantages to taking a position in an ongoing or recently concluded internal war, then an ideological rationale for doing so.

Oil in Gulf of Thailand

Late in 2006, news of potential oil reserves in the Gulf of Thailand sparked new interest in Cambodia. Chevron was reported to be planning to begin offshore drilling in the Gulf of Thailand in 2007, and several other companies were also involved. The World Bank says Cambodian reserves could contain as many as 2 billion barrels of oil and 10 trillion cubic feet of gas (Gentile 2006; also several web items on oil in the Gulf). This could change Cambodia's fate in either direction, oil being a notorious curse in some cases (such as Nigeria) and a great enabler in others (such as Norway). Either way, oil riches are in the future, and my study of Cambodia is about how it has been since the 1970s and as it is today.

A LONG VIEW OF HUMAN HISTORY

Taking a long and somewhat philosophical view of human history, we see physically strong groups killing off physically smaller or weaker groups whenever the resources or territory of the latter are wanted. Occasionally, the defensive groups have proved to be physically able to stop attackers. In both cases, command of current technologies and information has been crucial to forceful conclusions of wars, but sheer physical force has always been vital.

In contemporary terms, this same process occurs, for the moment within states rather than between them, but that is an artifact of the way human populations are organized. Intervention by a genuinely uninvolved world population in local wars is not "normal" in the sense of being frequent. If this is an accurate picture of human history, then we should assume that contemporary populations inherited their situations from those who "won" earlier wars. Thus, the contemporary concern with humanitarian intervention and aid, and with legal processes for dealing with perpetrators of wars, crimes against humanity, and genocide, is a truly remarkable and revolutionary development in human history. In what follows, I sometimes express skepticism and criticism of current attempts to save broken societies, but I hope it is clear throughout that I also admire our humane attempts to help them, whatever our motives or the outcomes. We are at the beginning of a world society, undoubtedly initiated by crass commercial, military, and nationalistic interests (paradoxical as that may be), but that is the nature of human development throughout its history: whether these crass interests shift into more humane developments is what matters.

2

"The Responsibility to Protect"

In 2005, the United Nations adopted a motion regarding the responsibility to protect innocent populations under siege (usually by their own governments). This was not a departure from earlier actions of the UN, though the declaration was clearly contrary to the UN Charter, which says that its component states cannot challenge the sovereignty of one another over their respective borders or control of internal populations. Even so, past UN history included numerous instances in which external states provided peacekeeping, then peace enforcement, and finally military force against states that, for various reasons, dominant UN members opposed. In any case, the motion on "responsibility to protect" did not threaten anyone: it included no promises of military support, and the conditions under which protection was to be offered were vague.

The motion on responsibility to protect was still in the future when the UN intervened after the slaughter in Cambodia. Observers and participants have contradictory views on whether the interests of the Khmer people took precedence over the global and national interests of the interveners. Even the final chapter, an international court, may be more to assuage outsider guilt than to genuinely help Khmer deal with their cruel history. Intervention in Rwanda was colonial in nature before the genocide and sparse during the genocide. A small UN peacekeeping contingent was sent there and then stranded without the capacity to intervene in an ongoing war. Intervention in the breakup of Yugoslavia was extensive, often haphazard, and the outcomes are debatable. In another theatre, Iraq, the Western nations intervened through the UN oil-for-food program, then NATO bombing, and later the US-led war. As the fog clears, all of these interventions are shown to have been disastrous for the bulk of the population and, in particular, for children.

At some point we – the elusive international community – may have to decide that our intervention is necessary and to impose force if we cannot otherwise end a civil war, war crimes, or crimes against humanity; but we should not assume that our interventions are blessed because we have good intentions. Humanitarian intervention may be an idea whose time has arrived, but it has arrived in the context of a failing state system, and the one organization that has the moral authority to address the problems lacks the military capacity and the political will to do so.

This chapter deals with the dilemmas faced by the international community in the last half of the twentieth century by offering a brief survey of interventions – including, especially, peace commissions. I pursue this subject further in the chapters dealing with Cambodia and the former Yugoslavia, but I begin now with a note on how states were constructed in the first place. I do this because interventions, by their nature, involve the concept of state boundaries and state sovereignty, and because interventions, for the most part, are conducted by states or combinations of states. I argue that state sovereignty has little credibility in view of history and that it has equally little value in terms of the global context of modern states; however, dispensing with this does not settle the question of how much responsibility the rest of the world has when the people of one state are under siege. Further, it does not provide prescriptions for which organization should undertake what kind of action. If intervention is to be undertaken only by the UN, then we know that some interventions – those that might be contrary to major power interests as defined by their governments, and often those that involve states whose geopolitical locations and resource endowments are marginal to world affairs as defined by those same governments – will not be undertaken. Other interventions – those that the major powers on the Security Council can agree to or that are in their common interests – are more likely to occur. If the UN is not the agency most responsible for these determinations, then who is? Coalitions of the willing are no more likely to provide world security, let alone strictly humanitarian intervention, than is the UN, and unilateral action will almost inevitably be driven by the national interests of whichever power initiates it.

In spite of its deficiencies and some well-known failures, the UN continues to provide vital services throughout the world. Some

107 countries contribute something to its operations. Some eighty-six thousand persons are either employed or serve as volunteers in UN-supervised peacekeeping operations, fifteen of which were in operation as of March 2006. It has provided peacekeeping forces to sixty countries since 1948 and has overseen elections in many other countries to the benefit of millions of people. Its sub-organizations have devoted themselves to the care of orphans and children otherwise lacking such essentials as food or education; women who have experienced violence, rape, or forced prostitution; and many others in need of the necessities of life in refugee camps or in war-torn regions. As well, it has provided the framework for the development of conventions concerned with global conditions such as the Law of the Sea, and its creation of the International Court of Justice and the International Criminal Court (discussed in chapter 3) are crucial to the dramatic changes in how states deal with conflicts. With insufficient funds and extremely ambiguous mandates, UN forces have frequently put their lives on the line to save embattled populations. Often those populations were under siege by their own state governments and armies, and thus, even without a mandate to protect the innocent, the UN has often done so. Further, it has done so when the states that make up its membership and that provide its resources and military forces regularly fail to meet their obligations, even when demanding of the organization that it meet their demands for action. This said, some of the actions I consider in this and following chapters indicate that the UN as it currently operates cannot meet the standards implied in "the responsibility to protect."

WARFARE AND STATES

Long before anyone thought about humanitarian intervention, modern states came about through warfare. Charles Tilly argues that these formations involved powerful groups establishing boundaries against other groups and that this included subjugating local inhabitants and, therefore, negotiating with them if either their people power or their allegiance were required to sustain these boundaries. The borders comprised the extent of land that the strongest groups of the territory could successfully defend over many hundreds of years. The objective was to control land and probably also to control local labour supplies. The complex historical processes led to divergent results, depending on the role of capital, the strength of military forces, and the interactions between contesting groups. Over the past five hundred years: "First, almost all of Europe has formed into national states with well-defined boundaries and mutual relations. Second, the European system has spread to virtually the entire world. Third, other states, acting in concert, have exerted a growing influence over the organization and territory of new states" (Tilly 1992, 181).

The new states were deliberately constructed by both colonial and indigenous groups. As Holloway and Stedman (2001, 169) argue:

The founding of the League of Nations, and then of the United Nations, ratified and rationalized the organization of all the earth's peoples into a single state system. Most of the existing states in the world came into being in the twentieth century, largely in three waves. The first wave followed the breakup of multinational empires at the end of World War I. The second resulted from the collapse of the European overseas empires in the years after World War II. And the third wave of new states emerged from the collapse of communist rule in Eastern Europe and the Soviet Union.

In the cases of colonies in Latin America, Asia, and Africa, and in the post-Soviet states of Eurasia, external coercion was often involved in the creation of states. Borders were delineated largely by officials of other states, who did not have to live with the new arrangements. The legacies of the European colonizers differed in significant respects, but several left behind states that had artificial boundaries, people with few skills and less education of a kind that would enable them to move forward in the global economy of the second half of the twentieth century, centralized state bureaucracies, and poorly developed economies. According to Holloway and Stedman (2001, 172):

The roots of Africa's violence lie principally with the political and economic conditions that existed after independence and the policies pursued by elites to gain and consolidate power ... Colonial governments neglected the cultivation of Africa's human capital; when independence came, few Africans were trained to step in and operate large state bureaucracies. Strategists of colonial control manipulated ethnic division and exacerbated group conflicts over political and economic resources.

The borders of Western European states and their white settler colonies are not in dispute today, though much else is contested inside those borders. Colonialism in its earlier form has disappeared, displaced now by global production chains. The implosion of the USSR left a large swath of territory in ambiguous circumstances. It was not simply a case of new states gaining independence from Russia; indeed, in some cases Russia encouraged formal independence, but these states remained closely tied to it through economic linkages. More problematic for some were wars over territories that had been autonomous republics within union republics. These had been prohibited from seeking independence under the USSR Constitution and were subject to its armed forces, but now the larger republics (or districts within which they dwelt) and adjacent republics fight over them. Such wars affected Armenia and Azerbaijan over the region of Nagorno-Karabakh, and Georgia over Abkhzia and South Ossetia. Chechnya was also an autonomous republic within the Russian Federation, and its vicious continuing war is over the bid to secede from Russia.

State Sovereignty

The argument over sovereignty is generally attributed to agreements reached between European nascent states in 1648 at the Council of Westphalia. It is claimed that they agreed that the secular rights of German princes took precedence over the claims of the Pope and, further, that they would not intervene in one another's claimed territory. Whether in fact the agreement did this is debatable. Victoria Tin-bor Hui argues that the Treaty of Westphalia and other treaties, such as those of Münster and Osnabrück, stipulated basic constitutional relations between the Holy Roman Emperor and various principalities and that they actually confirm the right of intervention as a means of enforcing those provisions. Further, every constitutional order promulgated by political organizations since then has provided legitimacy to intervene against those who disobeyed it. In addition to legitimate forms of intervention sanctioned by international treaties, many less open forms, such as assassination, bribery, subversion, and subsidies, have all been tried by diverse constitutional orders, whether under the Treaty of Westphalia, the Treaty of Berlin (1878), the Treaty of Versailles (1914), or the treaties that ended the Second World War (to name only the European varieties) (Tin-bor Hui 2004, 86–7; Krasner 1999). As Daniel Philpott (2001, 298) summarizes the critical view of the Westphalian tradition, "It is not that sovereignty no longer is; it is that it never quite was."

In any event, the presumed niceties of the Treaty of Westphalia did not include imperial extensions. Colonial powers used force to extend their territorial reach, and when words were required as justification they said, without a blush, that there were no real states in Africa, the Middle East, Asia, or wherever they were raising the flag, so sovereignty was not an issue. The demise of the Austro-Hungarian, Ottoman, and Russian empires in the First World War altered the groundwork for this agreement. In the interwar period, the League of Nations set up mandates to replace colonial territories of defeated powers: Rwanda thus came under the Belgian rather than the German mandate.[1] Another war, more changes in the ground rules. The establishment of the UN Charter was an attempt to manage a changed world, and agreement to respect sovereignty was the basis of the new international forum, which was deliberately called the United Nations. And it is well to understand that it is nations (and, more accurately, states), not peoples (however otherwise populations might be identified), that maintain this organization.

United Nations Charter on Sovereignty

The UN Charter, a post-Second World War attempt to construct a law-bound international community of states, recognized all its members as equal before international law. Equal, at least, on paper. The Security Council held power in the UN, and all states other than the dominant five of the time (the United States, Britain, France, Russia, and China) were unequal as far as voting was concerned. However, the legal framework set up by the UN Charter did something remarkable: it stipulated that sovereign nations did not have the legal right to wage war except in self-defence and with UN agreement. Article 2.4 of the UN Charter reads: "All members shall refrain in their international relations from the threat or use of force against the territorial integrity or political independence of any state, or in any manner inconsistent with the purposes of the

United Nations." This parallels the removal of the landed aristoc-
racy's rights to wage war in the feudal period in favour of placing
the monopoly of force in the hands of the central state authorities
(mostly monarchies), except that the UN has only moral authority.
To take any military action, it must have the approval of its member
states, who must contribute their troops to the united intervention.

States and Their Citizens

In the affluent and democratic states of the world, populations
have come to expect certain social services. Those who govern
them are supposed to look after them, provide a public education
system for all children, possibly even for university-age young people; a medical system with at least rudimentary universal health
care; a security system with police for internal security and an army
for external threats or unusual situations at the domestic level, such
as earthquakes and floods. Progressive taxation (or, more accurately, taxation with a few progressive features to offset the regres-
sive ones) is part of the package deal. To the extent that they
provide these goods and services, states have been a great organizational development in human history. But, obviously, not all states
provide these services. Indeed, most states of the world – that is, organizations for the governance of populations in given territories –
provide very little by way of citizen services. In many parts of the
world it is unsafe to walk along the streets at any time of the day,
and it is certainly unsafe to do so at night. Hospital and health services are scarce and poor; safe water supplies are inaccessible; education is available only to those with money; roads and other
physical infrastructure are either not available at all or are in a persistent state of disrepair.

  With such vast differences in the capacities of states and in the
willingness or ability of governors to bring about services to citizens, the term "state" already has different connotations for different populations. If one has to look out for one's own security at all
times, and cannot obtain either education or medical attention,
then the state is something of an abstraction for its own citizens.
Citizenship, in fact, is something of an abstraction as well. It merely
indicates where one was born or happens to reside (not necessarily
by choice); it confers nothing on the bearer and implies no responsibilities for the governors.

Multicultural States

The Ottoman Empire was, if nothing else, a multicultural conglom-
eration of peoples. It was not a state in the modern sense but,
rather, an assemblage of groups over a huge territory with a central
taxing authority. Not all groups were equal. Even all who professed
the Islamic religion were divided by other features of ethnicity and
history. Those who were both of another ethnicity and religion
(specifically Christian, whether of the Roman or the Orthodox variety) were not highly regarded, though, curiously, many Greek and
Armenian Christians found their way to wealth through merchant
activities despite ethnic and religious barriers. The empire was too
large and diverse and, for the twentieth century, too archaic: in the
decades leading up to and including the First World War, as it was
called (actually, the European War of 1914–18), it finally fell apart.
In the process of disintegration, Turkish leaders targeted the Armenians as enemies of the empire and chose to exterminate them
both by outright murder and by dispersal under conditions that
few would survive. Though modern Turkey denies that a genocide
occurred, the evidence does not support its wilful ignorance.

Yet for several centuries those peoples did live together, inter-
marry, carry on business, grow their crops, and celebrate life. The
society fell apart not because it contained many diverse peoples but
because its central government could no longer defend its territories or control its subject peoples when surrounding countries, pos-
sessing superior weaponry and desiring the lands of the "sick man
of Europe," began to take over parts of its territory. Then a curious
thing occurred: nationalism was born (or perhaps reborn, since
history does keep repeating itself). Nationalism meant that look-
alikes and think-alikes were to inhabit a given territory and that all
others were to be excluded. Stateless migrants became the hall-
mark of the twentieth century. The horror of Nazi Germany was the
epitome of a movement that was widespread. Nationalism became
pandemic, and it was not until late in the century, spurred on by
the few states that had not been so badly infected, that the ideologies of multiculturalism began to have homes. A state, in the early
twenty-first century, could be a state without a nation (where nation
implied common heritage), but this was still a tenuous notion and
was by no means universal.

INDIVIDUAL RIGHTS

The 1949 Universal Declaration of Human Rights, described in the next chapter, flies in the face of state sovereignty. It declares that individuals have rights irrespective of the rights of their sovereign states. If individuals are so entitled, then the state or nation in which they are citizens or visitors does not have the right to treat them inhumanely, and thus, it may be reasonably argued, the international community does have the right to intervene on their behalf. The adoption of the motion to authorize intervention for purposes of protecting individuals is consistent with the Universal Declaration. The establishment of juridical institutions, including the International Criminal Court, is based on the same general thrust – that the sovereignty of states is limited when they are doing harm to their own citizens. Genocide, likewise, poses an exception to the inviolability of states. The Genocide Convention identifies individuals as members of groups, so there are two levels of protection in these measures.

Yet even in the twenty-first century, neither of these declarations has the force one might expect on reading them. One might ask, why was the Genocide Convention ignored during the genocide in Rwanda, and why, also, as I am writing this, is it being ignored in Darfur, in Northern Uganda, and many other places where the conditions cited in Article 2 (quoted in chapter 3) appear to apply? The answer is embarrassingly obvious: the member states of the United Nations deliberately refrain from admitting that a genocide is occurring. By not using the "G word," as it came to be known, they could avoid sending troops to far-off countries in which they had no national interests to stop civil wars and state attacks on citizens. And, if individual states failed to contribute troops, the UN – lacking any armed force of its own – could not take action. By the mid-1990s, the same arguments as had been used with respect to Cambodia were put forward to justify inaction in Rwanda, including the claim that this was not genocide as defined in the UN Convention. Yet if the two contenders – Hutu and Tutsi – were believed to be different ethnic groups (as most reporters of the time assumed), then the war of 1994 was genocide. The pastoral Janjaweed's dispersal of the agricultural Fur people on the west coast of Sudan, apparently instigated and sustained by the Sudanese government in Khartoum, may also be genocide, although it is not clear that, apart from their occupations, the victims and the perpetrators are ethnically different. Again, however, the international community is loath to send in its armies; instead it is providing some funding and some training of troops from neighbouring African states, though there is little evidence that this is effective. The refugee camps in Uganda and Chad are filled with terrified survivors, many of whom are orphaned children.

SELF-INTERESTED INTERVENTION

Those who control state machinery, whether as warriors who won battles or as elected representatives, take ownership of "national interests." Genocide may be controversial as a cause for intervention, but "self-defence" and "national interests" are not. During the Cold War, interventions were routine affairs. When the Congo elected its first president, a combination of Belgians and the American CIA assassinated him (see below). Patrice Lumumba was too far left for Western tastes. The USSR sent in military troops when Hungary and Czechoslovakia thought about changing their lifestyles. African and Asian countries were regularly pulled and pushed in one direction or the other by the two superpowers, who were vying for hearts and minds as well as resources and markets. Central American countries were subjected to military intervention when they ventured too far from US interests, and South American countries sent their military officers to American and French military schools to learn anti-subversive measures and to drink in anti-Communist ideology (Marchak 1999). The Korean War and Vietnam War were interventions on the part of both superpowers, each taking sides in what amounted to proxy battles. The last major proxy war of the era was in Afghanistan, with the USSR taking the lead. But none of these events, even the wars, was examined as competing principles of sovereignty and universal human rights. The balance of power took precedence over any other international arrangements.

In light of Cold War history, skepticism may be the appropriate response to Vietnam's claim of humanitarian concern when it invaded Cambodia. Pol Pot's regime had become a nuisance to its neighbour. A puppet regime next door was in Vietnam's interest – also, as long as it kept China at bay, in the interests of the USSR. Other interventions in the same decade, beyond the usual Cold War conflicts, had been justified in terms of self-defence. Tanzania's overthrow of

Idi Amin's regime in Uganda in 1979 and India's invasion of East Pakistan in 1971 in support of Bangladesh independence are examples. What is of interest in the Cambodian case, unlike in the Ugandan and East Pakistanian cases, is that Vietnam claimed that it acted on humanitarian grounds. Humanitarian intervention had already developed a modest history during the 1960s and 1970s, but it was not yet a popular movement.

What was different between Cambodia and Rwanda was not the failure of the world to stop the mass murders but the reaction of the world when the events in Rwanda became known. The Khmer Rouge era in Cambodia had not been an issue elsewhere because its borders were closed and few outsiders had any idea what was happening there. By contrast, the story of Rwanda became seared on the world's consciousness as a terrible failure of Western humanitarianism. Samantha Powers (2002 and 2001) apparently shocked the American public by informing them that, throughout its history, the United States had failed to intervene in genocidal episodes elsewhere. For humanitarian reasons, she argues, this most powerful of nations should have launched military interventions against the perpetrators of such acts.

In response to Samantha Powers, some writers note the wide range and considerable number of interventions actually undertaken by the United States. According to a 1996 US Congressional Research Services Report, the US Armed Forces were engaged in what the authors call interventions on 234 occasions between 1798 and 1993, only five of which involved formal declarations of war. These included a major war of territorial expansion against the Mexican government; occupations in American Samoa, the Philippines, and Cuba; and interventions in Haiti, Guatemala, the Dominican Republic, Lebanon, Panama, and Grenada. After the Second War, the United States occupied and undertook the reconstruction of Germany and Japan (Bhatfia 2003).[2]

American presidents and other US leaders have frequently weighed in regarding conditions for military intervention. Secretary of Defence Caspar Weinberger argued in the mid-1980s that force should be used when interests vital to the national interest of the United States or an ally are at stake. He thought there had to be some reasonable assurance of congressional and popular support and that force should only be used as a last resort (Haass 1999).[3] Colin Powell, when chairman of the Joint Chiefs of Staff, suggested similar conditions, with an emphasis on whether the objectives are clearly defined and the balance weighed between costs and risks. He argued that if force was to be used at all, then it must be over- whelming force, and much of the debate since then (the 1990s) has focused on how much force is appropriate (Powell 1992–93, excerpts reprinted in Haass 1999, Appendix E). His comments were made in the context of US interventions in Bosnia and Soma- lia and in the aftermath of the (first) Persian Gulf War.

The senior George Bush hesitated when it came to deciding whether national interests alone should be the guiding principle for the use of military force, the grounds being that military force might not be the best tool for safeguarding them. Otherwise, he was well within the terms of the debate regarding when the United States should intervene militarily. Such interventions should only occur when they can be effective; they should be limited in scope and time; they should be based on the cautious measuring of risks and bene- fits; and they should necessarily be tied to clear objectives and realis- tic plans for ultimate withdrawal when the mission is over (Haass 1999, 16). George W. Bush Jr. was outside the boundaries of his pres- idential predecessors in his head-long rush into Iraq, even though the UN team appointed to determine whether it had weapons of mass destruction had found none, even though it posed no threat to the United States, and even though it was not a potential haven for Osama bin Laden. Indeed, Bush Jr. jeopardized the search for bin Laden in Afghanistan by transferring the bulk of his troops to Iraq thus allowing the man alleged to be responsible for the attacks on New York's twin towers to remain free.

Noting the numerous American interventions, some patriots argue that the United States has always been involved in humanitarian oper- ations. It is undoubtedly true that some of the major advances in hu- manitarian law originated in the United States, and American NGOs and sometimes the US government, through foreign aid programs, have contributed to the welfare of less developed nations. Although Marshall Plan aid for the reconstruction of Europe and similar aid to Japan in the immediate postwar period of the 1940s and 1950s was self-interested in the context of the Cold War and the need for mar- kets for American products, for a victorious country, these develop- ments were an extraordinary reaching out towards its former enemies. But precious few genuine interventions by the US govern- ment or armed forces were occasioned by humanitarian impulses, nor, as the deliberations noted above suggest, were they designed as such. Interventions in Central America were undertaken to protect property rights of Americans, to either protect or attack sources of illicit drugs, and/or to prevent left-wing governments from acting against corporate American interests.

The United States, in these respects, is no different from other countries, industrialized and otherwise. It is normal for states, and before them the multiple forms of political organization, to look after their own interests when dealing with peoples who are not regarded as "us." Indeed, when their stance is questioned, as by Powers's widely publicized book, they say – and they are honest in saying – that they see their task as protecting American interests abroad and protecting their citizens at home. When President Clinton refused to define the Rwandan massacre as a genocide and to send military interveners, he was acting within the guidelines for US presidents. As he stated at a UN meeting in the early 1990s: "The United Nations simply cannot become engaged in every one of the world's conflicts. If the American people are to say yes to UN peacekeeping, the United Nations must know when to say no."[4] The rest of the world may despair of the decisions their governments make in US interests, but we (i.e., other countries, including Canada) who have so much less military power to spread about are obliged to defer to US national interests when we argue in favour of humanitarian (or any other) interventions.

HUMANITARIAN INTERVENTIONS

Canadian diplomat (and, later, prime minister) Lester B. Pearson, who won the Nobel Peace Prize in 1956 for his role in negotiating a peaceful resolution during the Suez crisis, was also known for his participation in the development of policies for UN peacekeeping in war zones where keeping the contestants apart and holding them to peace pacts seemed idealistic but possible. Canada became one of the world's dedicated peacekeeping nations, following his lead. Scandinavian nations had long moved in the same direction, supporting peacekeeping actions rather than wars. At the time, Dag Hammarskjöld, UN secretary-general, was a major influence for peaceful resolution of disputes, and he strove to strengthen UN peace operations. For the next four decades, UN peacekeeping operations flourished, and in 1988 the UN Peacekeeping Forces

themselves won the Nobel Prize for Peace. But humanitarian operations are always subject to debate. How much of the impetus is really altruistic concern for the world at large, and how much is
determined by national self-interests? The underlying dilemma
plagues virtually all of the peacekeeping and other humanitarian
ventures under UN and other aegis.

The success of these operations depends on the contenders' requesting and being prepared to abide by the peacekeeping rules. UN
troops monitor their activities, maintain a ceasefire, and keep the
peace without themselves being equipped with weapons beyond
those needed for self-defence. Their strength is supposed to lie in
the very fact that they have no military weapons or support and, thus,
can be counted on to dispassionately operate as third-party interveners to gain and sustain peaceful resolution of conflicts.

Peacekeepers have acted as the Observer Group in India and
Pakistan in the Kashmir region since 1949, as the UN Truce Supervision Organization in 1948, and as the UN Disengagement Force in
the Middle East since 1974. One of their early and, despite difficulties,
most successful ventures was in Cyprus, where they were stationed in
1964 with the mandate to maintain a testy peace between Greek and
Turkish communities, each supported by the Greek and Turkish governments, respectively. However, a small group of peacekeepers is still
there (including one lonely Canadian from a force that used to number one thousand), and this raises a concern. It must be remembered
that the role of peacekeepers was to keep warring parties honest while
they created a non-violent solution to their conflict: peacekeeping was
not intended to provide a permanent police force for people too lazy
or pig-headed to create their own alternatives. Likewise, peacekeepers
stationed in Lebanon since 1978 have become fixtures instead of temporary aids. The world easily forgets what is done in its name until, as
happened in Lebanon during the Israeli-Hezbollah war of 2006, UN
peacekeepers are caught in the crossfire and killed.

Peace agreements are formal undertakings that specify the procedures and schedule of events involving disarming and demobilizing
combatants. The issues are actually easier to resolve when the conflict
is between separate states than they are when it occurs within a state.
As noted by Julian Ouellet (2005) regarding these agreements, "The
disputants must find a way to live together with a level of security and
justice that is acceptable to everyone. While ending violence is a start,
the long-term problems of building infrastructure and wealth and

revising the distributive policies of the government must follow if reconciliation and peace are to be achieved." The procedures are useful,
however, only if the protagonists are eager to settle their dispute and
to get on with recreating their society. Here Ouellet inadvertently un-
derlines a paradox of peacekeeping. He argues that the problem of
"failed states" is their loss of a monopoly on "legitimized violence"
and suggests that "third parties can, when so motivated, help to re-
store this monopoly," which "characterizes successful states." It is generally true that successful states have a monopoly on the use of
legitimate force (indeed, that is the major characteristic of states and
has been used as the prime definition of these phenomena for the
past century or so), but it is also true that many of the internal wars in
what might be designated as unsuccessful states are caused by state
oppression, including force, against minorities. Ensuring that those
who control such states are enabled by third parties to regain control
of the use of force is hardly a solution for an oppressed population,
though it may be the right solution when two groups, neither of
which is in control of the state, are doing battle.[5]

Peacekeeping costs have been a perennial problem for the UN.
The Congo operation in the 1960s put the organization into a cash
crisis because member states failed to provide the funds. Similar
shortfalls have plagued more recent interventions. In 1973, a for-
mula was introduced that put the costs for peacekeeping onto the
five permanent members of the Security Council (Jett 1999). In comparative terms, the actual cost of peacekeeping is small relative to the
amount of military spending by states, but UN operations are humanitarian by definition, and state military spending is about self-defence.

While the requests for peacekeeping increased during the Cold
War, the willingness of the parties to abide by the rules declined
markedly after it. In 1993, American peacekeepers in Mogadishu,
Somalia, were killed, and along with those deaths American enthusi-
asm for further peacekeeping missions sharply diminished. Rwanda
in 1994 was intended as a peacekeeping operation. It was initiated at
the request of the two signees to the Arusha Accords, and General
Roméo Dallaire expected that his job would be to monitor and maintain the terms of the agreement while the transition from Hutu government to shared government took place. He had no sooner
arrived than two things became clear to him: the invading Rwandan
Patriotic Front was still in war mode, and the government forces
were training a militia force (the Interahamwe) and planning a

genocide of Tutsi civilians inside Hutu-held territory (Dallaire 2003). Peacekeeping was impossible, and the UN forces were permitted neither to enforce the peace nor to stop the genocide.

With the Cold War behind them and the growth of the unipolar world, in which one hegemonic power possessed military power greater than the combined forces of the next twenty or thirty countries, peacekeeping lost its novelty; however, well into the twenty-first century, it is still quietly employed and quietly successful in many regions. Bruce Jones, series editor of the *Annual Review of Global Peace Operations 2006*, wrote in the *Los Angeles Times* that, in 2005, "the United Nations oversaw or assisted elections and referendums in various countries, affecting the lives of more than 100 million people. And it has proved adept at stabilizing small trouble spots such as Timor and Sierra Leone." But, warned Jones (2006), along with almost all others who investigate the matter, the UN is expected to do far too much on too thin a budget.[6] It is not adequately funded by its member countries.

Throughout the Cold War, the UN had been paralyzed by the incapacity of the Security Council to agree on any initiatives; now, abruptly, it was free to change the rules and seek new arrangements if it could dislodge the five powers of the earlier era, or at least persuade them to compromise, and obtain sufficient funding to do its job. Peacekeeping had always been a form of crisis management, but, when crises could not be averted and genocide or war crimes occurred, the UN had to decide whether to become an enforcer of peace; and, if so, how that might be achieved. Intervention was taking on a different meaning. Some of the combatants were choosing not to sign peace agreements because they were not interested in achieving peace, no longer having any stakes in the Cold War context, in which so many little wars were essentially proxy wars for the great powers. More and more, the warlords wanted to destroy the other side, not coexist with it. Either that, or they were competing for booty, and civilians who got in the way became just so much "collateral damage," to use the icy phrase coined by warlords in the Western countries. Peacekeepers under UN agency have found themselves in the middle of several wars, have been used as pawns, and have been killed either as collateral damage or deliberately (by way of warning the UN to butt out).

During the Cold War the UN occasionally contracted out command of a military operation to "coalitions of the willing" or even to single states. The Korean operation between 1950 and 1954 was conducted by the United States with voluntary allies, though it was run under UN auspices. Operation Desert Storm against Iraq, following the Cold War, was authorized by the Security Council, but the UN flag was not used while the United States led the forces. Similar arrangements were made after the Cold War for Somalia and East Timor. In this period, the UN developed a form of expanded peacekeeping, whereby its blue-helmeted troops were encouraged to seek out the root causes of the conflict and attempt to contain and de-escalate it. UN forces might even be mandated to establish more accountable forms of governance, promote the growth of civil society, and begin the process of economic reconstruction. As Trevor Findlay (2002, 5) discusses in his comprehensive study of UN operations, "In some cases this amounted to the resuscitation of failed states or nation-building." This expanded role troubled China and other developing countries on the grounds that it breached the sovereignty of independent states.

Peacekeeping with military support was always a contradictory stance: war for the purposes of stopping wars. Several operations demonstrated the paradoxes inherent in this position: the Congo between 1960 and 1964, the first Gulf War in 1991, Bosnia and Hercegovina between 1992 and 1995, Somalia between 1993 and 1995, and Kosovo in 1999. I detail the interventions in Bosnia-Hercegovina in chapter 9. Here, I briefly discuss the Congo during the Cold War and Kosovo following the breakup of Yugoslavia. Iraqi history deserves a special section not only because of its complexity but also because it obliges us, yet again, to consider whether the world should be holding leaders or whole states accountable. It also confronts us with the frequent appearance of great power complicity in the establishment of conditions that later become global problems.

The Congo, 1960–64[7]

An anti-colonial war erupted in the Congo shortly after it gained independence from Belgium in June 1964. Belgium air lifted its civilians and moved its troops to the mineral-rich eastern province of Katanga. UN secretary-general Dag Hammarskjöld treated this as a proxy war, between the Cold War powers and urged the Security Council to provide for UN troops with full capacity to wage war.

Over eight thousand troops eventually joined the military force, most coming from other African countries.

Prime Minister Patrice Lumumba was elected while UN troops provided security, although he was concerned about the failure of these troops to expel Belgians from Katanga and other military bases. In September 1960, a constitutional crisis emerged when President Joseph Kasavubu ousted Lumumba and the government. Lumumba was backed by the Parliament, and the constitutional deadlock was ended when Army Chief of Staff Joseph Mobuto managed to take over the reins of government. When Lumumba tried to join his supporters, he was not provided with UN protection. He was detained, jailed, and, by January 1961, assassinated. UN forces were criticized for failing to protect Lumumba, but their mandate did not permit them to do so. Both tribal war and civil war were now in the opening stages.

Throughout 1960 and 1961 UN forces and, on a notable occasion, the secretary-general himself, rejected the claims of Belgian and Katangan authorities who insisted on their right to intervene with force. In August 1961, the UN forces mounted a major operation to round up European officers serving with the Katangan forces. This was a successful and non-violent operation, though the threat of force was always in the balance. However, a month later, a UN operation, not authorized by Hammarskjöld, became violent. The secretary-general was killed in a plane crash shortly afterwards, and the following day a ceasefire that left the secessionists in power was announced.

Hammarskjöld's successor, U Thant, interpreted the mandate of UN forces in the Congo as necessarily supporting the central government against secessionists, and, thus, the whole affair moved towards further confrontation. Continued threats and conflicts finally concluded in January 1963, with the secessionist movement in Katanga defeated. But that did not end the internal conflict, chaos, and civil war in the Congo: it merely permitted the UN to withdraw with something akin to honour. In Findlay's (2002, 81–6) view, the lessons of the Congo operation, and of later operations in Somalia, the former Yugoslavia, Rwanda, and Sierra Leone, included, inter alia: that peacekeeping operations should never become peace enforcement operations; that the use of force is too blunt an instrument for promoting peace; that the military capability of peace operations "should match the expectations of their mandates (and the parties in the theatre of operations) with regard to the threat or use of force"; that timing of deployment and use of military force is critical; that peacekeeping operations are politically sensitive and need tight political control; that air power can be extremely inaccurate and dangerous to civilians; and that civilian police are invaluable in internal conflict situations, especially where anarchy more than armed conflict is the problem.

Kosovo

In flagrant contravention of UN rules, NATO forces bombed parts of Serbia in what was labelled a humanitarian intervention on behalf of Kosovo Albanians in 1999. Kosovo was then an "autonomous" territory within what remained of Serbia, and Serbia was still a sovereign nation. The UN Security Council had not authorized the attacks, the Milošević government had been elected, and Yugoslavia was not threatening international peace and security. Unlike the gulf states, Kosovo did not have oil or other resources essential to NATO forces, so at least this intervention may actually have been undertaken on genuine humanitarian impulses. Opponents of the war, however, have an argument that can't be lightly dismissed: by 1999, with the Cold War now long past, NATO had nothing to do and was in danger of falling apart. It needed a decent war to regenerate its batteries.

There is no consensus about the reasons for intervention in Kosovo. In the early stages the world press saw it, as NATO described it, as an attempt to save Albanians from Serb aggression. Europeans may have felt shame at their clumsy and inadequate response to the Bosnian crisis or seething anger at the repetition of Serb military action in another part of the former Yugoslavia. The mainstream press reported that, in the early stages of the action, the ethnic Albanian population was targeted and that upwards of 300,000 people were evacuated from their homes; many died, though the numbers are in dispute. NATO air strikes, which began on 24 March 1999 and were intended to end Serb violence in Kosovo, were instead accompanied by escalating violence on the ground and a large refugee outflow that included organized expulsions. Within nine weeks of the beginning of the air strikes, a reported 860,000 Kosovo Albanians fled or were expelled by Serb forces.

A different version of these events is provided by Diana Johnstone, who argues that Serbs, a minority of about 200,000 in the Kosovo population of about 2 million, were more the victims than the perpetrators. In her view, Albanian Kosovars, aware of the ill will the Americans and Europeans had for Milošević's Serbia, were successful lobbyists and propagandists who encouraged NATO bombing, which – they hoped – would rid their state of Serbs. Further, she argues, NATO's use of the term "humanitarian" to explain its intervention was an intentional attempt to deceive the media and liberal politicians, and even the anti-globalization movement, about the real reasons for this and other military operations: to ensure the hegemony of the United States and its allies (Johnstone 2002).

Whether one or the other of these reports is closer to the truth, the failure to resolve the problems in Kosovo – nay, more than that – the increased mess in Kosovo due to a botched intervention – suggests that if intervention is going to be attempted, there have to be some firm rules. Kosovo was left with a UN supervisory arrangement that barely kept the Albanians and Serbs from continuing their war. Finally, in January 2007, the UN granted Kosovo all of the capacities of an autonomous state except the name. Yugoslavia, which had just lost its hold on Montenegro via an election on separation, was initially fairly calm on hearing the news: journalists speculated that promises of better deals with the European Union might be forthcoming if it did not react with hostility. In any event, its nationalist leaders were gone (Milošević beyond earthly concerns) and no one chose to lead the opposition. But over the next few months the tension mounted. By August, Serbia warned of possible retaliation if Kosovo declared independence and if other nations accepted its separation ("Serbia Set to Retaliate against Kosovo's Declaration of Independence," *International Herald Tribune*, 31 August 2007). Russia, which opposed the granting of Kosovo independence, responded to Serb threats by saying that it was not the role of international mediators (Russia, the EU, and the US) to "force a particular solution" ("Russia Would Accept Kosovo Partition If All Sides Agree," Reuters report on Radio Free Europe, 31 August 2007). One option to be considered is a partition of the province to accommodate the Serb minority in the north, leaving the rest of the area for the Albanian population.

The Kosovo war illustrates some of the problems of armed intervention. The potential interveners have to have solid information about the situation on the ground. They need to know what caused the humanitarian crisis they propose to interrupt. They also have to develop an educated guess about the humanitarian and other costs of any intervention (because there is no crisis that does not have at least two sides) and the comparative costs of inaction. And they have to be genuinely disinterested, in the sense that the national interests of their own state, or their own careers and other interests, must not be the determinants of their action.

SANCTIONS AND WARS IN IRAQ

Sanctions are another form of intervention. They were successfully used against the apartheid South African government and the regime in Rhodesia. They are intended, or at least justified, as a means of bringing a country and leader into the normative culture of the international system so that these regimes would not continue to be a threat to international security. But such sanctions carry the potential to do great harm to innocent civilians for the crimes of their leaders. And this brings us back to the central conundrum that runs through this book: when a population allows a murderous regime to take over, should it pay the price of its own security because its leaders are unacceptable to outsiders? Especially when, in this case, as in many, the outsiders themselves were complicit in setting up the regime that they later toppled?

In August 1990, the Security Council, following the Iraqi invasion of Kuwait, imposed comprehensive sanctions on Iraq. These resulted in a humanitarian crisis, with many Iraqis unable to obtain sufficient food, medicine, and other life-supporting requirements. Further negotiations with the Iraqi government resulted in the "oil-for-food" program, through which Iraqi oil could be exported and food imported with the proceeds. This program went into effect in December 1990 and continued until the second invasion of Iraq in 2003. The stated objective was to prevent Iraqis from benefiting from normal market economic transactions involving their oil until they rid themselves of their president, Saddam Hussein. But the defects in the plan were that the actual oil available on a per capita basis was insufficient to provide food and other essentials for the population of Iraq. The causes of the deficiency included the fact that a substantial amount (estimated at 30 percent) was being siphoned off the top for the UN Compensation Commission (the organization that considered requests for compensation from governments and others who claimed victimization because of Iraq's invasion of Kuwait); general corruption involving companies and individuals associated with the UN and contributing governments of the time; and the disparities between aid for the northern (Kurdish) region of Iraq and for the rest of the population. In the view of Hans von Sponeck (discussed below), this occurred because the real objective was to punish the Iraqi people rather than to induce them to become part of the international community.[8]

If one reads American or UN documents about the program, one would probably conclude that it was a resounding success. However, that would leave one puzzled as to why two outstanding UN administrators in charge of the program resigned one after the other on the grounds that the Iraqi people were deeply harmed by it and that it was based on deliberate lies. Here is how career UN diplomat Hans von Sponeck, former UN humanitarian coordinator for Iraq and a man who had previously served with UN development programs in Ghana, Turkey, Botswana, Pakistan, and India, expressed it in an open letter to Britain's minister with responsibility for Iraq in December 2001: "Without a transparent political agenda and a determined end to contaminating information, I do not see an end to this costly human tragedy in Iraq." Von Sponeck countered false statements by British and American leaders, one being that a UN resolution had removed the ceiling on the amount of oil Iraq was allowed to export. According to von Sponeck, "This is a political ploy. Your government knows well from annual UN reports on the state of the Iraqi oil industry that Iraq cannot pump more oil unless the UN Security Council allows a complete overhaul of the oil industry." He responded to a statement by the British minister for Iraq, Peter Hair, to the effect that it is an outrage that the Iraqi government wilfully denies food and medicine: "Please forgive me if I say it is an outrage that against your better knowledge you repeat again and again truly fabricated and self-serving disinformation. Why do you ignore UN stock reports which give you the monthly distribution situation and which, verified by UN observers, show for food, medicines and other humanitarian supplies an average of over 90% distributed per month?"

He concluded a strong indictment of the British position with a condemnation that is rarely seen in diplomatic circles: "Lawlessness of one kind does not justify lawlessness of another kind! This has grave consequences not only for the suffering of the Iraqi people but also for the importance we should ascribe in Europe to the laws earlier governments have helped to create."9 In interviews regarding his position, von Sponeck noted that, "on average, according to UNICEF, 5,000 children are dying every month because of sanctions ... The Convention on the Rights of the Child is violated. The Covenant on Political and Civic Rights is violated. The Hague Convention is violated."10

Before going on to discuss Iraq, and the first and second Gulf wars, we need to pause here to consider what von Sponeck is saying in this interview and in numerous other talks and articles. He said he had resigned because "I increasingly became aware that I was associated with a policy of implementing an oil-for-food program that couldn't possibly meet the needs of the Iraqi people, and I felt that I was being misused for a United Nations policy that was punitive, that tried to punish a people for not having gotten rid of their leader."11 His rejection had two thrusts: that the policy itself was unjust to Iraqis and caused the deaths of many, including children, and that the governments of Britain and the United States were lying about what was happening. Both are of concern to us, but here I want to dwell on the first argument. If we deal with individual justice, then only the leaders – indeed, in this case, only Saddam Hussein and his immediate associates – should have been targeted. If we deal with collective justice, then it is fair to do harm to the entire population. But if most of the population has never had any capacity to determine who leads them, then actions that harm them still further can hardly be justified. This is all the more problematic when we consider the history of modern Iraq.

Brief History, Iraq[12]

Very briefly: Mesopotamia (more or less modern Iraq), which was part of the Ottoman Empire, came under Turkish control with competing British and German commercial interests during the late nineteenth century. Exploitation of oil in neighbouring Iran began in 1901, and the Anglo-Persian Oil Company was established in 1909. Lord Curzon, former viceroy of India, observed that the allies in the First World War "floated to victory upon a wave of oil." British control of Mesopotamia followed, and, despite promises to Iraqi leaders of full autonomy in return for military support, Britain entered into the British-French-Russian Sykes-Picot Agreement, which gave Britain a "sphere of influence" in Mesopotamia and France a sphere of influence in Syria. A rebellion of Mesopotamian Arabs in 1920 led to the establishment two years later of the state of Iraq as a kingdom, with a British high commission in supervision.

In 1928, Standard Oil of New Jersey and Mobil joined British and French oil interests in signing the "red line agreement" pledging cooperation in exploiting the Gulf's oil reserves. A Pan-Arab movement began in 1936 under King Ghazi, and, during the 1939–45 war, Iraq sided with the Axis alliance. It was defeated by the British in 1941 and re-established as a supply centre for British and American forces. At the end of that war, despite the red line agreement, four American companies took Saudi Arabian concessions for themselves and fought a legal battle against French and British oil companies to retain control of all Middle Eastern oil supplies. They promised to defend the Saudi monarchy in return for concessions. By 1951, the Iraqi pipeline was opened, producing a vast increase in oil, and, in 1954, the US government extended military aid to Iraq, followed, in 1957, by the Eisenhower Doctrine, which stated that the US would supply military assistance on request to any Middle Eastern government threatened by external or internal Communist aggression.

In 1959, Saddam Hussein, of the Ba'ath Party, failed in an assassination attempt on General el-Kassem, but within four years a CIA-organized coup led to the assassination of Kassem and the Ba'ath Party came to power. Saddam returned from exile in Egypt and became head of Iraq's secret service. There followed the mass murder of Kassem's supporters, with an estimated death toll of five thousand, the preponderance of these occurring in the professional class. The Arab-Israeli conflict interrupted the drama in 1973, coinciding with the emergence of the Organization of the Petroleum Exporting Countries (OPEC) and the oil embargo of 1974.

At this point, the United States began to talk about American military intervention in the Middle East.[13] In 1975, Henry Kissinger said that the US was prepared to wage war over oil. The 1979 overthrow of the shah of Iran coincided with the second oil shock. US president Jimmy Carter said that, if necessary, he would use military force to gain oil supplies, and the Carter Doctrine continued into the present conflict. Saddam Hussein became president of Iraq with US backing in 1979. Iraq under Saddam Hussein initiated war against Iran between 1980 and 1988, with the US supplying war materiel to Iraq. France supplied the planes. The US is said to have supplied chemicals for chemical warfare against Iran but its government must have realized that these could be used as well against Kurds in northern Iraq. By 1990, Iraq was accusing Kuwait of violating Iraqi borders to secure its oil resources. Within months, the US entered the war, calling it a "humanitarian intervention" on behalf of Kuwait. The United Nations authorized military action against Iraq, invoking the Carter Doctrine. Iraqi control of both Kuwaiti and Saudi oil fields would have threatened Western economic security, and, from this point on, Saddam Hussein and Iraq were treated as enemies.

First Gulf War, 1991

The United States claimed that the purpose of the first Gulf War, under the senior Bush administration, was to prevent Iraq from taking over Kuwait. This intervention was carried out under the auspices of NATO, as was the intervention in Kosovo in 1999. The US and "coalition forces" initially bombarded key targets in Kuwait and Iraq and, six weeks later, initiated a limited ground campaign. According to Richard N. Haass (1999, 34), director of foreign policy studies at the Brookings Institution and former assistant to President George Bush (Sr.), US forces "destroyed the bulk of Iraq's army." Haass also asserts that "Senior Bush Administration officials expected that surviving Iraqi troops would return home in March 1993 and, together with their fellow citizens, rise up against the government of Saddam Hussein" (35). That expectation was unrealistic: Saddam was capable of overcoming the Shia and Kurd uprisings of the period. Some months later, the exodus of Kurd refugees into Turkey necessitated a humanitarian intervention in the form of food drops. These were stop-gap measures. The problems were finally addressed by a "no-fly" zone for Iraqi aircraft, which allowed the repatriation of Kurds.

Iraq continued to be a thorn in the side of the United States until President George W. Bush (Jr.) determined to get rid of Saddam and to try to force his version of democracy on the Iraqi people in March 2003, even though this meant going against the will of the United Nations. The second invasion of Iraq was initially launched by the United States and Britain, along with a few soldiers from allied countries too frightened to say "no," on the grounds that Iraq posed a threat to the United States due to its possession of weapons of mass destruction. Later, when no such weapons were found, the administration claimed the war had been intended as a humanitarian intervention.[14]

I have gone on at some length regarding the invasion of Iraq because it and the attack on Kosovo have become the fulcrums in the debate about humanitarian intervention. In both cases the world was willing to accept "humanitarian concerns" as an explanation for the interventions. Yet if, indeed, their intention was to provide humanitarian aid to beleaguered populations under oppressive governments, it appears that in neither case were they successful.

CRITERIA FOR SUCCESS

Rushing into a bad situation may square with our collective conscience, but we are not well equipped to determine whether our activities are actually producing a desirable result – in part because we are not in agreement about what would constitute success. One researcher suggests four distinct criteria for a peacekeeping operation (PKO): completion of the mandate, facilitation of conflict resolution, containment of the conflict, and limitation of casualties (Bratt 1996, 64). These are not universally applicable. As Dennis Jett observes, containment is not an accomplishment if there is no danger of expansion, and limiting casualties is not a good measure if the action fails to terminate the conflict. He argues that "facilitation of conflict resolution is perhaps the most important thing a PKO can achieve, since it was conflict that brought the operation into being in the first place," but even that is not always attainable or even useful (Jett 1999, 20). Jett's analysis of the many problems inherent in the UN mandate, its process for decision making, its lack of resources, and the demands put on it suggests that, within the current organization, success is rarely possible.

RESPONSIBILITY TO PROTECT

The history of failed or, at least, not altogether successful UN operations might make us think twice about the prospects for humanitarian interventions. However, one group of researchers credits more modest UN interventions with having greatly reduced the incidence of violence in the world since the end of the Cold War. According to them, in a compilation of data on international violence: "Since the end of the Cold War the UN has led an upsurge of international activism that has played a critical role in reducing the number of violent conflicts" (Human Security Centre 2005, 146).

The International Commission on Intervention and State Sovereignty, appointed by the Canadian government and reporting in 2001, argued its case most eloquently, and its report formed the basis of the UN declaration of September 2005. The "core principles" identified by the commission are these:

- States are responsible for protecting their own people. If they fail to do so the international community must intervene.
- The Security Council of the UN, under Article 24 of the UN Charter, must take the responsibility for maintaining international peace and security and for maintaining international humanitarian law.
- The responsibility to protect involves: the responsibility to prevent (to address root causes and direct causes of internal conflict); the responsibility to react to "situations of compelling human need with appropriate measures, which may include coercive measures like sanctions and international prosecution, and in extreme cases military intervention" (xi); and the responsibility to rebuild.

The commission presented military intervention as a last resort, to be used only where all else had been tried and failed, where innocent populations were in grave danger, and where states had either fallen apart altogether or were the perpetrators of attacks on citizens. There is a strong and refreshing discussion about early warning and root causes, but there is no discussion of the scarcity of resources for curing the problems. In other words, in attributing to the UN the responsibility to take on the authority to react to abuses and to rebuild states, the commission moves into wishful thinking. Reform of the United Nations, and in particular reform of the Security Council (even when it is no longer stuck in the freeze of the Cold War), was not likely to occur when the commission wrote its recommendation that the council should be the proactive agent, and it has not occurred since, despite lengthy discussions of UN renewal and reform.

Between our notions of collective responsibility and the responsibility to protect, we are stuck in a no-man's land. The dilemma is not about sovereignty, though that canard is frequently invoked

and will be again as China, India, and Brazil become major powers
with problematic human rights records; rather, the issue is, on the
one hand, whether an entire nation can be held responsible for the
actions of its leaders and, on the other, whether the global community should be responsible for "saving" populations under leaders it
regards as unacceptable. In addition to these difficulties we have to
acknowledge that throughout the history of both inter-state and in-
tra-state wars, the developed nations and their leaders have not
been mere innocent by-standers. While arguing about the importance of dethroning non-democratic governments with lousy human rights records, they, themselves have rather often failed to
practice what they preach.

This discussion continues in Part 3. First, however, we need to
consider empirical examples of intervention, and this is done in
Part 2, which focuses on Cambodia and Bosnia.

AND FINALLY, THE SIMPLE
HUMANITARIAN ACTS ...

When the warriors have exhausted one another, humanitarians try to
feed the survivors in refugee camps and to bring perpetrators to justice. It is they and their legal allies who have developed the body of
international law that begins to govern wars and their aftermath. It is
they who have organized Amnesty International (AI), Human Rights
Watch (HRW), Oxfam, the Red Cross, Avocats sans Frontières (ASF),
Médecins sans Frontières (MSF), and many other humanitarian
NGOs; they who provide the fieldworkers for such organizations as
International Crisis Group (ICG), and who often (not always) are the
bureaucrats in the Organization for Security and Cooperation in
Europe (OSCE) and the mighty range of UN organizations or spin-
offs, such as the United Nations Education, Scientific and Cultural
Organization (UNESCO), the United Nations Development Program
(UNDP), and the United Nations High Commissioner for Refugees
(UNHCR). They may try to intervene between brutal forces and
potential civilian victims, or, if they cannot distinguish between the
opposing groups, they may at least help to care for the refugees.

3

International and Domestic Justice

Václav Havel, when asked if he agreed with the lustration laws that were presented in the new Czech legislature after the "velvet" revolution, said that he had received a list of individuals who had denounced him in the past and that that same day he had "lost" it and forgotten the names. He attributed this to the fact that he was a playwright and, thus, had been able to exorcise his ghosts in artistic ways before he took public office. But as a president, he said, he had to recognize that most people in society had to see some form of justice brought to the perpetrators of heinous crimes against them and their families. Eventually, Havel reluctantly accepted the lustration laws, which disbar individuals who were affiliated with the previous regime from obtaining public service employment in a successor administration, because, he surmised, the alternative – vigilante or frontier justice – was worse (Michnik and Havel 1993).

What is remarkable about this tale, besides Havel's philosophical disposition, is that Czechoslovakia managed to settle for mere lustration in the post-Communist period. In the post-Nazi era, the Czech record was as vicious as was any other in Europe (Frommer 2005). Was it wisdom, exhaustion, or a less terrible experience of communism than of Nazism that underlay the softer response? I'll opt for wisdom: both Havel and his compatriots have something to teach the rest of us. Revenge doesn't solve the long-term issues where large numbers of people are implicated in crimes against humanity.

OBJECTIVES OF POSTWAR JUSTICE

José Zalaquett, a leading member of the Rettig Commission on Truth and Reconciliation in Chile (1990)[1] and a former president of Amnesty International, suggests that policies whose purpose is to deal with past abuses should have two objectives: "to prevent the recurrence of such abuses and to repair the damage they caused, to the extent that is possible." He argues that other objectives, such as retribution or revenge, are not (and should not be) legitimate. The achievement of obliging accountability for previous human rights violations is invariably couched within other demands on a successive government, in particular, trying to achieve a measure of national unity and reconciliation, and developing the economy and institutions to strengthen and stabilize the society. In Zalaquett's (1992) view, a human rights policy within these limitations must have three conditions if it is to be seen as legitimate: the truth must be known, it must be complete, and it must be officially proclaimed and publicly exposed.[2]

Obliging former leaders and their followers to take responsibility for what happened can be extremely dangerous for a society. Sometimes it turns out that many are implicated in one way or another: few hands are entirely clean. This happened in Argentina and Chile after the military regimes were supposed to be out of office. Zalaquett is well aware of these difficulties and the restrictions placed on successor governments in their pursuit of justice or in their attempts to distance themselves from their predecessors. He considers the problem of impunity granted by democratic governments to persons accused of, or even tried for, the criminal behaviour of a previous government, and he also considers the possibility of arbitrary punishments and unfair trials. Paramount in these considerations is the problem of armed force and of military personnel who were not defeated when they were replaced by democratic governments. This problem is more closely tied to national than to international legal trials, where the government is both the instigator of the trials and the essential organization for creating and maintaining stability while an army bristles on the sidelines. This is noted as an obstacle to fair justice rather than as an argument opposed to trials or other forms of accountability.

Although Havel and Zalaquett both have the greatness of spirit and the experience to prefer justice based on empirical evidence and transparency, each has acknowledged that this is not always possible. The vast majority of human beings are afflicted with a desire for revenge when they have been sorely treated. An example is France after the Vichy regime. The resistance movement under

General de Gaulle, much eulogized in film and fiction, turned out to be as vicious in its revenge as the Nazis were in their repression. The liberation was declared in December 1944, but the punishment of collaborationists had begun a full year earlier, when several hundred individuals were interned in Algeria. Following the liberation, somewhere between eighty thousand and an estimated 400,000 were victims of what became known as the "Great Purge." During that period, the purging of collaborationists coincided with the power struggle between Gaullists and Communists (Macridis 1982; Novick 1968; Aron 1959). What happened in France resembled retribution scenes throughout liberated Europe at that time.

The insistence on accountability, however, is not necessarily a wish for revenge. Indeed, the arguments for making criminals accountable for their crimes are both more philosophical and more practical than is the argument for mere revenge. One of these arguments is that societies cannot be ruled by law if, after these terrible events occur, we fail to employ the full power of the law to protect the innocent and to ensure that the guilty are held responsible for their actions. The defence for trials or other forms of accountability for criminals is this: impunity must not be allowed to further destroy a shattered society. The truth about what happened must be given to the survivors so that they can close the chapter on their loved ones. War, genocide, and other mass atrocities destroy both individual lives and whole societies. When parents, children, or other loved ones are abducted, are known to have been tortured or raped, are maimed or killed – or when a childhood is spent in fear, hiding from brutalities or in refugee camps – finding out who was responsible and obliging those persons to face consequences is a necessary process. And it must be gone through before people can begin to repair their society and to resume their lives. Memories refuse to die.

Just like individuals, societies may also need to exorcise their ghosts, deliberately come to terms with the past, and see justice done so that they can move on. In the event of a civil war or revolution, the pressing need to reunify the society – or at least the survivors of the shattered society – ultimately rests on recognizing what happened through trials or truth commissions. On that basis, reconstruction becomes possible. If the ghosts are not faced head on, they may lie in wait and emerge a generation later in an even more ugly form. National or ethnic folklore will keep the flame alive, and sooner or later it will burn the descendents of those who failed to acknowledge their guilt.

These, then, are the arguments in favour of establishing formal accountability procedures for the leaders who planned, created the context for, and encouraged or ordered others to murder, maim, rape, or otherwise destroy the citizens of their own or another society. How far down the list of followers the hand of justice should go is debatable because many of the crimes are committed by groups or at least within a group context. What happens here has more to do with the herd than with discrete persons who happen to be part of it. It is not easy to deal with the issue of collective guilt: its history is ugly and its potential for harm most serious. Even so, as the studies of Cambodia, Rwanda, and the former Yugoslavia unfold, we can hardly avoid recognizing that many of the crimes were committed by gangs, militias, armies, or groups defined and defining themselves in ethnic, national, religious, or class terms. It may be true that one individual shot or raped a member of the group defined as the enemy, but when that one individual was completely immersed in groupthink and group action, our criminal procedures are not designed to deal with them, at least not in any way that recognizes the group context of the crimes.

Before considering the specific instances of how people deal with the history of these crimes in Cambodia, Rwanda, and the former Yugoslavia, I propose to provide a description of the current state of international criminal proceedings relevant to our concerns.

INTERNATIONAL WAR CRIMES TRIALS

War, by its nature, is a series of crimes against humanity. But by the middle of the nineteenth century, legal experts and statespersons were attempting to codify laws that restricted the barbarous acts of war even though they could not stop interstate war itself.

Geneva and Hague Conventions

Conventions at Geneva and The Hague began in 1856 and, at irregular intervals in the following century, rules were established for the conduct of war, including prohibition of the use of asphyxiating gas and bacterial weapons and the obligation to care for wounded soldiers. The Geneva Conventions (1949) spelled out how prisoners should be treated during wars, and they specified that the deliberate killing of civilians is a war crime (Geneva Convention IV, 12 August 1949).

However, with modern war technologies, the role of armies has changed dramatically, and, where aerial bombing is the modus operandi, civilian targets are unavoidable. Guerrilla warfare involves the outright targeting of civilians, and anti-insurgency operations likewise recognize no distinction between civilians (any one of whom might be a covert terrorist) and uniformed armed personnel. In the Iraq war since 2003 numerous mercenaries under contract to private companies have become armed forces whose actions have become front page news either when their members are killed or when they do the killing.[3] The Geneva Conventions are casualties along the way, as evidenced by Afghani and Iraqi prisoners in American jails located outside the United States. The general argument against playing by the rules is that the good guys are defending their turf (as well as virtue) while the bad guys are killing people. War crimes trials managed by the victors, then, are about obliging the bad guys to admit their guilt. Until the establishment of international criminal courts operated not by victors but by disengaged legal managers, it was impossible to put the victors of wars on trial. It is now theoretically possible but, in fact, very unlikely. Victors are notoriously difficult to rein in for purposes of justice.

Nuremberg and Tokyo Trials

War crimes trials were mounted during the days of empires and again after the First World War, but we generally think of the Nuremberg Trials and the Tokyo Trials as the prototypes. The advertised objective in these post-Second World War cases was to ensure that Nazi and Japanese leaders took full responsibility for initiating war and committing war crimes, but the speedy and theatrical trials, especially at Nuremberg, were as much about demonstrating the superiority of the victors as they were about obliging the defeated to accept their guilt. At Nuremberg, the tribunal took eleven months to prosecute twenty-two leading Nazis. They sentenced twelve to death, acquitted three, and imprisoned the others. The Court continued to sit another four years and secured 175 convictions.

Allied Crimes and Victors' Justice

Self-defence has always been an accepted rationale for what the protagonists call retaliatory acts of war, but even as defensive behaviour
the firebombing of German and Japanese cities and the atomic
bombing of two Japanese cities were war crimes. These actions killed
huge numbers of civilians and were designed to do so. No president
or prime minister or officer or scientist has ever been charged with
war crimes in connection with these events. These are, of course,
only the most spectacular of allied means of gaining victory. The argument that these actions saved many lives by foreshortening the war
may be valid, but it doesn't alter the fact that the victors engaged in
war crimes. This was acknowledged by American general Curtis
LeMay, who is reported to have told then US secretary of defence
Robert McNamara that, had Japan won its war with the United
States, LeMay and his cohort would have been tried as war criminals.
Instead, he was applauded for firebombing sixty-seven Japanese cities and approving the dropping of atomic bombs in 1945.[4]

If the aggressors win the war, there may not be any war crimes trials. In the past century, there have been numerous wars and atrocities for which no responsibility was ever accepted or assigned. The
Spanish Civil War in the 1930s left thousands dead and wounded,
but the international community accepted its outcome – the dictatorship of Franco – without a criminal court hearing. No leaders
have been indicted or otherwise obliged to account for their actions in the American war against Vietnam, with the exception of
lowly soldiers who were tried for war crimes in the village of Mai
Lai. Only one man at the top – Robert S. McNamara, then US secretary of defence – has had the courage to admit that US policies
were wrong and that the war should never have happened. Unfortunately, his retrospective bout of remorse was too late for the thousands of Vietnamese civilians and soldiers as well American soldiers
who were killed in the war (McNamara and VanDeMark 1995).

Prior to that war, the Indochina War – waged by France after the
Second World War in its disastrous attempt to regain colonial territories in what became Vietnam, Laos, and Cambodia – also provided no war crimes trials, though thousands were killed and
colonial policies did irreparable damage to the entire region. In
the American and British war against Iraq, we note the same process. Iraqis, if caught alive, might be tried for organizing suicide

bombing, but American and British forces are rarely called to account for their prosecution of war. When it became known that torture and humiliation of prisoners were frequent and even normal in American-managed prisons in Iraq, and also in Guantánamo Bay and elsewhere, soldiers at the bottom of the pile were prosecuted and penalized. Those who either explicitly or implicitly authorized the behaviour were left unscathed.

The USSR invaded Afghanistan in 1979 by way of propping up the local Communist government. As we now know, the United States became involved in that war by instigating and financing offensives against the USSR on the part of Afghan warlords and others, including one Osama bin Laden from Saudi Arabia. The Soviets finally departed in 1989, defeated in guerrilla warfare much as the United States had been in Vietnam a decade earlier. But war was not finished: by now the mujahedeen warlords who had been propped up and funded by the US continued with a civil war. Among the contending groups were radical Arab Islamists along with other warlords equipped with Stinger missiles and many other weapons courtesy of the CIA.

The US lost interest once the Soviets left, so the civil war raged on without further help or interference. An estimated 1.5 million Afghanis were killed before the Taliban, a fundamentalist Islamist sect, gained control of southern Afghanistan (the warrior tribes retained significant control of northern territories throughout the Taliban rule). There have been no international trials to determine responsibility for the instigation, funding, or continuation of the wars between 1979 and 1991. Indeed, most Americans and their usual allies had little knowledge of the region or its affairs. If a stray journalist caught their attention in all that time, it was with an article bemoaning the fundamentalism of the Taliban. The USSR had ceased to exist, and the US was engaged elsewhere before the infamous attack on the World Trade Towers and the Pentagon in New York on 11 September 2001.

Victors' justice in international wars seems, then, to be a non-starter if what is wanted is the development of an international justice system. However, victors' justice may be all we get in this world, unless every nation or other political unit is subject to the same international law. Without equal subjugation to the same laws, the system will oblige losers to accept responsibility and dissuade others from challenging the winners ever again. The skeptic might well argue that this system is no better than nothing with regard to international accounting. Yet if we look at the long brush of the history of jurisprudence, we might be a little more kindly in our assessment of contemporary justice. Victors' courts are a beginning of the process, not necessarily the form that will develop with greater maturity of the system.

HUMANITARIAN DECLARATIONS AND CONVENTIONS

In its finest moments, the United Nations made declarations about humanitarian objectives that would, its members hoped, prevent a repeat of such crimes as were committed during the Second World War. These continue to have resonance in today's world.

The Universal Declaration of Human Rights

The Universal Declaration of Human Rights (1949) was a significant milestone in the development of international law, even though it does not, itself, constitute a law. It is, rather, a declaration of intent, a humanitarian signpost. It declares that individuals have rights irrespective of the rights of their sovereign states:

> Everyone is entitled to all the rights and freedoms set forth in this Declaration, without distinction of any kind, such as race, colour, sex, language, religion, political or other opinion, national or social origin, property, birth or other status. Furthermore, no distinction shall be made on the basis of the political, jurisdictional or international status of the country or territory to which a person belongs, whether it be independent, trust, non-self-governing or under any other limitation of sovereignty. (Article 2)

The rights identified in separate articles include, inter alia, life, liberty, and security of person; equality before the law; freedom of movement; nationality; and absence of servitude, torture, cruel or degrading treatment, arbitrary arrest, detention, or exile. If individuals are so entitled, then the state or nation in which they are citizens or visitors does not have the right to treat them inhumanely as defined in the Universal Declaration, and, thus, it may be reasonably argued, the international community does have the right to intervene on behalf of individuals. As noted in the last chapter, a full half century later, the United Nations adopted a resolution called "the responsibility to protect," which asserts the collective right of other nations to intervene when individuals are beset by their own governments. Institutions including the ICC are based on the same general thrust – that the sovereignty of states is limited when they are doing harm to their own citizens. I consider the issues of national sovereignty and the practical limitations of these declarations in Part 2.

UN Convention on Genocide

States that, in 1951, signed and ratified the United Nations Convention on the Prevention and Punishment of the Crime of Genocide agreed to take action under UN auspices against perpetrators. Article 2 of the convention reads:

> Genocide means any of the following acts committed with intent to destroy, in whole or in part, a national, ethnical, racial or religious group as such. (a) Killing members of the group; (b) Causing serious bodily or mental harm to members of the group; (c) Deliberately inflicting on the group conditions of life calculated to bring about its physical destruction in whole or in part; (d) Imposing measures intended to prevent births within the group; (e) Forcibly transferring children of the group to another group.

For signatories, this is a legally binding obligation. Unfortunately, nations have found numerous ways of wriggling out of their obligations, particularly by quibbling endlessly over the definition of genocide. Also unfortunately, the definition is problematic. The chief obstacle has to do with whether the warriors (and outsiders) identify the different groups in terms of race, ethnicity, nationality, or religion. But there are other difficulties: we do not know, for example, whether numbers matter. If one hundred Croatian Serbs are killed by Croatian armed forces at Gospić, for example, is that the same crime as is the killing of seven thousand to eight thousand Muslims at Srebrenica by Bosnian Serb or Serb forces? As well, there is nothing in the definition that delineates the differences between premeditated murders and murders committed in the heat of battle or between mass murders committed by large numbers of armed persons and murders committed by relatively small gangs.

Crimes against Humanity

"Crimes against humanity" were originally defined in 1907 at the Second Hague Convention in connection with the 1915–16 genocide of the Armenians by the Turks in the Ottoman Empire. They were further defined and established in law by the international military tribunal at Nuremberg in 1945. The specific crimes included by the framers of the law pertaining to Nuremberg included:

> murder, extermination, enslavement, deportation, and other inhumane acts committed against any civilian population, before or during the war; or persecutions on political, racial or religious grounds in execution of or in connection with any crime within the jurisdiction of the Tribunal, whether or not in violation of the domestic law of the country where perpetrated. (London Charter of International Military Tribunal, para. 6c, issued 8 August 1945)

Rome Statute

Only crimes committed by European Axis powers were included in the earlier conventions, but by 2002, with the establishment of the International Criminal Court under the Rome Statute, a larger definition of crimes against humanity was formulated. This includes:

> any of the following acts when committed as part of a widespread or systematic attack directed against any civilian population, with knowledge of the attack: (a) Murder; (b) Extermination; (c) Enslavement; (d) Deportation or forcible transfer of population; (e) Imprisonment or other severe deprivation of physical liberty in violation of fundamental rules of international law; (f) Torture; (g) Rape, sexual slavery, enforced prostitution, forced pregnancy, enforced sterilization, or any other form of sexual violence of comparable gravity; (h) Persecution against any identifiable group or collectivity on political, racial, national, ethnic, cultural, religious, gender or other grounds that are universally recognized as impermissible under international law, in connection with any act referred to in this paragraph or any crime within the jurisdiction of the Court; (i) Enforced disappearance of persons; (j) The crime of apartheid; (k) Other inhumane acts

of a similar character intentionally causing great suffering, or serious injury to body or to mental or physical health.[5]

These conventions and legal acts have moved global society towards more humanitarian concerns. They have enabled us to identify specific crimes that may be considered crimes not just against a particular people but also against the entire human species. They have alerted people around the world to crimes that, in their own cultures, may not have been articulated as such. Yet all these conventions have been frequently criticized on the grounds of vague wording and the impossibility of enforcing them. Crimes against humanity were enforceable at the Nuremberg Trials only because the Court was set up solely to try Nazi war criminals. The term is now being used, tentatively, in the tribunals for Yugoslavia and Rwanda, but the difficulties of specification and proof remain as obstacles to justice.

INTERNATIONAL TRIBUNALS AND SPECIAL COURTS

The war crimes trials of the past were examples of victors' justice. It may be a fair assumption that an international court set up by disinterested parties on behalf of the "global society" would be less prone to bias and revenge politics than would either trials under the aegis of winners in wars or trials in domestic courts. In the wake of the wars in the former Yugoslavia and Rwanda, such new courts were established. Unlike the huge interstate wars of the twentieth century, these were both civil wars in relatively small countries.

In the case of the former Yugoslavia, there were no victors, only losers, and members of all participating groups are equally likely to be indicted if they committed crimes (though many Serbs would disagree with that judgment). In Rwanda, there were victors in the sense that the invading army of Tutsis won the war and became the government, a fact that greatly influences the conduct of domestic courts. It would also influence the international tribunal if only Hutus were being tried. Tutsi soldiers who took retaliatory action amounting to war crimes have not been indicted so far, the argument being that war crimes, even if meted out against a particular ethnic enemy, are not equivalent to premeditated genocide. Ordinary crimes, including murder, are to be dealt with in domestic courts, not in courts established for the purpose of judging genocide cases.

Whether or not the tribunals are dealing with genocide and war crimes in a fair way, our assessments must take into account that these courts are the beginnings of an international system. The judges, lawyers, police, and all other staff have had to learn as they proceeded. International law in the mid-1990s did not provide the information needed to base trials on established rules and precedents. As well, the courts had to take into account constitutions and legal precedents in the countries where the war crimes occurred. The record is not unblemished.

There being at the time no International Criminal Court, the tribunals established a legitimate interest by the international community in the affairs of these two pariah states. The International Criminal Tribunal for Yugoslavia (ICTY) was created in May 1993 at The Hague. It delivered its first sentence in July 1997 to Serbian Duško Tadić: twenty years for crimes against humanity. Both tribunals have been excruciatingly slow at getting the work done, and the cost has far exceeded original estimates. By comparison with the Nuremberg Trials, the ICTY completed trials for forty-six people, with another thirty-eight under way in mid-2005 (Edwards 2004). The Milošević trial was moving into its fifth year, frequently interrupted by the star player's illnesses. His death in March 2006 precluded the judgment that would otherwise have been presented just a few weeks later. Perhaps the disparity between the speed of the ICTY trials and that of Nuremberg is due to the greater willingness in more recent years to allow even despised war criminals the full rights of self-defence. The ICTY has not had an easy time gaining legitimacy in Serbia. Milošević was given up most reluctantly, and two of the world's notorious criminals, Ratko Mladić and Radovan Karadžić, were protected by Serbian colleagues and authorities through 2006 despite ICTY indictments.[6] While dealing with the death of Milošević, the European Union told Serb leaders that there would be no relaxation of punitive measures against Serbia if it failed to surrender Mladić.

The International Criminal Tribunal for Rwanda (ICTR) was struck in November 1994 in Arusha, Tanzania. Its first sentence was handed out in September 1998, to Jean Paul Akayesu, the former mayor of the town of Taba. He was found guilty of ordering the murders of two thousand people. Altogether by mid-2005, the

ICTR had delivered judgments involving twenty-five accused, of whom twenty-two were convicted and three acquitted. Another twenty-five individuals were currently standing trial as this was being written (mid-2005). The slow progress of these trials attests to the determination of the Court to be scrupulously fair. Witnesses have lodged numerous complaints about the personal cost of travel to Arusha and waiting to be called. Costs are also a concern for the international community, which is paying an estimated $US200 million per year for these trials,[7] an amount that, were it invested instead in the plumbing or electrical wiring for villages in Rwanda, could make a substantial difference to people's lives. Since many surviving rural Rwandans cannot read, they are dependent on radio transmissions for information on the progress in Arusha. It is unlikely that they are well informed. These trials may assuage the guilt felt by Westerners about their failure to intervene in Rwanda's genocide, but they may have no real impact on the lives of the majority of Rwandans.

Cambodia's terrible killing spree occurred twenty years earlier, but no international tribunal was set up for the Khmer Rouge leaders before 2007. The "Extraordinary Chambers," as the tribunal is known, are the result of many years of on-again, off-again negotiations between the country's government and the United Nations. With negotiations finally concluded, the Court issued its first indictment in August 2007 to an individual already in jail. The announced intention is to prosecute no more than five surviving leaders. Pol Pot died in 1998 of natural causes. As the chapter on Cambodia demonstrates, we are talking about a population that is largely illiterate and grindingly poor. We are also talking about a government that is notoriously corrupt. NGOs in human rights areas are divided about the wisdom of the proposed trials. Cambodian politicians and bureaucrats are dragging their feet, saying they favour trials but simultaneously setting up obstacles whenever it appears likely that the trials will actually go ahead.

My reservations about these particular tribunals do not constitute a principled rejection of them but, rather, a practical and critical assessment. These were set up as experiments, the rules have to be developed in situ, and the judges and all other personnel have had to learn how to proceed. In both Yugoslavia and Rwanda, the domestic courts would have had difficulty dealing with the most deadly of the criminals. But it is unclear whether justice is well served or whether the terms, as outlined by José Zalaquett (for example), have been met. When much of the population either learns nothing about the trials or sees them as a foreign imposition, the likelihood of them acting as a means of ensuring accountability and as a means of assuaging the pain of victims is much diminished.

UNIVERSAL JURISDICTION

In 2001, long after the bombing of Cambodia and his role in the coup against Salvadore Allende in Chile,[8] Henry Kissinger was served with a summons by a French magistrate at the Palais de Justice in Paris, requesting that he provide testimony regarding American knowledge of and involvement in Operation Condor. Condor was an infamous organized operation between Chile, Argentina, Uruguay, Bolivia, and Paraguay to capture and/or kill escapees from the military juntas of the 1970s. The United States was the mentor for army officers throughout Latin America before and during the state terrorist regimes. Whether or not Kissinger was instrumental in Operation Condor, he did not wait around after seeing the summons: he left for the United States immediately and referred the Paris court to the US State Department. Augusto Pinochet was less quick on his feet when he was served with a summons in London in the same year.

What was happening to both Kissinger and Pinochet, and what later happened to Slobodan Milošević, involves what we now call "universal jurisdiction." The concept is not new: it was originally applied to pirates and later to plane hijackers. But in its most recent form it applies to heads of state or other leaders deemed to have committed crimes against humanity, genocide, or other serious crimes. A group of American scholars and jurists may be credited with furthering the idea when they published an influential document called *The Princeton Principles on Universal Jurisdiction* (2001). This argues in favour of the establishment of principles of law to be applied in national or international courts equally for what the authors call "serious crimes," including piracy, slavery, war crimes, crimes against peace, crimes against humanity, genocide, and torture. These could be invoked anywhere, irrespective of where the crimes were committed, who committed them, and who were victimized by them, Essentially, it means that one state may exercise jurisdiction over crimes committed in another state. Kissinger (2001, 95), subsequently responding to the arrest of Augusto Pinochet, observed: "The notion that heads of state and senior public officials should have the same standing as outlaws before the bar of justice is quite new."

General Pinochet had created an impunity clause for himself and all others in power at the time of his murderous reign in Chile from 1970 to 1986. He had also stuffed the Senate with his own appointees for life to ensure that there could be no constitutional changes. The Commission on Truth and Reconciliation (Informe de la Comision Nacional de Verdad y Reconcilation), established by President Patricio Aylwin during the first democratic government following Pinochet's reign, identified nearly three thousand victims. But for constitutional reasons and because the armed forces remained so powerful in Chile, Pinochet and his closest advisors were not charged in Chile. When he went to London in October 1998 for medical treatment, he was detained on the strength of extradition papers authored by a Spanish judge. The case is complex, involving citizens of Spain who were "disappeared" in Chile. It involved the UK government, which had signed and ratified the international convention disallowing torture irrespective of the position of the accused.[9] London judges and the UK government took nearly two years to reach a decision to let Pinochet go back to Chile because, in the view of their medical specialists, he was suffering from dementia and thus unable to defend himself. The case received such publicity that, when he returned to Chile, jurists there determined that he was fit to stand trial. The concept of universal jurisdiction was finally established.

The principles are being tested and applied in the UK in other ways. A senior Israeli soldier was informed that he would face legal action if he travelled to Britain, and another officer stayed on his plane at London's Heathrow airport after being given similar warnings.[10] These legal actions can now be taken by individuals. One of the cases involved a general who was in charge of an Israeli warplane that dropped a one-tonne bomb on a building in which a Hamas leader was resident.

THE INTERNATIONAL CRIMINAL COURT (ICC)

The argument for establishing an international criminal court was mounted immediately following the Second World War, but the emerging conflict between the USSR and the Allied forces stopped further consideration. It was the 1990s, following the implosion of the USSR, before the idea was taken out of mothballs. The Rome Statute for an International Criminal Court was enunciated in 1998, and the ICC came into force 1 July 2002, with 139 signatories and eighty-seven ratifications.[11] Since then, other states have signed and ratified it, and have adopted comprehensive domestic legislation to comply with it. Among the arguments in favour of the ICC are the following: many states are incapable of judging their own heads of state and army after state-inflicted crimes against humanity because they have few jurists left, because their courts and other institutional structures are not up to the task, or simply because no one has the power to take on the criminals in their midst. The international community steps in, takes over, and allows the weak survivor community to move on to other tasks of reconstruction. There may also be among the victims citizens of countries other than that which is in turmoil. So, again, there is a reason for the international community to prosecute the perpetrators.

In this favourable view, an international criminal court becomes the global version of domestic courts within a country. Just as, at an earlier stage of history, political leaders had to struggle with theological leaders, monarchs, and aristocrats to set up courts and the rule of law, now international citizens must go through a similar struggle against the notions of inviolable national sovereignty to establish a court above nations and dedicated to equality before international law.

There are some caveats to this version. In particular, when earlier domestic courts were established, the juridical and the political boundaries overlapped. Our world is lacking the global sovereign to provide the political weight to a juridical system. The global sovereign could be supplied by the United Nations (preferably a reconstructed version) only if that body were able to mount its own military force and use it to enforce obedience to an international law. That's not going to happen soon, and meanwhile the ICC is flying solo with very little capacity to enforce its decisions if governments choose not to obey.

Many countries have signed and ratified the ICC, its precarious hold notwithstanding. But the United States is one of the few holdouts – under George W. Bush, the US withdrew its original signature. This puts the US in the same category as Iraq, China, and Libya. Even Afghanistan, Albania, the Democratic Republic of the Congo, and the Dominican Republic have signed up. Not only did the US choose to withdraw, it embarked on a global campaign to obtain immunity for US citizens from the ICC's jurisdiction, and President George W. Bush signed a supplemental appropriations bill that prohibits any US agency from cooperating with the ICC. This bill also restricts US participation in UN peacekeeping operations (the ICC has been jokingly referred to in the US as the "Hague Invasion Act"). The fear in the United States of having its officials taken to an international court for criminal behaviour in other countries may be well founded. Speculation on the legitimacy of taking Henry Kissinger to court has been around for many years, but it was not possible earlier because the ICC has jurisdiction only from the time of its establishment. If the US signed on with the ICC future US leaders might be accused of war crimes, defined as "grave breaches of the Geneva Conventions of 12 August 1949, namely ... acts against persons or property protected under the provisions of the relevant Geneva Convention" and including such acts as wilful killing, torture, wilfully causing great suffering or serious injury, extensive destruction and appropriation of property, wilfully depriving a prisoner of war or other protected persons of the rights of fair and regular trial, unlawful deportation or transfer or unlawful confinement, and the taking of hostages. Although the ICC can function without the endorsement of the United States, the fact that this great power is exempt from rules that pertain to other countries obviously weakens the power of the international court.

The ICC has jurisdiction especially for the crime of genocide. If a national court is able to prosecute citizens for their participation in genocidal acts, the ICC need not be involved. But countries are generally unable to proceed with criminal proceedings on such a scale; the establishment of a disengaged international court was essential to making genocide a prosecutable crime. Among the reasons that national courts are rarely in a position to take on such prosecutions is that most genocides are actually organized by persons in control of state machinery and armies. Their successors are seldom in a position to prosecute them.

As many commentators have noted, actions taken by Europeans between about the sixteenth and twentieth centuries that destroyed indigenous peoples throughout the world were genocide, and had these actions occurred after the enunciation of the Genocide Convention or after the Rome Statute came into force, virtually all leaders of European countries and their successor states, who were responsible for genocidal acts against indigenous peoples in Asia, Africa, Australia and New Zealand, and North and South America, would have been subject to trial under the law. They cannot be taken to court for these actions retrospectively, but the existence of the statute should deter other states from similar actions in future.

The mass murders in Rwanda were determined to be genocide as defined by the Genocide Convention, though there are ethnographers and historians who would argue that the two groups are not different races or even different ethnic groups (they share a culture, religion, language, and recorded history). Crimes against humanity is the more appropriate label for Khmer Rouge murders. The Khmer Rouge were ethnically and religiously the same as other Khmer people, and the victims were primarily other Khmer. Some genocide experts have argued that the Khmer Rouge should be tried for genocide in respect to Vietnamese and Cham Muslims, and that may be appropriate, but the vast majority of their victims were Khmer Buddhists like themselves. Another objection to the use of the Genocide Convention for the crimes in Cambodia is that, insofar as the actions of the Khmer Rouge can be deciphered, it does not appear that the intention was to destroy in whole or even in part a particular population. Though urban dwellers were targeted, they were not the only victims, and they were not defined in terms of consistent characteristics similar to ethnicity or religion.

THE INTERNATIONAL COURT OF JUSTICE (ALSO KNOWN AS THE WORLD COURT)

The International Court of Justice (ICJ), set up in 1945 as the principal court under the United Nations, was designed to provide pacific settlement of disputes between states. Like its predecessor under the League of Nations, the Permanent Court of Justice, it has dealt with civil cases such as disputes over fisheries jurisdiction, nationalization of private companies, and conflicts over territory. However, a case brought before it in 1993 and finally heard at The Hague between February and May 2006 was of a rather different nature: it was the "application of the Convention on the Prevention and Punishment of the Crime of Genocide" put forward by Bosnia and Hercegovina against Serbia and Montenegro. Public hearings concluded 9 May 2006, and in February 2007 a final judgment blamed the Serb government for failing to prevent a predictable genocide in Srebrenica; however it also said that the genocide was enacted primarily by Bosnian Serbs and thus the Serb state could not be held responsible. The judgment is controversial because of media speculation that Serbia managed to persuade the ICTY to withhold records it had, under pressure, provided for the trial of Slobodan Milošević.[12]

Jurisdiction Issue

The original claim was that Yugoslavia had "planned, prepared, conspired, promoted, encouraged, aided and abetted and committed" genocide against its population. As Yugoslavia disintegrated, the original claim had to be restated and submitted against the successor state of Serbia and Montenegro. That in itself is a legal issue since the actions took place prior to the breakup of Yugoslavia, and the rump state subsequently known as Serbia and Montenegro was not then in existence. Serbia was the strongest component republic within Yugoslavia, and its leadership was in control of the federal state when it initiated the internal war that finally resulted in the breakup of the country, but the changed status of Serbia since then is part of Serbia and Montenegro's rebuttal. Another component of the rebuttal is that Serbia was not then a member of the United Nations.

Serbia and Montenegro, in its final submission, argued that the ICJ:

> has no jurisdiction because the Respondent had no access to the Court at the relevant moment; or, in the alternative, that this Court has no jurisdiction over the Respondent because the Respondent never remained or became bound by Article IX of the Convention on the Prevention and Punishment of the Crime of Genocide, and because there is no other ground on which jurisdiction over the Respondent could be based.

That argument was dismissed when the ICJ earlier concluded that it did have jurisdiction for the case.

Bosnia-Hercegovina Argument

The summary statement in the resubmission by Bosnia-Hercegovina argued:

That Serbia and Montenegro, through its organs or entities under its control, has violated its obligations under the Convention
on the Prevention and Punishment of the Crime of Genocide by
intentionally destroying in part the non-Serb national, ethnical
or religious group within, but not limited to, the territory of
Bosnia and Herzegovina, including in particular the Muslim
population, by: killing members of the group; causing serious
bodily or mental harm to members of the group; deliberately
inflicting on the group conditions of life calculated to bring
about its physical destruction in whole or in part; imposing
measures intended to prevent births within the group; forcibly
transferring children of the group to another group.[13]

Subsidiary to this central claim are further explications regarding
complicity in genocide; aiding and abetting individuals, groups, and
entities engaged in acts of genocide; conspiracy to commit genocide;
inciting to commit genocide; and failing to prevent genocide.

During the proceedings of the ICJ, Bosnia-Hercegovina argued
that Serbia and Montenegro should be charged with: systematic
practice of "ethnic cleansing"; murder, summary execution, torture,
rape, kidnapping, mayhem, wounding, physical and mental abuse,
and detention of citizens; wanton devastation of villages, towns,
districts, cities, and religious institutions; bombardment of civilian
population centres, especially in Sarajevo; starvation of civilian population; interruption of, interference with, or harassment of humanitarian relief supplies; use of force; violations of sovereignty,
territorial integrity, or political independence; and support to
groups engaged in military or paramilitary actions against Bosnia
and Hercegovina. Said the defence lawyer: "The armed violence
which hit our country like a man-made tsunami in 1992 destroyed
the character of Bosnia and Hercegovina and certainly destroyed a
substantial part of its non-Serb population."[14]

Intentionality

Beyond the jurisdictional question there were two central issues in
this case – issues that will affect other and future litigations independent of the ICJ's decision on this particular case. One is
whether intentionality could be proven. By virtue of the legal definition of genocide, the Court had to be convinced that Serbia's

leaders intended to commit the crime knowing that it would cause death and destruction. Intentionality is difficult to prove even if culpability is clearly indicated. In this particular case, the charge of intentionality on the part of the Yugoslav state would have rested on proof that it was directing, financing, training, or otherwise enabling Bosnian Serbs to commit genocide. Yugoslavia's military forces (predominantly composed of Serbs) claimed innocence during acts of genocide. The evidence of intentionality was based, then, on urgings, funding, public statements, private correspondence (if located), and other support from Serbian leaders to Bosnian Serbs.

The prosecution had support in an earlier decision of the ICTY that the events at Srebrenica constituted genocide. The Bosnian Serb army was charged with responsibility for executing Muslim men and boys in July 1995. Two commanders of the Bosnian Serbs (Radislav Krstić and Vidoje Blagojević) were found guilty and were incarcerated. In June 2005, a video showing the executions of six Muslim men became public. It had been photographed in 1995 by one or more former members of the paramilitary group known as the Scorpions. Prosecutors claimed that the Scorpions were controlled by the Belgrade government at the time of the genocide. Since the video appeared, five Scorpions members were put on trial in Serbia. (Further information from the trial in April 2007 is discussed in chapter 11.)

Other evidence put forward by the prosecution included statements by Radovan Karadžić, the Bosnian Serb leader, and speeches by Milošević himself in which the support and funding from Belgrade to the paramilitary forces were acknowledged. Some documents vital to the case against Milošević at the ICTY were not included in the ICJ case. The reasons for this are in contention, but apparently the ICJ did not seek to obtain the same range of documents from Serbia: the ICTY was not obliged to share documents that were under seal at the Court (see chapter 11), and as the ICTY has pointed out, the two courts are independent organizations.

CO LLECTIVE RESPONSIBILITY:
CAN A STATE BE CULPABLE?

The second issue is whether an entire nation can be blamed for the crimes committed in the name of the Serbian people but not necessarily with their unanimous consent or even with their knowledge.

The judges had to be persuaded that, irrespective of popular knowledge of what leaders do, people are represented by their governments and must accept responsibility for what is done in their name. This case is about states, not individuals, even though it was individuals who acted. Those arguments could lead to a new interest in collective responsibility.[15]

A 1986 ICJ decision might have been a relevant precedent to this case. In that instance, Nicaragua sued the US for supporting the Contra insurgency against the Sandanista government. The Court supported Nicaragua's case. It ruled that Washington had contravened its treaty obligations by training and otherwise supporting military and paramilitary activities in Nicaragua. However, the Court also said that the evidence was insufficient to hold the US directly responsible for acts committed by the Contras. That decision was criticized by legal observers for setting an unrealistically high barrier for proof of proxy relationships. In a similar case in 2005, the ICJ ruled that Uganda had violated international law by supporting armed groups in the Democratic Republic of the Congo (Global Policy Forum, Institute for War and Peace Report, 24 February 2006).

Compensation

Bosnia's lawyers demanded huge compensation. If they had succeeded in persuading the seventeen judges (fifteen international judges plus one additional judge appointed by each of the parties) that their case had merit, Croatia – already making claims for compensation against Serbia – might have made a strong case for itself. As observed further on in the chapters on the former Yugoslavia, in addition to seeking justice for crimes past, there was a question of justice for the poor of Serbia as they dealt with crimes of past leaders. In any event, the decision was that the Serb state was responsible for failing to prevent a predictable genocide on the part of groups with whom it was affiliated but that it could not be held accountable for the genocide itself. Bosnians, particularly those whose loved ones were murdered at Srebrenica, were stunned by the Court's decision. Current Serb leaders were pleased but did acknowledge that the judgment still left Serbia stained by its former leaders. The hope as this judgment was rendered was that the Serb state as constituted in early 2007 would make the effort to capture and send to the ICTY the men most responsible for the genocide at Srebrenica: Ratko Mladić and Radovan Karadžić. The Court awarded no claims for compensation to Bosnia.

DOMESTIC TRIALS

International wars, certainly the one on the scale of 1939–45, are qualitatively and quantitatively different from small regional or civil wars that take place within a single country. In an international war, the victors may choose to hold the leaders of the vanquished accountable for the war or for human rights crimes (as in Nuremberg and Tokyo), but they are not obliged to go on living side by side with the people they have conquered. Typically, in smaller wars, the survivors have to find a modus vivendi because most of them, with all their memories, will continue to live in the same space. In both kinds of wars there are undoubtedly many shades of criminality on all sides, but at the conclusion of an international war the victors have much more control over how the events are conveyed to world populations and whom to blame for what has happened. In small wars, ambiguities are likely to overwhelm those who take control of the institutions of the state and who attempt to fully reconstruct the reality of what occurred. As well, the victors of international wars control the available wealth and can choose to finance international courts; rarely are the winners of small wars rich enough to sponsor justice, even if they would like to – which should never be assumed.

The difference between international war crimes trials and possible trials for small-scale war leaders is often lost in the debate about the ICC or the tribunals. The arguments in favour of international justice are strong: small societies are too close to the perpetrators to judge them fairly, the international community ought to be involved as an arbiter of universal justice, and the establishment of an international court spreads the costs to the more affluent societies. These arguments were put forward in 2005 with respect to the proposed special court for Cambodia.

But the arguments against international action, or at least action of the kind that involves an international court, are also worthy of consideration. A society that manages to dislodge a particularly nasty junta – as in Greece and later in Argentina (discussed below) and Chile – may be by far the best judge of its leaders. Of course, few societies on their own manage to get rid of an unwanted junta, but some do, and when they succeed, surely it is they, not the global society, that should decide what kind and how much support would be helpful in their dealings with history. There are alternatives to international courts that might well be better suited to small societies. Truth commissions inform, lay some ghosts to rest, lay blame and shame, and often serve the purposes of justice very well. International commissions may be more concerned with their own constituencies and funding agencies, with such bodies as the UN, UNPROFOR, NATO, and their spin-offs, and getting peace deals settled so they can get on with other matters. If it is justice that is wanted, simple domestic trials or truth commissions might do the trick.

The Greek Example

The trials of the Greek colonels in 1974 were an important beginning for twentieth-century societies trying to work their own way out of domestic crises. Although these, like Nuremberg, were trials by victors against alleged aggressors, the victors were ordinary citizens and the aggressors were their own military officers. The military junta that had seized power in April 1967 had a sorry record of repression, purges, media closures, intervention in universities, banning of books (nearly eight hundred, including Sophocles and Shakespeare), the incarceration of thousands of political dissidents, and the enactment of laws that effectively stifled public life in Greece. The conclusion to military rule came when the regime tried a coup on Cyprus in July 1974. Turkey, with its own interest in the half of Cyprus that was under its jurisdiction, responded by landing troops and bringing the two countries to the brink of war. Probable defeat for the Greek colonels moved them to oust General Demetrios Ioannides (who had replaced the original leader, Colonel George Papadopoulos) and began negotiations for a return to civilian rule.

The civilian government of Constantine Karamanlis spread its "dejuntafication" blanket over a wide terrain, dismissing or replacing an estimated 100,000 military personnel and bureaucrats at all levels of government. Six months after taking office, the government undertook criminal proceedings against over one hundred former officials for participation in the coup or in subsequent repressive activities or torture. The actions were supported by a clear majority of the civilian population. Nikiforos Diamandouros argues that Karamanlis pursued a carefully orchestrated gradualist course

to keep the surviving armed forces at bay, while satisfying the popular demand that its members be punished (Diamandouros 1986;
Psomiades 1982). He paced the trials so that they occurred after an
election that provided legitimacy to the civilian government, and
he ensured that civilians were installed in controlling positions
within the police force, security services, and intelligence agencies
as well as appointed chiefs of staff. A private suit against the protagonists of the colonels' regime preceded the elections, but even that
case was not tried until nine months later. An aborted coup in February 1975 provided the prime minister with the opportunity to
sideline sympathizers with the colonels, and at that point he proceeded quickly to criminal trials. The trial resulted in lengthy sentences for leaders and lesser sentences for others. Death sentences
were given to the major three leaders, but these were commuted to
life imprisonment. There was no retreat from the hard-line position nor were there any amnesties, and Greece has not since shifted
from the democratic forms that followed.

The successful transition from authoritarian military rule to democratic civilian government in Greece is generally viewed as a
model for how such transformations should and can take place.
But the conditions may have been unique: the population was overwhelmingly opposed to the colonels; the international community
was not supportive of them; several bloody confrontations between
military personnel and civilians had galvanized public opinion
against them; and they made the error (repeated in Argentina
many years later) of provoking a stronger power to the point of an
unwinnable war at the very moment when the internal cohesion of
the military junta was breaking down. The interim leader for civilian government was a strong anti-Communist right-wing former
prime minister (thus initially trusted by the military); and he was
skilful in devising winnable strategies and timing them to ensure
maximum popular support.

The Argentine Example

The Greek example was not an easy act to follow. In Argentina in
the mid-1970s, as in Greece earlier, a military junta had tried to
prevent leftist ideas from developing or flourishing. It had kidnapped ("disappeared" is the Latin-American verb) an estimated
thirty thousand individuals, had tortured and murdered many of

them, had imposed bans on books and burned them in public demonstrations (including such "revolutionary" items as Saint Exupery's *Little Prince*), had intervened in universities, and had finally been brought to heel by an external power after the junta had foolishly tried to wage an off-shore war that it could not win.[16] At that point, too, the junta had lost its internal cohesion, though not to the degree that had occurred in Greece. After it negotiated a peaceful transition to a democratic government, and in this respect it differs from the military in Greece, the military remained a force to be reckoned with. The new government was unable to dismantle the military apparatus immediately. In addition, unlike in Greece, in Argentina a sizable population still supported the military (or at least continued to believe that the country was threatened by subversives for whom no compassion was merited). For these reasons, the new government sponsored a truth commission with the intention of using it as a preliminary stage towards court trials.

The truth commission was successful – nearly nine thousand cases of disappeared, tortured, or murdered individuals were well documented by human rights groups within a year of the political transition. The proceedings were televised and inexpensive copies of the cases entitled *Nunca Más* (Argentina, Comisión Nacional sobre la Desaparición de Personas, 1985) went on sale in every kiosk in the country. The collective nature of the crimes was later described by one of President Raul Alfonsín's advisors in the democratic government that took over from the military junta in 1984:

Some participation in human rights violations, even if only through acquiescence by a failure to act, was universal within the military. By implementing state terror, the power of the military hierarchy had been great enough to compel compliance to its policies. Human rights violations were the result of a centralized nationwide policy. The method of terror was basically the same throughout the country. In the pursuance of orders, army officers enjoyed support from their comrades and were granted *de facto* immunity. When torture or summary executions were carried out, perpetrators could count on unlimited assistance from the entire state apparatus. No officer would attempt to stop or report abuses. Officers delivered prisoners to specified places at specified times, and commanders were briefed on how events developed. No opportunity for legal defense was ever accorded to those detained or abducted. Victims names were never made public nor even disclosed to their closest relatives. Lawyers who submitted writs of habeas corpus were threatened and some were killed. Police avoided reports or claim records of any sort and merely rebuffed claimants. When the military finally waived power and civilian rule reemerged, new armed forces did not replace the previous military establishment. (Malamud-Goti 1990, 189–90)[17]

The attempt to prosecute crimes perpetrated by military officers was controversial in Argentina in the mid-1980s. Democracy was not yet well embedded. The armed forces were not yet reduced in size (that occurred under the Carlos Menem administration, even though it was also Menem who granted amnesty to all 280 members of the security forces who still faced trial for human rights abuses, including the leading officers already found guilty and incarcerated). The Constitution of Argentina was lenient towards the armed forces, and, with time, the officers became ever more protective of one another, irrespective of their individual offences. In late 1986, the advisor quoted above, recognizing that the government was losing public support as the economy deteriorated, advocated the *punto finale*, or "full-stop," law that set a deadline with regard to when further punishments would be imposed. The new democratic government under Alfonsín had failed to establish the legitimacy of the trials, and before its electoral mandate had expired it was nudged out of power. Jaime Malamud-Goti (1995, 192) speculated on the errors of the government that he advised:

> The government probably failed to choose the politically best criteria for ascribing criminal responsibility. It probably lost the initiative at an early stage when, three days after being sworn in, the president as commander-in-chief of the armed forces decided to prosecute the army commanders-in-chief. Had he ordered the trials of sixty, eighty, or a hundred renowned officers instead of twelve, the populace might have taken the trials more seriously and the trials might have been more effective in enhancing the credibility of democracy.

Perhaps in the Argentine situation of that time more trials would have been efficacious, but this advice seems to fly in the face of experiences elsewhere. If one wants to engage in speculation, it is likely that arbitrary executions of the top twelve leaders would have sent just as strong, if not a stronger, message to the population and would have kick-started the era of democracy. The major contribution to global society of the new democracy in Argentina of that time was the truth commission's substantial and accessible report. However, human rights organizations representing survivors who still do not know the fate of their loved ones continue to demand justice, and even with the passage of time they have finally found ways to get around the precise wording of the amnesty. The record in Argentina is not closed.

Truth Commissions and Other Processes for Accountability

International criminal court trials and tribunals have global dimensions and formal procedures that are focused on single individuals or small groups of leaders who have been involved in mass atrocities. National courts may be equally formal, though their location is within the country in which the acts occurred and there is generally less participation on the part of non-nationals. Truth commissions are next in the line of formal inquiries and may be extensive or limited, involving international or only national participants. The objective of truth commissions, at least if they are intended to do their job (often they are intended only to take care of appearances),[18] is to get at what actually happened so that survivors can know what transpired and possibly find closure. Unlike trials, truth commissions do not have the objective of assigning guilt, obliging full accountability, or punishing transgressors. And, more than trials, they can be adapted to discover truths about groups as well as individuals. Other options for dealing formally with past crimes are discussed in chapter 12.

RETRIBUTION FOR COLLABORATION

The situation in France (mentioned above) was not dissimilar to that elsewhere following the Nazi era.[19] A chilling account of the eagerness of ordinary folk to deal out rough and unforgiving punishment in the interval between the Nazi occupation of Czechoslovakia and the Communist takeover documents a similar tale. Benjamin Frommer's account (2005) is chilling because it tells all too well how willing so many people were to denounce their neighbours or their relatives in order to curry favour with the Nazis (and how they were denounced in turn by their neighbours and their relatives when the cycle began again under Communist rule). They told the Nazis about friends who mimicked or mocked Nazi soldiers or listened to foreign broadcasts. They spoke against the annoying in-law or the imperfect teacher. Some managed to find fault with many fellow Czechs. When what went around came around at last, those who won awards and who were given money or goodies by the Nazis were roundly denounced by their neighbours. But so were the in-laws, the landlords, the corner grocery store owners, even one's own parents or children. Easier to denounce than to divorce: denouncing became the most popular political action of the immediate postwar era. The floodgates opened for denunciations and other forms of retribution during the final months of the war. As it became clear that Germany would lose, President-in-Exile Edvard Bénes encouraged Czechs to deal with their past. Punishment for both Germans in Czech territories and Czech collaborators was the first act of re-establishing an independent state. Not only in Czechoslovakia but all across the European continent the first victims were Germans and the well-known collaborators. The politicians spoke of "national cleansing" – a phrase we of later generations have attached to the horrors of the Yugoslav wars in the 1990s.

Summary courts and tribunals were established and staffed by ill-trained citizens who tried over thirty-two thousand alleged collaborators and war criminals and some 135,000 cases of "offenses against national honour." Thousands more were arrested and incarcerated but never charged. Before the Communist coup in February 1948, nearly seven hundred individuals were executed. Frommer (2005) observes that this was more than the total killed during the subsequent four decades of Communist rule. The postwar atmosphere that allowed sheer revenge to serve in place of accountability encouraged pettiness rather than justice, and political sympathies also played a role during this short interim. Leading intellectuals and many others have referred to the trials as perverted justice and as being among the saddest pages of Czech history.

Czechs, who behaved with such extraordinary courage and restraint throughout the war and occupation, must surely suffer remorse when they think about their meanness during the peace. To be fair, there were judges and politicians who steadfastly refused to parlay minor infringements into major offences. Since there were no adequate definitions of collaboration or other crimes, each court took on its own stamp of harshness or leniency, and this often depended on the sense of justice held by judges. As time passed, the proportion of those charged with crimes who were executed or incarcerated for lengthy periods declined. Perhaps the taste for revenge was finally satiated.

The usefulness of formal trials and Western justice in these circumstances may lie precisely in the fact that, as Havel suggested, they are prophylactics against more vicious forms of frontier or vigilante justice. But in the immediate aftermath of a prolonged war and repression, time-consuming courts based on Western notions of empirical evidence are rarely possible. Neighbourhood courts with untrained judges are quite possibly the best that can be managed.

RETRIBUTION FOR LONG-PAST CRIMES

Retribution for military occupation, with all the privations, torture, and other crimes involved, may be inevitable. But what about retribution for crimes perpetrated against one's relatives or friends a full generation or more earlier? Is this also inevitable? Consider the case of Yugoslavia. When Serbs began their war in Croatia, the soldiers were well aware of what the Croatian Ustashe had done to their ancestors in the 1940s. Though Tito pulled Yugoslavia together and obliged Serbs, Croats, Slovenes, Bosnians, Montenegrins, Kosovars, and others to coexist, the memory of concentration camps in which Croatians tortured Serbs, Jews, and many others remained alive, passed on from generation to generation. Were the resentments handed on to new generations the burning cause of the war nearly a half century later, as those who use the case as evidence that crimes must be judged and dealt with would argue?

The contrary argument is that, while the memories may have been imprinted on the brains of second generations, that in itself need not have led to the Yugoslavian civil war. In historical fact, Tito, as leader of the Partisans in the crucial 1940s, swiftly executed many (some reports would say "thousands") of the Ustashe leaders as well as the leaders of the main Serbian opposition guerrilla group (the Chetniks). There were no trials, no truth commissions, just a firing squad. Now, if trials had been held for the Ustashe but not for the Partisans, would the country have been safer, kinder, gentler, and more likely to survive past Tito's death in 1980? What happens when every organized group, and many individuals, are guilty of war crimes? Who should be purged, who should apologize to whom, and what would make the world safer for all survivors?

These questions beg answers, and we can't know for sure what might have happened if something earlier had not happened or if it had been dealt with through war crimes trials when it did. Suppose, for the moment, that we accept the argument that crimes must be dealt with, that we accept the assumption that impunity is destructive of both individuals and societies. Then we need to determine what forms of justice are appropriate. Since societies differ in their history, their status and location within the world system, their culture and their demography, we can probably assume at the outset that one size does not fit all. If it is to be just, the form justice takes must accommodate the particulars of the society in which it is to be applied.

What Follows

This chapter has offered a general discussion of the issues. In the next several chapters, I consider these issues at ground level in societies that have been affected by mass crimes during internal wars. I begin with Cambodia, a society that has the dubious record of having killed at least one-quarter, and possibly one-third, of its entire population and whose political and economic history since the end of the killing fields has been dismal. Among my questions is this one: will the proposed trials, thirty years after the events, bring about a release from that history and contribute to the welfare of Cambodia's people? Rwanda, by contrast, seems obsessed with making its génocidaires accountable for past events. So I ask: is this concern excessive and is it actually just? The convoluted events of the early 1990s in Bosnia concluded with NATO bombs and occupying forces under UN auspices. The wisdom of both the bombing and the occupation has been questioned by many observers, but even more questions have been posed about the tardiness and, on tragic occasions, the ineffectiveness of EU, US, and UN actions. Looking at the current situation, we see totally different societies, with Serbia, ironically, being a major victim of the disintegration of Yugoslavia.

PART TWO

Broken Societies

A Street in Kigali, Rwanda

4

Global Context for Cambodia

UN intervention in Cambodia occurred after the Khmer Rouge regime had been defeated in most of the country and the Vietnamese forces had left. It came with a great deal of money and an army of bureaucrats resolved to bring peace to the country and the region. It had majestic objectives when it organized a peace conference. The conference failed to bring peace, however, and the well-intentioned bureaucrats turned their attention to imposing an election instead. The election succeeded in the sense that it did occur and that Cambodians duly voted, but it would stretch the truth to say that it brought justice and democracy with it. The UNTAC (United Nations Transitional Authority in Cambodia) period, as it was known, did provide enough safety for the return of some 300,000 refugees, and it enabled the survivors of one of the most atrocious eras in modern history to gain a modest hold on a renewal of their society. But when the UN left, a guerrilla war continued in the northwestern region, and it was not until Pol Pot's death that the Khmer Rouge finally disintegrated.

This chapter focuses on the global context for Cambodia shortly before, during, and after the Khmer Rouge savagery of 1975–79, concluding with the lengthy negotiations between the Cambodian government and the UN over the establishment of trials of KR leaders. Internal dimensions of Cambodian society since the end of the Vietnamese occupation are the concern of chapter 5. While I in no way intend to treat lightly the responsibility of the Khmer Rouge for their savagery, I believe that that brutal period and the prolonged guerrilla war following it need to be seen within the global context. Cambodia's neighbours – Vietnam, Thailand, and China – and the United States, all acting in their own interests, had profound impacts on the little kingdom. Moreover, the United Nations, while ostensibly trying to encourage peace, not only failed to do so but also contributed to the prolongation of the war and to the spread of disinformation about it.[1]

BEFORE DEMOCRATIC KAMPUCHEA

Some four centuries after the demise of Angkar Wat, the French empire extended to what became Indochina, including Cambodia, Laos, and Vietnam, and controlled the entire region for about eighty years. Japan established a garrison in Cambodia in August 1941 but left responsibility for government to the French colonial authorities. Japanese occupation following the overthrow of the French (Vichy) administration was brief during 1945, and it was followed by another short period of independence before France was again in control of the region. Independence was finally declared on 9 November 1953.

The Geneva Accords of 1954 restored formal independence. Norodom Sihanouk ruled first as a constitutional monarch (he had been crowned by the French in 1941), then (from 1955 to 1960) as the elected prime minister while his father was named king; and, following his father's death in 1960, he ruled until 1970 as Prince Sihanouk and Head of State.

Civil War, 1970–75

The context for Sihanouk's rule changed in the 1960s as the United States prepared to fight against North Vietnam for what American leaders contended was a war against Communism. Sihanouk tried to play all sides in order to maintain an official policy of neutrality. He was deposed in 1970 by General Lon Nol, who was supported by the United States but not by the Khmer people, and by Prince Sisowath Sirik Matak. Sihanouk joined with the then small Communist party, which had hitherto sought to depose him. With his support, the National United Front for Kampuchea, as this party called itself, became better known as the Khmer Rouge (KR). Sihanouk's objective was to denounce the Khmer Republic, as Lon Nol's period was called. This is generally understood as the beginning of a civil war that lasted for the next five years. Craig Etcheson (2005, 6–7), a leading scholar of this period in Cambodia, claims that the KR had already established its trademark in the regions where it was strong, killing all whom its leaders regarded as class enemies.

While the KR was establishing its territory in the eastern provinces, the Lon Nol government established "Khmer-Mon" ethnic nationalism, which was directed against Vietnamese. During this period, as described by Australian scholar Jay Jordens (1996, 134), "thousands of Vietnamese were butchered by special Lon Nol military units, and many thousands more were deported or fled across the border into Vietnam." Much of this period is forgotten history, possibly because the successive period was so brutal that the killing of thousands lost its shock value in the face of the killing of millions. This is vital information, providing one of the threads in an explanation for the KR and post-KR relationships between Vietnam and Cambodia.

US Bombing

The United States, persuaded that Vietcong (North Vietnamese) bases were supplying their enemy through the Cambodian border with Vietnam, began intensive bombing of the border region. Recently released US Air Force data on all American bombings of Indochina between 1964 and 1975 indicate that bombing of Cambodian territory began on 4 October 1965 under the presidency of Lyndon Johnson, nearly four years before the acknowledged commencement date. Taylor Owen and Ben Kiernan published the data together with a map of bombed sites. The map shows that bombing was not restricted to the border region; rather, it spread throughout the entire country (Owen and Kiernan 2006). These newly released data show that, between October 1965 and 15 August 1973, an estimated 2,756,941 tons of ordnance were delivered in some 230,516 sorties (compared to just over 2 million tons delivered by the allies on Japan throughout the entire Second World War, including the nuclear bombs on Hiroshima and Nagasaki). Further, Over 3.5 thousand sites were listed as "unknown" targets, and over eight thousand sites were assigned no target at all (Owen and Kiernan 2006, 62–3).[2]

Under President Nixon, beginning in 1969, bombing escalated and continued even after the US Congress demanded that it be restricted to within thirty kilometres of the Vietnamese border. Owen and Kiernan argue that the rationale was to keep enemy forces at bay while US forces withdrew from Vietnam: the Cambodian population became "cannon fodder" to save American soldiers. Bombing escalated again between February and August 1973, presumably to stop the Khmer Rouge advance on Phnom Penh (Owen and Kiernan 2006, 67.) On 15 August 1973, Congress forbad the administration to carry on bombing.[3]

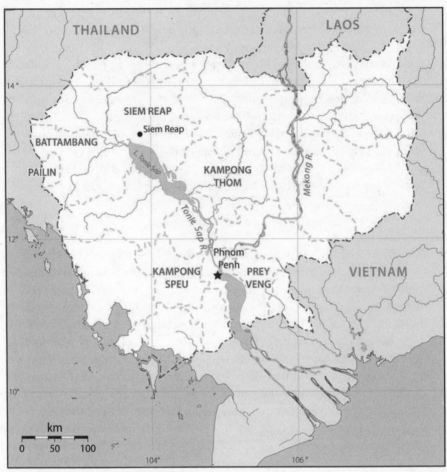

Cambodia – before the wars

By the time the bombing finally stopped, Cambodia was devastated. The bombs destroyed rice fields in the Tonle Sap and Mekong river deltas and, with them, the lives of many peasants. There were many thousands of civilian deaths. Before the new data were accessible to researchers, estimates were between fifty thousand and 150,000: obviously, these will now be revised steeply upwards but reliable data are not available and the actual death toll may never be established because this occurred within the period of the civil war, and the subsequent Khmer Rouge period erased evidence. In some villages, the destruction was so great that no one survived. Thousands of peasants were displaced, thousands more migrated to the scarcely functioning cities in hopes of gaining food sources or work.

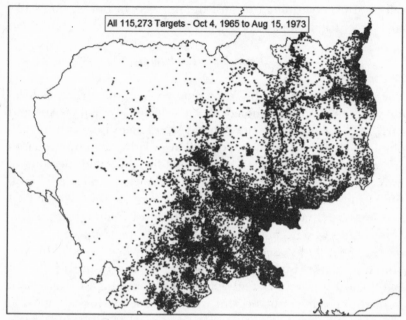

All 115,273 Targets - Oct 4, 1965 to Aug 15, 1973

Cambodia – bomb sites

Owen's maps, more than any literary source, indicate the absolute destruction of Cambodia at that time. Their lives, families, and villages destroyed, peasants were easily recruited into the revolutionary forces created by the Khmer Rouge. It was not Communist propaganda that enticed them: it was the death of their world. The KR was already established, but it is fair to surmise that its rapid growth was a direct consequence of American bombing.

KR recruits had other and long-standing complaints to go with their anger over the American bombing. They had been abused for many generations by urbanites – some of whom were ethnic Khmer, some of whom were Vietnamese, French, or other European. The abuse took the form of marks of disrespect. Peasants could not come into Phnom Penh, for example, in their traditional sarongs: they had to wear shoes and top-body clothing that was not part of their normal attire and that, further, was too expensive for many. They were frequently humiliated by urban people, made ashamed of their illiteracy, their poverty. They were also hungry. Much of their produce was going to urban centres or export markets through intermediaries, and the producers were left with insufficient food for their own families. When (former king and now prince) Sihanouk, whom they revered, made common cause with the Communists, they accepted his

call to arms, determined to oust the usurpers of power, Lon Nol's
government, and Americans.

Khmer Rouge Leadership

The revolution was not, however, led by Sihanouk; rather, its leaders were ideologues schooled in Paris during the late 1940s and
early 1950s. They had decided to test Mao's theories of cultural revolution. They apparently believed that only by abandoning cities
and modern technologies could people live pure and meaningful
lives. Their context included the rise of the Communist regime in
China and the proxy war in Korea. Saloth Sar (later called Pol Pot)
and Ieng Sary participated in a maelstrom of Communist politics.
Many others who became leaders of the KR a few years later, including Son Sen, Rath Samoeun, Hou Youn, May Mann, and Thiounn
Mumm, had likewise engaged in the feverish activity in Paris. When
Saloth Sar returned to Cambodia, he married Khieu Ponnary and
worked with others who became leaders of the KR, including Nuon
Chea and Tou Samouth (Chandler, DP 2000, 190).

Some of these compatriots were killed by government forces and
others were assassinated by the party for presumed relations with Vietnamese or other impure forces over the next couple of decades. But
those who survived the early period waged a successful war against
the state army led by Lon Nol (who himself escaped before the end).

DEMOCRATIC KAMPUCHEA, 1975-79

The civil war ended in April 1975. For the next forty-four months,
urbanites who had not been killed outright were force marched or
made to work in the fields. Many died from exhaustion, starvation,
or broken souls. Current estimates of deaths due to KR executions
and starvation range from 1.7 million to 2.5 million in a total population of 7.5 to 8 million – from a quarter to nearly one-third of the
total population. Torture prisons were established throughout the
country. One of these, the infamous Tuol Sleng – also known as S-21
– on the outskirts of Phnom Penh has been turned into a ghastly museum. An estimated seventeen thousand enemies of the state were incarcerated here for varying but usually short periods of time – short
because almost all died under torture. The corpses from Tuol Sleng
were dispatched to Choeung Ek, now known around the world as

"the killing fields." Professionals, especially teachers and professors but also medical doctors and nurses, virtually anyone who was literate, along with bureaucrats, those who ran the cities, and Buddhist monks were the main targets. Ethnic Vietnamese and Muslim Chams were also victims, but this was not primarily an ethnic war; rather, it was a war against urbanites and modernity. It was a peasant revolution, its leaders notwithstanding, a full-scale class war. The country under the KR regime was known as Democratic Kampuchea (DK).

Many of the soldiers were children, aged anywhere from six or seven to eighteen or so. Children were used in all sectors of the DK government as factory workers, prison guards, torturers, even executioners. They were given guns or other destructive instruments and scarcely any rules for using them. They were encouraged to kill urban slackers, bourgeois enemies, and useless intellectuals. Older soldiers patrolled borders against potential invasions from Vietnam. Purity being impossible to define or sustain, it was only a short time before the party turned in on itself, killing its own leaders and then its own followers, while ideologues claimed that this person or that one was insufficiently pure. Young soldiers were both killers and victims. Surviving cadres were still children when the KR lost control of the country, but they knew nothing except the fear, brutality, and horror they had experienced. They had been taught that the agrarian model of the KR was pure, that all else was polluted, and they had no capacity for distancing themselves from their experience. Those who survived are now adults and parents, unschooled, impoverished, and often ill. In the opening decade of the twenty-first century, hunger again stalks the land.

International Context, 1975–79

KR soldiers initially worked with North Vietnamese forces along the border in the early 1970s. But as Americans withdrew from Vietnam, and as the tempo of the Cambodian civil war intensified, the KR broke with Vietnam. Once the revolution was under way, KR leaders became increasingly hostile towards Vietnam and increasingly cozy with China. As early as 1977 the DK government was engaged in frontier skirmishes with Vietnamese forces. The skirmishes invited retaliation from Vietnamese forces, who occupied much of eastern Cambodia for a two-month period in 1977. The DK government broke off diplomatic relations with Vietnam at the end of that year. Pol Pot's celebrated paranoia may have played a role in this, aided by the general animosity that Cambodians felt towards Vietnamese, even though the two peoples had shared the long French occupation and the liberation struggles that ended it. But more immediately, the issue was Cambodia's close relationship to China and Vietnam's relationship to the USSR.

China provided Cambodia with money, technical aid, and training as well as an ideological model. This was the era of the Cultural Revolution, and Mao's opposition to intellectuals, professionals, and city dwellers more generally provided the inspiration for Pol Pot's Cambodian revolution. While these contributions were important for Cambodia, the benefit for China was more than neighbourly good feeling. The USSR supported Vietnam, enabling it to become an important actor in Southeast Asia; China's interests were best served by isolating Vietnam wherever possible. Cambodia was one small piece in the Chinese strategy.

DEFECTIONS, INVASION, AND THE PEOPLE'S REPUBLIC OF KAMPUCHEA

The KR regime was murderous by any measure. As time went by, it began to turn in on itself, capriciously killing off its own soldiers and leaders at any hint of disloyalty (or even with no hints at all). Sensing that they would soon be among the victims, several leaders, independently, escaped to the border with Vietnam, where they joined Vietnamese forces in an invasion of Cambodia in 1979. They fairly quickly gained control of Phnom Penh and established a puppet regime called the People's Republic of Kampuchea (PRK). KR forces retreated to the northwestern region and, with aid from Thailand, established bases across the western border and sustained guerrilla warfare throughout the next two decades.

Among the KR leaders who defected to Vietnam before 1979 were Heng Samrin, Hun Sen, and Chea Sim. Heng Samrin was a senior military commander; Hun Sen was a commissar for a troop regiment; and Chea Sim was a political leader. All had worked in eastern regions under KR control prior to their defections. Joining them were other Cambodians who had been trained in North Vietnam and who had stayed there or who, although residing outside Cambodia, were in other ways allied with the KR. Under the victorious Vietnamese forces in Phnom Penh, these individuals became major political leaders in the PRK. Heng Samrin became president, Hun Sen eventually rose to become (and remain) prime minister, and Chea Sim became leader of the National Assembly. Other defectors also gained new positions with the government in Phnom Penh or elsewhere in parts of the country no longer under KR control.

The new regime, under the party name of People's Revolutionary Party of Kampuchea (PRPK), extended public announcements inviting KR soldiers to defect, promising them leniency and re-education, and meting out severe punishments to those who chose otherwise. Cambodians, many of whom welcomed the Vietnamese invasion despite a long-standing dislike for the Vietnamese, were less than enthusiastic when the new regime turned out to be not much different from the old one.[4]

People's Revolutionary Tribunal

By way of trying to persuade the Khmer population that the PRK was not the same as the DK, in July 1979 the new regime set up a trial for two leaders of the KR – Pol Pot and Ieng Sary – on charges of genocide. Both were absent, and their (court-appointed) defence lawyers agreed that they had led the criminal forces. Both were convicted and sentenced to death. However, Pol Pot was never caught (he died peacefully in 1998). The PRPK maintained control of Phnom Penh and much of Cambodia through the following years until 1989. Ieng Sary was pardoned in 1996 in a deal that helped the government of that period to finally destroy the KR.

Cambodia in 1979

At the time of the PRPK takeover in 1979, the cities of Cambodia had been largely destroyed. There were no hospitals, no schools, no public transport systems. Roads within urban centres and throughout the whole country were severely damaged, many beyond repair. The technology of the twentieth century was gone: electricity, telephones, clean water, toilets, typewriters, and trains. Banks and all things connected to the financial sector had been destroyed.

Rural regions in the northeast were devastated, and many villages were emptied by KR forces who were in retreat from incoming Vietnamese forces. Villages in northwestern regions were subjected to

continuing battles between surviving KR and Vietnamese forces.
The KR took much of the rice harvest with them as they fled north-
ward, and they left few animals alive. Even the fishing industry was
troubled by a lack of boats and nets,[5] and landmines covered much
of the countryside. In the midst of the chaos thousands of people
frantically travelled across the country trying to find their families
or regain their homes. Crops were not planted and hunger was
widespread. In addition to the physical destruction, large numbers
of survivors had lost all hope for the future, were spiritually devastated, and were lacking in motivation to begin again. Orphans were
many, and, while parents grieved their losses, many of those families that did retain or find their children no longer had the capacity
to raise them in traditional ways or to overcome the training the
children had received in KR camps.

By one count there were only fifteen doctors in the country, and
intellectuals – indeed most members of what had been a middle
class – had been virtually wiped out. Where schools were reintro-
duced, they had to operate without books and managed only where
there were surviving teachers whose memory served in place of cur-
ricular materials (Mysliwiec 1988).

According to Sampong Peou, during the PRPK period the legal system, beginning with only five judges and a handful of law students,
was somewhat rebuilt. A new constitution was introduced in 1981,
and courts were created – at least on paper (Peou 2000). However,
police retained excessive control, torture continued to be practised,
and, according to the Lawyers Committee for Human Rights, referring to the period beginning in 1979, "the government ... has imprisoned thousands of persons for taking part in violent or non-violent
activities on behalf of the Khmer Rouge or the non-communist opposition" (quoted in Peou 2000, 68). KR prisoners who were initially
imprisoned were generally pardoned, provided they acknowledged
Communist leadership; leaders of non-Communist reform groups
were generally kept in jails or killed (Gottesman 2003, 53–5 and
chap. 3; Short 2004). There were no national elections prior to the
UN intervention in late 1991. Guerrilla warfare continued throughout the 1980s: the forces loyal to the KR in the northwest, now operating out of bases inside the Thailand border as well as Battambang
Province, were still strong enough to make the PRPK vulnerable
to takeover.

UNITED NATIONS: THE UNITED STATES
AND CHINA VERSUS VIETNAM

Despite its horrendous record of human rights crimes, Democratic Kampuchea retained its seat at the United Nations during this period, courtesy of politicking by the United States, China, and Thailand. In the Security Council, it was opposed only by the USSR. As Berdal and Leifer (1996, 29) argue with reference to the Vietnamese invasion of Cambodia in 1979: "At issue was whether or not Vietnam was to become the dominant state in the peninsula. That matter primarily involved a test of wills between Vietnam and China." Further, "the attendant invasion of Cambodia was interpreted in both Washington and Beijing as clear evidence of Soviet expansionist intent through political proxy" (ibid.). The proxy war between the mammoths was one of the last of that era; Mikhail Gorbachev soon began the process of withdrawing from Third World wars, and this included removing the USSR's support of Vietnam.

Thailand also felt threatened by Vietnam's invasion, which situated Vietnamese troops on its eastern border. Thus, it came about that China and Thailand agreed to support the DK, and, in a curious turn difficult for outsiders to comprehend, Prince Sihanouk went to the United Nations to argue the DK case even though some of its victims were his own children and grandchildren.

Part of the explanation for the UN's decision may lie in ignorance of what had happened in the little kingdom. Prince Sihanouk's initial support for the KR in 1970 had effectively silenced the rest of the world during the DK period. He appeared to be still heading a government in exile in Beijing, while the Lon Nol government took the Cambodian place in the United Nations under the new name of the state, the Khmer Republic. In 1975, and until he left office in April 1976, Sihanouk again appeared as head of state for Democratic Kampuchea. When the KR revolution succeeded in taking over Phnom Penh, apparently with Sihanouk's blessing, the world accepted the new government. To much of the external world, Sihanouk was still the personification of Cambodia. The harsh realities of the KR regime may not have been understood outside, and, until refugees began spilling into Thailand, very little news was available. Virtually all Western outsiders were expelled or hurried away before the revolution began, and few who chose to stay survived to tell the tale. While these events explain part of the world's failure to respond, other considerations were probably more influential. These include, for France, its own colonial record; for the United States, its own brutal record of bombing.

External fears mounted, however, when the DK was replaced in January 1979 with the establishment of the PRK and its PRPK government allied with Vietnam. The Khmer Rouge record was viewed at the UN, in the US, and, most significantly, in China as a manageable problem (indeed, as not their problem at all). For the United States, Vietnam was a Communist regime, and for China it was a local power that challenged China's hegemony in the region. The UN became involved in documenting Vietnam's invasion as a violation of the UN Charter. Despite the Soviet veto, the General Assembly demanded Vietnam's military withdrawal and accorded the KR the right to occupy the Cambodian seat. Although this is recorded as a win for the KR at the United Nations, it was, in fact, a win for both China and the United States – one of the many ironies of history in Southeast Asia.

Encouraged by the US and member countries of ASEAN, resistance movements emerged to oppose the PRK. Former prime minister Son Sann created the Khmer People's National Liberation Front shortly after the PRK was established. It and other groups formed an opposition in exile early in the 1980s, with Sihanouk as its president. Western military support was provided for continuing guerrilla war against the PRK. Vietnam responded with additional forces to support the PRK. A stalemate ensued. Meanwhile, Cambodia's poverty intensified as external countries isolated it. To this point, the horrors of Democratic Kampuchea under the KR were still not publicly acknowledged by world leaders.

WITHDRAWAL OF VIETNAM, BEGINNING OF PRK/SOC

External events finally altered the domestic circumstances of Cambodia. Towards the end of 1986, Vietnam decided to develop market economic principles similar to those started under perestroika in the USSR.[6] But to gain access to world markets it had to overcome the barriers established because of its occupation of Cambodia. Vietnam then began talks with other interest groups in Cambodia, particularly with the still symbolically powerful Prince Sihanouk, to develop a negotiated agreement on political power that would

allow it to withdraw. Glasnost in the USSR reduced Vietnam's status
and power as a regional force. Finally, Vietnam said it would withdraw unconditionally from Cambodia by September 1989, leaving
the PRK to carry on alone, now under the label of State of Cambodia (SOC). The transition to SOC also involved a commitment to
adopt private enterprise. Guerrilla battles continued in the northwest. Craig Etcheson attributes substantial strength to the KR
forces, aided by bases inside Thailand. Indeed, he claims that they
were "backed militarily, economically, and politically by China, the
United States, the Association of Southeast Asian Nations (ASEAN),
and most of the rest of the Western world." He attributes less
strength to the PRK/SOC military forces but observes that the degree of success they managed to gain "was no small accomplishment, and it did indeed prevent the return of the Pol Pot regime"
(Etcheson 2005, 29–30).[7]

THE UNTAC PERIOD

In view of the declaration by Vietnam, the United Nations chose this
moment to convene an international conference in Paris. Australia
presented a plan for a negotiated settlement. This included a council
in which all Cambodian factions would participate and that would assume the Cambodian seat at the United Nations. No agreement was
likely to satisfy either the PRK/SOC government or the Khmer
Rouge, and the agreement finally hammered out in Paris in 1991 depended in large part on miscalculations and deviousness on the part
of all concerned.

The 1990 UN Security Council adopted the Framework for a Comprehensive Political Settlement of the Cambodian Conflict, which advocated elections in preparation for which (and during which) the
UN would assume control of key ministries in Phnom Penh. Says
Etcheson (2005, 32): "Though the Phnom Penh government agreed
to this arrangement on paper, in practice, they had another idea altogether." The PRPK party renamed itself the Cambodian People's
Party (CPP), now formally shorn of its devotion to Communist principles. Hun Sen had become prime minister in 1985, and Heng Samrin was, about this time, replaced by Chea Sim as party secretary.
China did not object because Vietnam, shorn of USSR support, was
no longer a regional threat. Berdal and Leifer (1996, 35) say that
the KR leadership "almost certainly miscalculated that the Phnom

Penh administration would fall apart with United Nations' intervention." And they argue that the UN Transitional Authority strength-
ened the Hun Sen government.

Paris Conference

The international conference in Paris in October 1991 concluded
negotiations with the Comprehensive Political Settlement of the Cambodia Conflict. This settlement was to be implemented by the United
Nations Transitional Authority in Cambodia (UNTAC), whose primary task was to maintain the peace while developing the capacities
for electoral democracy. The objective was to disarm and demobilize
armed personnel, resettle refugees, and prepare for national elections. UNTAC was to take administrative oversight of Cambodia and
was to be provided with "all powers necessary to ensure the implementation" of the Paris Peace Accords.[8] These powers included
means of sustaining human rights, such as prevention of attacks on
refugees or combatants who had laid down their weapons, and caring
for prisoners of war (Schear 1996, 143–5). The total operation was
the most expensive of its kind in the history of the United Nations: it
cost over $US3 billion and involved more than twenty-five thousand
participants, some sixteen thousand of whom were troops (Chandler,
D.P. 2000, 173–4). It was the largest peacekeeping force since the UN
operations in the Congo in the early 1960s (Findlay 2002, 125).[9]

The extraordinary effort and allocation of personnel and money,
however, did not bring peace or even disarmament to Cambodia. Neither of the major parties involved in the peace talks and over the subsequent period attempted to keep promises. Etchesons's research,
based on the internal documents of the government of that time,
leads to the conclusion that the government was engaged in a deliberate and centrally organized process of obfuscation. As he states it:

> It was a highly organized strategy to create as much chaos as
> possible among those who were, under the putative protection
> of the UN, attempting to challenge the entrenched power of the
> Cambodian People's Party in an open electoral contest. These
> tactics revealed clearly the fact that the People's Party simply did
> not accept their former military opponents as legitimate political
> players. The People's Party operated as if by the credo that, in
> war by any means, anything goes. (Etcheson 2005, 51)

As well, by May 1992, the KR had reneged on agreements and had now removed its negotiator, Son Sen, from further interaction with UNTAC. The ceasefire was ignored during KR wet-season attacks on both government and UNTAC forces. In the northwest, the KR expanded its control, and large-scale fighting in some areas prevented peacekeeping forces from being deployed. UNTAC was staffed by soldiers from Australia, Japan, and Indonesia, and none of these countries was willing to risk troops' lives for the sake of peace in Cambodia: this was supposed to be a peacekeeping operation (Berdal and Leifer 1996, 42–3). Consequently, several northern regions of the country remained under KR control. Meanwhile, and this constituted the up-front reasons for KR refusal to cooperate with UNTAC, the CPP/SOC government was still in place, and it was still able to use its secret police for its own political objectives. Despite the obvious difficulties, UNTAC declared that an election should take place.

1993 Election

The political parties vying for office had not developed any capacity for mutual tolerance, and overlying all of the ideological and practical issues was now the question of Vietnamese "invaders." There had always been a substantial ethnic Vietnamese population in Cambodia. These people were targeted as enemies by all parties, and, while Hun Sen's CPP pointed the finger at other parties for advancing Vietnamese interests, other Cambodians feared that the CPP was really just a front for the renewed takeover of the country by Vietnam. UNTAC was unable to protect either ethnic Vietnamese or politicians and businesspeople who openly backed parties other than Hun Sen's CPP. The opposition parties were the Front Uni National pour Cambodge, Indépendant, Neutre, Pacifique, et Coopératif (FUNCINPEC), which was founded by then Prince Norodom Sihanouk but subsequently led by his son Prince Norodom Ranarriddh; the Party of Democratic Kampuchea (PDK), representing Khmer Rouge survivors who stayed with electoral politics; and two smaller parties.

Hun Sen's CPP was reputed to have had no hesitation in killing opponents. But the PDK may have won the championship in that regard: its violence was directed against its political opponents, anyone who was known to be their sympathizer, ethnic Vietnamese, and UNTAC personnel.

FUNCINPEC won the 1993 election, but no party had the required overall majority, with the result that a coalition government had to be installed. Since the main body of the Khmer Rouge had repudiated the electoral process it was to be excluded. Judy Ledgerwood (1996a), whose observation of this election provided many insights, said the victory of FUNCINPEC was, in part, a reaction to the violence: the beleaguered electorate longed for peace. The election marked the termination of what had been, in effect, a dictatorship of the Communist party allied with Vietnam. It marked the termination of the dictatorship – but not the end of the dominance of Hun Sen and the CPP. Coincident with these developments, Prince Sihanouk was restored as king in 1993, but he went into self-imposed exile a few months later and, citing health issues, abdicated the throne in October 2004.

UN descriptions of events under UNTAC, especially the peace talks and the 1993 elections, give the unambiguous impression of magnificent success. The United States was ecstatic. Craig Etcheson (2005, 51) expressed another view: "with the end of the Cold War, this proxy contest became an irrelevant irritant to Great Power relations, and so the Great Powers fashioned the peace process to extricate themselves from their 'Cambodia Problem.'" Regional powers directly affected by the process also expressed skepticism. Cambodia was still extremely impoverished, substantial battles continued in the northwest, the outcome of the elections created uncertainty for all parties, and corruption and cruelty still marked relationships between government and people: what exactly had the great UN spectacle accomplished?

In fairness, some benefits came from the UN intervention – not those anticipated by the original mandate, mind you, but modest help even so. Chinese military aid to the KR was terminated (Rodman 1994); over 300,000 refugees returned; human rights organizations were established and electoral processes were initiated. People actually voted, though they ended up with a wobbly coalition government.[10] Elections over, the UN withdrew.

International Disinterest after 1993

Although foreign powers were intermittently involved in negotiations regarding possible genocide trials of KR leaders (as described below), for the most part, the world, with the exception of China and Thailand, just forgot about Cambodia. Vietnam had enough problems of its own, and it was by now concerned with developing market relations with the United States. Russia was moving in its own direction, and Cambodia was not part of its sphere of interest. The US provided modest aid for rural development. In Washington, a group managed to put through the Cambodian Genocide Justice Act (CGJA) in 1994, requiring the US State Department to propose an international genocide tribunal. In response to this, the Khmer Rouge said that they would establish a "Commission to Review the US War of Aggression to Massacre the Cambodian People between 1970 and 1975" (Etcheson 2005, 43). Not much came of either proposal.

China, however, gently shifted its support for the KR to the Cambodian government and became the major investor in the new Cambodian garment industry as well as a source of aid funds. Thailand, which had supported the KR before and after the UNTAC period, subsequently joined China as an investor in Cambodia. It made substantial investments in tourism, transportation, banking, and resource sectors.

AMNESTIES, POL POT'S DEATH, AND COALITION GOVERNMENT

With the end of the UNTAC period, the country resumed its violent path. Although a free press had gained guarantees, in fact it was increasingly repressed, and government officials acted against human rights with impunity. In 1996, a journalist was shot and killed, two were arrested for what they wrote, and extrajudicial executions and torture were reported in the areas where the Khmer Rouge remained active. Trafficking of children and other abuses continued. Human Rights Watch (1996) reported that "the consensus among local and international human rights workers in Cambodia was that the human rights climate was worse than it had been at any time since 1993." The next round of local elections in 1997 and national events in 1998 erupted in widespread corruption.

The coalition government – actually dominated by the CPP – still had to deal with the continuing guerrilla war in the north. It managed to do this by first granting an amnesty to Ieng Sary, whom it

had condemned to death in the show trial of 1979. The Royal
Pardon granted by the king in 1996 at the request of Prime Minister Hun Sen and Co-Prime Minister Prince Norodom Ranariddh
was explained by Hun Sen as follows: "For the sake of the nation we
had to do it. To destroy 70% of the KR forces, we needed to pay a
price too – that was the amnesty provided to Ieng Sary" (quoted in
Fawthrop and Jarvis 2004, 137). By that time, the KR loyalists were
coming unstuck. Son Sen, who had been appointed by the KR to engage in the negotiations at the Paris Peace Conference, was assassinated at Pol Pot's order. His murder and that of fourteen members
of his family led to increasing opposition to Pol Pot's leadership,
even among the incredibly loyal remaining units. Hounded as a
traitor and running from his former troops, Pol Pot was finally captured in June 1997 and subjected to a show trial by Ta Mok (who
had been in charge of the southeastern region during the KR regime). Almost simultaneously, in June 1997, the Cambodian co-
prime ministers asked the UN to organize a Khmer Rouge trial, and
in December of that year the UN General Assembly adopted a resolution to consider assistance.

Pol Pot died on 16 April 1998 (apparently of natural causes,
though reports that he was poisoned continue to circulate.) Khieu
Samphan, former president of the DK, and Nuon Chea, known as
"Brother Number Two," surrendered in December of the same
year, and their armed forces were gradually integrated with the
Cambodian forces. They themselves were provided with police protection. Their compliance was understood by the government as
part of the deal, as was the amnesty for Ieng Sary, which finally
broke the back of the KR. Helen Jarvis, advisor to the senior minister of the Council of Ministers, Sok An, and her co-author bragged:
"What the UN with its huge budget and 12,000 strong peacekeeping forces had failed to do – disarm the Khmer Rouge – had now
been accomplished by the Cambodian government" (Fawthrop
and Jarvis 2004, 138).

A DECADE OF NEGOTIATION OVER TRIALS

In 1997, over twenty years since the reign of terror began, the Cambodian co-prime ministers requested the United Nations to organize a Khmer Rouge trial. On the face of it, this was because no one

had ever been punished or called to account for the deaths, the concentration camps, the mass executions, the mass famine, or the absolute terror experienced by the population. For the United Nations, another explanation for pushing ahead involved the shame that UN participant nations felt not only for their failure to act when these events took place but also for their bald-faced support of Khmer Rouge membership in the UN even after the terrors had been revealed. Explanations for the 1997 request by the co-prime ministers were probably even simpler and cruder, but readers can fill in the blanks.

In Cambodia, the amnesty had long tentacles. Trials initially considered in 1997 were put on hold while the UN and the Cambodian government continued negotiations through the following decade. Both are aware that the same individuals who were given amnesties are among the few likely to be tried in a renewed effort for legal justice. The government is over a barrel: if it continues to delay trials, donor countries might choose to opt out; if it complies with international pressure for trials, its deals with KR leaders will have to be revealed. However, if it delays long enough, the biological solution might kick in. After all, those who supported General Pinochet in Chile managed to delay his trial until his death. Meanwhile, the delays are blamed on the UN, which, indeed, did not rush into the task in 1997 and nearly opted out several times before commencement of proceedings in 2007.

Throughout the negotiations, the major obstacle to UN participation has been its insistence on a majority of international jurists and several provisions in international law, including independence of jurists and protection of witnesses. The Cambodian delegation, including Deputy Prime Minister Sok An, were unwilling to accept that level of international interference in Cambodian affairs. It has consistently argued for a majority domestic court under domestic rules. According to the Cambodian government version of events, on 20 September 1999 the prime minister informed UN Secretary General Kofi Annan that there were three options: the UN could provide judges and experts to modify the draft law "to achieve what is known as credibility, in conformity with procedures trusted by the international community, and can also provide judges to work with Cambodian judges in the court"; it could provide legal experts for drafting the law but "let Cambodian judges work alone at the trial stages"; or, finally, it "may withdraw and let Cambodia establish the draft law and organize the trial by itself" (Cambodia, Royal Government of, 2007). The differences between the two groups finally became unbridgeable, and the UN withdrew in February 2002. Cambodia, however, did not undertake its own trials. The same obstacles to agreement were evident in renewed discussions since 2005.

According to the chief of public affairs, Dr Helen Jarvis, the government was "concerned to ensure that society is not destabilized nor would the process degenerate into a witch-hunt" (Fawthrop and Jarvis 2004, 149). It is not clear why an international trial would destabilize the country, but in their book on Cambodia, Fawthrop and Jarvis (2004) accuse "right-wing US congressmen" who want "regime change in Cambodia." Curiously, the most influential American to negotiate with the Government of Cambodia regarding the proposed trials was Senator John Kerry, the 2004 Democratic candidate for president.

Fawthrop and Jarvis are not alone in fearing renewed violence. Iljas Baker of the *Bangkok Post* wrote in 2005 about the prospect of trials: "There are also fears of a renewal of violence instigated by former Khmer Rouge leaders who feel threatened by the trial. These fears are shared by the rural population and the educated urban classes alike, and they are by no means groundless."[11]

This message could be read as having a double-meaning since the government of Hun Sen includes former KR defectors, and others who were more than bit players in the former regime are now in important posts throughout the country. Hun Sen is not known to have personally committed human rights crimes, but speculators who argue that his government is playing a game with the United Nations, whereby he speaks in favour of the trials but undermines them every time they seem likely to proceed, are numerous. The trials might legitimize his government if they raise no questions beyond the culpability of the half dozen old men expected to be indicted. But then again, they might raise other issues that implicate either him or his government.

The 2005 proposal put forward by the UN was that these chambers should be conducted by three Cambodian judges together with two international judges. They would try crimes under both Cambodian and international law in what is described as a "hybrid" model.

There has to be a majority of four judges to make a decision, so an international jurist would always be required.

Only the surviving leaders would be tried. This plan was criticized by Steve Heder, a genocide researcher at the University of London, who argues that the "Nuremberg model" (i.e., blaming only the most senior leaders) shields many bloody hands, and in Cambodia the bloody hands include the Vietnamese, the Royal Cambodian Government, the United States, and the United Nations, all of whom have "knowingly" shielded many culprits from scrutiny. Among the difficulties of determining who is responsible in the tragedy is the amount of discretionary power left to district-level officials and other subordinates. While the party leaders ordered city inhabitants to move to rural areas, it was up to the local cadres to decide what to do with them. Many were starved or worked to death, and the local cadres were often absolutely ruthless in their treatment of urbanites.

We do not know whether the lower-downs were following actual orders, were interpreting orders according to their whims, or were simply eager to show how much power they (suddenly) had under the DK regime. Heder notes that "these lower-downs were certainly not 'just following orders' ... making district party secretaries key figures in responsibility for killings nationwide." Further: "The criteria for prioritizing prosecutions should be the seriousness of the crimes committed, not the official place in the hierarchy of the alleged perpetrator."[12]

Chea Sim is among those who have escaped scrutiny for possible crimes committed when they were in positions of power. When he was a district party secretary in the District of Kampong Cham there were thousands of killings during the Pol Pot years. Residents of the villages at that time and still there in 2003 told the *Cambodian Post* that Heder's claims that Chea Sim was involved were consistent with their memories. Many of them lost members of their family, especially during 1977 and early 1978 before a Vietnamese army incursion overran the district. One woman, aged sixty-three, said that some forty members of her family who had returned from Phnom Penh to her village were killed.[13] Chea Sim was responsible for recruiting former DK members to the new government backed by the Vietnamese and headed by Hun Sen.

Heder argued against the exclusion of lower-level administrators from criminal proceedings. But Hun Sen has made it clear, as have others of his government, that to go further (and to include himself and Chea Sim, for example) would reignite war. Others argue on simple pragmatic grounds. Craig Etcheson, another prominent genocide researcher, argues that "criminal culpability and moral culpability are not the same thing" and that those who are "morally culpable" would number in the thousands. A complete accounting might go into the low five-figure. In a published correspondence with Bill Bainbridge, Etchison argued:

> It is simply not feasible to try thousands and thousands of people in Cambodia's circumstances. Cambodia does not have enough lawyers, money or time to do it ... That said, the situation does cry out for some mechanism to address the culpability of the lower-level perpetrators, to find some way for them to confess their sins to their fellow citizens and seek social harmony for their own sakes as well as the sakes of the victims. (Cited in Bainbridge 2003, 5–6)

In another article, Etcheson (2003, 2) observes:

> "In villages all across the country, Cambodians live amid those who were responsible for their torment during the Khmer Rouge regime. Many hundreds, perhaps thousands, of former Khmer Rouge cadres who ordered and carried out the execution of loved ones still live freely everywhere. In many cases, these former killers are still in positions of political power."

He notes, however, that just bringing criminals to justice will never be enough. There are numerous cleavages within the Khmer population, not least of which is the chasm between rural and urban people that persists three decades after the terror. National reconciliation is necessary, but the question is how best to move in that direction.

Youk Chhang, director of the Documentation Centre of Cambodia (DCC), has relentlessly argued in favour of a UN trial. This non-profit organization, enabled by donations from foreign governments, trains researchers, enables foreign and domestic scholars to obtain research materials, and distributes regular email newsletters to many researchers and others throughout the world. One of its objectives is to ensure that a war crimes tribunal is established, and its persistence in calling for this has been an important reason for any success –

modest as it is – to date. The DCC is affiliated with several leading universities in the United States, Canada, Australia, and the United Kingdom, where research collections are being stored for future scholarly attention. Chhang spoke with me about Cambodia and the need for a trial:

> I call this a broken society, and we are broken persons. Because the KR managed to completely eliminate the family foundation in Cambodia. All of us have at least one family member tortured by the KR. All of us have a missing person in the family ... According to a psychiatric survey by GPO, some 75 percent of the people are having trouble. There is a lot of rape among youth and violence on the streets ...
>
> The government always uses the end of the KR as their good point. Well, we have survived now for twenty-five years. If we don't legally end the KR issue, the country will not grow. There is no trust. The KR even caused mistrust between family members. The wife would hide food from the husband. The husband would tell the village chief and the wife would be imperiled.
>
> I am pushing for the legal prosecution of the KR leaders because as a human you know it is wrong for anyone to take away your life. They took away 2 million lives. It is one of the grossest human rights violations in history. Even to prosecute the few who were responsible would not restore trust in this legal system. People will say, "I don't honestly know why I should be punished – look at the KR leaders."
>
> ... the problem with truth commissions is that they might work in Christian countries but not in Buddhist countries. In Christianity, god teaches people to speak the truth and to swear to speak the truth. In Buddhism there is no text saying that we have to swear to speak the truth ... it would be difficult to have a truth commission with legal authority here because people would not want to testify in public. Most of the former KR are in fact in the government now. So focusing on education and documentation might be a better way to focus a truth commission.[14]

Another local resident (who prefers not to be named) had this to say:

Who wants the KR trials? The CPP don't want it, the Vietnamese
don't want it, the Chinese don't want it, the Thais don't want it,
the KR don't want it. So there's your political will. It's amazing
that there's nobody pushing for it and that it's gotten this far ...
Thailand doesn't want it because then you have to forget that
they supported the KR after 1978 with military supplies at the
border. They want to bury that part. The Vietnamese, I think
they'd just rather bury the whole thing because they know it will
stress the relations between Cambodia and Vietnam. You can be
sure that the US was defending the country from the Vietnamese
and if they hadn't done that the Vietnamese would just gobble
up Cambodia.

I also asked Helen Jarvis why there had been such reluctance to
proceed with the UN trials. She disagreed with the phrasing of the
question: "I would correct you. I don't think the government has
been reluctant to come to an agreement. It insisted on certain conditions and that has ended up as a prolonged protracted negotiation. But not reluctance, indeed, if anything, the delay has been on
their side." Jarvis noted that the delay involved a dispute over
whether there could be a death penalty for murder, and there were
other delays due to the recess of the National Assembly. In their
book, Fawthrop and Jarvis argue that Western and ASEAN governments delayed the trials – the US initially because it was developing
its relations with China and maintaining its opposition to Vietnam.
They also claim that Thailand protected Pol Pot. All this time,
China would have vetoed a trial at the UN Security Council. They
suggest that China posed a persistent threat to Cambodian stability.
They have less to say about domestic politics and problems in Cambodia during the period from the takeover of 1979 to the 2003
elections (Fawthrop and Jarvis 2004).

Jarvis expressed her view again in a radio broadcast with inter-
viewer Anna Maria Tremonte on CBC's *The Current* on 17 May
2005. Again she argued that there was no foot-dragging on the government's side; rather, it was on the side of the UN negotiators. Immediately following her radio interview, Philip Short (2004),
author of a Pol Pot biography, strongly disagreed. In his view, the
Hun Sen government has a great deal to hide and would not benefit from revelations even at this late date. While Jarvis argues that

Hun Sen and his three top cabinet members had risked their lives escaping from the KR and then returning with the Vietnam forces, Short argues that their defection was more likely the result of the internal factionalism that had already led to the likelihood of their imminent assassination. In his view, all of them were major figures in the KR regime and easy targets for those who wanted to get past them. Also, those who gained power in Cambodia after the KR period ensured that an amnesty for KR defectors was passed in 1994. Even those who had been major actors in the KR for many years were given amnesty in the 1990s, precluding possible international court charges against them.[15]

Short also made the point that to proceed with an expensive trial when much of the country was still hungry, ill-housed, lacking employment or land, and immersed in poverty was a travesty, the more so when only a handful of leaders were to be tried. With Pol Pot dead, and the others creaking with age, just how much "closure" was this going to provide?

Among the continuing debates between Short and other writers more supportive of the Hun Sen regime is the question of responsibility for the more extreme murders. Were the central leaders in firm control all the time? Craig Etcheson (2005) argues that they were, but according to several eye-witness accounts now available, young cadres and supervisors in the districts to which the urban marchers were assigned went berserk, intoxicated with power over people they had long hated as abstract categories. When they had killed many and were sated with death, there were others clamouring to kill *them*. The histories of the young "comrades" is beyond sobering (see Ming-Try Ea and Sorya Sim 2001; Hui Vannak 2003). This does not absolve the central figures, but it raises doubts about the validity of trials aimed only at them.

Bringing only the leaders of the Khmer Rouge period to justice is problematic when one surveys the catastrophes that have occurred in this country over the past thirty years. There were the killing fields of the Pol Pot era, but there was a war before that, and before that war there was US carpet bombing, and before that there was a war for independence from the French. After all that, there was the invasion and occupation by Vietnamese forces and widespread famine. How can an international court separate these events, make sense of them, call this or that one to account? Who should be made accountable for the vast regional destabilization that provided the ferment for the creation and expansion of the Khmer Rouge?

One of the reasons it is so difficult to identify the perpetrators of the ugliest events is that many of them were killed by the very people who ordered them to so act. Youth who joined the KR, often under duress and without ideological leanings, and did all of the mean and beastly chores put upon them were then turned into victims themselves. The KR would promote people to some exalted post and then, without explanation and even without any acrimony between them, order their deaths along with that of all their family members. One of numerous cases reported by the DCC in Phnom Penh and the *Cambodia Daily* (and many books now reaching a wider audience) concerns a young woman, six months pregnant when she joined the KR in 1970 along with many other family members. In 1976, her husband was sent to China to work on a trade agreement, but, inexplicably, when he returned he was arrested and he, his wife, and their children were killed (Etcheson 2003). Thousands of similar stories or even more appalling ones have been methodically accumulated at the DCC as an archive for scholars and journalists but, most especially, for the future population of Cambodia.

The chief witnesses of any genocide or war crimes trials are survivors who lost family members or who themselves were nearly victims. But there are also those who served the perpetrators, survived, and have agreed to speak. In Cambodia, these last ones include the long-time minister of economy and finance, Keat Chhon, who announced in May 2004 that he was ready to talk about his past association with the KR. He was employed as an interpreter for Pol Pot, who did not leave the KR movement until the mid-1980s. According to Phelim Kyne of Dow Jones Newswires, reporting from South Korea during a meeting of Asian finance ministers, the French-educated Keat would "prove awkward for the current Cambodian government whose ranks are riddled with a cadre of former Khmer Rouge who have shown lukewarm support for UN efforts to form a tribunal."[16]

Even more awkward are the leaders who were granted a free pass after Pol Pot's death. When it seemed likely that a trial of the surviving leaders would eventually occur, former DK president

Khieu Samphan boldly claimed that he had no idea that murders and other terrible events had occurred on his watch, and, on human rights grounds, he asked for international aid to prepare his case should he be indicted in any legal measures taken by a UN tribunal. Ieng Sary, first tried in absentia and condemned to death along with Pol Pot in what the rest of the world regarded as a show trial with no claim to fair procedures, was granted amnesty as part of a deal with the remaining KR leaders (including Samphan) to stop the wars. Nuon Chea (Brother Number Two after Pol Pot) is now seventy-eight years of age and is hospitalized in Thailand.[17] Military leader Ta Mok had been arrested and charged with crimes committed by the DK forces in 1999, and a few months later, Kang Keck Iev, best known as Duch, former director of S-21 Tuol Sleng prison and chief of the KR secret police, was also arrested. Both were incarcerated without trial. In 2006, Ta Mok died peacefully, thus evading the trials and leaving the country with no explanation for his actions or for those of his comrades under the DK government.

Financing and Accommodating Trials

As the pledges to finance a tribunal or special chambers mounted, though ever so slowly and without the aid of the United States, practical questions arose: Where should the tribunal be located? Who should be the judges? The venue matters. Early in April 2005, Prime Minister Hun Sen proposed that, instead of theatres inside Phnom Penh, the whole tribunal should be moved to an army base about 16.5 kilometres from the city, known as the high command headquarters of the Royal Cambodian Armed Forces. Kek Galabru, president of LICADHO, said this would pose problems for witnesses and family members of victims. They would not feel safe, she said: "People feel safer at a theater in the city. I would like to go, but I would be scared out there, too ... Cambodians are so afraid of the military police, or soldiers, because they aren't there to protect you."[18] Another, perhaps more pedestrian, concern is that it would cost money to hire transportation to get to the outskirts of the city. This is not an American city, with interurban trains and frequent buses. Roads are often impassible, and public transportation is rarely available.

The 2007 Impasse and Recovery

In January 2007, just a few months from the scheduled beginning of the trials, the Cambodian and international judges were locked in an impasse over the tribunal rules. To the credit of the chambers, the draft internal rules governing the work of the Court had been released for public comment in November 2006. Many of the responses from internal and external human rights and other bodies were also made public. Cambodian lawyers disagreed about how international judges should be chosen: Cambodians wanted to have the right of approval; the rules for conduct remained under dispute; the rules for disqualification of judges were not yet agreed to; the provisions of the law concerning confidentiality and security of records were problematic; the rights of the accused were not yet clear; the rules for care of witnesses and confidentiality were in question. The list of disagreements went on at some length.

One further obstacle was a suddenly interjected demand by the Cambodian negotiating team for substantial entry fees to be paid by international lawyers acting for the defence. Although it is not unusual for lawyers acting in the jurisdictions of other countries to be obliged to pay fees, this demand at this stage of negotiations was understood to be thrown in to prevent resolution of the disputes. It would also have discouraged international lawyers from acting on behalf of the defence, especially from acting pro-bono.

Amnesty International called on the judges not to rush to adopt rules until agreement was reached, even though the schedule would thereby be disrupted. It said that there were inadequate provisions for the protection and support of victims and witnesses, that the rules for reparations were vague and inconsistent with international law, and that there was inadequate provision for prosecution of crimes of sexual violence or rules relating to the treatment of survivors of sexual violence. As well, Amnesty International argued that accreditation of defence lawyers must be conducted independently.[19]

Human Rights Watch also issued a public statement calling on the Cambodian government to end its interference in the tribunal. Other organizations and individual researchers and lawyers weighed in, some suggesting that the funding governments and the UN should withdraw if the Cambodian government continued to create what they called technical objections to international rules. Hun Sen assured the international audience that he most earnestly wanted to get the trials under way, but Cambodian bureaucrats, presumably operating on instructions from above, continued to object to requirements that the international judiciary and human rights organizations deemed essential to fair trials.

The question of who would be the judges is paramount since there is no independent and respected judiciary in Cambodia. Yet an entirely international judiciary is not wanted by those Cambodians, excepting former King Norodom Sihanouk, who speak freely. It is generally understood that participation by Cambodians is essential for the success of the tribunal. But in Sinanouk's view, trying KR leaders in Cambodia "insults the memory of the innocent victims of the Khmer Rouge while sparing the killers ... from being presented in front of an international court." And he asks, "How can one describe the court in question as serious, credible, honorable?"[20]

Earlier, in April 2002, Cambodia had ratified the Rome Statute of the International Criminal Court, indicating its intention to bring to trial those who had perpetrated grave crimes against humanity. But only a few months later, Prime Minister Hun Sen agreed to a reciprocal bilateral contract with the United States that would ensure that no US nationals in Cambodia or Cambodian nationals in the US would be prosecuted. In many other respects as well, Cambodia's government has shown an unwillingness to live up to the demands of the international agreements it has signed. (This, obviously, also implicates the US, but that is another issue.) This adds to serious questions about Cambodia's ability to proceed in a fair judicial manner with the proposed court.

Under Way at Last?

The negotiations did finally reach a conclusion mid-2007. Fees for international defence lawyers were reduced, compromises were accepted on both sides, and the court issued its first indictment to Kang Keck Iev, alias Duch, then still languishing in jail without having been previously charged. His indictment was somewhat overshadowed by the unilateral decision of the Cambodian government, contrary to its own Constitution, which required consultations, to reassign their leading judge to the Appeals Court at the same time.

The judge, You Bun Leng, said he would try to carry on both jobs for the duration of the Extraordinary Chambers. After petitions from international groups, the Cambodian government agreed that he could continue with the ECCC; but outsiders familiar with the process saw this as yet another attempt to set up an obstacle course against international investigation.

5

Cambodia after the Wars

This impoverished little country, home of the astonishing Angkar Wat city-state with its magnificent stone-carved heads and friezes, struggles with democracy at every turn, never quite managing to grasp the concept.

DEMOCRACY AND HUMAN RIGHTS

National Assembly elections, the third following the 1991 Paris Peace Accords, took place on 27 July 2003. Observers claimed that polling was more peaceful and orderly than it had been in previous elections but that arbitrary restrictions had been put on freedom of assembly and expression and that intimidation had again marked the campaign. According to the August 2003 report to the United Nations delivered by Peter Leuprecht, special representative for human rights in Cambodia:

> In confronting electoral fraud, vote-buying, intimidation and violence, the National Election Committee failed in almost every case to use its considerable power to impose fines and other sanctions. Although law enforcement officials took some steps to investigate killings of political party activists, the investigative and judicial processes of bringing the culprits to justice remained flawed and ineffective in the majority of cases. (UN, "Situation of Human Rights in Cambodia," 58th session, 22 August 2003)

There had been riots in Phnom Penh in January 2003, centred on the Embassy of Thailand and dozens of Thai-owned businesses.

One woman was killed, while other people were treated for serious injuries. Many were arrested, with some sixty people finally being charged with theft and property destruction or criminal incitement. This was a nasty event, but its repercussions went far beyond the tense relations between Thais and Cambodians. The government used it as a reason to prevent public demonstrations or assemblies in the months preceding the July 2003 election. Charged in connection with the Thai event were people whose political agendas were contrary to those of the government, including a radio station owner, a newspaper editor, and two student youth movement leaders. Over the next few months, members of the opposition Sam Rainsy Party and demonstrators at a garment factory were attacked, resulting in one death and a number of injuries. Radio journalist Chuor Chetharith and a pop singer, Touch Sonic, were attacked: both were linked to FUNCINPEC. The journalist and the mother of the pop singer were killed. In February, a senior monk and a FUNCINPEC politician were killed.

Without an investigation, the government's Ministry of the Interior stated that the motives for the murders were theft, and two military officers suddenly "confessed" to having accidentally killed during robberies. Other murders included that of an appeals court clerk and his wife, a municipal court judge, and a Chinese factory administrator. The murders were similar in style. In each case an armed man wearing a helmet jumped off a motorcycle whose driver slowed and waited. The helmeted man then shot the victim and escaped on the back of the waiting motorcycle. The victims were in public places or their own cars at the time of the shooting. No one was ever charged (UN "Situation of Human Rights in Cambodia," August 2003, par. 8).

With the election in progress, the government issued statements about the need for police neutrality and the like, but intimidation of voters and opposition party activists was widespread. By the time international observers arrived, violence had decreased. Still, the National Election Committee was generally slow to respond to incidents of election-related intimidation. And this intimidation was not restricted to the government party. Representatives of several parties used racist and xenophobic, more specifically anti-Vietnamese, rhetoric. Some Cambodian-Vietnamese were prevented from voting. In the end, the governing party failed to either convince or strong-arm voters to support its cause: it failed to gain the required two-thirds of the vote and was obliged to negotiate with its opponents to form a government. This led to a lengthy stalemate.

The three major parties continued to squabble publicly over the outcome of the elections, and along the way there were assassinations. Among the victims was a militant union leader who was gunned down in Phnom Penh in January. Sam Rainsy, whose opposition party carries his name, said that the union leader had been the target of the current regime because of his stand against corruption and human rights abuses. Rainsy was continuing with legal action, going back to a 1997 grenade attack in front of the National Assembly, which he claims was an attempt on his life initiated by the prime minister.[1] Prior to the 2003 election, Rainsy had said that the government was akin to the regimes in Zimbabwe, Iraq, and Kyrgyzstan, despite the substantial monetary transfusions from the international community into attempts to beef up democratic procedures (Bainbridge 2002, 13). Kem Sokha, then president of the foreign-funded Cambodia Centre for Human Rights (CCHR), also said he believed his life was in danger, and he travelled with bodyguards, not trusting the nation's police. He told foreign newscasters, "I fear the killing fields in Cambodia are still open."[2]

Finally, on 11 March 2004, the CPP and FUNCINPEC agreed to form a coalition government, with the two sharing 55 percent and 45 percent of cabinet seats, respectively. The lengthy stalemate held up the ratification of the agreement with the UN regarding the tribunal. Both Rainsy and Sokha were later charged with ideological crimes; Sokha was incarcerated. Rainsy went into voluntary exile, but in February 2006 he returned to Cambodia on a promise to cooperate with Hun Sen. Sokha was released "as a courtesy to the United States," though the charges against him were not dropped. He was charged with embezzlement by his colleagues at the CCHR, but he was free and, by January 2007, planning to start a new political party – with the blessings of Hun Sen. Such a party, it is speculated among Cambodians, would split the opposition. Meanwhile, the only other strong candidate for leader of the opposition, Prince Norodom Ranariddh, remained in prison and was charged with breach of trust by his party, FUNCINPEC.[3]

In late 2003, at the age of eighty-one, the king-father (as he was called) Norodom Sihanouk began writing a stream of "open letters" deploring what had become of his beloved Cambodia. He talked about criminal violence that resulted in journalists, entertainers, other public figures, and even uninvolved bystanders frequently being gunned down. By 2005, the mess that had become Cambodia was grist for the mills of French newspapers. *Le Monde, Le Figaro, Libération,* and *La Croix* noted the poor human rights records, corruption, and terrible poverty that had become characteristics of the Hun Sen government. *Le Figaro* went so far as to entitle an article "Rotten by Generalized Corruption." It also accused the French ambassador of doing nothing while the government attempted to sell off the state-owned hospital in Siem Reap City.[4] (It was unclear what the ambassador was expected to do as this is no longer a French colony.) Such critiques notwithstanding, in early 2005, the government announced its intention to privatize management of the killing fields (Choeung Ek) for thirty years in exchange for US$15,000 for the first year, with a 10 percent escalation each year thereafter. The buyer was a private Japanese company.

Legal and Human Rights

Human rights are guaranteed under the Cambodian Constitution, 1993. But the Constitution is regularly ignored, and laws are promulgated that are inconsistent with it. Freedom of expression and freedom of assembly are regularly outlawed or simply prevented by police and soldiers. The judiciary has neither the independence nor the competence to counteract such behaviour. There is a Cambodian human rights committee, but it is not adequately provided for and so is unable to do its job. Public accountability, institutionalized and transparent mechanisms for dealing with information, guarantee of the right of access to information, and other aspects of a responsible government are still not implemented – perhaps not even understood.

Following the 2003 election, the United Nations, then again deliberating about whether to establish a tribunal for Cambodia, heard strong criticism of the state of human rights in the country from its special representative for human rights, Peter Leuprecht:

Equality before the law and before courts and tribunals is not a reality in Cambodia. Impunity for those responsible for human rights violations, especially the police and military and those in positions of political and economic influence, remains a serious problem. Use of available resources in the justice sector is often skewed and discriminates against the poor. Lack of transport to courts means that trials and appeals are often delayed – exacerbating overcrowding in prisons and extending pre-trial detention – or held in absentia, violating the right of defendants to be present at their own trials. (UN, "Situation of Human Rights in Cambodia," 22 August 2003, para. 27)

Cambodia's prisons remain overcrowded, with heavy prison sentences being the standard punishment for even minor offences ... overcrowding, lack of access to potable water, poor sanitation, disease and inadequate nutrition continue to jeopardize the health of prisoners. Visits by the families of prisoners continue to be restricted and regularly subject to unlawful demands for payment. The United Nations Standard Minimum rules for the Treatment of Prisoners, which are incorporated into Cambodia's law and prison procedures, are routinely ignored. (UN, "Situation of Human Rights in Cambodia," para. 30)

In this 2003 report, the UN observer noted that "even such basic principles as the presumption of innocence and other guarantees contained in article 14 of the International Covenant on Civil and Political Rights are routinely violated." Further, he complained that "torture and cruel, inhuman and degrading treatment of persons in police custody remain a serious concern, as does the failure to prosecute and appropriately punish responsible officials" (UN, "Situation of Human Rights in Cambodia, 22 August 2003, para. 26).

LICADHO (Cambodian League for the Promotion and Defence of Human Rights), a leading human rights NGO in the country, monitors elections, informs the citizenry of its rights, and teaches police and military personnel about human rights. LICADHO was established in 1992 by Dr Kek Galabru (a Cambodian who returned after the Khmer Rouge period) to monitor the Khmer Rouge following the peace agreement. Since then, it has created a curriculum for school children that includes a translation of the Universal Declaration of Human Rights into Khmer. Books on the subject are illustrated with cartoons not only for children but also for the many adults who are not able to read complex texts. LICADHO also monitors and investigates human rights complaints and puts complainants in touch with lawyers at legal aid NGOs. It assists children who are trafficked for prostitution, adoption, or labour.[5] It seeks legal aid and medical assistance for people in the twelve of twenty-seven provinces where there are medical doctors who are willing to help.[6] Sometimes the organization petitions the king for mercy. It tries to arrange for food for prisoners, whose supply is insufficient and many of whom contract beriberi, thus being in immediate need of vitamin B1.[7] In addition to food and many other problems, the prisons themselves (built during the French colonial era) are in danger of collapse.

Other NGOs also monitor human rights violations or help people who are in trouble. There are, however, so many problems in Cambodia, so many victims in need of help, that the dozen or so NGOs are far from enough either in number or in capacity. No matter how dedicated these people are to human rights and to positive changes in Cambodia, they have very little power. They harangue, they cajole, they complain to the international press, they try to help the victims and to teach children their rights, but in the end they are overwhelmed by a society stuck in a culture of impunity and privilege.

PROSPECTS FOR RECOVERY AFTER 2003

The outstanding features of Cambodia during the first decade of the twenty-first century are widespread corruption and the debilitating poverty of its rural population. The Vietnamese army took over Phnom Penh and most of the country nearly thirty years earlier. Pol Pot died in 1998, and his chief lieutenants surrendered the following year. But the extreme brutality of its history – a long history capped by the KR period – is still with the people. And, as the previous section documents, the peace is pockmarked by assassinations and other signals that all is not well in this realm. In chapter 1, I suggested a range of indices that provide perspectives on whether a country might move on after a civil war. Using them to examine the Cambodian case shows that Cambodia's record to date is not promising.

Control of Military Force

The government has control of the legitimate use of military force, and there is no organized military opposition. This is the essence of the "peace dividend," as the World Bank calls the period of state control. Having control of the military does not guarantee that the military is a professional body above politics, but neither is it a contestant

for taking control of government. The military in Cambodia constitutes no immediate threat to continued civilian control of the country: it is weak and neither skilled nor well organized. Although not a
formidable force, both the military and the police are deemed by
most observers to be corrupt and very much involved in local politics. Opposition leaders have been assassinated or eliminated from
political roles by tactics that required force and control of it, so it is
not surprising that the charge of corruption is widespread.

Corruption and the Rule of Law

According to the World Bank report of 2004, "Cambodia ranks
(with respect to the rule of law) among the bottom quartile" of all
countries, and "domestic surveys confirm that corruption is endemic and high" (World Bank 2004, 6). The rule of law has never
been implemented, courts and honest police forces are not part of
the social fabric, and even if the population wanted them, trained
jurists and police staff do not exist. Corruption is widespread. Pay-
offs, bribes, and threats are normal; assassinations occur fairly frequently. The legislature, though called democratic nowadays, is far
from that of a functioning democracy: its leading members fight
with one another through the press and, from time to time, the
noise is temporarily silenced by another assassination or by an incarceration that has come about without much evidence of the rule
of law. The 2006 World Bank Report concludes:

> Corruption keeps people poor; they have to pay (or pay more)
> for goods and services. Benefits intended for them are diverted
> and they are unfairly disadvantaged and dispossessed in conflicts
> with other groups who can afford to pay more for official decisions
> that favor their cause. Services are under-funded as revenue collec-
> tion is foregone; and investment is deterred and employment sup-
> pressed. The cumulative effect of corruption in constraining
> economic development is immeasurable but undoubtedly very
> high. (World Bank 2006, xiii)

Amnesty International's Charges, 2005 and 2006

The Amnesty International report for 2005 (covering 2004) summarized its charges against the Kingdom of Cambodia: "Human

rights violations continued to be reported against a background of
political instability. A weak and corrupt judicial system remained a
serious obstacle to human rights protection. A prominent trade
union leader and political activist was assassinated" (Amnesty International 2005, 69–70). It also noted that:

> Cambodia remained one of the world's poorest countries, with
> 36 per cent of the population living in poverty and a high mortal-
> ity rate among under-fives. Land disputes increased, with mem-
> bers of the wealthy elite and military involved in land grabbing
> and speculation. The number of reported injuries caused by
> landmines rose dramatically as poor people seeking land moved
> into affordable areas that had not yet been de-mined. The preva-
> lence of HIV/AIDS continued to be a serious problem; Cambodia
> was reported to have the highest infection rate in Asia (ibid., 69)

The terse summary for 2006 began: "Peaceful criticism of the
government was curtailed. Immunity was lifted for three opposition
parliamentarians; two were subsequently sentenced to imprisonment. Criminal charges were brought against trade union leaders
and a media representative. Human rights defenders and opposition politicians faced threats. Restrictions on freedom of assembly
were maintained" (Amnesty International 2006, 81–2).

Resources: Land Tenure

The World Bank declared in 2003 that corruption continued to be
endemic through all levels of Cambodian society; further, that,
though existing provisions of the criminal law relating to corruption, bribery, and embezzlement are adequate, there is a failure of
will and capacity to prosecute offenders. Among the several areas
discussed in World Bank and UN papers, land conflicts are particularly troublesome. This is outlined in the UN report of 22 August
2003, paragraph 46:

> The Special Representative continues to question the Govern-
> ment's policy of granting large-scale agricultural, forestry and
> other concessions to private companies, in particular their ad-
> verse effects on the livelihood and fundamental human rights
> of affected communities. In the case of large-scale agricultural

plantations, concessionaires are permitted to clear private State land for exploitation, including forest land, and have rights of control over land almost as expansive as those of owners.

About 20 percent of Cambodia has been given over to forest and land concessions, with dubious benefits to the communities that depend on the land and without reference to either access or sustainability for the general population. Private companies have destroyed forests, limited agricultural development, and forced local inhabitants to abandon their traditional agricultural activities. In some regions, formerly independent subsistence farmers have become wage workers for the concessionaires; in some regions, not even that option is provided. Companies often employ armed guards – former military personnel in many cases – to defend their interests against their neighbours, whom they designate as "encroachers." As stated in the 22 August 2003 UN report: "since most concessionaires pay neither the required deposit nor rental fees to the State, it is hard to see what contribution they are making to the country and the welfare of its people" (para. 47).

The UN special representative investigated several land concessions in the late 1990s and the first years of the twenty-first century, noting several areas where companies had bulldozed large tracts of primary forest, preventing access to local people and to the agricultural land on these concessions. One concession, in Tum Ring commune in Kompong Thom Province, comprising a 6,400-hectare area of forest, was classified by subdecrees as a "State public establishment rubber plantation," operated by the Chup Rubber Plantation Company. Local communities were not consulted before this occurred, and some two thousand inhabitants who had earlier subsisted on ricefields in the area, and through tapping resin trees and collecting forest products, suddenly had their livelihoods destroyed. In addition to the legal activities, the company has illegally felled hundreds of resin trees and bulldozed land while transporting logs to an external sawmill, contrary to the moratorium on transporting round logs out of the area (as described in the 22 August 2003 UN report, para. 50).

Good agricultural land is scarce. Secure land tenure is noted in the World Bank report entitled *Poverty Assessment 2006* as one of the problems for rural people (World Bank 2007).[8] Title to land differs greatly by income class. While the richest 20 percent of the population have title to 29 percent of the agricultural land they own, the bottom twenty percent of households have title to only 15.6 per cent of the land they work. Another 20 percent of rural people have neither title nor informal ownership in land. The land owned by the richest class is closer to all-weather roads and permanent markets; households have water pumps and plots with access to irrigation in dry season. For all of these measures, the poorest rural people have less favourable conditions (World Bank 2007 Table 1, v). Even more problematic, a substantial part of the land owned by the richest 20 percent is not in use. It is owned by urban dwellers in Phnom Penh who intend to hold it as an investment. They do not rent it to poor rural people for fear that the renters would claim ownership. This fear is realistic because much of the land under cultivation is not governed by legal deeds; indeed, the World Bank report shows clearly that the lack of legal title is one of the reasons for the low productivity of small farms in Cambodia compared to those in nearby Laos, Vietnam, Thailand, Indonesia, Malaysia, and China.[9] Cambodia's rice yields are the lowest of the region, as are value-added per unit of labour or profit per hectare. Other reasons for the low productivity of the agricultural sector are a lack of irrigation, a lack of infrastructure to transport and sell produce, and a lack of access to common property resources such as forests and fishing waters. The access problem is partly due to the increased privatization of formerly open-access resources and partly due to population increases and commercial interests that lead to over-exploitation. In some districts, farmers are dependent on rainwater: when it fails, the yields dramatically decline (World Bank 2006, x).

Different parts of the countryside have different experiences of growth and poverty reduction, as measured by the Economic Institute of Cambodia and reported in the World Bank report. For example, in Siem Reap Province, where the urban centre is experiencing the economic benefits of tourism, a combination of poor soils, lack of funds for fertilizer, lack of water control infrastructure, and poor roads have prevented local farmers from selling foods to the restaurants and hotels of the growing tourism sector. By contrast, in the District of Malai on the Thai border, former KR lands were distributed to local households. They have relatively rich soil and access to export markets in Thailand, so their average incomes are much greater than are those in other regions. Phnom Sruoch District in Kampong Speu Province has poor-quality soils, and land tenure is not secure. According to the World

Bank report, "There has been a steady accumulation of land in the hands of the rich, many living in Phnom Penh, while the situation of the local poor has changed only marginally, and may now be declining as further forest clearance becomes impossible" (World Bank 2006, vi, box 2). Another very poor district in Prey Veng Province is described as "encountering the limits of traditional livelihood strategies based on rice cultivation and common property resources" (ibid.). Some 40 percent of the poor live in this district, and families are sending members to Phnom Penh to seek employment in the garment industry, construction, or transportation.

Poverty Reduction and Differences Between Rural and Urban Populations

The World Bank (2006, vii) records that Cambodia had, overall, a 7 percent increase in household incomes between 1994 and 2004. While 47 percent of the total population fell below the national poverty line in 1994, that proportion had dropped to 35 percent in 2004.[10] However, these data are problematic because the surveys in the early 1990s did not include villages still controlled by the KR, and even where the same villages were included in both surveys the questions and approaches differed. At best, the rise has to be understood in the context of a baseline that, in the World Bank's terms, was "of very low output and very high poverty at the start of the 1990s" (World Bank 2006, i). Even with these caveats, the World Bank argues that poverty had declined in rural areas, that women as well as men have benefited (especially where garment factories are established), and that there have been improvements in primary education. It credited the improvements to continuing peace and the introduction of market openings.

The report observes that further poverty reduction will not rest on the "peace dividend" and will require further investments in infrastructure; the establishment of secure property rights to private land; "emphasis on small holder agriculture"; "equitable access to common property resources"; and "improved human development and human capital achieved through the pro-poor delivery of basic services in education and health" (World Bank 2006, xvi and throughout the assessment).

As the data in the World Bank report document, there is a growing gulf between the relatively rich people in urban centres, particularly Phnom Penh and Siem Reap, and the vast majority of the population.

There are also differences, as cited above, between rural regions. Ninety-one percent of the population was still rural, and agriculture still contributed 71 percent to the GDP in 2004 (World Bank 2006, vii). There has been some economic growth since 2003, when one-third of Cambodia's people survived on less than US$1 per day. Per capita gross national income in 2003 was reported as US$260. But the World Bank report says that Cambodia's growth over the last decade is dependent on export-oriented garment manufacturing and tourism, both of which are urban-centred.

Where poverty is endemic, trafficking in women and children for prostitution, drug abuse, petty corruption, and illegal logging of the remaining forest resources are all part of the daily grist. Referred to as a "hopeful" or "happy" development, the garment factories established by Chinese, Taiwanese, and Hong Kong investors employ some 200,000 Cambodians, mostly women, who earn a minimum wage of US$45 per month plus overtime in Phnom Penh.[11] This is a magnificent sum compared to the average wage of schoolteachers and police officers, at about US$25 per month. The employers are the usual companies to be found in poor societies: The Gap, Old Navy, Banana Republic, Columbia Sportswear. The United States is the major customer. Cambodian exports enjoyed preferential access until the end of 2004.[12]

Physical Infrastructure

Reducing rural poverty will require land tenure reforms and enabling investments to create market access for rural produce. The physical infrastructure throughout the country is as poor as one can find anywhere in the world. In the northern regions, roads are either non-existent or impassible for much of the year. Even the road from Phnom Penh to the killing fields monuments only eighteen kilometres away is a rough ride, and it is very difficult to travel far from the capital by road at any time. Ferries and other boat traffic are frequent modes of travel along the Tonle Sap and Mekong rivers. Although a few of these ferries are comfortable modes of travel for tourists (at tourist prices), most are extremely uncomfortable and dangerous; however, they carry the bulk of human traffic and goods from south to north and back again. Sitting atop an overloaded general traffic ferry for a five-hour journey from Phnom Penh to Siem Reap, where it seems safer to perch precariously on

the roof rather than to take the chance of being stifled in the hold
(where, if there were a mishap, one would have no chance of escape), I have watched the passing scene of small craft, fisherfolk,
houses on stilts, handsome teenagers pushing poles to move their
narrow boats from one location to another. If one ignores the poverty, this is a rustic picture of Cambodia – almost of a Cambodia
past, a Cambodia that barely hangs on while the bigger fishers in
Phnom Penh chase metaphorical barracudas.

A part of the population is still engaged in fishing on the two major rivers and lakes. Extremely agile, the fishers travel by small
boats, and, if they wish to go to a more distant location or to send
something beyond their region, they hitch their small craft to a
ferry for the few moments it takes them to jump aboard. They live
in small wooden houses resting on stilts above the river. When the
river is at its low levels, they may keep chickens under the houses.
There are also many city dwellings built on stilts, even where the
river is not close by. The advantages are substantial: during the hot
season, many people spend their days in the shade under the buildings, where they also keep chickens. These ancient residential customs serve the people well, but they are not so well served by
modern amenities or services.

As the World Bank (2006, x and xi) report summarizes:

The challenges facing the Government in managing rural development serve as a microcosm of broader national development
challenges. In the economy as a whole, investment that might ac-
celerate and diversify economic growth to the benefit of the poor
is constrained by low capacity, lack of transparency, and inappropriate and arbitrarily-applied regulations. These phenomena
contribute to a low level of official accountability and thus a low
level of incentives to achieve results. They also create opportunities for corruption. This increases the costs and decreases the
competitiveness of businesses operating in Cambodia, deterring
investment and constraining the expansion of small enterprises.

Population Growth and Demographic Profile

The United Nations estimated the 2005 population at about
14.5 million, with a growth rate of 1.74. This is higher than the
world average rate of 1.17 but much lower than many other poor

countries. However, the population is contained in an area of about 181,000 square kilometres, ranking its overall density at 111 on the list of 230 countries. Since much of the land is mountainous and covered by a tropical forest, the actual density in fertile agricultural areas is greater than this (UN 2006).

The median age is 20, with over half the population younger than 25. The World Bank estimates that the dependency burden (number of dependents per 100 economically active adults) is 97 percent amongst the poorest sector of the population, compared to 54 percent amongst the richest class (Table 1,v). Further, the sex ratio, female to male, is 1.6 to 1, implying that many women are sole earners for dependent children and the elderly. (WB 2006). As children become adults small land holdings are often divided, providing even more marginal returns to the rural population.

Social Infrastructure

Evan Gottesman, who lived in Cambodia for three years trying to find a way of developing a code of law, called it "a blank slate of a country." He said that it had no social infrastructure – "no bureaucracy, no army or police, no schools or hospitals, no state or private commercial networks, no religious hierarchies, no legal system" (Gottesman 2003, x). Having discovered a cache of documents regarding internal debates within the government, Gottesman came to the disturbing conclusion that the "Western" concepts of human rights were well understood and that the failure to apply them was a deliberate decision, not a cultural misunderstanding (xii-xiii). As he summarized this revelation:

> As it turned out, most of the arguments that I and other foreigners had been making, especially about human rights, had been the subject of extensive internal debate for years. I found this revelation reassuring because it confirmed that human rights was not a foreign concept. It was also depressing. Cambodia's top leaders were clearly familiar with the concepts of human rights and the rule of law. Having thought through their political and legal options and having already made what they felt were informed policy choices, they were unlikely to alter the way they governed the country merely in response to Western advisors. (xiii)

Other policy decisions likewise suggest that Cambodia's problems are not only due to its tragic past but also to a government that has not put its people's welfare at the top of the agenda. In connection with the World Bank review of poverty, the director of the Economic Institute of Cambodia observed that poverty-reduction goals could be achieved if the country were to implement critical reforms in land tenure, civil services, and the judicial system (World Bank 2006, xviii).

As of the middle of the first decade of the twenty-first century, there still are insufficient public schools, especially in rural areas. Primary school completion rates have significantly increased since 2000 from near 47 percent to near 82 percent of the relevant age group, but secondary school levels have not similarly improved. For those who can afford them, there are private schools and some thirteen small private universities (these would be regarded as single-building colleges elsewhere) plus another dozen or more advanced training schools, most of which were established by foreign investors and NGOs.

Medical facilities have not improved. According to a World Bank report in 2004, some 36 percent of the population still suffered from hunger; malnutrition was prevalent and access to health care meagre; child mortality increased over the previous decade largely due to preventable diseases; the maternal mortality rate was high; sanitary conditions were poor; and only 30 percent of the population had access to safe drinking water (World Bank 2004).[13] For the poor in rural regions the cost of illness can amount to giving up whatever small gains in land and food supplies the family has struggled to achieve. Under the circumstances, few children can afford to stay in schools, even if these happen to be close enough for them to attend. The impact of illness has been documented in many studies (World Bank 2006, executive summary and chap. 6).

Two small English-language newspapers in Phnom Penh,[14] both produced by individuals who were not born in Cambodia, and several other Khmer newspapers or other publications provide the news services. Electronic media are essentially controlled by the CPP. Independent lawyers, doctors, and other professionals provide services in the cities, but their ratios tell the tale: for example, there is one medical doctor per 16.3 thousand people. Many have been recruited from abroad for temporary periods or have returned after prolonged absences during the civil war and KR period. Small businesses – beauty shops; cafes and restaurants; mechanical services; ferry, bus, and car services; and other service outlets – are mostly owned and operated either by returned Cambodians who were not present during the KR period or by Vietnamese and Thais. A fledgling internet business provides services for tourists and an exciting new worldview for local youth in cities, and the private universities are offering training in computer skills (but computer usage is not yet well developed). Foreign chains maintain a few large hotels alongside locally owned and generally smaller hotels and guest houses.

In Siem Reap there are numerous tourist facilities, and the range of small businesses includes such retail and service operations for tourists as photographic supplies, guides and tours, books and other publications, clothing, and souvenirs. The ubiquitous outdoor markets in poor countries are the best places to buy pirated goods at cheap prices and souvenirs of all varieties and qualities. The visitor is always invited to spend time at "crafts schools," where much junk and occasional artworks are sold. In less tourist-friendly regions of the country, journalist Tom Hilditch's description of the road into Pailin in 2000 described "scenes from medieval Europe" and "burned-out tanks" overseen by fifteen-year olds with AK-47s (Hilditch 2000).

Those who retreated to the forests of the northwest and the home base of Pailin have expressed no regrets. Pailin has become a proverbial den of iniquity – prostitution, gambling, dope, illegal trade over the nearby Thai border, and general corruption – but the ironies of this are apparently lost on the remaining KR loyalists. One who talked with Hilditch solemnly informed him that he was just doing his bit for the country. Asked why Pailin was a fly-infested "resort" of porn, hookers, and gambling, he said he couldn't really explain that but blamed it on the Vietnamese. Said Hilditch (2000, 14): "It is beginning to dawn on us that Pol Pot's real legacy is the abolition of responsibility."

Social and Human Capital

Among the consequences of events nearly three decades ago was the evisceration of Cambodia's educated middle class. Children following that period had few people to teach them. Many important tasks, whether performed by private or public agencies, require education and training. In Cambodia, these tasks are either left undone or are done badly because of a lack of teachers and trained managers. The rural sectors of the society were always impoverished, and this has not changed: killing off the urbanites did not improve the situation for the 80 to 90 percent of the population that lived, and that still lives, in rural regions, but it did deprive them of the possibility of change. Today the literacy rate for those aged fifteen and over is only 35 percent. Some 41 percent of the population is under that age, so with a renewed effort to provide these youngsters with a primary school education the overall development of the country could improve. But this depends, in large part, on the ability of parents to keep their children in school, and income, the cost of illness, and the paucity of the social infrastructure all work against them.

THE EXTRAORDINARY CHAMBERS, 2005+

It is probable that, for some survivors of the KR period, some kind of accounting would be helpful. It would, perhaps, provide closure with regard to what happened to their families at that time; it would, perhaps, remove the strong climate of impunity in the country, which leaves victims with no recourse under law and that benefits the criminals. But the corruption in Cambodia is so pervasive and of such lengthy duration that trials alone, and especially trials of only the few remaining live leaders, will not heal the wounds. Truth commissions are, we have heard, not likely to succeed because they run counter to Buddhist cultural norms, but there has been no testing of that argument: in fact, no alternatives have been seriously discussed in Cambodia or (apparently) in the United Nations. It would be impossible to legislate or enforce any rule preventing criminals from taking public office as the prime minister and many others in his and other parties are accused of being among them. Many Cambodians consider the government to be a Vietnamese import, and they regard it as essentially illegitimate even if legally constructed. In short, this is not a society in transition: alas, it is a society mired in its own sad history, unable at this stage to emerge and to begin again. Possibly there will be no new beginning until all who lived through the 1970s are dead. And perhaps not even then, if the succeeding generations cannot overcome the legacies of that era. My questions, then, are: Will trials of the few surviving leaders of the KR help ordinary Cambodians to deal with the past? Is the investment of some $us56 million the best way to enable Cambodia to recreate a viable society?-

Whether or not these trials take place before remaining KR leaders die, this long tragic story says one thing clearly: Cambodia is still a very long way from recovery.

6

Rwanda: Democracy
after a Genocide

The thirtieth of September 2003 was the day of a general election to choose the president of Rwanda. I was excited because, by accompanying a Canadian Embassy officer as a foreign observer, it was an opportunity to observe the election. With much hope that all would go well for the Rwandan people in this important event, I began the day at 4:00 AM and watched the women in their brightly coloured dresses prepare polling stations in bare schoolrooms. These jobs are almost always done by women. I tried to convey my good wishes through a smile as I saw the people lining up to vote, but I soon realized how pointless my smiles were in a land that had very little trust for "white" people, regardless of our origin or personal history. I found myself rebuffed at several polls, where the electoral officers were reluctant to accept my credentials as an observer. Rwanda had agreed to have foreign observers, but that did not make us welcome. Eventually, they accepted the evidence – the badge, the papers – but reluctantly. And it was clear that I was there on sufferance. My francophone male companion was more readily accepted, and he did his best to defuse the distrust for his anglophone colleague.

The election seemed to go well. We saw no serious irregularities in our polls, nor were problems noted by other Canadian observers throughout the country. However, the next day's papers informed us that electoral authorities were angry with foreign observers who, in their opinion, were obstructing them in the conduct of their duties. As I document further on, the validity of the elections was somewhat compromised by government actions prior to the voting, but the voting itself was deemed fair by observers.

Rwanda is the exact opposite of Cambodia in terms of accepting accountability for genocide. Victorious Tutsis – who, by the time they won the war, were supported by the world – seem to be determined to make every Hutu alive responsible for the events of 1994. Not only were the leaders rounded up if they were still in the country, but so were their followers, members of the army, members of the Interahamwe (militia), and others suspected of having been present at the crimes. And while those inside the country were corralled, the armed forces proceeded to go after the runaways in the Democratic Republic of the Congo, Burundi, Uganda, and anywhere else where they might have fled. The war did not end in 1994, even if it was officially concluded by the victory of the Rwandan Patriotic Front (RPF). Eventually, leaders were taken to Arusha, Tanzania, where the International Criminal Tribunal for Rwanda (ICTR) was established. Others, soon over 120,000, were put into makeshift jails inside Rwanda. Within a few years there were so many people in jail, most of them men, all of them Hutu, that the jails were bursting and the countryside lacked not only a balance between men and women but also an essential labour force. When it became clear that Rwanda could not, in a century, mount Western-style court cases for this many people, the country reinvented neighbourhood trials known as gacaca courts. However, as I note further on, these did not reduce the number of prisoners; instead, these trials implicated still others.

In what follows, after a very brief description of Rwanda's earlier history and 1994 genocide, I discuss various features of the society in the opening years of the twenty-first century and then go on to concentrate on the government's obsession with (selectively) eliminating impunity. There were interventions in Rwanda before and during the 1994 genocide, but they are best considered in the context of that event, and for this reason I have not turned them into a separate chapter.

THE GENOCIDE OF 1994

The world's mass media told a story of tribal wars in Rwanda, culminating in the terrible slaughter of 1994, but that story was not accurate. The populations called Tutsi and Hutu were not then and are not now tribes; there is doubt that they are even distinctive racial groups.[1] Those called Tutsis were, traditionally, herders; those called Hutus were, traditionally, subsistence farmers. Throughout known history, the two groups had the same language, religions, customs,

Rwanda and neighbouring countries

and other features of culture, and many were intermarried. Belgian colonial authorities chose to treat them as races and introduced identity cards labelling them as either Tutsis or Hutus. The Tutsis – about 15 percent of the population – were regarded by the colonial authorities as superior, and it was through them that Rwanda and Burundi were governed. Unfortunately, many Tutsi came to believe they were a natural ruling class, and many Hutu came to believe they were the victims of a takeover by an alien group. Yet, in 1934, because the actual physical differences between the two groups were highly variable, the Belgians used ownership of cows as the criterion for determining race. Indeed, it was those who were intermarried and their progeny who suffered most as the spouses and children deemed to be Tutsis were targeted for death.

Over time, the two categories became embedded in legal practices. Individuals were obliged to carry identification cards, and schoolteachers or other adults would remind children which of the two groups was theirs. During the colonial period this worked in favour of Tutsis, but, with the advent of democracy and the exit of Belgian administrators, the advantage swung to Hutus because they were a large majority. And they had long-standing grievances against the Tutsi. The Tutsi king was assassinated in 1959, and some 150,000 Tutsis immediately went into exile in neighbouring countries.

Violence erupted in 1963, 1966, 1973, and the early 1990s. Over those years, some 700,000 Tutsi left Rwanda, many going to neighbouring Uganda. They, and the children who were born in Uganda or raised there, formed the revolutionary force known as the RPF. By the time they returned, the RPF was a well-trained army. They chose their moment well: the Hutus were not united behind the presiding president; they were (and may always have been) divided by regional alliances. Outsiders familiar with the situation assume that Hutu forces deliberately shot down President Habyarimana's plane on April 1994 as he returned from Arusha, where he had signed the Arusha Accords with the Tutsi RPF. Hutus, however, blamed Tutsis and used the assassination as the cover for a planned and well-orchestrated genocide.

The planning was meticulous, even if the instruments were primitive. The names of all Hutus likely to try to prevent the event had been recorded, and many of them were killed instantly. Tutsi leaders were similarly identified in advance, so that the population would have no leaders. The youth who had been trained as a militia force, the Interahamwe, were given orders and machetes, and they were backed up by Forces Armées Rwandaises (FAR) soldiers with guns. There was no going back for any of them; they would have been killed had they tried to retreat. Roads were blocked off, and Tutsi or Hutu who tried to flee were stopped and generally hacked to death on the spot. Some tried to find safety in the Roman Catholic churches that dotted the countryside and were the strongest physical and spiritual legacy of the Belgian colonial power. Terrible tales are told of church leaders who worked with Hutu militias to ensure that all the huddled survivors became corpses, often burned to death when the doors were locked and the wooden buildings set to the torch. Tutsi women were brutally raped and mutilated. Men and women, the elderly and children alike, were killed in ways too gruesome to report. The Khmer Rouge slowly starved its captive population; the FAR and militias killed them one arm or leg or breast or penis or vagina at a time, with machetes and broken beer bottles.

The underlying reasons for this terrible assault? Clearly, colonial context was influential in creating the "ethnic" groups. Beyond that was the fear of losing land when the RPF returned to claim its lost properties. The population already exceeded the carrying capacity of the land (Gasana 2002). The National Unity and Reconciliation Commission claims that "most of the killings during 1994 were done with a promise of getting the victims' property" (Oppenheim and van der Wolf 2001). Perhaps for some it was economic decline of a more general nature: coffee and tea, the only export products of Rwanda, were suffering market setbacks. Fear of the RPF was articulated in hourly state radio services, replete with calls for murder of the Tutsi "cockroaches," and by the Hutu army and militia. After four months of mass murders, the FAR and the Interahamwe were defeated by the incoming RPF.

The rape of women left few survivors, but those who did emerge were scarred psychologically and physically, often pregnant with unwanted children. After the war, they had to head families consisting of their siblings, children of their deceased neighbours and kin, their own children (if they had them prior to the onslaught and if those children survived), and the child born of the rape (who often began life with HIV). Many of these women were themselves children when the war occurred, and they are often ill. Surviving women, despite ill health and burdened lives, have become the strongest force for change in the country.

By way of explanation for the genocide, one woman told me:

Some people did it out of fear. A lot of people were threatened with death and prison, with being killed or having their family killed. There were some people who did try to stand by their friends and family, and strangers even, but the threats they received made it difficult. I think they are definitely suffering their own kind of grief. I mean, I can't imagine people just being happy to pick up a machete and cut off others' limbs and there are some people who say "Once I killed one person, the first time it was difficult, but the next time I think, well it is possible, so I just go ahead and do it." A lot of people who are confessing say they don't know what was happening to them or what possessed them.

Professor Simon Gasiberege, the psychologist who created gacaca training manuals, provided this explanation of what happened:

> Conscience is what somebody has of self and belonging to a community. Persons now tell me they don't know who they are, what is their identity. They have no trust of anyone and they ask if they have relationship to other Rwandans. That shows what has been destroyed. Why is this? There was a long period of destruction [before 1994], and a culture of impunity. Colonialism changed the social system, the culture, et cetera. This blocked Rwandans from developing their own culture … The culture of impunity is a process, a process the lets people do things until such point that they don't know what is right and what is wrong for themselves.
>
> Before the colonial period, the head of the family would bring people together in a small gacaca. During the colonial period, the elders of their families, instead of going to their own system, went to classical justice. And the education system, which used to be conducted by the elders, lost control …
>
> The genocide planners, most went to the same secondary school as myself … There was a conflict between the traditional values and the colonial system, and that conflict never was solved. On the contrary, that conflict developed into a system of division. This created divided personalities, an internal and an external division. There was division in the peoples' hearts, and it was turned into an ideology by the politicians but it didn't stay at the level of politics. It was taught in the school and in the families. From that time the Hutus began to not like Tutsi children, and the [Hutu] children felt they were just excluded and began to ask themselves why and how they were different. It affected their identity. It was like a culture. Someone who harmed Tutsis did not get punished. On the contrary they were rewarded. We have people who began to harm Tutsis in the 1960s, and they became "great personalities." So they develop an "anti-value" of themselves. This was combined with the manipulation of a very poor population. The leaders said, "If you kill this man you get his property."
>
> People do not necessarily see what is objectively before them, they see through the veil of their preconceived ideas, their imagination. If they think that someone is a Tutsi – long-faced, tall – then they kill him because they imagine him as the enemy whether or not there is any validity in what they think is true.[2]

In Kigali, unlike in cities in many other countries where atrocities have occurred, people continue to talk about what they've been through. One researcher even mentioned that she was tired of hearing the stories of survivors. Then, on reflection, she said: "But you know it's only nine years old. What do you expect survivors to talk about? Survivors of the holocaust are still talking about it and it is fifty years old, so I think it is still appropriate to be talking about it."

INTERVENTIONS

As the previous section indicates, Rwanda had been a Belgian colony before independence. France had long-standing trade relations with the Habyarimana regime – trade relations that included supplies of arms and military expertise. French support for the Hutus was based on two main pillars: the belief that they were democratic and the fact that they spoke French. Lieutenant General Roméo Dallaire, in charge of the UN Assistance Mission for Rwanda (UNAMIR), claims that France's support escalated to outright intervention against the incoming RPF forces from 1990 to 1993, though by 1994 it attempted, in concert with the United States, to bring the president and the leaders of the RPF to the negotiations that led to the Arusha Accords (Dallaire 2003, 436).

As the world knows, the United Nations sent a small peacekeeping force to Rwanda just before the 1994 genocide. UNAMIR personnel understood that its task was to maintain the ceasefire while negotiations proceeded for putting the Arusha Accords into action. They were scarcely in place when it became clear to Dallaire that peacekeeping was not what was needed. Government forces were preparing for something much worse, and soon the horror of genocide was being enacted. The small UN force was ordered to take no military role, and it was obliged to witness thousands being murdered and raped. Dallaire has described the tragedy in his book *Shake Hands with the Devil: The Failure of Humanity in Rwanda* and films have brought its impact to a wide audience.[3] The genocide ended when the RPF took over Kigali and stopped the war. The American president of the period, Bill Clinton, and his secretary of state, Madeleine Albright, have both apologized to the victims and to whomever else challenges their wilful ignorance of the period. Their claim remains that they did not realize it was a genocide until too late.

To Dallaire, the task in these impossible circumstances was to maintain neutrality and to attempt to bring the government and the RPF together for a negotiated ceasefire. But neither side wanted a ceasefire: the RPF, much the superior army of the two, was marching towards the capital sure of its victory. The government forces, the FAR, and the militias they had trained focused on killing remaining Tutsi rather than on direct fighting with the RPF. The massacres they had witnessed took their toll on the involuntary UN witnesses who, in addition to dealing with scenes of sheer horror, had to cope with poor accommodation, putrid canned food, and interrupted sleep. Dallaire persistently informed UN headquarters and his own superior officers in Canada that a genocide was in progress. Just as persistently he was rebuffed or given instructions that, in the circumstances, were absurd.

Towards the conclusion of the one hundred days of madness, suddenly, France, apparently with UN and US agreement, created Opération Turquoise. This consisted of 2,500 members of elite units, including the French Foreign Legion, marines, paratroopers, and special forces. They were well equipped. They had apparently been informed that the RPF was invading the country and killing Hutu civilians. Their lengthy history of warm relationships with the Hutu government and traders supported their interpretation of who was committing genocide. They essentially told Dallaire that they would take over and that the UN forces should not get in the way. France, though it had voted in favour of UN peacekeeping forces in Rwanda, had not backed up its vote with troops or equipment, and now its troops were coming in on the pretense of humanitarian intervention with massive quantities of equipment. Some of the soldiers had been military advisors to Hutu forces in times past: in short, the French at this stage were not neutral (Dallaire 2003, 420–60).

Dallaire's account from the perspective of the UN mission is matched by the account provided by the scholar Gérard Prunier, who was seconded by the French government to provide cultural advice to Opération Turquoise. Prunier recognized that this was not a humanitarian gesture, except insofar as it was designed to support the FAR and the interim Hutu government. He attributed this last-minute attempt to save Hutus from their inevitable fate to language politics. The RPF leaders all spoke English, as did the whole region of East Africa. They were representative of the "Anglo-Saxon world," and if the Hutu were beaten, one of the last French-speaking former colonial territories in East-Central Africa would be anglicized (Prunier 1995, 281–311). French authorities regarded

Prunier as a heretic, but internal politics in France suggested that he be included in the operation so as to give it greater credibility as a humanitarian effort. The UN Security Council gave the French an intervention mandate under Chapter 7 of the UN Charter, which allows for military efforts towards gaining peace. UNAMIR, meanwhile, was still operating under Chapter 6, which allows only for peacekeeping.

In Rwanda, Hutus warmly welcomed French intervention, even to the point of hanging the Tricolour on lampposts, grateful to have those they considered allies take over from the faltering FAR. They expected the French forces to go into direct combat with the RPF, but French authorities and the UN had not given approval for a more expanded operation. The French met with RPF leaders and assured them that this was a humanitarian and neutral operation designed to end the war, though the huge number of heavy weapons and other equipment seemed incongruent with those intentions. Constrained as they were by inconsistent rules – they were, after all, a well-equipped army being told they couldn't engage in direct aggression – they ended up protecting a region in the southwestern section of the country as Hutu refugees poured in following the RPF victories.

The near conclusion of the war came with the RPF taking Kigali and installing a temporary government. Thousands of refugees streamed out of the city and regions held by the RPF. Prunier says that over a million people crossed into Zaïre in one week. About 10 percent of the total population had been killed, and another 30 percent had gone into exile. Tutsis who had been living in exile in Uganda and Burundi were simultaneously returning, bringing their cattle with them.

In the overcrowded and unsanitary refugee camps cholera broke out. An estimated thirty thousand emigré Hutu died. The French legion buried some twenty thousand of them in their region: this was not the task they had expected to perform. Prunier observes that the Western press told the world about these tragic events, even comparing the deaths by cholera to deaths by genocide. The effect was to obliterate the horror of the genocide and to reduce the world's sense of its own failure to respond when support for the UNAMIR operation could have saved many lives (Prunier 1995, 302–3). When the French legion, which had held the southwestern region of the country, withdrew, they left some 1.5 million people without defence. Those refugees headed for Bukavu. After the war, but while thousands of refugees were still in camps, the United States dropped food parcels.

RPF ATROCITIES

The incoming RPF was generally well disciplined, but its troops also committed atrocities during the course of the war and afterwards. One that was recorded occurred at Kabgayi. RPF soldiers who had secured the area entered a monastery and killed an archbishop, three bishops, and ten priests. Of this, Dallaire (2003, 414) wrote: "The rebel troops had been travelling for weeks and encountering everywhere the effects of the Hutu scorched-human policy, and they were well aware that the church was very intimate with the Habyarimana family and members of the former government. Quite simply, they killed the princes of the church out of vengeance, their discipline frayed to the breaking point by the atrocities they'd witnessed."

Another mass killing by RPF soldiers included several hundred people in Butare towards the end of the war. The RPF showed no inclination to charge them with the crimes, and the new civilian government did not have the police force or other means to do so. Other incidents that have been recorded appear to have been individual acts of revenge or what Prunier (1995, 306–7) calls ordinary banditry. Whether or not there were more revenge killings than were reported between 1994 and 2000, when an interim government with RPF participation was established, rumours of RPF atrocities were running high. Hutus in refugee camps were still trying to escape anticipated reprisals on the same scale as they had inflicted. The RPF subsequently entered neighbouring countries in search of Hutu génocidaires, and again, there were reports of vengeance killings.

Just a word about the refugee camps: before long they were under the control of leaders of the genocide. Hutu who failed to support the demands and brutality of those who took control were killed or tortured. As well, there were some Tutsi in the camps, people who had somehow survived and escaped along with the Hutu refugees. Caught out, they, too, were executed. The aid agencies who set up the camps could not control them: the refugees were too frightened of these leaders to speak up (Prunier 1995, 312–20).

IMMEDIATE AFTERMATH OF GENOCIDE AND WAR

The country that emerged from the massacres had a poverty rate of over 50 percent, a human life expectancy of about forty, and a rate of malnutrition of 29 percent for children under the age of five years. Half the population aged fifteen and over was illiterate. GNP per capita, as measured by conventional means and in US dollars, was about $210 per year. Added to these indicators of human misery was a high rate of HIV/AIDS affecting both males and females. More males than females were killed in the genocide, and the majority of perpetrators were also male; those apprehended were incarcerated, others became refugees in nearby countries. Thus, for some time following 1994, women were more numerous, particularly in the age group between twenty-four and twenty-nine. Many of these women had been raped, some gang raped, and the result was unwanted children, HIV/AIDS, and emotional traumas (Institute for the Study of Genocide 2001; see also Fein, Brugnola, and Spirer 1994). Psychiatrist Athanase Hagengimana, who conducted a large study of trauma in Rwanda, noted: "Both Hutu and Tutsi feel victimized by events of the genocide and subsequent migration. The fate in 1994 of up to 800,000 Tutsis killed in the genocide and tens of thousands of Hutu killed in extrajudicial executions and reprisals in Rwanda and others killed in the Democratic Republic of Congo (DRC) or during counterinsurgency activities have created a sense of mutual victimization and a climate of mistrust" (Institute for the Study of Genocide 2001).

Among the psychological problems encountered are post-traumatic stress disorder and chronic traumatic grief. The symptoms of these disorders include fear of uniformed men, inability to deal with the loss of loved ones whose bodies have never been recovered, persistent grieving, and various other traumatized states. A 2004 study of trauma and post-trauma symptoms showed that, of 2,074 respondents with data on exposure to trauma, 75.4 percent were forced to flee their homes, 73.0 percent had a close member of their family killed, and 70.9 percent had property destroyed or lost. Just short of 25 percent met symptom criteria for post-traumatic shock syndrome. Respondents with these symptoms were "less likely to have positive attitudes toward the Rwandan national trials, belief in community, and interdependence with other ethnic groups." They were also less likely to "support the Rwandan national trials, the local *gacaca* trials" and various measures of openness to reconciliation (Pham, Weinstein, and Longman 2004, 602).

Psychological trauma was not the only after-effect of the genocide: physical dislocation was also a major problem. Internal refugees, terrified of going back to their homes, tried to settle on land and premises left by those who had fled to other regions. Some survivors tried to find new accommodation where their original homes had been destroyed. There was much dislocation and many attempts to begin again in new places, and this inevitably created confusion and fear among villagers in both places.

Another spillover effect of the genocide was the exodus of many Hutus fearing reprisal. As these new refugees flooded into neighbouring countries, the latter were destabilized by the now displaced war between the Hutus and the RPF soldiers in pursuit of them. The continuing war exacerbated an already anarchic situation in Ituri Province in the Democratic Republic of the Congo (DRC), where warlords and nationals of many countries vied for a share of mineral wealth, and both the Hutu refugees and their would-be captors were blamed for much of the looting and violence.

The physical infrastructure of Rwanda was destroyed. Nothing worked. Government coffers had no money in them because the former government members had taken everything with them when they fled. There were no functioning utilities, banks had been looted, stores had been emptied, and transportation was non-existent. Because so many Hutu farmers had left, crops were not harvested and the remaining or returning population had little food. Houses had been destroyed so that when refugees and displaced people returned, they had no lodgings. And, to make matters more difficult, foreign aid was slow to materialize because outsiders were unsure of the new government, unsure who had committed genocide, and unsure how the current rulers would deal with the previous ones. The rumour was that this was a double genocide, a civil war, that both groups had been its perpetrators, that no one was innocent and no one could be trusted.

GOVERNMENT OF NATIONAL UNITY, 1994–2003

A "Government of National Unity" staffed by both Hutu and Tutsi was established after the war in 1994. It was extended in 1999 for another four years. In 2000, the leading RPF general, Paul Kagame, was sworn in as president. A transitional national assembly, with Prime Minister Bernard Makuza and a new constitution, was put in place. Human rights organizations complained that the government did not apply either former or new constitutional regulations to its own behaviour. For example, it banned a new political party and put its organizer, a former president, under house arrest. Street gangs attacked him and other supporters of his party. Several persons in the custody of military authorities "disappeared," several civilians fled the country for fear of being killed, and at least two persons were assassinated (Human Rights Watch 2000). In the circumstances, these events caused consternation but not surprise in the international community. Revenge killings occurred, though not on a scale that would have merited the designation of civil war, and the government was dealing with a volatile situation.

Changing Identity Codes

Although one of the first acts of the government was to ban the terms "Hutu" and "Tutsi," the fact was that the country, after the war and through the following decade, was run by Tutsi, primarily Tutsi who came in with the RPF or following it. The rules – whether fair and just or otherwise – were seen to be Tutsi rules, and the courts were viewed as symbols of victors' justice. Elections in 1999 and 2003 notwithstanding, observers claimed that the government became increasingly centralized and authoritarian. However, apart from claims of looting in the DRC, there were few claims of generalized government corruption.

New Institutional Infrastructure: The Imidugudu Process

The Arusha Protocol, signed in June 1993, stated that refugees who had been out of the country in excess of ten years could not claim back their property but that they would be assisted to resettle in villages with basic infrastructure. This agreement had been reached between the leaders of the RPF and the Hutu government prior to the assassination of President Habyarimana. The question of land rights for returnees became an emergency following the genocide, and the proposal to create new villages became, by the end of 1996, the National Habitat Policy, known variously as *imidugudu* and "villagization."[4]

Arguing that it was impossible to provide schools, plumbing, electricity, and other services to a scattered population, the government ordered both the displaced and the returnees to relocate. Small-lot owners were forcibly moved to more central locations, where they were promised new houses and services. This was implemented initially in the most volatile regions in the northwestern prefectures of Gisenyi and Ruhengeri. The implementation was extremely slow, and families, having been obliged to destroy their earlier homes, sometimes found themselves homeless and impoverished in strange locations. They were far removed from their subsistence plots and had to travel back and forth by foot, using up valuable hours just travelling so that they could grow their food. Human Rights Watch accused the government of "violating the basic rights of tens of thousands of people," a claim strongly denounced by the Rwandan government as "baseless and full of lies."[5]

In the following years, hundreds of thousands were moved, many against their will, and aid workers claimed that the massive displacement was primarily designed to prevent any new insurgencies. Simultaneously the government displaced more than 650,000 people who had lived in the northwest into camps, "more to keep them from supporting the insurgents than to protect them from attack," according to Human Rights Watch and other aid groups. Civilians living in those regions were caught in the crossfire between the remaining armies of the earlier government army (FAR) and the Interahamwe, on the one hand, and the now reconstituted RPF, known as the Rwandan Patriotic Army (RPA), on the other. Persons collaborating with the RPA, genocide survivors, local civilian authorities, and returnees were often targeted, and those attacks were then followed by RPA counterinsurgency operations, with high casualties among civilian populations. According to several aid agencies and the Global IDP (Internally Displaced Person) Database, as of July 2003 there remained some 200,000 relocated families living in precarious conditions.[6] The Rwandan government, however, responded that it had invested heavily in new villages and also in a new land system that should mitigate future land disputes. International aid was also invested, though by 2003 those funds were diminishing.

An average family plot in these years was 0.6 hectares, and families kept partitioning their tiny plots to accommodate family growth. Some 90 percent of the population was involved in subsistence agriculture, and naturally people preferred to reside next to their plots. Because of the massive displacement of populations, customary law was no longer capable of dealing with land conflicts, and the *imidugudu* process may have exacerbated rather than relieved the pressures. The Land Policy and Land Bill introduced in

November 2001 were consistent with the government's attempt to guarantee security of land tenure, provide for land earmarked for *imidugudu* sites, and ensure private ownership of land. The government stated that one objective of the law was to promote equal distribution and access to land so that women would no longer be discriminated against. Another objective was to monitor land management in order to avoid speculation and exploitation.

The claims of the government had to be measured against a continuing concentration of property without compensation to original owners and charges of corruption in the villagization process. Although cases of abuse were noted in the human rights literature, they did not appear to be frequent. Yet those documented, especially in a lengthy study by Human Rights Watch (2001c), were certainly serious: they included a case in which a military officer took over land declared as a military zone, then grew cash crops on it. He employed former landholders as wage labourers. Another case involved a millitary officer displacing 166 families from the commune of Nyarubuye so that he could used it to pasture his cattle.

Gap between Intentions and Funds

Some of the reforms adopted by the government established by the RPF immediately after the conflict, and maintained until the elections of 2003, were claimed to have been intended to develop social services across the country that, a generation hence, would result in an educated population and in villages with electricity, plumbing, and other modern amenities. Had there been funds to actually implement these reforms, the country might have benefited enormously. As it happened, people were moved but the promised services often failed to materialize. Even where they were implemented, they involved the forced movement of people from isolated locations far from their subsistence plots. Part of the unstated objective was to oblige Hutus to abandon outward indications that they recognized the difference between themselves and their Tutsi neighbours.

Deforestation, overgrazing, soil exhaustion, and soil erosion were continuing problems in the country. A pressing problem that preceded the genocide and may well have triggered it was the high population growth rate: by 2000, it was still 6.8 per annum, with a total population of 8.0 million. Life expectancy at birth was 40.9 years, and

5.1 percent of the adult population was infected with HIV.[7] As one of the most densely populated countries in Africa, Rwanda appeared to be on the cusp of a huge ecological disaster.

Education

Primary school education was viewed by the new government, and possibly by the majority of Rwandans, as the key to a peaceful and more prosperous future, but after the genocide over half of all adults were illiterate. By 1995, most children of primary school age were enrolled in schools (94.1 percent, compared to 63.1 percent in 1985). However, few completed primary school, and even fewer continued to secondary school (11.0 per cent by 2000). By 2000, the adult literacy rate was about 60 percent.[8] The quality of education was poor because of a lack of qualified teachers and teaching materials (African Rights 2001). Not surprisingly, with that record at the primary and secondary levels, very low enrolment in university and technical schools resulted in a continuing failure to develop a more skilled and knowledgeable labour force. On the positive side, the government gave education high priority in its budget decisions and launched programs for training teachers, examining students, and creating a national syllabus. The new Kigali Institute for Science and Technology was established, and the National University of Rwanda at Butare was trying to develop stronger capacities.

Human Rights

The Commision Nationale des Droits de l'Homme was established in March 1999, and its seven elected commissioners were in place by May of that year. The mandate was to investigate all violations of human rights, but the specifics of the task were not clearly outlined, and Human Rights Watch was unable to get straightforward answers about the procedures or scope of inquiries in 2001. At that time, Human Rights Watch (2001b) implied that the commission (like other commissions in Africa) was more of a "Pretender" than a "Protector."

The government imposed new limits on NGOs and other organizations during 2002, and it promulgated a law giving authorities broad powers to control the management, finances, and the projects of local and international NGOs. Although independent publications were permitted, staff who were critical were harassed. All of the human rights groups reporting on Rwanda said that freedom of speech was effectively curtailed (noted, for example, in Human Rights Watch World Report 2002; International Crisis Group 2002; Amnesty International 2002 and 2003) The major opposition party was dissolved in April 2003. The opposition Mouvement Démocratique Républicain (MDR) was accused of propagating a "divisive" ideology. Forty-seven individuals were named by a parliamentary commission report and the party was purged. In addition, the Ligue Rwandaise pour la promotion et la défense des droits de l'homme (LIPRODHOR), the leading human rights NGO in Rwanda, was accused of obtaining foreign funding for the MDR (Human Rights Watch World Report 2002).

During 2002, according to Amnesty International, freedom of expression was severely curtailed, and journalists were imprisoned, deported, or driven into exile (Amnesty International 2003, 212). As well, all political party activity, save that of the Rwandese Patriotic Front, was effectively banned and leaders were jailed. Religious freedom was reduced, with demands from government that religious organizations submit to various new legal requirements. Leaders of the Association of Pentecostal Churches in Gikondo District, City of Kigali, were arrested and detained for two weeks in November 2002. Some members of the congregation were attacked by local defence forces and national police (ibid).

Women Survivors and Their Associations

One cannot be in Rwanda long before realizing that women's organizations are the most critical tools of renewal and development in this society. Many NGOs headed by women and designed to help other women or help orphaned children have been established. Some are branches of international humanitarian NGOs, and many are funded by outside foundations and governments; however, the daily work, the persistent empathy, sympathy, physical support, skills training and retraining, love and care are all provided by strong women working together to change their society and, especially, to raise and educate the children.

At the individual level it is also women who are carrying the load of enabling families to survive. As previously mentioned, due to the genocide and imprisonment policies, there were many more women

than men in Rwanda after the genocide, so women were carrying a
double burden, trying to maintain the remnants of a household and
also trying to grow or obtain food for their dependents. This is all the
more difficult because the legal system in the country is patrimonial,
even though (as interview data made clear) women have always been
and still are the stronger pillars for families and communities. Even
so, a woman often had to contend with surviving members of the
husband's or father's family, who would claim the land and attempt
to evict her and her children.

The government must be given much credit for recognizing that
the education of women and legislation designed to enable women
to head families would be crucial to recovery. Women have been
encouraged to stand for Parliament, to vote, to attend schools, and
to take the initiative to lower birth rates. Obstacles for women, such
as patriarchal property customs, run contrary to government initiatives, so it may be some time before the old habits are overcome;
however, the government is providing leadership in this respect.

At many stops along my way I asked whether there were any NGOs
or government offices who provide counselling or other aid to men
who suffered trauma and dislocation during the genocide. The answers were always vague or negative, which suggests that male survivors are adrift without support. Perhaps more seriously, both because
of their numbers and their guilt, the men who killed and raped, if
they are not incarcerated already or in exile, have no route by which
they might call out for help or receive it. Given the other information
that comes via confessions of the accused during the gacaca process,
many of these men had little understanding of what was happening:
they were simply caught up in it. Now they are obliged to live with
knowledge of their past deeds in a culture that no longer approves of
what they did. The level of fear and frustration many experience cannot be healthy for their society, the more so when the government
pushes them to give up the privileges of patrimonial society, to relocate to locations where they are not known, and to accept the rule of
persons they still regard as "cockroaches."

THE 2003 ELECTIONS AND
THE RPF GOVERNMENT OF PAUL KAGAME

The government met its promised deadlines of August and September
2003 to hold national elections for the president and Parliament,

respectively. The Kagame party (known still as the Rwandese Patriotic Front or RPF) was voted in by substantial majorities throughout the country. As noted earlier, I was one of many international observers to the 30 September election. The international observers were tolerated – not welcomed – and their rights were limited, but even so I have no doubt that the Kagame slate had a whopping majority of the votes in the polls I observed. The final report gave 95 percent of the vote to the government, a suspicious level of support in any democratic country, but foreign observers did not provide evidence of fraud during the voting.

The actual fraud had occurred prior to the election. Other parties were not permitted the same range of recruitment or activity, leaders were obliged to run as independents when their parties were banned, and individuals could be jailed or put under house arrest because of claims that they used the words "Hutu" and "Tutsi" or were otherwise "divisive" in their behaviour as judged by the government party. The chief opposition party was banned, and its leader in the presidential elections was labelled "racist." While other countries expressed guarded criticism of the government's actions, the Netherlands froze aid for the elections because of concerns about the disappearance of opposition politicians.[9] The government's position was that there must be a transformation in mind-sets before full civil and political rights could be extended.

In March 2004, Paul Kagame was confronted with new accusations that it was he, not Hutu extremists, who ordered the killing of former president Juvénal Habyarimana, thus triggering the genocide. His office dismissed the allegations, and the United Nations denied that it had launched an investigation into the assassination. But Le Monde and Canada's National Post claimed to have UN documents showing that an investigation was under way and that the UN's chief war crimes prosecutor for Rwanda in the late 1990s "abruptly ordered the investigation closed."[10] Nothing further has come to light on this wavelength. The majority of analysts, whatever else their orientation, have long since concluded that it was Hutu extremists who killed the president and then launched the genocide in the wake of his death. The supposition is that the RPF, with the Arusha Accords in hand, was harmed by the assassination; the Hutu extremists of that moment were the beneficiaries. One might otherwise speculate that, if the RPF believed more could be gained by continuing the war, then killing the accords in this fashion might have been a means of doing this, the more so since the reasonable supposition would be that the assassination had been planned by Hutus. The speculation does not take into account the level of organization and instant readiness to respond by the Hutu forces intent on committing genocide.

By July 2004, the Parliament was recommending that LIPRODHOR and five other NGOs be disbanded. This recommendation was based on the report of an ad hoc committee regarding the murder of genocide survivors in Gikongoro in late 2003 and the continuing harassment of people willing to testify at gacaca hearings in that district. The inquiry brought forth accusations that the NGOs and some church groups were fomenting anti-government ideas in the guise of education or development work.[11] These persistent human rights violations notwithstanding, the same government established a ministry of justice, a human rights commission, and educational policies whose purpose was to promote positive acts of reconciliation and to demolish the sectarian versions of reality that had thrived under the previous racist categories of Hutu and Tutsi.

The Unity and Reconciliation Commission as of the 2003 Election

The National Unity and Reconciliation Commission has, among its obligations as set out by law, the responsibility to "denounce any written or declared ideas and actions aimed at or based on disunity" – a responsibility that leads not only to preventing the dissemination of hate literature and/or speeches but also to preventing debate about government initiatives. Unity and reconciliation are, in effect, whatever the government – and only the government – deems to be acceptable. Another of the commission's responsibilities is to "monitor whether political parties, leaders and all the people in general do respect and observe the policy of national unity and reconciliation." The actions of government officials regarding the *Imigudugu* policies (described above) provide further examples of an increasingly self-righteous government determined to reform a tragically flawed society through repression (African Rights 2000, 97).

The Unity and Reconciliation Commission monitors government and civil society institutions, both private and public, to ensure that what they do does not contravene government policy. As well, it trains people in the field of conflict management, peace-related issues, reconciliation, and peaceful resistance. Teachers are trained in the United Kingdom, Sweden, and the United States. The commission works closely with gacaca towards the goal of restorative justice. It deals with such issues as poverty reduction, refugee problems, and transitions from war to peaceful relations. It holds hearings and consults with people on issues of justice, reconciliation, corruption, and distorted history.[12]

What is highlighted in the debate that consumes Rwandans is something that Germany is still debating half a century after its war. And that is this: can democracy, civil liberties, human rights, and all that goes with a free society be advanced by repressing thought, speech, publications, assemblies, and actions that are contrary to what the leading authorities believe is good for social development?[13] The debate occurs because, ultimately, the elite that controls the government and economy does not trust the population to make choices that would keep it in power. As I write, in 2006, we are seeing the same development of distrust and de-democratization occurring in the United States and Britain and, to a lesser extent, in Canada, Australia, and many European countries, with terrorism being used as the excuse for forms of repression that would not have been tolerated between the 1950s and at least 1990, perhaps even as late as 2000.

Continuing Conflict in the Democratic Republic of Congo and Rwanda

Though the mass destruction of the 1994 events ceased as the RPF gained control of the land, violence erupted again and again in the following years. These eruptions were often associated with the conflict in neighbouring Democratic Republic of the Congo (formerly Zaire and, before that, the Belgian Congo), where soldiers of both groups carried on their battle. Hutus in the defeated FAR and in the Liberation Army of Rwanda (ALIR) fled to the DRC, and the victorious army went after them. The violence intensified after the mass repatriation of refugees from the DRC in November 1996 and Mobutu Sese Seko's fall from power. Insurgents moved into the northwestern region of Rwanda, while others held on to bases in the eastern DRC. Terrible massacres tore apart refugee transit camps throughout 1997 and 1998, and, even later, guerrilla attacks continued to terrorize Rwandese in the northern territories (African Rights 1998). In 2000, Amnesty International reported that, while the number of killings inside Rwanda decreased after 1998, thousands of unarmed civilians were killed in the DRC in armed conflicts that included the Interahamwe militia and FAR soldiers (Amnesty International 2000, 202–3).

The battle in the DRC was not only by way of evading or enacting rough justice. The DRC is rich in many minerals, and both groups lusted after those riches. Child soldiers were reported to be reinforcing both the FAR and the Rwandan Patriotic Army (the reconstituted RPF, now incorporating Hutu soldiers) in the DRC. Reports of extensive abuses of human rights crossed army lines. A UN panel called on the Security Council to impose bans on timber, diamond, gold, coltran, and other exports from Rwanda, Uganda, and Burundi. And it also called for a suspension of aid to Rwanda and its neighbours (Human Rights Watch 2001a; Human Rights Watch World Report 2002). Repeatedly, the United Nations objected to the role of the RPA in the Congo and called upon Rwanda and other signatories to the Lusaka Accords to withdraw their troops. Paul Kagame responded that Rwanda would not withdraw troops as long as its security was threatened.[14] Again in 2002, the United Nations accused Rwanda, Uganda, and Burundi of looting the DRC's mineral wealth, to which the Rwandan government retorted that the report was an attempt to smear Rwanda's army and top leadership. Although the government claimed to have withdrawn its troops in the following year, there are frequent reports of continued fighting involving Rwandese troops in the DRC.

Justice?

Clearly, the Kagame government, together with the United Nations and the many NGOs now dominating the scene in Kigali, wants to enact justice through the courts, including the innovative gacaca system. Impunity is eschewed – except with respect to former RPF soldiers and their members now in government or holding other important positions within Rwanda. In defence of the new system, we must note that this society is functioning – not magnificently, but, considering what it has gone through, reasonably well. The government works. The justice system is clogged and inefficient, but it, too, more or less works. Numerous NGOs, both domestic and foreign, fill in the gaps with social work, education, grief counselling, and skills training. Inflows of development aid from countries belatedly expressing grief about the genocide they failed to notice earlier keep the economy alive.

But to say that this is a successful transformation is, I suggest, more than the circumstances merit. Beneath the changes – and I do not underrate them, they are miraculous in many ways – but beneath them lie the continuing hatreds of the have-nots for the haves, and the people still refer to each other as Hutu and Tutsi. This is not the society that Habyarimana governed, no: it is closer, in many ways, to the society that existed before the Belgians left. The governors now, recruited from the Tutsi army and its followers, are working hard and honestly to create a new society and to banish the old one; however, as long as the renewal keeps them, and only them, at the top, the underlying frustration remains. Even if this were not so, there is the continuing problem of the failure of this society to develop industrial capacity: this matters where the land, used only for agriculture, is not capable of sustaining the growing population.

The ubiquitous memorials all over the country, the persistent reminders about the genocide, and the constant casting of blame on the previous government and Hutu extremists keeps the Kagame government strong; however, it is not so obvious that these state flourishes are helping with the recovery of traumatized survivors. In contrast to Cambodia, where amnesia is a prevalent disease, Rwanda seems determined neither to forget nor to forgive. It is obsessed with accountability, while seeming to re-establish the kinds of policies and the relationships of dominance and subordination that, long ago, were the prelude to what became genocide.

Amnesty International Reports 2005 and 2006

Amnesty International summarized the situation in Rwanda during 2004 as follows:

> The government continued to suppress the political opposition and those critical of government policies or government officials. Members of the banned Democratic Republican Movement (Mouvement démocratique républicain, MDR) continued to be arrested and detained. At least one MDR member was extrajudicially executed. Family members of some alleged MDR members or supporters had their land confiscated or were denied social services by local authorities. Some top officials who worked for Faustin Twagiramungu during his 2003 presidential campaign were arrested and unlawfully detained.

Further, the report detailed what it called the "suppression of civil society," whereby human rights NGOs were accused of supporting genocide or working with populations seen to be hostile to the government. It also alleged that freedom of the press was severely restricted by the intimidation and harassment of journalists. Further, it said that the trial of Pasteur Bizimungu was not carried out by international standards of fairness and that similar unfairness characterized the trials of many others. Finally, it noted that some sixty thousand refugees remained outside Rwanda, fearful of being forcibly returned (presumably to jails) or unsure of their reception were they to re-enter the country. According to the UN High Commissioner for Refugees, nearly 8.5 thousand refugees were repatriated in the first six months of 2004 from African countries. Some of those who were repatriated left again, seeking asylum elsewhere (Amnesty International 2005, 214).

In the 2006 report, Amnesty International was slightly more optimistic, though the charges were still serious:

Human rights organizations were prevented from working freely and activists were harassed and attacked. Journalists continued to face intimidation. Trials continued of people suspected of involvement in the 1994 genocide: some 36,000 of the more than 80,000 detainees awaiting trial were provisionally released in August. There were concerns about the fairness of some of the trials. (Amnesty International 2006, 218)

Amnesty International's 2007 report was more critical. It's summary of findings noted that:

The government maintained tight control over all sections of civil society, whose work was conducted in a climate of fear and suspicion. Trials continued of people suspected of involvement in the 1994 genocide. There were concerns about the fairness of some of the trials. Several thousand detainees were held in long-term detention without trial in harsh conditions. Six hundred people remained on death row. (Amnesty International 2007, 220)

The detailed charges in the Amnesty International report of 2007 were serious. Attacks on independent journalists and human rights defenders were depicted. Some of the gacaca courts were described as being staffed by "poorly qualified, ill-trained and corrupt" judges (Amnesty International 2007, 220). There were still many people in overcrowded and unsanitary jails who had never had a chance to appear in court (after twelve years, two Roman Catholic nuns were still in detention without trial) (221). According to Amnesty International, thousands of Rwandans fled the country because they feared the outcomes of the gacaca system. Fears of vindictive charges by neighbours and charges based on rumours were reported. Some seven thousand refugees were in Burundi by the end of 2005, and the 2007 Amnesty International report says that UNCHR reported that twenty thousand Rwandans fled from southern Rwanda to Burundi early in that year (ibid.).

A French judge who was investigating the shooting down of the plane carrying President Habyarimana in 1994 issued international arrest warrants in November 2006 for nine high-ranking Rwandan officials and requested that the ICTR issue a warrant for President Paul Kagame's arrest in connection with that crime. As well, a Spanish judge, looking into the deaths of Spanish nationals and other crimes committed between 1990 and 2002 in Rwanda, was reportedly assessing the participation of sixty-nine RPF members (Amnesty International 2007, 221). These events suggest that the current government of Rwanda is not free of international suspicions regarding its actions during its invasion and the genocide of 1994, nor, apparently, of what has happened since then.

7

Rwanda: Too Many Criminals

Since the war in 1994, Rwanda and the international community have dealt with the génocidaires on a scale that no other society in history has ever attempted. There is the International Criminal Tribunal for Rwanda, run by the United Nations and located in Arusha, Tanzania. This court is designed to deal with only the leaders of the genocide; national courts deal with lesser criminals. But with over 120,000 prisoners still awaiting trial in the first few years of the new century, and time being of the essence, the Rwandan government initiated the gacaca (neighbourhood or community) courts to try prisoners for lesser crimes. Unlike Cambodia, then, Rwanda is dedicated to erasing impunity and to making both leaders and followers accountable for their crimes.

This stance, applauded by most in the international community, is problematic in many ways. The international court at Arusha is a problem unto itself: it is notoriously inefficient, bureaucratic, and Western-oriented. Many Rwandans point out that the leaders are kept in relatively affluent conditions while awaiting trial, yet the lower-downs are kept in appalling conditions inside Rwanda. Its cost has far outstripped the original estimates, and compared to the paltry $56.3 million estimated for the Cambodia trials, this one costs a fortune at over $2 billion so far and still counting. That money, say many Rwandans, ends up in the pockets of international lawyers and does not help Rwanda. Why was the international tribunal located outside Rwanda in the first place? The answer is that in 1995 there was no guarantee that the peace would stick, and the international community was determined to make the leaders of the genocide accountable.

From day one, the new government of Rwanda said that it would insist on trials for all persons accused of crimes against humanity or genocide. This was strong in principle but short in practice because the society, at that stage, lacked trained and trustworthy judges, adequate prisons, appropriate courtrooms or court staff, and all other features of an independent judicial system. Many of the potential judges – either those legally trained or simply educated persons identified as moderates or neutrals – had been murdered or had left the country. If the government was to keep its promise of no impunity, it would have to draw on international aid and begin a massive training program for its citizens. The deficiencies of the justice system were widely recognized. Indeed, many of the same deficiencies characterized judicial institutions before the genocide. Independence from government had not been achieved then, with the result that the legal system was used to cover up politically motivated assassinations and attacks against political foes and Tutsi. Police inspectors and other personnel in the judicial system were easily persuaded to hide murders and theft.

As government troops sought out and brought home the accused génocidaires, the domestic courts soon became clogged, and they are still overburdened a decade later. Keeping so many prisoners behind bars in an impoverished country is a major problem. The country does not have the funds to maintain them in anything approaching decent conditions. Some of these prisoners may be murderers, many are probably implicated in mass murders and rape whether or not they instigated them, and many more are guilty primarily of lesser crimes and theft. But at the current pace, most may well spend much of their short lives awaiting charges, let alone trials. As well, the prison system is abysmal. Thousands of individuals were imprisoned in 1994 and 1995 without charges or court hearings. As their numbers mounted, the capacity of the courts was so strained that the government extended the period of incarceration without trial for an additional eighteen months – a total of seven years for many of them. Beyond these detainees, there were civilians as well as soldiers held in military camps, often in unofficial sites, where relatives could not find them and where human rights were not recognized (Amnesty International 2000, 202–03).

The judicial process began in 1996, with the Organic Law on the Organization of Prosecutions for Offences Constituting the Crimes of Genocide or Crimes against Humanity Committed since 1 October

1990. The government divided suspected génocidaires into four categories. The first category consists of organizers and instigators of the genocide, people in positions of authority who might be notorious murderers and rapists: these are to be judged by conventional courts, and the major instigators are to be tried in the International Criminal Tribunal in Arusha. The second category includes the crime of murder, the third the crime of conspiracy, and the fourth the crimes of assault and looting. Initially, these last three categories were to be tried in conventional Western courts in Rwanda.

Persons apprehended under the law, except where categorized as major instigators, were given the opportunity to confess in return for reduced sentences. These confessions had to be deemed by judges to be complete, and the confessors had to name their accomplices. Two assumptions guided this development: (1) that these confessions would lead to information about the organizers responsible for category one offences and (2) that the surviving victims would understand the wisdom of the process. From the start, it was recognized that impoverished Rwanda had no other way of dealing with the thousands of apprehended suspects in a timely and fair manner. It turned out that very few prisoners chose to confess. This was possibly because the reductions in sentences were short, but it was also because, in the early years, there was still hope that the RPF would be routed by Hutu forces moving in from the Congo. No doubt there was also pressure from the instigators of the genocide within prisons. In April 1998, twenty-two prisoners were executed in Rwanda, and the probability of secular salvation was now remote. This spurred the confession business.

Officers of the United Nations and external NGOs whom I interviewed in 2002 and 2003 observed that, during this period, Hutu were suffering economically and politically. Virtually all of the staff of these organizations were Tutsi, even though Tutsi were such a small fraction of the total population. The government was regarded as being in denial about the problem. There is an acknowledged paradox: nearly a million Tutsi were killed in a three-to-four-month period, and there is one person in jail for every ten persons killed. But the (Tutsi-dominated) government cannot recognize that it is setting up the same problems that created Hutu distrust under the Belgian regime. It insists that any Hutus who object or criticize are engaging in "divisionism" and must be jailed or otherwise punished. The Hutu remain the underclass; yet again they are uneducated and discriminated against. To add to the problems, the Tutsis who came in from Uganda do not speak French: they speak English, and they are trying to recreate the society as an English-speaking domain. Paul Kagame speaks English, not French. But the French fear that Anglo-Saxons would take over was greatly exaggerated. The population speaks Kinyarwanda, and some of its members also speak French; virtually the only speakers of English are returned Tutsi, whose external sojourn was in English-speaking countries.

GENOCIDE CASES IN REGULAR COURTS, 2000–03

As of 2000, according to Amnesty International (2000, 203), "at least 1,420 people were tried in Rwandan courts on charges of participation in the 1994 genocide. At least 180 people were sentenced to death." However, in a report dated 4 August 2003, only twenty-six out of four hundred who had received the death sentence had actually been executed: "Some prosecution and defence witnesses were subjected to pressure and intimidation. In some cases, false testimonies were delivered in court. Some trials were repeatedly postponed; the process for hearing appeals was often especially lengthy" (Amnesty International 2003, 210–11). In 2003, a tribunal convicted one hundred people of rape, torture, murder, and crimes against humanity in a mass trial involving 139 defendants in all.

The Case of Pasteur Bizimungu

The judicial system underwent an overhaul in 2004 because of serious errors on the part of trial courts. The reforms might have reflected a growing recognition of what exactly the Western notion of the rule of law is about. Some of the cases tried earlier were eventually forwarded to the Supreme Court. In January 2006, however, one of these raised questions about the continuing control that political powers were wielding over judicial procedures. This was the case with regard to former president Pasteur Bizimungu and seven others who had attempted to have their convictions dismissed because of egregious errors in trial courts. Pasteur Bizimungo deserted President Juvénal Habyarimana in the 1980s, eventually joined the RPF, and later became the transitional president of Rwanda. In 2000 he was pressed to resign, and Paul Kagame became president. The following year, he and several others, some Hutu and some Tutsi, created the new Party for Democratic Renewal-Ubuyanja (PDR-Ubuyanja), with the intention of running in the presidential elections of 2003. They were harrassed, and one of their number was assassinated. Tutsi members of the group withdrew, leaving only Hutu, who were subsequently arrested and accused of creating a criminal association and plotting to overthrow the government. Bizimungo was also accused of embezzling government funds and tax fraud (Human Rights Watch 2006c). In February 2006, his sentence of ten years imprisonment was reinforced. The Supreme Court found him guilty of "misappropriating public funds, inciting civil disobedience and criminal association mainly by having formed a political party that authorities accuse of promoting ethnic division" (Gabiro 2005). Many observers saw this decision as a step backwards, a political decision enacted by a court that was still not independent.

Confessions

African Rights (an NGO) researchers interviewed ninety-nine imprisoned genocide suspects in several prisons throughout the country in 1999 and 2000. They reported that very few genocide suspects chose to confess. Their findings suggested that ringleaders gained leadership positions within prisons and pressured others to withhold information. Intimidation was rampant. However, that was not the only obstacle. As the researchers state: "Some prisoners regard themselves as innocent of the charges against them, while others still believe that the genocide of Tutsis was justified and thus see no need to admit to participating before what they view as a Tutsi government" (African Rights 2000, 5). Further, "The conviction that by killing a Tutsi they were carrying out their civic duty is bound to be difficult to eradicate, since it was powerful enough to persuade people to kill their friends and even relatives in 1994" (16). Another disincentive for confessions prior to 1998 (or even later) was the belief that, with so many potentially productive workers in jail and costing money for food and custodial services, the government would finally relent and grant an amnesty just to save the economy. There also remained the forlorn hope that the Interahamwe would manage to return victorious and free everyone. Finally, there was the possibility that none of the survivors would be able to produce evidence to convict the prisoners – indeed, it was even possible that there were no survivors from the villages in which the crimes occurred (15–22).

With the introduction of the gacaca courts, more confessions were forthcoming, in part because prisoners were informed that, if they expected to gain shorter sentences, they had to confess before they would be tried by these courts. But even with this incentive, few suspects indicated any remorse or guilt. According to the researchers, the relationship between the suspects and the government was more sympathetic than was the relationship between the survivors and the government. The suspects understood that the government was actually trying to reduce the number of prisoners and speed up the judicial process; the survivors understood that the government was being too lenient with the génocidaires.

Approximately 1,300 people were put on trial in national courts during 2003. In the Specialized Chambers, some 7,700 persons were tried and forty defendants were sentenced to death, but there were no judicial executions. These numbers were similar to those of 2001 and 2002: they had not risen – in part because of the introduction of the gacaca courts and in part because of the "progressive disengagement" of Avocats sans Frontières and other NGOs.

JUSTICE AND RPF WAR CRIMES

The criminals tried for genocide and genocide-related offences were Hutu. RPF soldiers who retaliated or initiated crimes are recognized as being offenders under different categories: they are not génocidaires. But trying them in Rwandan courts was problematic. Neither the judges nor the processes were regarded as fair and above prejudice. Corruption was frequently alleged, and the processes were transparent to local or international observers.

But the argument is not restricted to national courts. The ICTR has also had to deal with the persistent claim by Hutu prisoners that this was a civil war, not a genocide. They say that the RPF won the war and is now treating its adversaries as génocidaires rather than as opposition soldiers. The interplay between court cases at the ICTR and the relations between Hutu and Tutsi is revealed in many ways. An ICTR electronic public press item, as shown in the boxed text, gives some indication of this:

GENERAL NDINDLIYIMANA DEMANDS THAT CHARGES AGAINST HIM BE DROPPED

Arusha, May 21st, 2003 (FH) – The former chief-of-staff of the Rwandan gendarmerie, Augustin Ndindiliyimana, has demanded that the International Criminal Tribunal for Rwanda (ICTR) order his release and drop all charges brought against him, because of what he calls "policy of selective prosecution" by Carla del Ponte, the ICTR prosecutor.

General Ndindiliyimana, 60, was arrested in Belgium on January 29, 2000 and jointly charged with three other officers of the former Rwanda Armed Forces (FAR) in what is known as the "military 2" case. They are charged with genocide, crimes against humanity and war crimes committed in Rwanda during the 1994 genocide. They have pleaded not guilty to all charges.

In a press release sent to Hirondelle news agency, Ndindiliyimana's Canadian lawyer, Christopher Black, said that he filed a motion on behalf of his client because they considered that del Ponte abused the process "by which only members of the former Hutu majority regime in Rwanda are targeted for prosecution while Tutsis, belonging to the Rwandan Patriotic Front (RPF) and its allies, who have committed similar war crimes as those alleged against the Hutus, including genocide, are granted effective immunity from prosecution".

Black explains that even though the prosecutor has conducted investigations into the alleged crimes, by members of the RPF, not one indictment has been brought against any of them.

Ndindiliyimana's lawyer continues that Carla Del Ponte's policy "has no legitimate criminal justice objective, only a political one ... The role of the Prosecutor, currently in breach of her mandate under the statue of the tribunal, should be referred back to the Security Council to seek clarifications of its intentions and provide instructions to the tribunal with respect to all those who committed war crimes in Rwanda during the events of 1994."

In order to keep on course with the tribunal's mandate that expires in 2008, the prosecutor will put a lid on her investigations in 2004. This has pushed her to drastically alter her programme on the number of investigation she intended to conduct, reducing them from the initial 136 to 14. Ten more investigations are under way.

Last year, the prosecutor was severely criticised by Rwanda when she reaffirmed her intentions to pursue some members of the current military, arguing that "a crime is a crime," adding that she saw no reason why she should not conduct her investigations if they lay within the bounds of the mandate of the Tribunal which covers the whole of 1994.

Last November, Del Ponte told British Members of Parliament that Rwanda's reluctance to cooperate with the ICTR, emanated from those investigations in which, she accused, the Rwandan government was unwilling to render any help whatsoever.

Apart from Ndindiliyimana, the second military trial also groups together the former chief-of-staff of the FAR, General Augustin Bizimungu, and two commanding officers in the reconnaissance battalion, Major François Xavier Nzuwonemeye and captain Innocent Sagahutu.

The first military trial, currently in progress, groups together four senior officers of the FAR, including the former director of cabinet in the ministry of defence, colonel Theoneste Bagosora.
KN/AT/CE/FH (ML'0521A)

African Rights (2000, 94) quotes the justice minister in the interim government that oversaw the genocide, Agnes Ntamabyarioro, to this effect:

The President's death united extremists of every kind – Hutus, Tutsis, FAR as well as the RPF. That's how the so-called genocide took
place. I say that because I don't agree with the term. By "genocide,"
they mean that the Hutus killed the Tutsis. RPF soldiers and some
of their civilian supporters killed Hutus but that isn't mentioned ...
Everyone has been affected. Before there is any progress towards
reconciliation, the entire Rwandese tragedy should be taken into
account. I, too, have lost around 20 of my relatives. How can they
ask me to confess while nothing has been asked of the man who
killed my family? I loved them too and I'm suffering at losing them.
The massacres carried out by the Hutus are the same as those carried out by the RPF as far as cruelty and numbers are concerned.
The only difference is that the RPF were more careful.

African Rights argues that there were, indeed, RPF criminal activities and that these should be investigated. Perpetrators should be
called to account, but, it argues, these activities were never on the
scale or of the character of the carefully planned and executed
genocide perpetrated by the Hutu (African Rights 2000, 93–5). In
my interviews with bureaucrats in high places, I asked about this issue. This is a composite of their responses (individual respondents
were promised anonymity and confidentiality):

People who ask that are undermining the process. Genocide
is a terrible crime. Other crimes will be handled by other courts.
Military courts handle war crimes. Some have been severely punished. The international court is just there to eat money, for diplomatic purposes, and what we have done ourselves – we have done
much more ... France supported the regime and the genocide,
using state money to kill Rwandans. France was embarrassed when
we showed films of French soldiers training the Interahamwe.
France is part of the Western family, the EU ... Many Americans
who hold power are in solidarity with France. The international
system is a network, influenced throughout the network.

Rwandans have profound deep sorrow about the country, including the perpetrators who now know they are misled, their forefa-
thers lived together for centuries, we are all Rwandans ... You stop
genocide by killing the killers, not by prayers. It is a mockery to
punish the army man who stops the perpetrator. Especially the

people in Kibuye in the church where men were killed and the
women raped … if you found that person and killed him you say
it is a war crime? To the Western world, they are thinking the army
who saves the people are worse then the real killers! For example,
a young boy who escaped at the beginning of the genocide was
given a gun and training by RPF – the killers of his family are identified and he kills them. Then he is put in jail. Some are still in
jail … Some of the Hutus pretended they were women gardening,
but actually were soldiers, then they shot at RPF when the RPF
turned away, thinking they were women. We find it very difficult
to answer the question of Westerners.

France was involved for economic and cultural reasons. France is
more powerful economically than the Belgians. If you have strength
in Rwanda, you can control the Congo. At least 50 million speak
French in the Great Lakes Region: 30 million are also Kinyarwanda
speakers. So control of Rwanda equals control of the GL region. But
now we speak English. The RPF soldiers were educated in Uganda,
and we are opposed to the Belgians and French who trained the
Hutu militias and procured their arms. We propose to ensure that
the new generation speaks English first, maybe also French, but
certainly English.

All states are oppressors to some extent, and have oppression capacities. In the third world we lack institutions, channels, a dicta-
tor can arise, kill half of the people, no matter – he wants power.

The church said "killing a Tutsi is not a crime" so the people
thought it was okay … but we will not forget individual priests
who did this, even if we understand the difference between a
priest and the Catholic Church as an institution.[1]

THE ICTR IN ARUSHA, TANZANIA

The ICTR was established in Arusha in November 1994 to provide
some distance between the scene of the crimes and the judicial trials
of the perpetrators. Perhaps it was established to allay the guilt of the
many governments and the UN, all of whom had failed to come to
the rescue of Rwandans during 1994; perhaps it was established
because a parallel institution had been set up for Yugoslavia some

eighteen months earlier. In any event, its mandate was to indict and try leaders of the genocide.

The Tribunal was scarcely started before it ran into objections. Genocide survivor organizations called on prosecution witnesses to boycott it for, among other reasons, alleged mistreatment of witnesses. Then the government imposed travel restrictions on prosecution witnesses and withheld necessary documents from the prosecution of soldiers in its RPF (also now known as RDF and RPS) ranks. A UN commission of experts established by the Security Council in July 1994 concluded that some members of the RPF "perpetrated serious breaches of international humanitarian law" and "crimes against humanity" during the takeover of Rwanda in 1994. Carla del Ponte, the senior judge in the Court, attempted to try RPF members for violations of humanitarian law, but she was replaced (whether or not for this reason is unclear). Rwanda's foreign minister in 2003 said: "No tears would be shed if the UN Security Council does not renew her mandate" (Lobe 2003).

Human rights groups have pressed the UN Security Council to ensure the independence of the ICTR, but they allege that the United States and Britain are protecting the RPF government and that the government is protecting its armed personnel. The international protection is said to be based on the supposition that Rwanda may be an ally in the "war on terrorism" in East Africa. In short, Rwandans are Catholics, not Muslims. As well, of course, there is the US opposition to any international criminal court.

By the end of 1999, thirty-eight individuals were detained in Arusha, and two leading members of the former government and the Interahamwe militia were sentenced to life imprisonment. (Unlike the Rwandan courts, international law does not allow for the death sentence.) The Court was able to issue only eight judgments in total between January 1997 and October 2002. Although rape was designated as a major offence, and thousands of rapes were committed during the genocide, only two defendants of crimes of sexual violence had been convicted, and one had his sentence reversed on appeal (Human Rights Watch World Report 2003).

However, in the next two years, the rate of trials and convictions increased. As noted in chapter 1, the ICTR convicted twenty-two and acquitted thirty-two individuals, with another twenty-five awaiting trials by the end of 2005. The international community has made it clear that no further individuals should be indicted and

that, when these trials are completed, the Arusha Tribunal will close
its doors. Gradually the ICTR is transferring indictees to national
courts for prosecution. Relations between the international court
and the national government are deteriorating, with the ICTR accusing the government of "failing to cooperate with the tribunal,"
specifically with respect to enabling witnesses to attend in Arusha,
and the government accusing the ICTR of "mismanagement, in-
competence and corruption." Further, the government has stated
that it will not cooperate in investigations of alleged war crimes
committed by RPA soldiers (Amnesty International 2003, 211–12).
Among the many irritants between Rwanda and the ICTR is that, at
Arusha, prisoners live in relatively luxurious conditions, are able to
hire international lawyers at public expense, and can cause lengthy
delays in the procedures by changing lawyers or pleading illness.
Survivors do not generally understand the trials in Arusha or the
prison arrangements there and in Rwanda. They are asked to go to
Arusha as witnesses, but they have never before left their small communes, and they are intimidated from the very beginning. Women,
in particular, are frightened because this is a society that has not listened to them in the past. One of the individuals I interviewed said:

I know one witness who went to Arusha and the judges laughed.
They were not laughing at her but were laughing at a defence
lawyer who was asking irrelevant questions and things like that.
I watched and I realized what was going on but she didn't know
what was happening, so she thought they were laughing at her ...
well, the news came out saying that all the judges were laughing
at witnesses. They should have explained things to her, told her
what was going on.

Another woman talked of a rape trial:

There were two women who were witnesses, they had been raped
and were being asked all these questions and obviously rape is
always contentious in any court. But they didn't really have any
support ... they just wished they had someone with them who
spoke their language, who knew how difficult it was and knew what
they were going through ... However, since that case, a landmark
case, now there are some people who are trying to make changes.
They have a sexual assault team now, and things are improving.

[re women survivors] They didn't get instant death but ... years later, you find you have AIDS, and it is difficult to link the HIV directly to the rape because we are not using scientific methods. But you are raped then HIV positive. (Fieldnotes, from my interview at African Rights)

I asked this individual about women who lived in the same district with the man who killed their husbands or children. She responded:

In talking to some of the women in this particular project, what sometimes comes out is that they are very lonely and there is nowhere for them to go and they have to live there. The release of prisoners frightened them because it meant that those people would return to the community. They [the released prisoners] were elderly, chronically ill or had confessed, there was no point keeping them in prison, but women who feared for their safety were bitter and afraid.

GACACA COURTS

Impoverished Rwanda would not have been able to deal with the cases under conventional Western law in less than a century. In 2003, a new judicial process was introduced. Named gacaca, it was a reprise of neighbourhood trials as they had existed prior to European intervention. The intention was to make close neighbours (the cellule) responsible for determining the guilt of, and choosing the appropriate penalties for, persons accused of the less serious crimes. The category of crime is also determined at the cellule level.

These gacaca courts were initiated in 2003–04, and, by 2005, they were finally in place throughout the country. They have met with mixed reviews on the part of international observers. While they have the merit of giving power to the communities of both victims and perpetrators, they lack any of the normal Western precautions that are believed to make trials fair to the accused as well as to the accusers. Gossip may become evidence; ill will may become motivation for accusations without evidence. At least as problematic is the fact that traditional communities were severely disrupted by the genocide. Many people were killed or fled the country. Many women and children were raped. Neighbours turned on neighbours, and many of those encounters were vicious. The inhabitants of what might be "villages" or "neighbourhoods" today are not necessarily linked to their neighbours in amicable relationship or, indeed, in any relationship. They may not have been in the country at the time of the crimes; they may be Tutsis who have taken over land vacated because of the deaths or emigration of previous owners. The new courts involve thousands of individuals in voluntary positions as a combined judges/jury arrangement. Though initiated in order to reduce the number of prisoners, the experience to date has actually increased their number because each case seems to implicate yet others who are then apprehended and incarcerated.

The appointment of judges for gacaca courts raised further pertinent issues. In some cellules, either there were few literate individuals or the surviving ones were suspected of being among the criminals. According to the Department of Gacaca Courts, there were very low literacy rates in some districts: Said one trainer: "Not more than 50 per cent of the judges really knew how to read and write ... The daily tests (at the training sessions) showed that a lot of them have not remembered anything" (quoted in African Rights, 2003a). The judges – called *Inyangamugayo* in Kinyarwanda – are elected by their cellule, supposedly for their fine qualities of fairness and integrity. But popularity does not necessarily rest with good judgment, particularly when the judges are expected to deal with such extreme issues of life and death. The original gacaca courts dealt with such matters as the theft of a goat, not genocide. In addition to this problem, the trainers themselves were sometimes incompetent, and their students were critical of them.

The sheer scale of the operation engages the whole country in the process of accountability and justice. One of the authorities charged with maintaining the gacaca process informed me that there were over nine thousand cellular courts, 1,545 sector courts, 106 district courts, and 12 provincial courts for appeals, for a total of 10,673 courts established for the conduct of gacaca trials. In all, there were 248,209 judges at the cellular level. In each cellule there were nineteen judges, five of whom had to be literate. The population base determines the boundaries of the cell. Some villages don't have enough people to maintain a cellule; there have to be at least one hundred people to make it work. I asked him, "Will this work?" He answered confidently, "Yes, it is necessary. People have to live together and they need to get this solved, they need resolution."

The process obliges everyone to attend sessions and speak about their own experiences. It is the people who must say whether the accused is guilty. Although gacaca processes prevailed in the country before European intrusion, the current process of dealing with mass murders and rape is not really based on the same form of procedure as once dealt with individual petty crimes at the village level. Consequently, they do not have as much credibility as they might have had if the continuity had not been disrupted. As well, villagers do not automatically approve of what a government imposes on them, and they know that the thing called gacaca is not their creation.

During our interview, Simon Gasiberege, one of the central architects of the revived gacaca system, defended the process in these words:

About the gacaca ... the classical justice may be replaced by participative justice. The gacaca tribunals are part of Rwandan culture. It involves what neighbours did to one another. And it is seen by everyone. If it goes well, each will just say what he exactly saw and experienced. Now the victim will know what really happened. The important thing about justice is to let the victims know what happened and that what happened to them is also important to their community and society.

We have to negotiate the gacaca with foreigners – European and North Americans. They do not understand that participative justice here now has to begin with people who have no experience. My job has been to create the new communication for this participatory justice, to make a process of training, of education after two years, two or three years, so that the people can know how to do it. So the critics from outside do not have an understanding of this reality. After the destruction of the society in Rwanda, recognizing that the people who committed this had experienced school and were experienced in classic justice, they are génocidaires – they cannot make decisions about the future, we have to train the people of Rwanda in how to live together in the future.

Suicides

One of the side effects of the gacaca proceedings has been an unprecedented number of suicides. Individuals whose lives had been

reconstructed in the wake of the 1994 events have since been implicated by others during the trials. The increase in suicides was reported soon after the gacaca hearings began, but it was not until
March of 2005 that the state began to keep track of them. Between
March and December of that year, there were sixty-nine identified
suicides and over forty attempted suicides involving men accused of
having committed rape or murder. In all these cases, as in those of
convicted rapists and murderers, women and children are left to
fend for themselves, and the community is further torn apart by
both the suicides and the tragedies of their survivors. One of the
unsympathetic survivors, the executive secretary of Rwanda's largest association of genocide survivors, denounced the suicides: "No
person has the right to punish themselves. They have to suffer for
what they have done." But this has to be seen in the context of the
event. Another accused militia member who had confessed and
named others who were with him when he committed crimes said
of one of the suicide victims that he had been a gentle, honourable
man and was not a violent person before or after the event: "He
just found himself in the atrocities, like many others."[2]

Community Service

In order to reduce the number of prisoners and to help the convicted re-enter society, several courts have ordered the latter to perform community service as their punishment. Those so sentenced
are called tigistes (travaux d'interet géneral), and they are ordered to
build houses, crush rocks for road building, and perform other community work. The punishments are controversial: survivors and their
associations have denounced them as being inadequate. Said one of
the victims of mass rape who witnessed the murders of seven members of her family, "How can you expect me to live in the same community with murderers who exterminated my family?" The tigistes are
not paid for their work, but they claim they should be so that they
can provide for their families while they serve their sentences.[3]

Prisoners Released

In 2002, 23,863 prisoners were released. They were people without
dossiers. They were not defined as criminals; they may have been accidental observers at the scene of the crime or have been falsely accused. Some were terminally ill with AIDS or other diseases, and the

government was not prepared to pay for their health care. Some were over seventy years old or under fourteen, and these the authorities decided to let go. Some were simply common criminals, and they would be brought back later. As noted above in one of the interview excerpts, their release added to the anxiety of women who feared the return of men who had killed or raped their kith and kin.

Survivors and Reconciliation

The Rwandan government attempted to promote reconciliation, hoping that confessions would facilitate that route to national healing. Survivors, however, have been less than lukewarm to these initiatives, often on the grounds that confessions are given in return for sentence reductions. As in South Africa, so in Rwanda: confessions of guilt do not necessarily include any signs of remorse or apology. A journalist describes his attitudes:

> I lost my father, my mother, my four brothers and many of my cousins in the genocide. I still don't know any of the people who killed my family, so I regard all the Hutus on my hill as murderers. I see them like that because they all claim they don't know who killed my family. So I must assume that they all took part, directly or indirectly, in the crimes that led to my present situation. If they had confessed straight away, I could concentrate on the criminals, and regard everyone else as innocent. But they did not, and there is an impressive conspiracy of silence. They were there during the genocide, and my relatives were targeted, not them. (African Rights 2000, 97)

Many of the survivors have lost families and homes. Civil damages awarded by judges are inconsistent and are rarely paid because most prisoners are impoverished and the state has no capacity to assume liability.

INSTITUTIONAL ROLES

The Roman Catholic Church

The Roman Catholic Church, to which the majority of the Rwandan population belongs, became complicit in the crimes against humanity perpetrated throughout the early 1990s and, particularly, in 1994.

Priests were implicated in aiding Hutu killers to destroy churches
where Tutsis had sought refuge. RPF armed fighters are implicated in
zeroing in on priests who might have aided the genocide. It may not
surprise anyone, then, that the Church has not been at the forefront
of those asking the guilty to confess or facilitating a process of reconciliation. As expressed by the assistant prosecutor in Kigali, Edouard
Kayihura: "The Church in Rwanda is itself split as a result of the genocide. Some members of the clergy took part in the genocide, others
deny that genocide took place and still others are surviving victims of
it ... Before it could [aid reconciliation] it would have to admit the
role played by some members of the clergy, and the whole Church
would have to apologize" (African Rights 2000, 111). The assistant
governor of one prison, Jean-Paul Munyankore, said: "I'm dubious
about the role the Church might play in reconciliation. It would even
be a contradiction for the same churches which supported the genocide to take the lead in reconciling the Rwandese. But those churches
could help prisoners to confess" (ibid.).

Ibuka: National Survivors' Organization

Many survivors feel that they have been excluded from the judicial
process. As one of them commented:

> The government gave the detainees a much higher priority than
> the genocide survivors in its campaign in favour of confession.
> Justice officials carried out a large-scale campaign in the prisons
> but hardly bothered to campaign in the community of genocide
> survivors who were usually the plaintiffs. Yet, Ibuka would orga-
> nize meetings between survivors and detainees if government
> officials asked us to. (African Rights 2000, 120)

African Rights Investigations

In 2003, African Rights researchers published the first of a planned
set of studies of the genocide as experienced by participants in the
twelve original pilot sectors. These sectors, or communes, included
several cellules, but the commune boundaries were not necessarily
the same as they had been in 1994. They interviewed the accused and
the survivors and witnesses as two separate groups. Those involved
were shown the initial draft of what they had said, and they were

invited to determine the veracity of the rendition regarding the events of that time. The objective was to provide background for the trials and a parallel document that would be a "shared point of reference" for residents. They found that there was a fair degree of consistency with regard to many of the atrocities, even where the perspectives on them differed. However, the victims of the genocide in one sector or commune were not necessarily residents at the time of the genocide; the same was true of the killers. Often bands of killers preyed on residents in nearby communes rather than in their own region. The redrawing of commune borders further complicated the issue. The gacaca courts were mandated to deal only with events in their own commune, so the court process might well either be truncated or, because of the pattern of killings across boundaries, duplicating nearby court processes.

2007: TRANSFERS TO DOMESTIC COURTS

The ICTR is scheduled to close in 2008. It has begun the process of transferring remaining cases to the national courts in Rwanda. How this society is going to handle more cases is hard to imagine. The Hutu have been forced to accept responsibility for their collective crimes, but reconciliation is not in evidence in Rwanda. Even truth may be elusive when many people claim they were simply doing what they were ordered to do by the leaders of their neighbourhoods – either that or that they somehow got swept up in the hatred of the crowd and now simply cannot comprehend what happened to them.

8

Interventions in Yugoslavia, 1992–95

General Roméo Dallaire, among others, argues that the crisis in Yugoslavia was taken more seriously by Western democracies than was the crisis in Rwanda. The clear implication is that Westerners looked after ethnic Europeans rather than Africans, or at least that they were more concerned with a region of Europe than with a region of Africa. The charge is fair. Certainly more energy and anxiety were expended on the breakup of Yugoslavia than on Africa then (e.g., Rwanda and Burundi) or now (e.g., Sudan and Ethiopia), but with exceptions since 9/11 where "Islamists" are perceived to have taken power (as in southern Somalia during 2006). Bosnians, however, might question whether their interests were protected by the concerns of outsiders during the 1990s.

Prior to its breakup, Yugoslavia consisted of six republics and had a population of close to 23 million.[1] Its capital, Belgrade, was situated in Serbia. Also included in Serbia were two autonomous provinces, Vojvodina and Kosovo. Bosnia and Hercegovina (often called simply Bosnia, or BiH) held the central interior, with a small share of the Adriatic coast at Dubrovnik. Croatia was to the north of Bosnia but also along the Dalmatian coast of the Adriatic, thus cradling Bosnia from both north and west. Slovenia was a relatively small northern republic hugging its border with Austria, while Montenegro sat at the base of Bosnia and had a larger share of the Adriatic coast. Macedonia was further east, cushioned between Albania, Greece, Bulgaria, and Serbia.

Each of these republics, except Slovenia, included Serb and sometimes other minorities. Bosnia was particularly complex, with a majority of Muslims (43.3 percent), together with Serbs (31.3 percent), Croats (17.3 percent), and others (7 percent).[2] The term "Muslims" was first used in the census of 1971 to designate those who did not identify themselves as either Serbs or Croats, even though neither of them was classified by religion. Later, Muslims preferred to call themselves "Bosniaks," in reference to their geographical location and historical origins.[3] Because of the war, other Bosnians became differentiated as Bosnian Croats or Bosnian Serbs. In what follows, I use the term "Muslims" for events prior to the end of the war and the term "Bosniaks" for the post-Dayton period (except where cited sources retain the term "Muslim"). Wherever confusion could arise, I use the terms "Bosnian Croats" and "Bosnian Serbs." Where the qualifier is not present, the text refers to Croats resident in Croatia and Serbs resident in Serbia. And, just to make it all a little more like a mad hatter's tea party, the reader should be aware that the war in Croatia was between Croatians (unqualified) and Croatian Serbs (also sometimes called "Krajina Croatians" or even "Krajina Serbs").

This chapter focuses on the interventions and the Dayton Agreement, providing only enough detail on the wars to indicate the reasons for the interventions up to 2006. The next chapter focuses on the societies that have emerged from the wars in Bosnia and Hercegovina, and in Serbia. The war in Kosovo in 1999 is not be dealt with in any depth. The reader should be warned that virtually everything written or said about the wars in the former Yugoslavia is disputed by one group or another: over a decade later there is still no agreement between the warring parties about what caused the conflict, who led it, where the arms came from, or who should be prosecuted at The Hague or in domestic war crimes courts established in what are now separate states to take over from the ICTY. Paranoia is widespread, but its chosen enemies differ by ethnicity and location. My version of the history is inevitably partial because no version can be otherwise: this is contested territory. But my partiality is not born of personal animosity towards any of the contestants: this is my reading of what occurred, open, as all readings must be, to correction through new evidence.

A BRIEF HISTORY TO 1991

Marshal Tito's Yugoslavia was created in the backwaters of the Second World War. Tito led his Partisan forces to victory not only over Nazis and their allies, the Croatian Ustashe, but also over their rival guerrilla forces, the Serb Chetniks. The Ustashe was already infamous for its brutal treatment of Serbs, Muslims, and Jews in Nazi concentration

Yugoslavia – before the wars

camps. Those responsible were not charged, and there was no equivalent to the Nuremburg Trials in this territory. The culminating circumstances were grisly and often omitted from the story: large numbers of Croatians and Chetniks were killed as the war wound down and as Tito gained control of the country. Tito himself was Croatian by birth. His was not an ethnic crusade; rather, it was a nationalist movement to unite the Balkan states and others in the region that had been variously organized under Byzantine, Ottoman, Austro-Hungarian, and German empires and states throughout the previous four hundred years. The initial attempt to unite the people of the region after the First World War had failed, but the idea of creating a nation out of a population that spoke the same language, used two alphabets but shared both, and had similar customs and ancient ethnic and geographical origins might have found its time at last. Tito's Yugoslavia was a bold attempt to get rid of ethnic identities and divergent religions (all imported from previous empires) and to create in their place a new identity as Yugoslavs.

To keep this boat afloat, Tito had to navigate most carefully between the shoals of the Cold War. He created a socialist state, but not within the USSR orbit; he created (to some extent) a market economy, but certainly not within the US or British orbit, and much of its small industries consisted of workers' cooperatives. He successfully negotiated compromises between southern Orthodox Serbs and northern Catholic Slovenes and Croats; and between Muslims, Croats, and Serbs in Bosnia. He kept the whole piece together from the late 1940s until nearly 1980. As his health deteriorated, the regional leaders of the different regions began to worry about what would become of them when the captain died. Each had ambitions. Serb leaders nursed hopes of a Greater Serbia, which would include Croats and Muslims, all of whom were descended from the same Slavic groups who migrated south from what became Russia, Czechoslovakia, and other northern regions in the sixth and seventh centuries. Croats, however, wanted a separate state, not a subordinate role in Greater Serbia. Albanians in the Province of Kosovo, where they formed a large majority, also wanted independence.[4]

It was not only the ambitions of leaders that drove the move towards the destruction of Yugoslavia. At least as influential was an unhealthy economy: industrial development had not grown, unemployment had. The political structure was not facilitating the emergence of either a new generation of leaders or economic solutions. Strikes and demonstrations had become frequent. The Communist Party was losing its credibility, and, gradually, the central government was disintegrating. As well, there was the problem of what might occur when the Cold War ended, as, even in the 1970s and early 1980s, was a possibility to be contemplated. Yugoslavia would no longer be necessary to the Western nations as a buffer state, and its leaders, shorn of Tito, had no perch in what would become the former USSR. They began to jostle one another by way of taking over control of the land and resources of what had been Yugoslavia.

Serbians had long been the major component of the Yugoslavian army. As tensions rose in the 1980s, other trained soldiers began to move out of the army, anticipating their utility to republics that could become new states. Simultaneously, Serbs began to oust others, anticipating the need for loyal Serbian troops in the future wars that now seemed unavoidable.

Short History of the Rise of Milošević

The odd history of Slobodan Milošević has often been told, but always by puzzled biographers – puzzled because they cannot find anything about the man that really explains how (or, for critics of the mainstream versions, whether) he mesmerized the Serb population and talked them into engaging in an aggressive nationalistic war against their neighbours. True, both his parents committed suicide – something bound to affect a fellow. True, he and his wife, Mirjana Marković, joined forces while still teenagers, and she piloted their ship through all rough waters. Still, he seems to have become a demagogue almost by accident: he never showed any inclination to actually believe the ideologies he spread about. He was an opportunist, apparently with no capacity for self-reflection or any sense of responsibility for what he was doing to Yugoslavia. The trial records at the ICTY might eventually provide a narrative that can reveal the role this man played, even though his guilt or innocence will never be legally established.

According to historians – and their collective understanding on this point is at least consistent one with the other – Milošević gave a speech in Kosovo complaining that Serbs had been cheated of their birthright there. This struck a resonant chord that reverberated throughout Serbian territories, and he may have concluded that he had composed a great symphony. His speech was preceded in 1986 by the publication of a nationalist document written by academics in the Serbian Academy of Sciences and Arts, which articulated Serbs' sense of being victimized by Croats and Slovenes in Yugoslavia. The fate of minority Serbs in Kosovo, described as unbearable, was identified as the iconic fate of all Serbs living outside the Republic of Serbia. Kosovo was one of two provinces of the republic that had been given independent powers under the 1974 Yugoslav Constitution. The Constitution had reduced Belgrade's authority over it and Vojvodina and had supported a "balance of power" within Yugoslavia as a bulwark against Serbia, the largest of the republics. Kosovo, however, was actually regarded by Serbs, or was reincarnated by the academicians and Milošević, as the Serb national homeland, even though for some five centuries it had been populated largely by Albanians.

The particular event that promoted Milošević as the leader of the Serb nationalist movement came about by accident. Ivan Stambolić, then president of Serbia, was scheduled to speak at Kosovo Polje on 24 April 1987, but he sent his junior colleague in his place. A Serb demonstration, replete with stones thrown at police, turned the rally into an episode of mass hysteria from which Milošević emerged as the new czar for Serbs. Within a few months, Stambolić, who had not only been Milošević's steadfast friend for the previous quarter century but also his political mentor and promoter, was pushed out of public life by his protégé. He was later assassinated (the case is discussed further in chapter 10).

There followed speeches and events accompanied by brute force in other republics. Gradually, Milošević gathered power within the vacuum left by Tito's death, aided by the centripetal forces engendered by the Constitution as much as by feuding leaders of the various republics. Separatist forces developed in Slovenia, Croatia, and Bosnia, even while Serbian minorities in the latter two prepared for battle with the aid of the Yugoslav-turned-Serbian army. Slovenia was spared an internal war because no Serb minority was lodged there. The wars of the 1990s were fuelled by Milošević's speeches, now in his capacity as president of Serbia, and fanned by the Serb army and paramilitary forces. But, as Slovenia, Croatia, and then Bosnia split off, Milošević's dreams of empire became stunningly inconsistent with what, by 1995, was left of "Greater Serbia": two republics – Serbia with 7.5 million people and impoverished Montenegro with 650,000.

Slovenian Independence

Slovenia had always been close to Austria, with families divided between the two regions. After its declaration of independence in 1991, there was a brief war between Slovenian soldiers (who had been trained apart from the Yugoslav army) and the Yugoslav army (Jugoslovenska Narodna Armija [JNA]). It wasn't much of a war, and Slovenia departed, later to become a component of the European Union. It took its wealth with it – not a magnificent fortune but substantial relative to the rest of Yugoslavia.

Croatian Move Towards Independence

Croatia tried to replicate the Slovenian feat through an election in which the ethno-nationalist party led by Franjo Tudjman commanded

Croatian votes, while the Serb-dominated parties abstained in protest. Croatia's Serbian minority, resident in the Krajina region bordering Bosnia, an eastern region known as Slavonia, and along the western Dalmatian coast, formed a majority in eleven communes. Ancestors of these Serbs in the Krajina region had been induced by Austria in the sixteenth century to settle there and act as a frontline against Ottoman incursions. Serbs remembered, during this war of secession, all the terrible deeds of the Ustashe during the Second World War and these were murderous deeds. However, the news of Partisan killings of Croats and Chetniks had never been disseminated in the country's political forums or classrooms. Possibly, the failure of Serbs and Croats to communicate with one another was built on the failure of both to face their history and to deal with it, though this argument (frequently stated in the postwar literature) rests on assumptions that are speculative. Both had a history of murder against the other: the history books, even those written outside the country, focus on the Croatian concentration camps and genocidal attacks on Serbs; however, Serbian Partisans also killed Croats at the conclusion of the war, and that history is only now becoming unearthed – literally, as it turns out. A mass grave near Maribor, Slovenia, has been discovered that apparently contains the corpses of nearly two thousand Croatians who were trying to escape retribution at the end of the war.[5] An undeclared war began in the Krajina region, and the JNA moved to defend Croatian Serbs.

Karadžić and Mladić

Radovan Karadžić, a psychiatrist and university professor, was now the president of the Serbian Democratic Party (SDP) of Bosnia, leader of Bosnian Serb nationalists. Ratko Mladić began his infamous career as the JNA leader posted to defend Krajina Serbs; he emerged later as the commander of Bosnian Serbs in Goražde and Srebrenica.

INTERVENTIONS, 1991–92

In September 1990, in an illegal referendum, Serbs in the Krajina region voted overwhelmingly for the creation of a sovereign and autonomous country. Following this there were repeated attacks by Croatian Serbs and Croatian security forces both on one another and on civilian populations. The former Yugoslavian army, the JNA, now under Serb command, was allied with local Serb Croatian forces. A year later, two months after Slovenia's separation and co-incidental with the undeclared war in Croatia, the federal government of Yugoslavia obtained a UN resolution to establish an embargo against the sale of weapons to all Yugoslavian republics. Serb forces had already removed the arms that had always been stashed in case of emergencies in each of the republics. The embargo thus had no impact on Serbian forces but effectively prevented Croatia and Bosnia from legally obtaining arms. From this point on, a black market in arms flourished throughout the region. At a later stage of the wars, Iran was smuggling in arms with the foreknowledge of US authorities (Burg and Shoup 1999, 338–9).

The Cutileiro-Carrington Peace Plan, 1991

Becoming concerned about the possibility of full-scale war in Croatia, the European Community (EC) appointed an English diplomat to intervene, anticipating that he needed only to bring Croatian president Tudjman and Serb president Milošević together to work out a constitutional agreement. As soon as Lord Carrington met with them, he recognized that neither wanted peace: both wanted to carve up Bosnia, and, he said later, "they weren't worried too much, either of them, about what was going to happen to the Muslims" (Silber and Little 1996, 197). Together with Portuguese ambassador José Cutileiro, he drew up a plan for a renewed Yugoslavia, organized working groups, and attempted to get the whole matter solved. The Cutileiro-Carrington Plan provided for six republics, each with considerable autonomy. Individuals were to be guaranteed civil rights, thus ensuring that Serbs residing outside Serbia would be protected. The plan even went so far as to entitle those Serbs, where they formed a regional majority, to have their own parliament, police force, and judiciary. Initially welcomed by all sides, the plan shortly thereafter failed to please either Bosnian president Alija Izetbegović or Milošević. Milošević said bluntly that what he wanted was a unified Yugoslavia, not a group of independent republics.

EC Recognition of Slovenia and Croatia

By November of 1991, with Croatia appealing for international troops and Serbia arguing that the conflict was a purely internal matter (Yugoslavia was still a sovereign nation and Croatia was still a republic), an EC summit considered trade sanctions and the United Nations appointed a former US secretary of state, Cyrus Vance, to work with Lord Carrington. Vance advocated the deployment of UN troops in Croatia. By this time, the JNA had most of the Serb regions of Croatia under its control. If a UN-brokered peace agreement were tied to sovereignty for Croatia, the JNA would be ousted as a foreign army. On the other hand, UN troops would then be required to protect the Serb minorities against Croats. Serbian president Slobodan Milošević, realizing that separation for Croatia was now inevitable, agreed to UN troops, but the Croatian Serbs who had fought to stay in Yugoslavia resisted that decision and battles continued.

Germany, meanwhile, had become the chief protector of Croatian interests, pushing the EC towards acknowledging Croatian sovereignty despite its failure to provide adequate safeguards for Serbs and Muslims. By December 1991, the peace negotiations ended in failure. The following month, the EC recognized both Slovenia and Croatia as independent countries, thereby reducing the incentive for Croatia to negotiate with Serbia or to comply with the UN peacekeeping proposals (Burg 2004, 51–2). Macedonia, which also wanted independence, was rejected: Greece worried that it might try to annex the Greek northern province of the same name. The United States did not recognize Slovenia and Croatia at this time, treating the region's battles as a European problem.

The Vance Plan

Cyrus Vance now proposed to the UN that twelve thousand peacekeepers (subsequently known as the United Nations Protection Force [UNPROFOR]) be deployed to Croatia to supervise a ceasefire, disarm the Serb militia, and monitor the withdrawal of the JNA from Croatia. The agreement included the creation of United Nations protected areas (UNPAS), where the ceasefire was to be maintained by UN aid until the combatants reached a settlement. These areas were in Krajina and western and eastern Slavonia, where Serbs were either in the majority or a substantial minority. The UN secretary-general expressed doubts that the disputants would agree to a ceasefire and a negotiated peace. Milošević expressed his approval of the plan, apparently thinking that his aims in Croatia were achieved and that the JNA could be redeployed to Bosnia. However, Milan Babić, elected president of the recently founded separatist movement, Srpska autonomna oblast (SAO), rejected it. Milošević prevailed, obtained a vote in favour of the Vance Plan at the Republika Srpska Krajina Assembly, and withdrew the JNA army from the region. The vote notwithstanding, Krajina Serbs continued to fight, and soon the Vance Plan was no longer relevant. UNPROFOR soon learned that a traditional peacekeeping operation was not possible. According to Frederick Fleitz (2002, 138) in his study of UN peacekeeping operations:

> From the beginning it was clear that neither the Croatians
> nor the Krajina Serbs planned to cooperate with the UN force.
> The UNPAS ... were not demilitarized, there was never a stable
> cease-fire, few displaced persons were able to return, and lawless-
> ness prevailed. Moreover, the UNPAS destabilized the region
> by serving as launching pads for armed incursions into Bosnia.
> The Krajina Serbs saw UNPROFOR, and its successor, UNCRO (UN
> Confidence Restoration Operation in Croatia), as helping them
> set up their own independent state. Croatia, on the other hand,
> regarded the UN presence as an opportunity to build up arms
> to take the UNPAS by force.

The Croatian army launched an offensive in several zones of concern to the UN monitors in early 1993. Shortly afterwards, Serbs broke into some UN weapons storage areas in the UNPAS and removed heavy weapons. More palaver and resolutions followed this. Fighting continued sporadically in the border area of Slavonia and in Krajina. Serbs in these regions fled to Serbia. Croatian Serbs declared the Republic of Serbian Krajina (RSK) as a state 1994. Their declaration was ignored, and the battles continued. Croatians suddenly crushed the Krajina Serbs in August 1995 and regained the land they occupied. Richard H. Ullman (1996, 16), professor of international relations at Princeton, summed up the situation: "the Croats were the beneficiaries of an extensive buildup of arms, mostly surplus equipment from former Warsaw Pact countries, imported in violation of the UN mandated arms embargo, almost certainly with the help of Western intelligence agencies." He also claimed that American senior officers provided training to Croat soldiers.

BOSNIA AND HERCEGOVINA

It was the third war that finally destroyed Yugoslavia and any hope of regenerating the idea of a federation of people whose ancestors came from similar northern Slavic roots. The third war was over the interior republic of Bosnia and Hercegovina. The republic was populated by three groups who shared one another's lives and ceremonies, married one another, and, at the 1984 winter Olympics, provided the world with what appeared to be a happy united people. They all spoke Serbo-Croatian (with minor idiomatic and accent differences), and though they had two alphabets – Latin and Cyrillic – all schoolchildren were taught both, and this caused no concern during the happier days of Yugoslavia 11.

The chief difference between the groups was religion, yet, in all three cases, these religions came via colonialism during the age of empires. The Austro-Hungarian Empire indoctrinated the northern regions – Slovenia and Croatia – with Roman Catholicism; Serbia had been submerged in the Byzantine Empire, and its majority had adopted the Orthodox version of Christianity; and Bosnia and Hercegovina had been more influenced by the Ottoman Empire.

Richard A. Clarke (2004, 136–40), former counterterrorism czar in both the Bill Clinton and George W. Bush administrations, claimed that Osama bin Laden had a well-developed al Qaeda network in Bosnia and that this was why us officials made stopping the war in the Balkans "its highest foreign policy priority, introducing us forces and hammering out the Dayton Accord." He does not explain why such a sophisticated al Qaeda organization failed to have any noticeable impact on the war or its immediate aftermath.

Charles Shrader (2003), a military historian, argues that some foreign-born Muslims aided the Muslim Bosnians as they fought with Croatian Bosnians as well as Serb Bosnians, but he does not go so far as to argue that a large-scale al Qaeda network was in existence in the territory. Edgar O'Ballance (1995, 94), though blaming President Izetbegović for trying to turn Bosnia into an Islamic country, concludes that foreign Muslims were more talked about than actually involved: "The presence of foreign Muslim volunteers in Bosnia, even such a tiny handful, alarmed Serbs and Croats alike, fearing this was just the tip of the iceberg. It also dismayed thoroughly Westernized and liberated Bosnian Muslims, who had no wish to be forced to tighten up their lax attitude toward their religion."

Bosnia and Hercegovina, 1995

Those who see ideology as the reason for wars will argue that this one was caused by nationalist and religious sentiments, beliefs, and memories that an adult population could not put aside when leaders emerged who were willing to risk all in a bid for power in independent states. I am inclined to the view, however, that this was a war over territory. Everyone knew that the federation was in a terminal phase, and the leaders of all three groups wanted to tie down their own territory against invasion and grab what they could of the neighbour's land and resources. Long-standing religious and perhaps other ethnic differences were submerged in the culture, but they were not the source of hatreds so intense that people would kill others who did not share their worldview. It took skilful politicians and propagandists to use that kindling to make a roaring fire. It also took an international context that pushed Bosnia to declare independence without providing it sufficient protection to exist as a separate nation.

Independence and Recognition

When Slovenia and Croatia declared their independence and the EC recognized them as states, the UN dropped Yugoslavia from membership. This left Bosnia in an untenable position as the largest remaining republic outside Serbia. The future was all too apparent: it would be dominated by Serbs. While for Serb Bosnians that might have been acceptable, it was anathema to many Croat and Muslim Bosnians. Indeed, Bosnia was already caught in a vice between the Croatian Serbs still at war with Croats on its northern border and the Serb army on its eastern border. When Bosnia's Muslim president decided to hold a referendum on independence, Bosnian Serbs accused him of trying to turn the republic into a Muslim state. However the EC, the UN, and the US agreed, even though it was obvious that a declaration of independence could prove to be the beginning of another war. Only as hostilities turned into war, war crimes, ethnic cleansing, and genocide did the international community begin to move beyond peacekeeping operations.

Bosnian Muslims, as the largest single ethnic group, had already won the election in November 1990. Bosnian Serbs proclaimed themselves a separate republic, and a couple of weeks later they voted to "stay in Yugoslavia." They boycotted the referendum, but it passed. The EC and the US recognized Bosnia as a state early in April. Predictably and simultaneously, the ethnic cleansing and internal civil war began. As one analyst observed: "In the absence of *either* a constitutional agreement on status among the conflicting Bosnian parties (and their neighbors) *or* an international commitment to defend the newly recognized government of Bosnia, or better yet *both*, recognition contributed to a rapid escalation of the conflict" (Burg 2004, 51, emphasis in original).

UNHCR, IDPS, and UNPROFOR

UN intervention in Bosnia and Hercegovina began in October 1991, when the UN asked the United Nations High Commissioner for Refugees (UNHCR) to assist with internally displaced persons (IDPs) and refugees from Bosnia and Hercegovina. By the following year, the

UNHCR became the lead agency in helping some 300,000 displaced persons. In mid-June of 1992, UNPROFOR's mandate was extended to protect the airport at Sarajevo, and for the remainder of that year air lifts of food became central to humanitarian aid for the population of Sarajevo. But UNPROFOR had fewer than nine thousand troops, most of them NATO personnel under the UN flag. These were not enough to ensure the effective implementation of UN resolutions, and it was not always possible to secure the airport. Airlifts of food and medicines dropped by US planes saved many lives after UN land forces were blocked from entry, but, as Sarajevo's people soon realized, UN forces were there only to provide humanitarian relief, not to stop the bombardment (Weiss 1999, 107; Weiss 1996 59–96; Durch and Shear 1996, 227–35).

Attacks on Rural Villages and Urban Centres

Though Bosnian Serbs were the primary aggressors, those who knew the country well and who witnessed the wars say that none of the combatants was innocent of war crimes. Civilians were not spared, and the militias – Bosnian Serbs, Bosnian Croats, and Bosnian Muslims alike – were brutal in their dealings with one another. Rape was a deliberate and frequent act of war. Torture, dismemberment, mass killings, and burning of occupied dwellings were committed by all groups. Concentration camps were maintained by Serbs. The Western media was rarely helpful to outsiders in telling the story because so few of its members knew much about the country before the war. There was a general presumption of Bosnian Serb guilt, ambiguity about Bosnian Croat complicity, and a conviction that Muslims were always the victims. In later tellings of the story by military and social historians a more balanced version has appeared. Muslims were, indeed, the major victims, but they were not innocent of committing war crimes themselves. As the ICTY cases are being written into the record, and as new cases are being processed by war crimes tribunals inside each of the states that succeeded Yugoslavia, the murderous deeds of all parties are becoming known. That all parties were complicit is no longer speculation; on the other hand, only Serbia as a state and Serbs as component peoples in Bosnia have been accused of genocide, an act that involves advance planning and considerable organization. Croatians and Muslims have been accused – and in the courts, found guilty – of war crimes and crimes against humanity.

The five largest towns of Bosnia – Sarajevo, Banja Luka, Tužla, Ženica, and Mostar – had only a quarter of the citizens in 1992 (Bose 2002, 14).[6] Many rural people were killed or evicted as armies strode across the terrain, taking villages and isolated farms as they moved. Survivors whose villages and farms were destroyed fled to the urban settlements. Then fierce encounters occurred in the urban centres to which they had emigrated.

Sarajevo was bombed from its surrounding hills by Serbian forces for some four months, and it was intermittently bombed over the entire three-year period from 1992 to 1995. Anyone who tried to get out of their homes to get food or whatever else they needed was in danger of being shot. Streetcars were bombed. Any public event was in danger of being terminated by bombs. UNPROFOR soldiers and NATO airlift supplies were vital in saving many people from starving or being killed by snipers. Banja Luca, situated in a northern enclave of Bosnian Serbs, became a centre of ethnic cleansing. Some Serbs left the city rather than contribute to the ethnic cleansing of their neighbours, but, even so, many Muslims were killed and women raped. Mosques were dynamited.

Economic Sanctions, 1992

The UN Security Council imposed economic and political sanctions on Serbia in May 1992. But it did not authorize military force as well. The UN said that it would send thousands more peacekeepers to protect relief convoys in Bosnia, and it warned Serbia that it would be isolated and ostracized by the world if it did not withdraw its forces from Bosnia. Milošević managed to persuade the Serb population that fundamentalist Muslims and fascist Croats were to blame for the sanctions. His successful message throughout the wars was that the JNA was heroically striving to save Yugoslavia while these other factions were destroying it.

UN Forces under Attack

Attacks on British soldiers under UN auspices near Tužla broke out in November 1992. On this occasion, the UN forces returned fire, leaving some eighteen Croats and Muslims dead. In the same region, the Nordic Battalion fought with the Bosnian Serbs. There was concern that these factional fights prevented the UN from getting aid through, so the UN troops tried to de-escalate; however, the line was thin between becoming a party to the war and self-defence (Findlay 2002, 222). Trevor Findlay, describing the war blow by blow, observed:

> From the outset UNPROFOR's humanitarian mission was thwarted by physical obstruction, mine laying, hostile fire and the refusal of the parties, particularly but not exclusively the Bosnian Serbs, to cooperate ... Access to populations in need was repeatedly denied for political or military purposes, especially by the Bosnian Serbs and Bosnian Croats. Infuriatingly to outside critics, lone individuals with a single weapon on occasions held up convoys for days as negotiations took place. (ibid.)

The Vance-Owen Plan

By the spring of 1993, the economy of Serbia was a shambles. UN sanctions were working, though Bosnian Serb militias and the JNA relentlessly carried on their wars against Muslims. The Security Council passed another resolution to free Belgrade's assets abroad. Cyrus Vance and Lord David Owen were authorized to prepare a new plan for ending the conflict. By this plan, Bosnia was to exist within current frontiers, but each of its ten provinces, defined in ethnic terms, would have substantial autonomy. Three provinces would be dominated by a Serb majority, two by a Croat majority, three by a Muslim, and one by a mixed Croat Muslim. Sarajevo would continue with all three groups having equal powers. The proposal would have obliged Serbs to give up territory it had already "cleansed" of Muslims but would guarantee that much of the territory Serbia had already claimed – Republika Srpska – would be retained. Milošević was worried that the plan would obstruct Serbia's control of a corridor linking Serb-held lands in Croatia as well as Bosnia, but the negotiators claimed that Russian troops would be brought in to safeguard their passage.

The carrot on the stick for Serbia was a promise to withdraw financial sanctions then pending at the UN. The threat of financial penalties appeared to sway Milošević, but his agreement was contingent on acceptance by Bosnian Serb militia leaders. Radovan Karadžić and his cohort rejected it. They later claimed that Milošević had said the plan could not be implemented so they would not have to actually obey it. Said Laura Silber and Allen Little (1996, 281), who prepared the script for the BBC television series on the wars, "For the first time, Lord Owen realized that Milošević had lost control of the war in Bosnia. The Vance-Owen

Plan, together with the financial sanctions' package, had succeeded in splitting the Serbs."

Another meeting, this time in Athens, included Karadžić and other Bosnian Serbs, but this time they were met by the Vance-Owen team, Milošević, Izetbegović, and Tudjman, all of whom were determined to force them to sign on to the plan. They were subjected to threats to bomb all Serb positions if they refused, and finally, many hours later, Karadžić signed but said that his agreement had to be ratified by the "Parliament" in the Bosnian Serb stronghold of Pale. Owen was sure that this had no importance, Milošević was sure he could sway public opinion among Bosnian Serbs, and Cyrus Vance took the occasion to retire on a happy note. The note faded within a few days, when the Bosnian Serbs strongly rejected the plan, insulting Milošević in the process. General Ratko Mladić succeeded in demonstrating, with military logic, how the Vance-Owen proposal would adversely affect Bosnian Serbs.

The Vance-Owen Plan, rejected by Bosnian Serbs, was dead. In any event, it would have required the deployment of about fifty thousand troops over a long period to maintain the peace, and even at that the peace might not have been enforceable. American secretary of state Warren Christopher tried to persuade NATO leaders and Russia to provide weapons to Muslims and to undertake air strikes on Bosnian Serb positions. European leaders rejected the idea because, they pointed out, *their* troops were on the ground. Even the rhetoric of retaliation slowed down, and by May 1993, US, Russian, and several European countries proposed a policy of containment that, in effect, ensured that Republika Srpska would be a permanent fixture, leaving what amounted to only half of what had once been the Republic of Bosnia-Hercegovina to the other two ethnic groups. Bill Clinton, US president through all of this, though earlier much concerned to create a solution for Bosnian Muslims, abandoned the project and said that it was up to Europe to make decisions about Bosnia.

By the end of 1993, the Security Council publicly recognized that the situation in central Bosnia and Hercegovina had deteriorated. A UN description of the events notes: "Although numerous cease-fire agreements were signed by the warring parties in Bosnia and Herzegovina, practically none of them were implemented and the military situation remained grave" (United Nations, Department of Public Information, n.d., 9). UN forces tried what they called "tough" strategies, threatening NATO air attacks against Serb roadblocks that prevented convoy deliveries of humanitarian aid, but their bluff was soon called when it became clear that they would not follow through. Indeed, Serb forces started to take UN peacekeepers and others hostage in order to prevent air attacks. NATO air strikes against Serbs in Sarajevo invited retaliation, which took the form of kidnapping some 370 UN peacekeepers as hostages. Some were handcuffed to Serb military equipment. Possibly the UN negotiations with the Serbs for their release included a promise not to use NATO air power again: there are different opinions about whether such a promise was made.

The chief result of the attempted tough stand was further denigration of UN forces, now seen by many Bosnians as useless appeasers. In Findlay's (2002, 226) view, "despite calls by successive commanders for reinforcements and better protective capability, UNPROFOR was never given the explicit mandate or the requisite forces or firepower to comprehensively and robustly protect the civilian population." Insult was added to injury in the black comedy film *No Man's Land*, in which UN peacekeepers were depicted as frightened boys under the charge of incompetent and pompous idiots.

Mostar and the Breakdown of the Croat-Muslim Coalition

The initial conflict in BiH involved allied Muslims and Croats versus Serbs. The now independent Croatia supported the temporary coalition, and Serbs from the Republic of Serbia supported their ethnic brothers and sisters. The alliance broke down in Central Bosnia, turning the Bosnian war into a three-sided conflict.[7] Having obliged Serb forces to retreat from the ancient city of Mostar in 1993, Croat soldiers turned on their former allies. One of Europe's most celebrated cosmopolitan cities lost its sense of itself, and whole city blocks were destroyed as Muslims and Croats were transformed into bitter combatants. A decade later, a Muslim student showed me his family's former Mostar home. It had once been a spacious and elegant building, but now it was a ruin, with the Croat checkered flag painted on the external edifice to mock its former inhabitants. Throughout his former district and throughout much of Mostar, homes, apartment blocks, and public and private buildings were destroyed or so pocked with bullet holes and unstable as to be unusable. In January of 1994, the prime minister of BiH said that up to five thousand Croatian armed personnel were supporting Bosnian Croats in military actions within Bosnia. Croats have since claimed that Muslims were being aided by imported warriors from Saudi Arabia or Iran. As noted above, some observers support that claim, but the number of imported fighters was apparently small.

UNPROFOR attempted to reach a ceasefire agreement, but when it became clear that their own troops were in danger, the UN withdrew its forces. The establishment of safe zones might have prevented the escalation of hostilities, but it became apparent to everyone that the UN and NATO were not prepared to provide military defence to back up their decisions. The consequences of misplaced idealism were painfully apparent. UN troops were peacekeepers with only enough military equipment to protect aid deliveries and themselves. They could not move about the country without the permission of the warring parties. Peacekeepers were told to escort humanitarian aid convoys and to provide guaranteed safety in what were called UN "safe areas," including Srebrenica, but Serbs continued to commit what is now called "ethnic cleansing" secure in the knowledge that UN troops were incapable of stopping them. UN troops were authorized to request NATO air strikes when needed, but both NATO and UN officials in Bosnia had to agree to them, and the UN representative was generally opposed to them (Fleitz 2002, 140–1).

Serb attacks on Belgian forces near Sarajevo in 1993 brought a stiff warning that further attacks would be met by military responses. By February of that year, the entire operation was put under Chapter VII of the UN Charter for the first time, allowing for enforcement to protect a peacekeeping force. But the UN at that stage did not actually have the capability to enter a protracted battle (Findlay 2002, 220–1).

Mortar Attack on Sarajevo Marketplace

A mortar attack on the busy marketplace in central Sarajevo in February 1994 may have been the pivotal event of the war. It killed sixty-nine and wounded over two hundred people. Radovan Karadžić denied responsibility, suggesting that the Muslims had done it to themselves in order to gain international attention. President Izetbegović saw this as proof that the Serbs and Croats were determined to destroy Muslims in Bosnia. Though over eleven thousand Bosnians (including all ethnic groups) had been killed in Sarajevo before the marketplace bombing, this one event caught the world's attention. These were people desperately trying to find food in a besieged city, bombed while they looked for carrots and eggs. Now the question of NATO air bombardment moved forward even in Europe; however, the NATO ultimatum against Serbia evaporated when Russia and the United Kingdom sided with one another against further NATO action.

Goražde, Srebrenica, and other Safe Areas

Fighting had intensified in BIH during 1993, especially in the eastern sectors close to the Serb border, including Srebrenica. One of the more fatuous demands of the UN Security Council, moved 6 May 1993, was that all parties must stop taking territory by force. It had no apparent effect on what was happening on the ground. In the same resolution, it declared Sarajevo, Tužla, Žepa, Goražde, Bihać, and Srebrenica and their surrounds as "safe areas," promising dire consequences should any party bring them harm (resolution 824).

A couple of weeks later, the UN Security Council established the International Criminal Tribunal for Yugoslavia (ICTY) to deal with any violations of international humanitarian law committed since January 1991 in the former Yugoslavia. Neither act had a deterrent effect on the warriors. Serb militias attempted to force civilians to leave Srebrenica, an action condemned by the UN but that had no other consequences. An attempt to demilitarize forces in Srebrenica was backed by UNPROFOR troops, civilian police, and military observers; while the UN reported that this action had been successful (United Nations, Department of Public Information, n.d., 14–15), subsequent events made it evident that such was not the case.

In March 1994, a month after the bombing of the central marketplace in Sarajevo, Bosnian Serb forces launched an offensive against the UN safe area in Goražde and its surrounding villages and rural areas. The UN had authorized UNPROFOR to protect the civilian population and to promote withdrawal of military and paramilitary units, but it had not authorized military action against Bosnian Serb paramilitary units that were attacking the towns. The UN authorized the threat of air power and found a few thousand additional troops for the safe areas; however, as the additions were insufficient and as the air power was not guaranteed, not surprisingly the commanders on the ground understood that they could not adequately protect the civilians in safe areas.[8] In the fight for Goražde, UN commanders were caught between their directive to engage in peacekeeping, being strictly neutral in their actions, and the pressure on them to engage in war against the Bosnian Serbs. As well, the international differences between Russia and Western countries had to be taken into account: Serbs enjoyed some protection from Russia, though both Russian and American representatives in Bosnia were determined to avoid a conflict that could lead to a larger East-West war. Further, there were differences between British, French, and American positions on whether NATO air attacks should be used while European ground troops were the UN forces in place. It soon became apparent to the Bosnian Serbs – Mladić and Karadžić again – that UN forces had neither the ground troops nor the willingness to order a serious air strike to maintain the safety of the region. Limited air strikes did not deter them. When the Bosnian Serbs had already seized the area they wanted, a ceasefire was finally achieved. The UN had lost all credibility, and its members were in considerable disarray.[9]

Both Bosnian Serb and Muslim leaders used the UN as cover for their own military offensives. Serbs signed agreements to stop shelling Sarajevo but continued to do so until August 1995, when NATO finally launched massive air strikes. Muslims used the UN safe area in Srebrenica to re-equip themselves and to rest between forays against Serbs. In the opinion of UN Secretary General Boutros-Ghali and others, Bosnian Muslims provoked Serb retaliation while using safe areas for their troops. They refused to evacuate Srebenica in 1994 when it was clear that the UN could not hold it as a safe area. Leaders may have known that it was not safe, but many other Muslims from surrounding villages and towns had gathered at Srebrenica because they believed they would be protected. Some three hundred Dutch soldiers who were on duty there vacated their location when they realized that the UN would not provide sufficient air protection in the event of an anticipated attack by Serb forces.

When the attack came, Bosnian Serb forces, possibly backed up by Serbian forces, detained men and boys while putting women, the elderly, the infirm, and infants on buses that took them to Tužla. Some women escaped to nearby forests, where they were hunted down and shot (there is a warehouse near the cemetery where they were killed; it is still there, with blood stains, and is open to the public). An estimated seven thousand to eight thousand detained males were then shot and buried in mass graves around the region. Ratko Mladić was the commander in charge of Bosnian Serb forces at that time, and it was he who directed the siege of Srebrenica. He is reported to be alive, and he remains free as of September 2007, though the ICTY issued a warrant for his arrest and the European Union put Serbia on notice that failure to produce him would bring about sanctions. Muslims will generally inform an inquirer that they assume he is protected in Serbia, together with Radovan Karadžić, the Bosnian civilian Serb leader during the war. Informed Serbs, however, point out that neither Mladić nor Karadžić was highly regarded by Milošević or other Serb leaders; they are, in consequence, more likely to be sheltered by Bosnian Serbs in Republika Srpska.

Because Muslims were categorized as a separate ethnic identity and because they had a different religion, the Serb attacks on Muslims in Bosnia are regarded as genocide.

Bosnian Serb attacks on Srebrenica and Žepa on the eastern border of Bosnia in mid-summer 1995 were final proof of the inadequacy of UN peacekeeping efforts. A later inquiry in Holland concluded that the UN forces had been inadequately briefed, were inadequately prepared and equipped, and were unable to act appropriately against Serb military power at the time.

Peace Enforcement in Contrast to Peacekeeping

One issue here is that the UN still had in its belly the notion that peacekeeping was possible, while the combatants had no complementary notion: they were not interested in initiating, let alone in maintaining, a peace. They wanted a war over territory, and that was what they had from 1992 to 1995. Through 1993 and 1994, Europeans preferred negotiation to force, and the Western countries were divided on how best to proceed following the failure of the Vance-Owen plan.

Many observers of these wars discuss the vacillating interest in Balkan events of the 1990s, but George Kenney, senior diplomat on the Yugoslav desk in the State Department up to 1992, wrote this damning observation:

> The positions of the Bush administration on the Yugoslav crisis
> between February and August represent the worst kind of hypocrisy. I know this, because I wrote them for seven months in addition to other duties ... My job was to do this in such a way that
> the US would appear active and worried about what was going on

there, and at the same time not give the impression that the US were (sic) actually ready to do anything about it. (Kenney cited in Divjak 2001, 166)

Jovan Divjak argues that other governments were also reluctant to move beyond peacekeeping. Russia and Greece blocked any action that was contrary to Serb interests. Britain and France were slow to concern themselves with the gravity of the wars. They and the media that arrived on the scene kept treating the events in Bosnia as a civil war with no side being the primary aggressor. Everyone wanted to give "balanced interpretations" and act as neutrals. Given the substantial difference in armed capacities between Serbs, together with Bosnian Serbs whose armaments were provided by the JNA, and Muslims, balanced reporting became obfuscation of actual events during the early 1990s. As well, governments and international media persisted in treating the conflict as the result of ancient hatreds and ethnic conflict. Divjak (2001, 168–69) interprets these beliefs as being Serbian propaganda that was accepted by Europeans and Americans because they could then say that they were unable to stop such a war. The genocide at Srebrenica finally altered outsiders' versions of the war in Bosnia.

The Finale

The creation of a UN rapid reaction force in May 1995 was the beginning of a serious counter-offensive to Serb attacks, though Britain and the United States were not enthusiastic about the initiative on the grounds that it blurred the distinction between peacekeeping and peace enforcement (Findlay 2002, 254–6). With much hand-wringing, dissention, and discussion over the interim, an agreement was reached three months later to allow for NATO air strikes in what was finally called a peace enforcement operation, though peace imposition might have been a more apt label.

An air campaign was directed to stop the siege of Sarajevo. Then NATO air attacks in early September hit a larger range of targets against the Serbs. The air strikes continued until mid September, successful by then in weakening the Bosnian Serb military and enabling a joint Croatian-Muslim offensive in central and western Bosnia (Burg and Shoup 1999, esp. chap. 7, 254–6). These air strikes coincided with the Croat offensive in the Krajina area of

Croatia. The largest military operation in NATO's history to that time was launched at the end of August 1995 on Goražde, with other operations directed at opening the Sarajevo airport and other transportation routes. It was brief, but it persuaded Serb forces that they could no longer gain ground through force. At the height of the war, some sixty thousand UN and NATO troops were deployed to Bosnia.

The weakness of the United Nations, which has no armed force of its own and is dependent on contributions by member states and NATO, was always painfully apparent to the combatants as well as to latter-day observers such as ourselves. In notable instances, UN interventions saved people who might otherwise have been killed, but they failed to persuade the various groups to stop killing one another. The confusion about peacekeeping, peace enforcement, and active military intervention was never resolved. NATO bombing ended the wars, but none of the underlying issues was resolved by force. Serbians obtained a large part of Bosnia in the form of Republika Srpska, a clear indication that their aggression had paid off in additional territory. Croatians in Bosnia and in Croatia continue to voice opposition to the agreed-upon governance and agitate for a settlement similar to that obtained by the Serbs. Bosniaks are caught in the middle, with a small island between their large neighbours. Not surprisingly, they have been offered and have accepted external support from Muslim countries.

THE DAYTON AGREEMENT

Following the air strikes, the war in the former Yugoslavia ended, and, in November 1995, American diplomats stepped in to negotiate a peace agreement. According to Burg and Shoup (1999, 316), "When the US leadership was compelled to deal with [the situation] it imposed a settlement shaped as much by US concerns as by the requisites of stabilizing the region." The US, in their view, was eager to stop the fighting rather than to settle political differences. "Thus," they continue, "it produced an unstable peace under which the parties continued their pursuit of fundamentally incompatible goals by other than military means, while they prepared for what appeared to be an inevitable resumption of fighting" (ibid.).

The agreement – the General Framework for Peace in Bosnia and Herzegovina (better known as the Dayton Agreement) – divided

Bosnia and Hercegovina into two parts. The Federation of Bosnia and Hercegovina (FBiH) is composed mainly of Muslims and Croats, and Republika Srpska (RS) is composed mainly of Serbs. The borders are consistent with much, though not all, of the territory that Serbs won through war. Bosniak leaders (i.e., Muslims of Bosnia) were obliged to sign the agreement, but it meant that half of the country they had once inhabited was now controlled by Serbs, and the half that they still held was shared with Croats not only by custom and culture but now also by legal authority. The settlement was similar in substance to earlier European proposals: division of the territory by ethnic designation.

The Organization for Security and Cooperation in Europe was authorized to implement elections. Some fifty thousand troops under NATO command, a majority from the United States, took over peace-keeping duties in what, in 1996, became known as the Stabilization Force (SFOR). The agreement was signed not by representatives of the Serb and Croat communities in Bosnia (who were deliberately left out), but by the presidents of Serbia and Croatia – now separate nations – and the (Muslim) president of Bosnia. In Sumantra Bose's (2002, 53) view: "The cold, sinister, yet thoroughly compelling logic of 'ethnic cleansing' provided the essential framework for the *General Framework Agreement on Peace in Bosnia & Herzegovina.*" In his opinion, there was a "conscious strategic compromise with the two individuals most directly responsible for former Yugoslavia's descent into war and the Bosnian tragedy – Slobodan Milošević and Franjo Tudjman" (ibid.).

Complexities for Bosnia and Hercegovina

The Dayton Agreement created an enormously complex administration for a total population of about 4.4 million (as of 1992). Just over one-half of the territory that used to be known as Bosnia and Hercegovina is now called the Federation of Bosnia and Hercegovina (FBiH), a state of about three million people, or 63 percent of the total.[10] Its population is predominantly Bosniak (70 percent), with a minority of Croats (28 percent) and Serbs (1.4 percent). Three towns, predominantly Muslim, are included in its territory: Sarajevo, Tužla, and Ženica. Mostar is partitioned into Muslim-controlled and Croat-controlled zones (Bose 2002, 74–5). Forty-nine percent of former Bosnia and Hercegovina is now Republika Srpska (RS), where 88 percent of the population is Serb and 11 percent is Bosniak.

At the top of a pyramid of bureaucratic positions is the Office of the High Representative (OHR), which coordinates and implements the civilian provisions in the agreement. The separate duties involved in civilian implementation are allocated to an array of international organizations, including the OSCE, the UN Mission in Bosnia and Hercegovina (UNMIBH), and the UN High Commissioner for Refugees (UNHCR). The ICTY at The Hague also has its vital role, though it is not embedded in the pyramid inside Bosnia and Hercegovina (Chesterman 2004, 76n83,84).

A parliamentary assembly also tops the separate entities (FBiH and RS) with two houses and a constitutional court. The judiciary for the court consists of two Bosniaks, two Croats, two Serbs, and three people from non-BiH countries chosen by the president of the European Court of Human Rights. The Constitutional Court has exclusive jurisdiction on any matters in dispute between the two entities. Like the Constitutional Court, the Central Bank of BiH operates for the entire region, and it is headed by a non-Bosnian who is appointed by the International Monetary Fund (IMF). The governing board has one Bosniak, one Croat, one Serb, plus one outsider who can cast a decisive vote.

Beneath the parliamentary arrangement for the whole, the two entities operate in most respects as separate sovereign polities. Each has a parliament of its own and a judiciary. Both components have a president and vice-presidents. In the FBiH, virtually every public unit has representatives of each of the three major ethnic groups, along with rotating presidencies or heads. However, the armies of both the FBiH and the RS were united, as of the beginning of 2006, under a new state-level ministry of defence. Police forces are scheduled to be united by 2010.[11]

FBiH is further divided into ten cantons, each with many of the powers of a separate state. Ethnicity is a major criterion for the divisions. The whole entity obliges Bosnian Croats and Bosniaks to work together; however, in the regions where they are equally numerous, their civil war still permeates the atmosphere.

Republika Srpska, with its de facto capital in Banja Luca, has a parliament, ministries to deal with external relations, interior matters, and police. The region covered by the RS was largely rural before the division, and it remains rural except for Banja Luca and a few smaller towns. It was poor before the war, and it was even poorer afterwards. The population is about 1.25 million. The RS depends not on BiH for its economic development (or lack thereof) but on what was the Republic of Serbia and what, subsequent to the wars, became known as the Federal Republic of Yugoslavia (FRY), then as Serbia and Montenegro, and, in 2007, as Serbia.

The Constitutional Court ruled in 2000 that the constitutions of both entities were ultra vires. The FBiH Constitution had been claimed to be for Bosniaks and Croats exclusively, and the RS Constitution for Serbs. The Court ruled that both constitutions were in conflict with the BiH Constitution. Both entities were ordered to change the wording so that in either place all citizens of the country had equal rights. However, changing the wording is unlikely to change attitudes or behaviour. Though the constitutions of the two entities have to provide for equal rights, they are permitted to run their own school systems. In Serbia, this means that history will be viewed from the Serb point of view. In FBiH, it means that, in Croatian cantons, history will be viewed from the Croatian point of view; in Muslim cantons, it will be viewed from the Muslim point of view. The experience of the generation that went through wars because its members could not communicate with one another is thus being fostered for yet another generation.

The High Representative

The High Representative (HR), appointed with sweeping powers, was to be appointed "consistent with relevant United Nations Security Council resolutions," but the United Nations was gently pushed aside as the governing body. According to Simon Chesterman (2004, 76–6), "key states saw the United Nations as so discredited by its peacekeeping performance in the Balkans that the drafters never seriously contemplated appointing a UN special representative instead of an independently constituted High Representative." That not withstanding, what the diplomats call "mission creep" provided more control to the UN mission in BiH, and, ultimately, UNMIBH had numerous functions involving law enforcement, coordination of humanitarian relief and refugees activities, de-mining, human rights, elections, and both physical and economic reconstruction.

The OHR turned out, in practice, to have less authority than it needed, and the Dayton Agreement was ambiguous in a number of ways. As Chesterman (2004, 77) puts it, "The mandate thus assumed a degree of cooperation and commitment to reconciliation between the parties that simply did not exist. This changed at the Bonn Summit of the Peace Implementation Council of December 1997, after which the High Representative began to take decisions against the will of the parties." Another feature of the agreement was that the HR, by informal agreement, had to be a European, and the two chief deputies would be, respectively, European and American, while the OSCE head of mission would be an American (Cousens and Cater 2001, 46; Chesterman 2004, 129–30).

Although the HR's assignment was to facilitate and coordinate efforts to reconstruct an independent society within two years of the signing of the Dayton Agreement, the High Representative attempted more. Between 1998 and mid-2003, the HR "dismissed, suspended, or banned from public office over 100 elected officials at all levels of government – including a former Prime Minister of the Bosnian Federation ... a President of Republika Srpska ... and a member of the Bosnian Presidency."[12] David Chandler (1999) and the International Crisis Group (2000) both argued that the consequence was to create a protectorate under the pretence that it was a democracy. The format did provide sufficient support to create a peaceful reintegration of the eastern Slavonia region into Croatia, but it failed to solve the continuing problems in BiH.

Croatian Claims

The wars in Central Bosnia and in Mostar were particularly brutal. As the Serbs retreated, the relationship between the allied Croats and Bosniaks broke down. Extremist Bosnian Croats still argue that the Dayton Agreement has jeopardized their collective existence. They continue to demand a territorially defined Croatian entity similar to that created for Bosnian Serbs in Republika Srpska. They want to gain the City of Mostar, even though they were outnumbered there before the war by four to one. They point out that the Serbs were given Banja Luca. Since the war, their numbers have steadily decreased due to emigration. After the war Mostar had two distinctive classes that overlapped with ethnic groups: the relatively wealthy Croats on one side and the relatively impoverished Bosniaks on the other. Not surprisingly, there is great bitterness in this arrangement, and since Croats continue to demand more than they got from the Dayton process, Bosniaks feel vulnerable, and, they, too, are losing population to emigration.

In stark contrast to the prewar reputation for mutual tolerance are the self-reported attitudes during and since the war. In 1998–99, the International Committee of the Red Cross sponsored a study that found 87 percent of Serb Bosnians, 72 percent of Muslim Bosnians, and 70 percent of Croat Bosnians identified with their respective ethnic groups during the war.[13] This division could not have happened overnight, and even if this was a retrospective version of what they felt during the war, it screams out just how fragile is the federation.

A less quantitative but nonetheless strong indication of this fragility consists of comments such as this, by Jadranko Prlić, foreign minister of BiH from the end of 1996 to early 2001 and reckoned as a Croatian moderate: "For us Croats the Federation is the ultimate goal and an acceptable form of association. The Bosniak side, however, attaches only a temporary position to the Federation on the way towards a centralized state with their own domination" (from *Hrvatski Glas*, Mostar, September 1996, cited in Bose 2002, 88). Author Sumantra Bose (2002, 88) argues that Bosnian Croats demand equal representation in the FBiH despite their smaller numbers and that there is a "network of parallel structures financed by Croatia, which make official Federation institutions redundant in most of Croat-controlled Bosnia, and which are well-financed even after reductions in Zagreb's funding following the death of Tudjman and the fall of the HDZ in the mother-country."

With Republika Srpska on one side taking up 49 percent of the territory and Croatian Hercegovina on the other, what remains of old Bosnia is a centrepiece nestled in the mountains and inhabited primarily by Bosniaks. Try though this tiny state does to move forward, one senses everywhere the feeling of futility and grief at what was lost. Young people migrate to European and North American cities if they can. One of the ironies is the growth in the number of people adopting the dress and habits of Islam, aided by grants and the building of mosques by Saudi Arabia and possibly Iran. Before the war, religion here was muted and was not regarded, either by Muslims or by Serbs and Croats as a matter of great importance in human relations.

Military Issues

The original sixty thousand NATO troops deployed to BiH were halved in number by 1996, but the United States decided, the following year, to keep troops in Bosnia indefinitely. The Dayton Agreement instituted measures to limit the military activities of the entities involved, but willingness to abide by these depends on the continuing presence of international forces (Burg and Shoup 1999, 378). Arms control provisions allowed the Bosnian government to increase its military capacity, with training and equipment provided by the US, but all of this was with a view towards integrating the armed forces.

In December 2006, Bosnia joined NATO's "Partnership for Peace" program, and entered talks with the European Union on stabilization processes with a view towards eventual EU membership. October elections were as divisive as ever, with opposing ethnic positions, but with the growing awareness that international agencies planned to reduce their activities in Bosnia during 2007, there was renewed internal pressure on the three major ethnic groups to come to some agreements. During 2005, reforms of police forces throughout BiH had gradually taken shape, though without the robust support of the RS Parliament. In July 2006, Bosnia began the process of merging the armed forces into a unified Bosnian army. The obstacles have not disappeared: the RS continues to look to its eastern borders for support, but these changes in defence arrangements, slow and halting though they are, suggest that a future might become possible for the three entities that, for the moment, are obliged to co-exist within the BiH borders.

Migration, Refugee, and Settlement Issues

The wars in Croatia resulted in some 200,000 refugees and 350,000 internally displaced persons in addition to the estimated twenty thousand dead. The Bosnia-Hercegovina war provided an estimated death toll of 100,000, and up to 2 million people became refugees or IDPs (Woodward 1995).[14] The Dayton Agreement stipulated the right for IDPs and refugees to return to their homes of origin. Further, it stipulated that they had the right to have their property restored. These and various human rights were to be supported by the UNHCR. NGOs were invited to assist in tracing missing persons, distributing food, and providing medical aid.

An estimated 330,000 refugees lived in Germany at the end of the wars, and another 450,000 IDPs lived in regions of the former Yugoslavia other than their earlier place of residence.[15] In Bosnia, the largest single group of refugees was comprised of Muslims who had resided in the eastern Serb-dominated regions of Bosnia (post-Dayton RS) and in Croat areas within Bosnia. Croats fled to Croatia if they had to leave territories taken over by Serbs or, in some cases, Bosniaks. Serbs expelled from Bosnia-Hercegovina went to what became Repulika Srpska or Serbia. Muslims had nowhere else to go.

Implementation of the Dayton Agreement and UN stipulations was no easy task. Only a little more than eighty-eight thousand refugees were repatriated in 1996, contrasted with an expected return of 400,000 refugees. Over the next four years, the same low numbers returned. In reality, refugees were returning only to areas where their ethnic group formed a majority. By 2000, only one-third of Bosnian refugees had returned, and another 300,000 still had no durable solution. Others – nearly half of the refugee population – had moved abroad or to other countries in the former Yugoslavia.

Many reasons militated against minorities' returning home. As noted by Cousens and Cater (2001, 76):

> Freedom of movement was restricted by a maze of illegal police checkpoints and rumors of long "lists" of Hague indictees who could be apprehended without due process; illicit tolls at inter-entity crossing points; the scattering of 600,000 active landmines throughout Bosnia, particularly along the IEBL; and actual violence in the form of attacks on individuals and small groups of travelers. These last were often reported as spontaneous acts by "mobs" but in almost all cases were shown to have been organized by political authorities.

The UNHCR provided a bus service to shuttle between the entities and to enable returnees to move across borders. It was moving some nine thousand people per week by 1997. But even with this and many other efforts to bring people back to their homes in both the FBiH and the RS, the returns were never as high as international authorities had anticipated. Fear, lack of housing, roadblocks to reclaiming property, various legal impediments, unemployment rates, lack of trust in local authorities, and the schooling situation were all cited as reasons. The last of these was seen as a major problem: many Bosnians cited the lack of a single curriculum for all children, irrespective of their ethnic origins, as their reason for looking elsewhere for settlement options. The roadblocks and other legal impediments were attempts to stop minority returns, and these impediments continued, illegally for the most part, through all of the 1990s and into the twenty-first century. The UN and SFOR troops tried numerous schemes to remove the barriers and enable people to return to their homes. They tried both incentives and penalties, but to little avail.

Patriarchy and Land Rights

Among the many disincentives to return are those erected against women. Although property laws have been reformed, the culture is still patriarchal, and most property is formally owned by men, not women. Women who have lost husbands have the legal right to a share of the husband's property, with equal shares going to the children of their marriage. But there are impediments to women gaining access to this property. If the majority group has taken over the property, it may try to prevent the returnee from getting it back. She has to prove that she has legal right to inherit it, and she may have to go to court to make her claim. She may also have to take legal action to evict others. Further, if other male members of the husband's family are alive they might claim the property.

In Srebrenica today, Serbs constitute the majority of the population. Only two thousand Bosniak returnees were registered as of 2003, when I conducted an interview with the mayor. He said that, in 1996, some seventeen thousand persons said they wanted to return. The two thousand people who returned were mainly women and children. According to him, during the first few years following the war there were "all sorts of scenes, difficult scenes, incidents, situations. On a few occasions buildings that had been renovated, reconstructed, were again burned and mined. There were even physical and verbal attacks on the returnees." However, he said, such situations were no longer happening. "The last one was around the New Year this year [2003]." I asked who were acting against the returnees. He speculated that they included members of the Chetnik movement, some followers of the Serbian Radical

Party, and certain members of the Serbian Democrat Party, but to the best of his knowledge Serbia (the country) was not supporting the attacks. I asked him to what he credited the cessation of violence, and he responded: "Time. The extreme members of the Serbian people realized that these actions harmed themselves."[16] One hopes he is right.

Triple Education Systems

The Dayton Agreement led to the creation of three different educational systems in the FBiH. Croatian children might be taught on one floor of a school building, Bosniaks on another, and Serbs elsewhere. Space would be allocated according to numbers in the population, though the arithmetic might be frequently revised because of the continual migration of families to wherever their ethnic group is in a majority. Some students lack sufficient funds to get to a school where they will be included, and so they get no schooling at all. Opinion polls cite this extreme isolation between ethnic student groups as a major reason for people choosing not to migrate back to any region where families with school-age children would be in a minority. In a handful of villages, the parents have quietly rebelled and held joint festivals and developed theatre troupes without separation by ethnic group. In one village, parents have integrated their schools, and the authorities be damned.

Economic Reconstruction

Bosnia's prewar economy was already in a deep slump. What little it had before was now destroyed: infrastructure and industrial base gone, half the population displaced or killed, the most skilled class emigrated. At the end of the war, unemployment was the lot of 80 percent of the remaining population (Cousens and Cater 2001, 87). Young people are especially harmed by the lack of economic reconstruction, and many seek opportunities to emigrate. The rates for poverty and unemployment are greater in Republika Srpska than in FBiH.

The World Bank and the IMF intervened following the war, and some fifty countries and twenty-seven international organizations pledged a total of $615 million for immediate reconstruction. More came in the next couple of years, and, in total, international donors provided over $5 billion for physical reconstruction, institutional development, and other essentials for the redevelopment of the economy (Cousens and Cater 2001, 88–9). Although the donations were substantial, the process was slow, in part because the donors could not agree on "conditionality" (see chapter 11 for a discussion of conditionality). Republika Srpska, in particular, was either unable or unwilling to meet conditions specified in the Dayton Agreement or further incentives for investment. The World Bank was prepared to invest in the RS as in the FBiH, irrespective of political developments or impediments, but the international community was not of one mind on this. Some of the World Bank and IMF demands on the FBiH increased insecurity and competition over scarce resources. Finally, the pressure to privatize state properties, according to Cousens and Cater (2001, 97), "had a very problematic impact in Bosnia, exacerbating corruption and thereby discouraging increased FDI while not spurring enough new economic activity to compensate." High unemployment rates throughout the FBiH have boosted the emigration rates for young people and professionals, leaving the country bereft of the very people it most needs for economic reconstruction and for leadership.

Corruption

During the war, as in most wars everywhere, material humanitarian assistance often ended up being sold on black markets or hoarded by the privileged. In mid-war, the Bosnian government could not be counted on to deliver food aid to the residents of Sarajevo, even though many countries provided it and the airport was guarded by UN personnel at considerable risk to themselves (Weiss 1999, 117). Corruption is a leading problem in postwar Bosnia. Says Bose (2002, 37):

> As can be expected in a broken post-war society facing severe economic hardship, corruption is rife at all levels of Bosnia's political structures, administration, and police services. Taking advantage of this semi-anarchic climate and the porous nature of Bosnia's external and internal borders, trans-national criminal networks have turned the country into a haven as well as major east-west transit point for trafficking in smuggled cigarettes, stolen cars, contraband narcotics and desperate human beings from Iran, China and Turkey, among other places.

The environs of the City of Mostar are particularly prone to criminal activities. Bose (2002, 102–3) informs us that the town of Stolać "is controlled by hard-line Croats with a symbiotic nexus to transnational organized-crime rackets. The town sits astride a notorious smuggling route leading from Montenegro through the Serb and Croat-controlled areas of Herzegovina to Croatia and beyond." Further on, he discusses the town of Grude, "a western Herzegovina town synonymous with Croat paramilitary and organized-crime networks" (102–3). He claims that, in Mostar itself, "various forms of criminality and corruption permeate much of the economic and business activity that does exist, and organized crime rackets are deeply entrenched on both sides of the divide, invariably in collusion with local political power-brokers" (108).

One of my interviewees brought to my attention the fact that the NATO soldiers who were tied to military equipment during the war were French. The major region in which organized crime operates is under French supervision, and it is there, he said, that Radovan Karadžić and Ratko Mladić are hiding. My respondent observed that many people (he seemed to exclude himself, acting merely as a reporter) thought that the French reached an agreement with the Serbs that they would not capture or prosecute Serb soldiers if their soldiers were freed. In his words, "ordinary citizens think there was a deal. We let your people live freely and you let us live the way we want to." I have no independent evidence of this.

The complexity of this agreement emphasizes the differences between the three populations. Perhaps, in 1995, there was no alternative other than to acknowledge the enmity between them and to create a constitution and territorial map that would govern their relationships but do nothing to heal their mutual hatreds. Sumantra Bose (2002, 4) thinks that this strange state can be maintained, and he refers to his position as a "carefully qualified affirmative." Others are more critical. Taking the position that the wars in Yugoslavia were prolonged by "Western leaders' interference, at times individually under the patronizing illusion that they could step in and settle this trivial 'Balkan tribal squabble,' and so gain personal kudos for their wise statesmanship," Edgar O'Ballance (1995, 248) concludes his study of the wars with condemnation for interfering outsiders. In his opinion, the Balkan war was caused by the determination of President Izetbeković to create an independent (Muslim) country and the opposition to this on the part of the two large minorities in

Bosnia. When the Europeans and Americans acceded to his unilateral announcement of independence, they encouraged him to proceed and ensured that the other parties would struggle against his leadership. However, they were not of one mind on how to proceed and were squabbling among themselves as Bosnians engaged in war. Ceasefires were declared and regularly ignored. All groups engaged in propaganda and made the most of the mass media to argue their case. In O'Ballance's opinion, the US proposed to use air power much earlier, with European allies providing the troops (and thus taking most of the casualties). Not surprisingly, Europeans were not keen on that approach. Although he is critical of the UN, O'Ballance acknowledges that UN forces "saved at least one million people in Bosnia from death by starvation and exposure; fed and sheltered countless thousands more; and delivered many tons of humanitarian aid, often at great personal risk" (ibid.).

The Dilemmas

It seems to me that saving many lives is an achievement of some note, so I find myself out of sympathy with O'Ballance's negative appraisal of UN action. He might, however, be right about the attitudes of outsiders insofar as they saw this war as a "trivial tribal squabble." Earlier, I argued that the causes of the war were not even genuine ethnic differences; rather, they were an unworkable federation, political paralysis at the national level, substantial regional inequalities, economic deterioration, and the lack of statespeople who might have countered the invented ethnic labels. These are not trivial issues, and similar problems were frequently in place when other states disintegrated over the past century. Neither European nor American statespeople and the negotiators they sent to deal with the conflict seemed able to understand the gravity of the civil war until they were shocked into realization with the slaughter at Srebrenica.

The incoherence of UN and NATO actions was, in large part, a reflection of the incoherence of the international community with respect to the nature of the conflict. From the beginning, some Western observers, journalists, and scholars were sure that what was happening was a Serb attack on Bosnia. It was not clear even to them whether the warriors were all JNA soldiers or whether they were paramilitaries and thugs. The difference between Serb forces under Serbian authority

and Bosnian or Croatian Serbs who might have had support from the
Serbian state but who were also merely self-organized armies was not
generally understood at the time. It was not clear whether the UN intended its forces to be simply peacekeepers when obvious massive
crimes were being committed: were they supposed to simply witness
and report or could they intervene? They were not well enough
equipped to be more than peacekeepers, but they found themselves
in the middle of an ongoing war, and there was no peace to keep. In
these respects, the UN's intervention in the Balkans was similar to its
intervention in Rwanda.

9

Opening Graves
and Closing the Past in Bosnia

Amor Masović, head of the Bosnian Commission for Missing Persons, invited us to attend the opening of a mass grave near Srebrenica, where he and a forensic team would be going the following day. He said the commission was set up to locate missing persons dead or alive, but that now, ten years after the beginning of the aggression and seven years after its termination, it is reasonable to assume that all missing persons are actually dead. To May 2003, the bodies of 27,731 Bosnians earlier listed as missing had been located and had either been identified or were in the process of DNA testing. In contrast to the Red Cross, the commission goes to the gravesites. It has its own laboratory in Tužla (a short distance from Srebrenica) and conducts forensic studies there. Discoveries of mass graves continued through the following years. Some of these are located near Srebrenica, where the mass slaughter of Muslim men and boys occurred. That this event occurred is no longer speculation: the ICTY has elicited evidence through numerous trials.

In the midst of our interview in June 2003 the telephone rang, and Dr Masović answered. He then explained: "I received a call from one of the workers at a mass grave. They found a document by the bones of one dead body with the name and surname on it. I ran a check and established that that man disappeared on the ninth of April 1992. So – after a full eleven years and more – we managed to find him." The group tries to obtain information about missing persons from all sides of the past conflict, but it has not been successful in obtaining cooperation from all sides. Better results have come through identifying persons whose bodies were exhumed. Bodies at the burial site are carefully assessed, and all

possible identifying information is attached to the burial bag containing the corpse (e.g., clothing, any jewelry or other items). At the
Tužla site the corpses are wrapped in bags and stored in a refriger-
ated room until identification can be achieved. The Tužla centre
tries to match up the identifying information and DNA with family
members' DNA and descriptions of the missing person. Masović di-
gresses from his depiction of the process, moving in a direction that
is close to my concern about whether judicial processes are essential
after civil and other wars:

> I am convinced that the vehemence with which the groups, or
> maybe it is better said, individuals, were getting even with the
> members of the other side was a consequence of the fact that after
> World War Two no one dealt seriously with the problem of missing
> persons, because many victims ended up in holes. These holes were
> sealed and cemented, all this time the frustration of the surviving
> relatives was building because they were not able to obtain those
> skeletal remains and bury their loved one decently ... These people
> lived for forty or fifty years with such frustration that fathers, uncles,
> et cetera were killed by the members of that other nation and were
> thrown in some hole. They were not allowed to bury their loved
> ones and start a proper period of mourning ... The territorial ten-
> sions were the cause of the war, of the aggression, but in the individ-
> uals, we would still be getting even, we would still be shooting each
> other, we are enemies. The intensity, and the horrible ways that
> people were killed and buried in holes, explains the grief and anger,
> even though the war was caused by territorial tensions.

In Masović's view, after the Second World War and after the end of
violence in Yugoslavia in 1995, Europeans were disinterested in financing or supporting a project to find missing persons. He believes
they were of the opinion that the search for the missing slows down
the process of reconciliation. He rejects the idea of a truth commission, observing that he is not the right person to address that possibility because he had personally handled over eight thousand bodies,
touched dead women in the seventh month of pregnancy, disin-
terred "children who didn't have names because their parents didn't
have time to give them one." As to a commission for truth and peace
and reconciliation, which outsiders are trying to implant, he thinks it
is important for the victims and the criminals to solve it between

themselves. A truth commission, however, would be about "the programming of truth." The reason he speaks thus is as follows:

> The Dayton scheme is such that the legal organs are disabled, incapacitated from doing their job from one side, and from the other side – in the Republika Srpska – there is no political will to produce the people for whom it is known that they were at the lower and even at the highest levels of the crime ... From Radovan Karadžić all the way to some guard in Foca who stole food from the packages that arrived for the war prisoners and who, in many other ways, tortured the war prisoners, over there, there is no political will for that to be done. There is no political will in the Republika Srpska.

It is difficult to estimate the numbers of people killed because corpses from different locations have been thrown together and often moved.

> We have proof that one and the same man, his parts, three parts, his head, arms, and legs, we found him in three different locations separated by about thirty kilometres. There is proof that they [the criminals] move in before the forensic teams in order to hide and cover the tracks of their crimes, after the wars, today. Also they threw explosives after the bodies, causing massive amounts of rocks to cave in.

In one hole they found seven skeletal remains from this war, and another twenty remains left over from the Second World War; and maybe this act came out of the "frustration in those who threw those seven down there." In another instance the team found 144 victims of this war and two Bosniaks "whose trail was lost in 1944." They were found via genetic testing through their offspring. In both cases, the burial holes were the same as those used by the enemies in the last war, and the criminals were never brought to justice. Said Masović: "So we are trying to show, by our acts, that these crimes cannot be hidden anymore. We can now detect the crimes. In the case of crimes in Mostar, where there were also mass graves to be found and opened, the victims were buried in a civilized way," even though the "Croatian government is not prepared to tell us where the bodies are."

SREBRENICA

Recovering Bodies

The next day, with Amor Masović in the lead car of a convoy including several UN vehicles, we travelled from Sarajevo to Srebrenica, now located in Republika Srpska. We spent the better part of a hot day watching forensic specialists carefully remove bodies from a mass grave – eighteen in this location, and it was only one of many. Each body was sheathed, together with any artifacts found near it and with its clothes (or, by now, rags) attached to it. The smell was hard to bear for the workers, and the heat made the job more unpleasant, but they were used to it. It was their vocation, and they knew that what they did matters. If the bodies can be identified – which is why the care is taken to retrieve even the smallest ring or scrap of clothing – they can be properly buried by their surviving relatives; moreover, the evidence can be taken to the International Criminal Tribunal for Yugoslavia in The Hague to be used in trials of Serb leaders of the Srebrenica massacre. Almost all of the bodies we saw at the mass gravesite were male, and they included boys as well as adults.

Forensic analysis will provide information to survivors so that they can determine whether or not a body is that of their relative or close friend/associate. The forensic team at Tužla includes archaeologists, anthropologists, and medical specialists from all over the world, many donating some time to the project.[1] Once the bodies are identified, a formal burial is undertaken in a memorial cemetery at Pontecari, close to Srebrenica. Amor Masović, who has been honoured by other countries for his dedication to this task, is compelling in his description of what happened at Srebrenica and the current work of disinterring the bodies.

Women of Srebrenica

Men and boys were separated from their womenfolk at Srebrenica. The women were forced to leave on buses that took them to Tužla. Those who fled Srebrenica on their own were hunted down and killed. Those who arrived in Tužla waited, hoping that their sons and husbands would make it out safely. The widows eventually established a family centre in Tužla, where the surviving women help each other to cope with their impoverished lives and inform others about what happened. On the walls are the pictures or descriptions of the men

Opening a mass grave near Srebrenica, 24 June 2003.
Photograph by the author

who disappeared. Among their tasks is the provision of DNA and information about their menfolk to enable the forensic laboratory at
the Centre for Missing Persons in Tužla to identify corpses.

The Mayor of Srebrenica

In 2003, the mayor of Srebrenica was a Bosniak, a man who, as a teen-
ager, had fled the town during the war and had since returned. I asked
the obvious question: how, as a Bosniak who had returned to a town
occupied primarily by Serbs, had he become the elected mayor? He
said that, under the rules of the period, those persons who had been
born in the town but who were living elsewhere and who registered to
vote in the municipal election were able to do so. In the 1997 election, there were fourteen thousand registered Bosniak voters, most of

whom did not live in the town; there were about ten thousand Serb voters. The mayor said that time would change these conditions. In his opinion, Serbs were becoming cognizant of the need to get on with the tasks of building a united community and country. He thought maybe 70 percent of Serbs in Srebrenica now thought he was doing a good job, and their opposition to Bosniaks in their midst or even in public office was gradually diminishing. In the Federation of Bosnia and Hercegovina as a whole, it would eventually disappear once everyone began building common institutions – schools, the army, the economic system, the taxation system, and so on. He also thought that, when The Hague began shifting much of its work to lower-level courts in the FBiH, local courts would be able to handle the cases.

Srebrenica, 2007

But all is not well in Srebrenica, despite the mayor's incredible optimism and tolerant good will. In 2007, as in 2003, unemployment is still the lot of virtually all inhabitants, and repaired housing is sparse. In early March 2007, a dozen years after the genocide, Bosniak survivors threatened a mass exodus unless their town was granted special administrative status within Bosnia i Hercegovina rather than in the Republika Srpska. Their threat came in the wake of the World Court decision (described in chapter 3). Said one Srebrenica politician, "If there is any morality in the international community, it will not allow the victims of genocide to be ruled by those who committed genocide on them."[2] The prime minister of the RS, Milorad Dodik, expressed regret, apologized to victims for "heinous crimes," and promised to allocate more funds to the town. Said the politician, "You can't put a price on the denial of genocide ... We wouldn't budge even if the RS entity allocated its entire budget to Srebrenica." At this time, there were about four thousand Bosniaks in the municipality (town and environs), constituting some 30 percent of the population. In 1991, before the genocide, the same municipality had some 36.6 thousand residents, of whom over 75 percent were Bosniaks.

BOSNIA: TRYING TO MOVE BEYOND THE WAR

Rape Victims: Speaking Up

Finding and identifying the dead is a beginning to recreating a society. But the dead were not the only victims of genocide; rape is another way of destroying a people. Many women were raped during the war. Gang raped. Some survived and have chosen to tell the story. And the story is even more frightening because the men who did this have not been charged, are not incarcerated, and are still living among the population, still (if only silently now) threatening to further harm the victims should they tell. Several brave women organized a group called Women Victims of the War. Its members speak publicly about what happened to them. Here is an example:

> At the beginning of June [names three individuals] came to my village and they raped me in front of [names several people, including a policeman in Višegrad] and my son. My daughter who was hidden in the "trap" (an underground space for potatoes in winter), was also watching. Then they killed my son. They dragged me by my hair and threw me into a car and took me to hotel "Vilina Vlas" in Višegrad. There I was raped numerous times daily by those whose names I cited and many others whose names I would not like to state now. To this hotel were brought young men and women of Bosniak nationality every day. All of the women were deformed, bloody, from the rapes and abuse, from being beaten up.[3]

Rape was regularly practised as an instrument of war. It was intended to demean not only the women but also the entire ethnic group to which they belonged. Men were shot, women were raped. The women with whom I spoke explained why: "this is a patriarchal culture, if they shoot the men it will reduce the reproduction capacities of the entire group." Women survivors, especially after rape, were unlikely to have new partners or more children beyond any conceived during the rape itself. When the world looks at statistics of war victims, we count the dead if we can, we seek the missing in what Masović calls "holes," and we tally up those known to have emigrated or who are still living in the limbo of displaced persons. But we never have accurate data on rape victims: it is rare for them to speak up, rare for them to be listened to, and, during a war, there is little chance that justice will reach them. So when these women take the stand and tell what happened, even though the culprits have not yet been charged and years have passed, they are saying: "we exist and we will not be silenced."

Police Reform

Police reform has failed to take place, and this is due in good part to RS reluctance to cooperate. In October 2005, the parliaments of both the FBiH and the RS, along with the combined BiH, endorsed a police reform agreement based on principles laid down by the European Union. All legislative and budgetary competencies for police matters were to be vested at the state level; political interference with operational policing was to be abolished; and functional local police areas were to be determined by technical policing criteria, with operational command exercised locally. The RS was not yet ready for these reforms. The High Representative tried to point out the advantages of honest police officers in his weekly sermon published in local papers.[4] But, by March 2007, the talks on police reform ended yet again in failure.[5]

Military Integration

Police – not yet; but military forces – surprisingly, yes. The RS and the FBiH both approved a historic agreement for reform of defence in mid-2006. This agreement ends conscription, integrates ministries of defence at the state level, and establishes a united professional military force. The force will not only focus on regional security but also meet requirements for participation in NATO.

Ethnic Identities and Perceptions, 2003–04

Ethnicity – even where the language, customs, and other aspects of culture are almost identical – continues to dominate local politics and much of the institutional structure of Bosnia. One hopeful sign appeared during 2004, when it was reported that a few schools had managed to integrate their classes despite the Dayton Agreement and the prevailing fears each group has of the others. A small beginning, perhaps, but a hopeful sign for the future.

Most Bosniaks and Bosnian Croats whom I interviewed saw the war as Serbian aggression – a statement that will cause no surprise to anyone who has listened to both sides. A typical comment: "It was classical aggression, Serbian aggression, they wanted to dominate other groups. It was not civil war, it was not pure ethnic conflict, there was a long history of Serbian nationalism." They were impatient with the

contrary argument that President Izetbegović's determination to create a Muslim state was the basic cause of war. A few Bosniaks mentioned Croatian nationalism as a cause, pointing especially to Mostar.
Although most interviewees said they thought the three ethnic
groups could again coexist, there was, in all the interviews, an underlying doubt, a certain measure of distrust for the others. Following
are a few excerpts from interviews. Interviewees are identified only
by collective names; personal identities were protected.

A civic leader on the war: ·

> Definitely a genocide, launched by nationalist programs of Serbs
> and Croats. It came out of the fifty years of communism, denial
> of individual identities. People were looking for new anchors
> for identity in post-Yugoslavia. The political elites defined ethno-
> nationalist politics … At present elites would block a truth com-
> mission. The Belgrade regime continues within Bosnia, same
> ethno-military structures as were created during the war … Now
> with Dayton, we have apartheid, nobody is ready to change this.
> The children at school do not even play together. And the uni-
> versities are now means of maintaining the status quo, we need
> to reform them, they are now dead structures. The criminals at
> the Hague were educated in these universities – they became
> eloquent speakers for ethno-nationalism. Almost all the
> politicians are university professors.

An imam:

> There are differences in what is written in the Dayton Agreement
> and what the politicians are promoting, also between those and
> what the people want. Three realities: the Dayton Agreement,
> the politicians, the folk … How can somebody go back to his own
> house where the police are not protecting him? And where we
> still have war criminals who have not been apprehended?

A (Roman Catholic) nun:

> Forgiveness is a moral law of Christianity … Muslims also have
> a code that says they must live together, but Islam also has ideas
> how to expand territory. [I asked, "Are Muslims less tolerant then

Christians?"] Yes, I think so. If some one does not know tolerance
from the inside, they can't act tolerantly. In Bosnia there are not
many reconstructed factories, but there are many new mosques.
That shows the way others want to help us. Expansion of Islam ...
but there are no evil persons here, no one is evil. There are Serbs,
Muslims, Croats – forcing the war came from outside, not inside.
International forces. Dayton is destroying us. People outside think
we hate each other, but we are simply hungry.

A university professor:

There is no need for them [SFOR] to be here because the
Bosnians are weaker than the Serbs and Croats. The Croats and
Serbs are so powerful now, they have no need to take over Bosnia
at this time. No need for war now. The Croats have territorial
aims. This undefined situation is good for them – they control
the economy, they have money, they control the media and
export and import businesses and they own the Croatian media.
Bosniaks own very little. We have no strategy, there is no consensus among us, we are divided into different parties. If NATO withdrew, the only area affected would be the problem of returning
refugees. Refugees from Bosnia have gone all over the world.
Refugees don't want to return, they have horrible memories,
no money, unemployment, wrecked houses. The money [from
donors] created a Lebanization of Bosnia; Palestinization of
Bosniaks, and made an instant Arafat of Izetbegović.

An opinion leader in Kresevo:

Kresevo was a thriving small town west of Sarajevo before the war,
with a population about 80 percent Croatian and 20 percent
Muslim, plus a very small number of Serbs. After the war property
rights were sustained for refugees and although most of the Muslim
population left during the war they returned and got their jobs back.

Another opinion leader in Kresevo:

The best way to prevent returns is a lack of employment, but here
in Kresevo, there are private companies that are unconcerned
about the religion of workers. Before the war there was high

employment in several factories – meat, steel, car parts, and mines, also smaller factories making steel items.

And I had an animated discussion with a Croatian-Bosnian in the same small town of Kresevo about the economic and spiritual problems of Bosnia. What most struck me was that this individual could tell me that seventy-five Bosnian Croatians from this town had died in the war, but he had no idea how many Muslims had met the same fate. This is not surprising to Bosnians (of all religions), but to a Canadian it screams out how the institutions of this society are pegged to ethnic positions. This individual said he could not judge the Serbs, but he could say that FBiH's economy had a particular problem with the banks because the international community was causing violence. "We," he said, "do not have our own banks. They are all Austrian or German or American. Ours were all destroyed."

A Bosnian journalist provided a lengthy commentary on refugee returns, Dayton, and the banks. In this person's view, the population in Republika Srpska, where he spent time because of his work, was not interested in Bosnia as a state and was unlikely to want re-unification. Most returnees to that territory were old people who went back to die or to sell their properties. Young people did not return because they had little opportunity to find work, and children were unable to attend schools when their parents were chronically unemployed. He spoke of one village where there were six hundred inhabitants and all were unemployed. He summarized these observations:

> The political leaders of all groups agreed to separation, they talk about living together in one state but in practice they are focused on their own areas. All minorities are in a difficult situation, nobody wants to help them. So the logical solution for minorities is to go where their ethnic group is in a majority. They often exchange flats or houses with people in the other ethnic group so they can survive.

He blamed the international community for the separation:

> The international community wants all people to be dependent on them ... The western area of BiH was not much hurt by the war and during the war it was economically strong. This disturbed the

international community and so SFOR destroyed the Bank of Hercegovina three or four years ago. They claimed the bank was acting illegally. The media said that over ten banks in Bosnia had more illegalities. The illegalities of this bank were never made public. So we think that the real reason for the destruction was because this bank was economically supporting the [Bosnian] Croatian population.

This individual gave examples that, in his view, proved that the international community, in the form of its representatives in BiH, had a geopolitical interest in destroying local initiatives and businesses. In his view, outsiders already owned telecommunications and banking industries; they often acted as advisors immediately after the war and then later came in as private businesses. He concluded that the international community's reason for being in Bosnia was to control the country, "although," he said, "officially no one will ever admit that." The international community was the de facto government of the country, having prevented the three component communities from arriving at an agreed upon integration. In short, he said, "very simply, if NATO, that is, the High Representative, can make laws without consultation with anyone and can remove anyone from power in this country, he does not need any other instruments of power."

Interview with General Jovan Divjak[6]

During our 2004 interview in Sarajevo, General Jovan Divjak lamented that government in Bosnia and Hercegovina was "not functioning." Divjak is a local hero in Bosnia. Born in Belgrad to Serb parents but with ancestral roots in Bosnia, he chose to fight the war on the side of Bosnia, against Serb and Bosnian Serb soldiers with whom he had spent his professional life. He is wanted as a war criminal in Republika Srpska and Serbia, but in the Federation of Bosnia and Hercegovina he is honoured not only for his courageous service in the war but also as the patron of an orphanage for children bereaved during the conflict. His autobiography, *Sarajevo mon amour* (Divjak 2004), is a hit in France as well as in Bosnia. Our discussion was about corruption and criminal behaviour at all levels. He commented: "There is a black or a grey market, so-called because there are individuals who are buying and selling and the state has no benefit from that, they are not paying taxes or anything like that." And he stated baldly: "I fear that the Bosnia-Hercegovinian government is corrupt."

We were sitting in a booth at a restaurant in the centre of Sarajevo during this interview in 2004. He pointed to a café nearby and said, "A young man owns that café. He was a war profiteer. What did he do to deserve to have it? The state is not ready to fight crime. They, themselves, are a part of the criminal structure, the ones who are in power." After some discussion of international organized crime, he observed: "the mafia has no nationality, they are a nation of their own."

According to Divjak, "During the war some people obtained a lot of money, they got rich partly by entering other people's premises or stealing their property." There is also the drug trade and trafficking in children and women. The money illegally obtained might expand legal businesses such as car dealerships. A Bosnian Croatian who was a member of the presidency was arrested and finally imprisoned on criminal charges, but many are not caught. Divjak names several who have become rich: "These people were members of government until two years ago, so it cannot possibly be that they were not connected to the mafia at the time they were in the government." Another example is the Hercegovina bank. As he says:

It was receiving funds from Zagreb for the salaries of Croatian soldiers, but the funds were just put away somewhere and nobody knows what happened to them ... To a certain extent during the war those who were in charge of ammunition, guns and food and so on were in league with the mafia. Now, a process has started to investigate troops who were selling guns in Kosovo after the conclusion of the war here.

And the general has other insights into the wars:

When the [Bosnian] Croatians were bombing Muslim properties in Mostar, the [Muslim] mayor asked Ratko Mladić (Serb military leader later charged with war crimes but still free as this is written) to bomb the Croatian ammunition storage. In Ženica in 1993 the Muslims and [Bosnian] Croats were at war. The Serbs had no salt and the Muslims had no ammunition. So, the Serbs said, give us two truckloads of salt and we will bomb the Croatians. And so they did.

During the war here the black humour was that one life was worth twenty-five Pfenigs because that is what one bullet was worth. But those who stole ammunition from somewhere and had it for themselves were selling it at three (Deutsch)Marks per bullet, so it was a huge, huge business. The United States was involved in supplying ammunition, but all of the ammunition trading was going through Croatia during the time of the war. And it is a fact that the Croatians kept for themselves one-third to one-half of everything that was going through to Bosnia ... The people who are in power are the ones who are responsible for the war and they are cooperating extremely well with each other.

NGOS re: Human Rights

There are several international and local NGOs in Sarajevo and other towns in BIH dealing with human rights violations. Their reports cite numerous issues, particularly respecting women, children, and religious groups. In confidential interviews, their members spoke of the corruption of the police and elected officials. Even when the war is long over, they said, and even with media exposés, the police do not act to stop criminal behaviour. Repeating the same regrets as did General Divjak, they speak of a "mafia" whose members have purchased formerly public businesses under the new privatization arrangements. One said he could name the largest businesses in Sarajevo but could not find out who owns them or where they got their money. The situation was not, in his opinion, getting worse, but "people are losing patience, especially young people, and morality is completely shattered. The social and cultural values that once guided us are gone."

DOMESTIC COURTS IN BIH

Domestic courts in Bosnia and Hercegovina are following the lead of the ICTY and Western legal procedures. They face a classic dilemma: they have little capacity to handle too many cases; their judiciary is weak; and they have insufficient funds to maintain the judiciary and the courts. FBIH is willing to conduct trials, even though hampered by incapacity; however, prior to 2005, the RS was balking at the prospect.[7] The Human Rights Chamber under the Human Rights Commission, mandated under the Dayton Agreement, was supposed to operate for five years after its signing. In June 2002, the Office of the High Representative disbanded the Chamber but did not complete the transfer of some ten thousand remaining cases to the Constitutional Court until December 2003. The Constitutional Court was not yet robust: there were many difficulties in appointing judges and dealing with the overload of cases (International Crisis Group 2002). However, the War Crimes Chamber (WCC) in Bosnia finally began operations in Sarajevo in March, 2005. It took on a limited number of cases from the ICTY, acting as one of the new hybrid courts mixing domestic and international law. It will concentrate on alleged crimes of lower-level perpetrators, while the ICTY continues with the higher-level leaders (Freeman 2004a). By way of indicating the kind of cases being transferred from the ICTY to the WCC in Bosnia, the first boxed item shown below is provided by the electronic public information services of the international court.

(Exclusively for the use of the media. Not an official document)

The Hague, 5 April 2007
RH/MOW/1153e

The Tribunal's Referral Bench today rendered a decision to refer the case of Milan and Sredoje Lukić to Bosnia and Herzegovina in accordance with Rule 11*bis* of the Tribunal's Rules of Procedure and Evidence. This decision can be appealed.

According to the indictment, Milan Lukić was the leader of the "White Eagles" or "Avengers", a group of local Bosnian Serb paramilitaries in Višegrad, south-eastern Bosnia and Herzegovina which worked with local police and military units in exacting a reign of terror upon the local Bosnian Muslim population during the 1992–1995 conflict. Sredoje Lukić, Milan Lukić's cousin, was a member of the unit.

Milan and Sredoje Lukić are charged with multiple crimes, including murdering approximately 70 Bosnian Muslim women, children and elderly men in a house on Pionirska Street in Višegrad by barricading the victims in one room of the house, setting the house on fire and then firing automatic weapons at those people who tried to escape through the windows, killing some and injuring others.

In addition, they are charged with murdering approximately 70 Bosnian Muslim women, children and elderly in a house in the village of Bikavać, near Višegrad, by forcing the victims into the house, barricading all the exits and throwing in several explosive devices.

Milan and Sredoje Lukić are also accused of beating Bosnian Muslim men who were detained in the detention camp at the Uzamnica military barracks in Višegrad.

Milan Lukić is separately charged with several other counts of murder, according to which he on multiple occasions led groups of Bosnian Muslim men to the bank of Drina river near Višegrad where he murdered them. He is also charged with brutally murdering a Bosnian Muslim woman in the Potok neighbourhood of Višegrad.

By way of showing how the two courts interact, this same case was subsequently returned to the ICTY for reasons explained in another press release:

(Exclusively for the use of the media. Not an official document)

The Hague, 20 July 2007
MH/MOW/PR1176e

The Tribunal's Referral Bench today rendered a decision revoking the referral of Sredoje Lukić's case to Bosnia and Herzegovina. This means that the cases of Milan Lukić and Sredoje Lukić will be tried jointly at the ICTY. The Referral Bench considered that this was in the interest of justice, as the two cases are factually very closely related. It also noted the Prosecution's argument that separate trials would have risked increasing the trauma for witnesses, who would have had to testify twice.

The Referral Bench had originally on 5 April 2007 issued a decision referring the case of Milan Lukić and Sredoje Lukić to Bosnia and Herzegovina. Milan Lukić, however, appealed that decision, and his appeal was last week granted by the Tribunal's Appeals Chamber, on the grounds that the gravity of crimes charged, in combination with the level of responsibility, demands that he be tried before the Tribunal. The Appeals Chamber considered that the Security Council had intended for the Tribunal to try at least some paramilitary leaders, and based on the allegations in the indictment, Milan Lukić would be perhaps the most significant paramilitary leader tried by the Tribunal to date.

Sredoje Lukić's transfer to Bosnia and Herzegovina had been suspended pending the outcome of Milan Lukić's appeal. In its 11 July decision, the Appeals Chamber held that in light of the fact that Milan Lukić would be tried at the Tribunal, it would be open to the Referral Bench to reconsider its decision relating to Sredoje Lukić. The Referral Bench issued today's decision revoking Sredoje Lukić's referral after his defence, the Prosecution, and the Government of Bosnia and Herzegovina had all agreed that the two cases should be tried together.

According to the indictment, Milan Lukić was the leader of the "White Eagles" or "Avengers", a group of local Bosnian Serb paramilitaries in Višegrad, south-eastern Bosnia and Herzegovina which worked with local police and military units in exacting a reign of terror upon the local Bosnian Muslim population during the 1992–1995 conflict. Sredoje Lukić, Milan Lukić's cousin, was a member of the unit.

Milan and Sredoje Lukić are charged with multiple crimes, including murdering approximately 70 Bosnian Muslim women, children and elderly men in a house on Pionirska Street in Višegrad by barricading the victims in one room of the house, setting the house on fire and then firing automatic weapons at those people who tried to escape through the windows, killing some and injuring others.

In addition, they are charged with murdering approximately 70 Bosnian Muslim women, children and elderly in a house in the village of Bikavac, near Višegrad, by forcing the victims into the house, barricading all the exits and throwing in several explosive devices.

Milan and Sredoje Lukić are also accused of beating Bosnian Muslim men who were detained in the detention camp at the Uzamnica military barracks in Višegrad.

Milan Lukić is separately charged with several other counts of murder, according to which he on multiple occasions led groups of Bosnian Muslim men to the bank of Drina river near Višegrad where he murdered them. He is also charged with brutally murdering a Bosnian Muslim woman in the Potok neighbourhood of Višegrad.

Milan and Sredoje Lukić were initially indicted together with Mitar Vasiljević. He was tried at the Tribunal and sentenced to 15 years' imprisonment by a final judgement on 25 February 2004.

The Tribunal has to date referred a total of 8 cases involving 13 persons to courts in the former Yugoslavia, mostly to Bosnia and Herzegovina. No further cases are under consideration by the Referral Bench.

*****

The full text of the Decision is available on the Tribunal's website.

Courtroom proceedings can be followed on the Tribunal's website www.un. org/icty.

The Bosnian court also has to deal with postwar cases. Among the many forms of corruption today is the trafficking in human sex slaves. Young women from Eastern European countries are tricked into service in the brothels and nightclubs of Bosnia. A case that went to trial in January 2004 concentrated on Milorad Milaković and seventeen others who were indicted on eighty-five criminal allegations, including conspiracy, organized crime, trafficking in humans, sexual slavery, human smuggling, and international procurement in prostitution. The judges in the case came from the United States, France, and Bosnia. The Canadian prosecutor to the state court of Bosnia-Hercegovina drew up the charges. He noted: "This has never happened before on this scale ... The drafting of the indictment and the detention of the principal accused has never occurred in Bosnia on that scale."[8]

The prosecutor in this case was one of several who were inserted into the Bosnian process by other countries. They have full authority in Bosnian state courts. The understanding is that they are less likely to be influenced by local gangs than are domestic lawyers and judges. The same Canadian quoted above, Jonathan Ratel, said that, in his opinion, "Organized crime and corruption in Bosnia-Herzegovina comprises the single greatest threat to regional peace

and security ... These criminals are opportunists, extremely organized, very aggressive and pose a significant threat ... Organized
crime in the Balkans reaches into every level of government, civilian institution, police and security service."9

War crime prosecutions began to take place in Republika Srpska
towards the end of 2005. Up to that time, only two war crimes trials
had taken place in the RS, compared to over fifty in the FBiH.
Within the next year, trials were scheduled in Banja Luca, Trebinje,
and other areas of the RS. This is in part due to a change of perspective in the RS regarding war crimes, but it also has to do with
the creation of the new WCC, which will require the participation of
both parts of BiH. Human Rights Watch notes that the impetus towards prosecuting war crimes in the RS creates opportunities for reform of the justice system. The reforms might include more
international funding for criminal trials, more specialist prosecutors, assistance for better police forces, and more support staff (Human Rights Watch 2006a).[10]

THE ICTY

As of mid-2006, the impact of the ICTY on the Federation of Bosnia
and Hercegovina has been profound, but it has had little impact on
Republika Srpska (South East Europe Democracy Support 2002).[11]
Two important cases addressed the killings at Srebrenica in 1995.
The former RS president, Biljana Plavsić pleaded guilty and accepted
an eleven-year prison sentence for her role in the Bosnian conflict.
She is a rare Bosnian Serb to take responsibility for what happened
during the war; she refused, however, to name others who had participated (ICTY 2003b; ICTY 2003c; Combs 2003). In the case *Prosecutor v. Krstić*, the ICTY Appeals Chamber unanimously ruled it was an
act of genocide. The Chamber stated:

By seeking to eliminate a part of the Bosnian Muslims, the
Bosnian Serb forces committed genocide. They targeted for
extinction the 40,000 Bosnian Muslims living in Srebrenica,
a group which was emblematic of the Bosnian Muslims in
general ... The Appeals Chamber states unequivocally that
the law condemns, in appropriate terms, the deep and lasting
injury inflicted, and calls the massacre at Srebrenica by its
proper name: genocide. Those responsible will bear this

stigma, and it will serve as a warning to those who may in future contemplate the commission of such a heinous act. (ICTY 2004)

Other indictments at the ICTY include those against Bosnian Serbs for the bombardment of the civilian population of Sarajevo (ICTY 2003a);[12] against Bosnian Serbs for numerous violations of international humanitarian law, including torture at the Omarska concentration camp in June 1992 (ICTY 2001); and against Ratko Mladić (ICTY 2002) and many others, Croats and Muslims as well as Serbs. One after another the indictments give a description of events at a particular place or places, dates, and what is called a "statement of facts." Mladić, not yet captured, is described as follows:

> In June of 1991, Ratko MLADIĆ was posted to Knin as Commander of the 9th Corps of the JNA, during fighting between the JNA and Croatian forces. On 4 October 1991, he was promoted to General Major by the President of the Socialist Federal Republic of Yugoslavia (SFRY). On 24 April 1992, Ratko MLADIĆ was promoted to the rank of General Lieutenant, and on 25 April 1992 he was assigned to the post of Chief of Staff/Deputy Commander of the Second Military District Headquarters of the JNA in Sarajevo. He assumed that post on 9 May 1992. On 10 May 1992 Ratko MLADIĆ assumed the command of the Second Military District Headquarters of the JNA ... On 12 May 1992 Ratko MLADIĆ was appointed Commander of the Main Staff of the VRS [Serbian Republic of Bosnia and Hercegovina/Republika Srpska], a position he held until at least 22 December 1996. On 24 June 194, Ratko MLADIĆ was promoted to the rank of General Colonel.

After describing Mladić's role in Srebrenica, the Bosnian Krajina, and eastern Bosnia, the prosecution zeros in on his command in Srebrenica and Žepa. His position as second in command to Radovan Karadižić (then president of the Bosnian Serb Assembly) is described by way of indicating his leadership role in the events and his individual criminal responsibility. The indictment frequently uses the phrasing "Mladić, acting individually or in concert with other participants in the joint criminal enterprise," as in the following charge:

General Ratko MLADIĆ, acting individually or in concert with other participants in the joint criminal enterprise, planned, instigated, ordered, committed or otherwise aided and abetted the planning, preparation or execution of the intentional partial destruction of the Bosnian Muslim national, ethnical, racial or religious group, as such, from Ključ, Kotor Varos, Prijedor, Sanski Most, and Srebrenica.

In July 2007, the ICTY undertook a new case against a Bosnian Muslim army chief. By virtue of his command responsibility, Rasim Delić has been charged for the murder, cruel treatment, and rape committed by his subordinate forces. He is charged with failing to take necessary and reasonable measures to punish soldiers who executed captured Bosnian Croat civilians and soldiers in two villages in Travnik municipality in central Bosnia, and with failing to prevent the torture and murders committed by his soldiers at Kamenica Camp, a detention centre for captured Bosnian Serb soldiers in central Bosnia.[13] This case is being tried while I write, so its conclusion cannot be included here, but that it is taking place demonstrates that all of the combatants in the Bosnian wars are subject to international and national court proceedings. Moreover, it is a particularly interesting indictment because this commander is not being tried for murder, rape, or torture he personally committed: rather, he is being charged for failing to prevent soldiers under his command from committing such acts.

Amnesty International, 2005

Amnesty International's annual report in 2005 (covering 2004) stated:

Impunity for war crimes and crimes against humanity committed during the 1992–95 war continued to be widespread. Thousands of "disappearances" were still unresolved. While perpetrators of wartime violations continued to enjoy impunity, victims and their families were denied access to justice and redress. Lack of cooperation with the International Criminal Tribunal for the former Yugoslavia Tribunal, particularly by the Republika Srpska (RS) was a major obstacle to justice. The efforts of the authorities to tackle impunity in proceedings before domestic courts remained

largely insufficient, although some war crimes trials were
conducted. (Amnesty International 2005, 58–9)

The report for 2006 was no gentler in its narrative about Bosnia
and Hercegovina:

> Impunity for war crimes and crimes against humanity during the
> 1992–95 war was widespread. Thousands of "disappearances"
> were still unresolved. Victims and their families were denied ac-
> cess to justice. Lack of full co-operation with the International
> Criminal Tribunal for the former Yugoslavia (Tribunal), particu-
> larly by the Republika Srpska (RS) remained an obstacle to jus-
> tice. Efforts to tackle impunity in proceedings before domestic
> courts remained largely insufficient, although some war crimes
> trials were conducted. The first convictions for war crimes com-
> mitted by Bosnian Serbs were passed by RS courts. Of the one
> million refugees and internally displaced people who had re-
> turned to their homes since the end of the war, many continued
> to face discrimination. (Amnesty International 2006, 73)

A TENTATIVE ASSESSMENT

Various perspectives reported above regarding the situation in
Bosnia-Hercegovina were sobering in their acknowledgment of corruption and ethnic divisions. Even in different ethnic groups the
blame placed on the international community was widespread. No
one I interviewed expressed any support for international institutions or gratitude for the number of lives saved during the war. One
has to recognize that these wartime interventions were not spectacular successes and that many since then are of dubious merit. The
state apparatus was unwieldy; the combination of external governors and local leaders from three mutually distrustful communities
was not working well. The persistence of ethnicity as a determinant
of virtually everything was destructive; it fed distrust and paranoia,
and it kept the "international mafia" in business.

The most problematic aspect of the Dayton Agreement and the
process since 1995 is the border between the FBiH and the RS. Although Republika Srpska has begun to relax its opposition to accountability for war crimes, it is still (as of March 2007) hesitating to
integrate its police force with that of the FBiH and is not yet prepared

to publicly call the Srebrenica events a genocide, despite two court statements to that effect. Leaders in the RS are still tied to Serbia, still looking for a union to the east rather than the one they have now. Ironically, what is to the east is crumbling. Its internal divisions are not ethnic (except as imagined in Montenegro, which has voted to exit the partnership with Serbia, as described in the next chapter). The major cleavage there is between a majority who cling to the belief in a Greater Serbia and a minority who wish to be citizens of the world. The RS is still allied with the majority of Serbs, all the evidence of decay in that position notwithstanding.

Meanwhile, BiH is moving towards negotiations for the country's Stabilization and Association Agreement with Europe, and if it manages to persuade the Republika Srpska to accept the integration of police and judicial functions as well as military forces, it would be well on its way to normalizing relationships as an autonomous state within the European Union (United Nations Security Council 2006).

But population data suggest another issue that no one discussed. According to UN 2005 population estimates for Bosnia, the growth rate is 0.13, one of the lowest of the 230 countries on the list (ranking at 193rd). This is far from a rate that would allow the population to replace itself, and with emigration of young people still advancing Bosnia could cease to exist as a secondary consequence of the war: depopulation. It might be small comfort for its people to know that Serbia has the same rate. (UN, 2006).

Despite all of its difficulties, the Federation of Bosnia and Hercegovina has begun to dig its way out of the mess. Its physical infrastructure was not destroyed, though many buildings and some towns were deeply shattered. Its institutional structure, divided and fraught with problems, is functioning again. The Sarajevo Museum of Archaeology is an example: despite falling plaster and lack of funding, the doors remain open and visitors can see artifacts of a long history. Dr Žilka Vejžagić, the curator, suffered through the siege of Sarajevo. Herself Croatian and her schoolteacher husband Bosniak, they emigrated to Canada, but she soon realized she couldn't abandon her home: she returned and works long hours with very little pay. This is human capital, and despite the wars, FBiH has enough of it to keep its social life alive. If the integration of military forces succeeds, perhaps the Republika Srpska will eventually come on board in other ways.

Serbia and Montenegro, 1992–2007

One might see the Yugoslav wars as a manifestation of the enormous transition taking place in the Balkans, as in Eastern Europe more generally. It was simultaneously moving from a centrally planned economy to a capitalist one, and from a predominantly rural to a more urban society. The transition was occurring within a single generation, whereas in Western Europe it occurred over three to four centuries (and is not complete everywhere even now). Martinez and Diaz (1996) suggested a similar rapid shift as a way of explaining the conflict in Chile during the 1970s. Some societies managed to bridge the gaps without excessive violence, and some did not; but surely the difficulties in Yugoslavia were exacerbated by the complicated history of empires occupying the territory, creating ethnic/religious identities that were in conflict with one another. Tito's attempt to build a federation was possibly doomed as long as these identities persisted, but one has to credit Serbians with the continued faith that the whole of the Balkans could be sustained as a single country in the post-communist era. Their problem was that other Yugoslavs with different identities did not share the Serbian project, and Serb leaders – along with the leaders of Croatia and Bosnia at the time – were unable to imagine a future together without those identities.

Since the wars, which were disastrous for Serbia, this former republic, unlike Slovenia and Croatia, has slightly improved its economy but has not managed to transform itself. Partly, this is due to the geographic advantages enjoyed by the two northern republics; partly, it is due to continuing failures of political and economic leadership in Serbia itself; and, partly, it is due to inconsistent international policies towards Serbia. The World Bank, the IMF, the United States, the European Union (through the OSCE and component states), Russia, and the United Nations have all participated, in some form or another, in attempts to reconstruct this portion of the former Yugoslavia. But as they vacillate between trying to enable Serbia to survive and trying to punish it for failing to give up war leaders indicted by the ICTY, they have not so far helped it to establish a new identity as an independent state.

This chapter is concerned primarily with Serbia following its wars in Croatia and Bosnia. It does not dwell on events in the Kosovo battle of 1999, except to note NATO's intervention and the impact of international reactions to Serbia under Milošević. Rather, it is concerned with how Serbs and the Serbian state have coped with the disintegration of Yugoslavia and with the role of the state in that process.

FEDERAL REPUBLIC OF YUGOSLAVIA

The Federal Republic of Yugoslavia (FRY), comprising Serbia and Montenegro as united but separate components, was established in 1992 following the disintegration of the Socialist Federal Republic of Yugoslavia. The United Nations, the United States, and other states did not recognize it as the successor to the former Yugoslavia because there was disagreement on the disposition of federal assets and liabilities, including the national debt.

Serbia had not itself been seriously disabled in physical terms by its wars with Croatia and Bosnia. Its young men had suffered as armed male forces usually do in battles, but in no part of the territory had Serbians suffered the kind of horrors experienced in Bosnia between 1992 and 1995. So the issue here was not large-scale reconstruction of the physical infrastructure, although, as time went on, the physical infrastructure deteriorated because no funding was available for its renewal. The social infrastructure that was in need of mending was related mainly to state institutions, government, and the economy as discussed below. From 1995 to about 2000, Serbia's economy declined due to international sanctions that were kept in place as long as the Serb state failed to produce leading candidates for criminal proceedings, including Slobodan Milošević. The state introduced a stabilization program that reduced inflation and increased foreign reserves toward the end of the 1990s, with modestly positive results in per capita growth rates appearing during the early 2000s. Ups and downs during the next few years left much of the rural population and refugees in poverty but urban dwellers enjoyed some improvements in their standard of living.

Because he was not allowed, under the Serbian Constitution, to have more than two terms as president of Serbia, Slobodan Milošević took on the presidency of the FRY in July 1997. His place as president of Serbia was taken over by a close ally.

Kosovo and NATO

As Serbia moved towards confrontation with Albanians in the autonomous Serb province of Kosovo, the West became increasingly belligerent towards Serbia and Milošević. From 1996 to 1999, Serb forces clashed with a guerrilla militia calling itself the Kosovo Liberation Army (KLA). Albanians comprised over 90 percent of the population in Kosovo, while Serbs formed a small minority of the population. Westerners were generally ill-informed about internal events there, and, because of their experience of Milošević's Serbia during the Croatian and Bosnian wars, they assumed that Serbs were responsible for atrocities against Albanians. As well, in the mid-1990s, the West had not yet developed its anti-Muslim stance, so the fact that Albanians were Muslims was not then an issue. Observers' accounts are mixed as to whether Serbs or the KLA began the wars and as to which civilians suffered most, but subsequent reflection in the West suggests that KLA atrocities were underreported and generally misunderstood at the time.

In 1999, NATO mounted air strikes against the FRY, with US foreign secretary Madeleine Albright declaring that this war was no longer an internal matter for the FRY. Although Belgrade experienced relatively little physical damage due to NATO bombing, the war produced substantial economic damage for Serbia as well as physical damage in rural areas. The limited foreign aid that had trickled in before the war was cut off following hostilities in 1999.

Milošević and Djindjić

The FRY Constitution called for an election in two stages, whereby candidates were to be eliminated in the initial stage and only the leading candidates for the presidency were to continue to the second round. In 2000, the same year that the UN finally admitted the FRY to membership, Vojislav Koštunica was ahead of Milošević, but neither was able to command 50 percent of the vote. Koštunica was favoured by NATO powers, but perhaps for that very reason it was possible, as claimed by Milošević allies, that many people who had voted otherwise on the first round would vote for Milošević on the second. On such grounds, Milošević rejected claims of an initial round victory for Koštunica. This led to mass demonstrations in Belgrade on 5 October that went on for eighty-eight days and brought about the eventual collapse of Milošević's authority.

Koštunica took office as Yugoslav president in October. He had essentially launched an unconstitutional coup, backed by Western powers: it might not have won the second round. This continues to be a rallying cry for nationalists who had backed Milošević. The demonstrations were reported in the Western press as evidence that the population wanted democracy and was eager to be rid of its long-serving helmsman.

Žoran Djindjić, the candidate of the Democratic Serbia (DS) party, was elected prime minister of Serbia on the Democratic Opposition of Serbia (DOS) ticket with Koštunica as president of the FRY. But soon Koštunica and Djindjić were in conflict over how to reform the country. Koštunica was labelled "nationalist" in contrast to Djindjić, who was labelled "pragmatic."[1] In 2001, Djindjić handed over Milošević to The Hague, after charging him with abuse of power and corruption, in contravention of the Constitution (put through by Milošević) prohibiting extradition of Yugoslav citizens. Koštunica formally opposed the transfer.

Now orchestrated street demonstrations proclaimed support for Milošević and shouted "treason" to the world, but how representative the marchers were of the larger population is open to debate, and voting patterns since then indicated that no one political position prevailed. Contrary to what the West would have preferred, a substantial part of the population clung to the position that Milošević was still their leader. And another substantial part of the population was either politically apathetic or deliberately boycotted electoral politics.

Following the handover of Milošević to the ICTY, the European Community, the United States, and the World Bank between them pledged between $1.28 billion to $1.3 billion (varying estimates in different newscasts) to rebuild the Serbian economy. But much of this went to international creditors, who were owed a total of about $12.2 billion. So only about $800 million actually reached Yugoslavia for the rebuilding of roads and bridges. It wouldn't pay much of the teachers' salaries or those of medical and other public servants. At the time, before Djindjić was assassinated, the World Bank spokesperson observed that "the country is in total chaos, there are major problems in every aspect of the organization of the economy."[2] Unemployment in 2001 reached 30 percent, and foreign and domestic debt was far beyond the capacities for internal generation of funds. Nonetheless, after Serbia surrendered Milošević to The Hague in 2001, foreign embassies reopened and the FRY regained a seat in the OSCE. Then the UN began to cooperate and the IMF and the World Bank reentered the picture. A modest economic recuperation began.

Presidential elections in 2002 failed twice because of insufficient voter turnout (at that time, Serbian law required the turnout of over 50 percent of registered voters), signalling either apathy and dismay with the politicians and their seemingly eternal squabbles or a disinclination to engage in democratic politics.

SERBIA AND MONTENEGRO

By February 2003, the effort to sustain the FRY became too difficult, and their respective leaders agreed to create a looser confederation with a new constitutional charter under the name "Serbia and Montenegro."

Assassination of Djindjić

Though by international standards one would not have considered Serbian prime minister Djindjić a radical, by Serbian standards he was too liberal: he was assassinated on 12 March 2003. A massive crackdown during the state of emergency following the murder, with some four thousand people arrested, resulted in indictment. The alleged assassin, police specialist Žveždan Jovanović (Žveki), was a member of the Red Berets and held the police rank of lieutenant colonel. He had been active in the Yugoslav wars of the 1990s and claimed he had killed Djindjić as a traitor to Serbia (because Djindjić had sent Milošević to The Hague). The murder was allegedly organized by Milorad Ulemek (nicknamed Legija in honour of his service in the French Foreign Legion), an ex-commander of the special police unit founded by Milošević's secret service and affiliated with the Serbian mafia. Ulemek had already been sentenced for his part in two attempted assassinations of opposition politician Vuk Drašković (who survived to become the foreign minister) in 1999 and 2000, and for assassinating Ivan Stambolić, the former president of Serbia, in August 2000. He had been the trainer for the Special Operations Unit (the JSO), a paramilitary force known as the Red Berets that had been prominent in the wars in Croatia, Bosnia, and Kosovo.

The Stambolić case had come before a special court in Belgrade. For the first time, Slobodan Milošević was directly implicated in the crimes of the Red Berets. Rade Marković, head of the secret service under Milošević, was earlier found guilty of having hired Ulemek for these executions. The trial for the assassination of Djindjić was started in 2004 and resumed in September 2005. Ulemek was sentenced to forty years imprisonment, including fifteen years for the attempted murder of Drašković. Marković was given fifteen years for his part in the murders. An alleged co-conspirator, Aleksandar Simović, was arrested in Belgrade in November 2006.

Elections, 2003

The vice-president of Djindjić's DS party took over the prime minister's position and new elections were scheduled for November 2003. Again, elections were declared invalid because of insufficient voter turnout. Under the new Charter, most federal functions and authorities devolved to the republic level. Milošević's Socialist Party (an offshoot of the former Communist Party) won twenty-two seats in the December 2003 elections for Parliament. Milošević's colleague in penitentiary at The Hague, Vojislav Šešelj, won eighty-two seats for the Serbian Radical Party. The interim leader of the Serbian Radical Party, Tomislav Nikolić, seeing that this was the largest single win among the parties, credited "Šešelj and other Serb inmates in The Hague." A minority government coalition between Koštunica's Democratic Party of Serbia (DSS) and several other democratic parties prevented the extremists from taking over Parliament, but it was, and continues to be, an uphill battle for moderates.

INTERVIEWS AND SOCIAL DEVELOPMENTS
IN SERBIA, 2004

My fieldwork in Serbia began in 2004. I encountered in Belgrade, once the capital of Yugoslavia, a generally poor infrastructure. Although the downtown core had the patina of other European cities – cafes, outdoor restaurants in good weather, hotels, shops, and service providers of many kinds – the legacy of the bureaucratic state lingered. I was often reminded of Soviet cities during the 1970s and early 1980s. The elderly gentleman at the cashier's desk in my aging hotel said he could not possibly provide me with an interim bill that would allow me to check the charges: his computer could only provide the final one when I was ready to leave. He had to have my passport and could not return it until the bill was paid. Room service could not supply a plug for the bath, sorry, they didn't have any. The elevator was not working today. No, madam, you cannot have your breakfast at tables near the windows of the hotel restaurant, those seats are reserved (apparently for the men in dark suits). These were useful reminders: this society was only yesterday released from the centralized state; much of the city was still controlled by the same bureaucrats, now privatized.

I could not escape an atmosphere of profound dejection that seemed to envelop Belgrade. Taxi drivers were belligerent, hated American tourists (as a Canadian, I'm always tagged as "one of them"), though they hated Europeans even more. The European Community accepted Slovenia in 2004, and it held out a potential invitation to Croatia if it cleaned up its human rights record. But Serbia was not even on the horizon. "They meddle," said one driver. "They don't understand," said another. "They don't understand" might have been closer to the truth. It is very difficult for an outsider to understand the mindset of a society whose leader is in jail at The Hague, charged with crimes against humanity, yet whose people (at least many of them) voted for him even so.

Bosnians will explain that they had to resist Serbia because otherwise Serbs would have dominated and transformed Bosnia into a Serbian province. Serbians, however, find this kind of thinking muddled. "They are all Serbs" is a frequent statement. They are, indeed, from the same roots, all South Slavs originally, but the history of four empires interconnecting on the territory of the former Yugoslavia has created something different for all of them, even though Serbs cannot fathom why others choose a different path. Had these internal wars been avoided, the country might have been able to move from a centrally planned economy to a market economy and to make the transition from the political leadership of Tito to a full parliamentary or republican democracy. But the wars did happen, and before they happened the elites of the various regions had reached an impasse. A virulent form of ethnic nationalism replaced communism. My interviews in April 2004 evoked dispirited responses to the political impasse in the country. The situation is such that most people do not want to be identified, though they may be willing to express themselves to outsiders. Typical of the segment of the population that would prefer a more liberal democracy, one individual observed:

> After the outcome of the December parliamentary elections, Serbian society has been backsliding. As you know we have a kind of restored Milošević regime. Actually we have managed to backslide to the time that brought about Milošević, so I think we need to pinpoint the threats … There is always a need throughout history to blame things on someone else. At the beginning of the Yugoslav crisis we had Slovenians, we had Croats, we had whoever to blame. We had the international community and then Milošević to blame. Milošević was not the only one to blame for what happened to Serbia. I hate to use the term "what happened to Serbia" actually – because the population encouraged him. They didn't blame him for the war until he lost it. So with Milošević gone we got a parliament and the new government with Premier Djindjić. And all at once there was another person to blame. Djindjić was primarily blamed for having a vision of another Serbia. He had a vision of what Serbia has to do to join the mainstream and that was misunderstood. He tried to privatize some of the state assets.

Another interviewee agreed with this general perspective:

> Since his assassination his successors are trying to recover whatever was sold, and that tells foreign investors to back off. So now Serbia has restored the *ancien regime*. Serbians are deeply afraid of otherness. They are afraid of everything foreign. Reforms are seen as something imposed on them rather than something they

have to do to become part of the European realm. There was a court case to judge the men who assassinated Djindjić. Several men turned up wearing red berets, the uniform of the paramilitaries who fought in Croatia. Were they trying to intimidate the judge, the jurors, the witnesses? Was it a way of giving support for the genocide that the Red Berets were involved in during the wars, and for the general who was convicted of genocide at The Hague? But people admired these guys, and the police refuse to acknowledge that this was a threatening gesture, they refuse to acknowledge any involvement in crime.

Yet a third person said that Serbs had not yet realized their guilt in the Yugoslav war: "They did not witness the victims or their crimes. So in the end, only the NGOs actually talked about the crimes." As a consequence, this individual concluded, Serbs think they are being forced or blackmailed into giving up indicted war criminals to The Hague. They blamed Djindjić and the international community for this: "They do not want to blame themselves, to accept responsibility for what was done. So now they simply wash their hands and say, 'Oh no, we never supported Milošević's ideas.'"

Said another, referring to the Djinjić trials: "Well now there is no one else to blame so they criticize dissonant voices and [human rights] NGOs. Serbia has not made any progress and will not unless it breaks with its past – unless it faces its responsibility for the past developments. Serbians don't want to change. Deeply underneath they are nationalists. They are conservative and they do not want, they cannot change. They cannot perceive the world any other way."

The problem of punishment inequities is noted by many Serbs. One who expressed his opinion said, "If horrible war crimes happened on all sides, why are they [the international community] punishing people unequally? Serb commandants go to the Hague, okay, but why don't others go as well? Serbian citizens are left with the impression that the international community is more strict with the Serbian side than with the others."

Croatian Serbs who fled to Serbia and who attempted to return have often discovered that their properties in Croatia (primarily in the Krajina region) have been taken over by others and that they have to endure legal battles to reclaim or reoccupy previous homes. In some cases, their homes have been destroyed and need to be rebuilt. The Social Democratic Forum (SDF) in Serbia represents their interests to the Croatian government. Its spokespersons say that Croatian laws discriminate against Serb refugees. The SDF also tries to obtain accommodation in Serbia for those who stay, but there is no legal arrangement for integrating them into Serbian society, and Serbia lacks the economic capacity to look after them. Many are elderly and they are poor; they escaped with no assets to enable them either to live in Serbia or to emigrate elsewhere.

Organization for Security and Cooperation in Europe

The European Union has recreated intervention in the form of a mission to provide assistance and expertise to the Yugoslav authorities in the areas of democratization, protection of human rights and minorities, and media development. Its central task is to advise on the implementation of legislation, development, and processes for democratic institutions, including, particularly, law enforcement agencies and the judiciary. According to its 2003 report, the mission redirected its efforts in law enforcement, following the assassination of Prime Minister Djindjić in March 2003, to the fight against organized crime.[3] This project is preemptive in nature, attempting to prevent further internal wars between the component republics of the former Yugoslavia. The OSCE has offices throughout the region, but in the rump state of Serbia and Montenegro it has been particularly active since the conclusion of the wars.

The Law on War Crimes adopted by the Serbian government in April 2003 was generated through a supportive relationship with the OSCE, and investigations of war crimes and support for war crimes trials began in Serbia early in 2003. Prison reform measures and the training of trainers among prison staff and prison governors are all part of the OSCE investment in Serbia. The OSCE documents applaud these initiatives despite the dismal record of the courts and police in actually implementing the war crimes investigations and trials.

A Serbian anti-corruption council was established by the Serb government in December 2001, again with the support of the OSCE, but it has not reduced corruption. At the same time, the OSCE organized roundtables, seminars, training, and special programs for Serbian officials to enable democratization and the incorporation of refugees. Among the developments supported by the mission was the Charter on Human and Minority Rights in the State Union Constitution for Serbia and Montenegro. Further, a human rights task force was established in 2003. Special measures for working with Roma were created in the National Strategy for their integration. Programs initiated by the mission addressed trafficking in human beings. Other measures were actively implemented to develop media capacities and to introduce measures to sustain the environment. A major effort was introduced for ecological conservation and security, with European mentors trying to develop local processes to implement and monitor conservation and environmental protection measures. Opposition voices argue that these "mentors" are doing nothing of the sort. NATO bombing in Serbia in 1999 (as is the tendency of bombing anywhere) was destructive of flora, fauna, rivers, and human industrial complexes. The particulars notwithstanding, the actual conflict is over jurisdiction: some Serbs want to know: does the OSCE have some god-given right to tell Serbs how to behave? Given the record of NATO and Europe vis-à-vis Serbia, why should Serbs kow-tow to Europe's initiatives?

Independent Media and Popular Responses

Although the state media took a nationalist line, after 1989 there were, in fact, several independent media outlets that provided information on the war in Sarajevo and, belatedly, what happened in Srebrenica. Serbs who wanted news could get it, but many chose not to know. There was a big demonstration in Belgrade called "Black Flowers for Sarajevo."[4] The demonstrators sent food packages and medical aid to the people of Sarajevo. Since the demonstrations were public, it was clear that, had they been willing to listen and take their share of responsibility, city dwellers had access and exposure to information. Obviously, some did listen: otherwise, no demonstration would have taken place. There were penalties, however, for speaking out. Everyone knew that assassinations of NGO leaders and politicians as well as army generals and dissidents had occurred. In the early twenty-first century, the media were still not governed by transparent rules and procedures. The state-run stations were seriously overstaffed and were going broke. External agencies and the OSCE continue to work with Serbs to revise broadcasting rules.

Perceptions of Corruption and "Greater Serbia"

The socialist press is not alone in making the claim that the privatization projects, the assassinations, the gangster capitalism that prevails today (and, despite popular belief to the contrary, was in full bloom under Milošević) are destroying the country.[5] Corruption may have been rife during the 1980s, when the elites were scrambling to dominate the country by whatever means. Leaders of OTPOR (in English, "resistance"), a dissident non-violent student opposition group that formed on university campuses talked openly of the problem in 2004. Funded in large part by the US government and NGO organizations, OTPOR became the opposition to the government from 1998, when it was founded, through the next decade. Its initial priority was to get rid of Milošević and what its members called "the old regime." It succeeded, although its spokesperson told me, with a laugh, "not because of our pressure but because of US pressure" (personal interview). That done, the tasks OTPOR set for itself were to improve transparency in government, get rid of the secret police, and disable organized criminal groups. Its spokespersons say that these objectives are still in force. Of interest to anti-globalization activists, OTPOR argues that, in Serbia, perhaps unlike in other places, globalized economic measures would be progressive and would oppose the tribal measures preferred by current elites.

Other interviewees went further in their discussions about the links between the public sector, political parties, the police, and drug-dealing criminals. These cannot be quoted by name even as late as 2006, but the general argument that I heard from several respondents was along these lines: criminal groups would stage an incident – a shooting, an illegal demonstration, something of that sort – and while the local police were concentrating on that, their lorries, full of illegal substances, would cross the border. The civil war hid much of this activity while simultaneously providing it with its capacity for growth. As one person put it, "If you put nations into conflict, and they establish secret police and other armed groups, and they do business while people are fighting, they do very well, yet ordinary people are killed in the process." One might discount reports of this kind, but their frequency, and the fear of being named in connection with such charges, cannot be ignored. Corruption is a serious impediment to recreating a viable society in Serbia and in Bosnia-Hercegovina.

Several interviewees in Belgrade observed that Serbia and Croatia had always considered the territory of Bosnia their own. In their view, the leaders of these republics had never accepted the multicultural republic of Bosnia, nor would they ever accept it as a state. For Serbs, Turks (as Serbs still call Muslims) remain the enemy that they were over a century ago, despite the simultaneous claim that they all came from the same sources. The twin dreams of a "Greater Serbia" and a "Greater Croatia" were in opposition to Bosnia. They leave the impression that Bosnia will not be allowed to survive until its neighbours come to terms with the legitimacy of its survival – and that may never happen. As one historian told me, referring to the enmity as being at least 150 years old, "it is not a question of Tudjman and Milošević, it goes back long before they emerged as leaders of Croatia and Serbia."

A minority of Serbs, people who have travelled outside the country or who read widely, recognize that the Serb army and government were aggressors; moreover, that the governing elites since Tito's death have been and are unwilling to tell the population the truth about their actions. But, judging from the voting patterns in Serbia and the interview data I gathered in the spring of 2004, there are still many – perhaps no longer a majority but many – Serbs who have become ever more parochial, ever more nationalistic, and they take no personal responsibility for the breakup of Yugoslavia. They are angry and puzzled about the war waged against them by NATO in 1999 (over Kosovo). Serb hardliners, and possibly the majority of the less politicized population, argue that Serbia was the source of genuine Yugoslav sentiment and that its army (the rump of the former Yugoslav army) was only attempting to keep the union of South Slavs together, while others – Slovenians, Croatians, Bosniaks, and Albanians – were determined to tear it apart. Those who defend Serbia point out that The Hague (i.e., the ICTY) has indicted more Serbs than any other group in the former Yugoslavia. This may be true. It is also true that Serbs fought four wars – in Slovenia, in Croatia, in Bosnia, and in Kosovo. Slovenians, Bosniaks, and Albanians, however, fought only one war and fought it on their own territory. Croatians fought more than one war, the second in Bosnia. Only in the Kosovo war were any buildings in Belgrade destroyed, and in that case the destruction was wrought by NATO air bombardments. Other Serb buildings and rural areas were also targeted by NATO bombs, with serious consequences for local populations and industries. The scale, however, was much less than that in Bosnia. On the other hand, many young men in Serbia were killed in the various wars, and their absence is noticeable as one observes public places.

One of my informants had left Belgrade in 2001 and chose to return with her husband a year later. They decided they could get better jobs in Serbia than in Canada, the land they had intended to adopt, because they are both educated and their skills are scarcer in their homeland. She told me that she didn't really know what had happened in Croatia except for what she heard from refugees who came to Belgrade and from friends who told them about that war. She knew nothing about Bosnia-Hercegovina. "Maybe," she said thoughtfully, "we don't want to know; we might feel ashamed. And yet, how could I feel guilty if I didn't do it or know about it?" Regarding Kosovo in 1999, she said she knew only that Serbs there were evicted and were discriminated against and finally forced to flee as refugees. When the Kosovo war was in progress and bombs were dropped on buildings in the centre of Belgrade, she and her husband, like many other citizens, stood on one of the bridges of the city to watch. It was like a display of fireworks.

Individual memory is slippery enough; collective memory is wonderfully malleable, persistently changeable, lying like raw sewage at the base of the brain ready to be recreated into political fodder at the instigation of a demagogue. Thus, though they insist "we are all Serbs," and though, if history is traced back to the sixth and seventh centuries the historians corroborate that judgment, when it comes to the 1940s Croats are suddenly very different from Serbs, and Muslims are beyond the pale. Croats, with Muslims as accomplices, created the Yugoslavian holocaust, replete with concentration camps and terrorism: Serbs were its primary victims. Serbs who speak of this might concede that perhaps not all Croats were complicit, but, as their collective memories, reactivated by Slobodan Milošević, recreate that terrible event, forgiveness is out of the range of possibility.

2004 Elections and Language Laws

Presidential elections were held in June 2004, following changes in the electoral law to allow for a turnout of less than 50 percent of registered voters. This time a moderate, Boris Tadić of the Democratic Party (DS), won with 54 percent of the vote cast by an estimated 48.5 percent of the eligible voters. Koštunica supported him when his own party's candidate finished fourth in the first round. Was this the sign that Serbia was en route to a more democratic state?

Democracy involves equality between voters, but does it also require that small differences be enshrined in law? Serbia and Montenegro enacted a law called "mother tongue," according to which all children must be taught in their mother tongue. Serbo-Croatian, with its minor variations between all the new states, is suddenly seen as several languages. Albanian is another. So anyone not speaking Serbian will be taught in separate classrooms. This makes for even further divisions throughout the country. Still, it shows a willingness to accommodate differences that was not apparent under the more nationalist regime.

Was There a War in Srebrenica?

The massacre of 7,500 men and boys by Bosnian Serbs in the UN-protected Muslim enclave of Srebrenica between 14 and 17 July 1995 was the subject of a Bosnian Serb (Republika Srpska) government commission in June 2004. The commission was appointed in response to the demand of the Human Rights Chamber of the ICTY for information on Srebrenica. While the report avoided calling the event a genocide, it provided numerous details that would lead to the arrest of Ratko Mladić and other Serb Bosnians (see Republika Srpska 2004).[6]

The report seemed to support the argument in Serbia that the massacre at Srebrenica was conducted primarily by paramilitary Bosnian Serb forces rather than the regular Serbian army. The two infamous leaders, Radovan Karadžić and Ratko Mladić, were Bosnian Serbs. The Serbian understanding of events was jolted in June 2005 by a videotape run at the ICTY in The Hague and rebroadcast on Serbian television that showed a Serbian paramilitary police unit known as "the Scorpions" killing six emaciated Muslim men at a location close to Srebrenica. Two of the men were tortured in a nearby house before being killed with machine guns. It is emphasized that these were Serbian police, not Bosnian Serbs. The current prime minister, Vojislav Koštunica, ordered the arrest of those shown on the video. He did not say what would be done, if anything, to the Serbian Orthodox priest who blessed the Scorpions before their mission (also shown on the video). Before this event, pressure on the Serbian government finally encouraged the transfer of sixteen war crimes suspects to the ICTY, but this was the first time that Koštunica had publicly ordered arrests for the Srebrenica crimes.

The director of the Humanitarian Law Center in Belgrade – a human rights advocacy group – said that the tape would change state strategies for dealing with war crimes. But both the politicians and the human rights community in Serbia (mostly in Belgrade) note that public opinion is still strongly nationalistic and either unaware of or unwilling to believe that their own troops committed crimes. An opinion poll published by the Belgrade-based Strategic Marketing Research in April 2005 indicated that over half of respondents "either did not know about war crimes in Bosnia, or did not believe they had taken place."[7]

The *New York Times Online* article on the event quotes passers-by in Belgrade as saying: "The footage will not change anything because people knew what had been happening. Everyone knew about the siege of Sarajevo all along. Unfortunately people don't care about it. They only care how to feed their family." And: "The footage might change some people's opinion about Srebrenica, but the majority knew what had happened there. People knew what had happened in Srebrenica more than any other place as it has been often raised in public."

Bosnian Serbs who still reside in Srebrenica can hardly avoid knowing about the massacre. The trucks containing the corpses go by fairly often as they take the day's excavations to Tužla. Yet even there denial is widespread. Still, the Srebrenica Research Group argues that the official version of events cannot be correct because "the math does not add up." They claim that it is "mathematically impossible for 8,000 men and boys to have been massacred – to get this figure there would have to have been at least 48,000 people in Srebrenica." But, in their count, there were only forty thousand people in Srebrenica when it fell to the Bosnian Serb army, and thirty-eight thousand of these survived.[8] These opinions are losing force in Serbia as new information comes to light.

IMPACT OF MILOŠEVIĆ'S TRIAL AND DEATH

March 2006: Slobodan Milošević died – end of an era and all that. But in Serbia that may not be true. He had become the icon of the era. He was the leader, the hope after Tito expired; he was the demagogue who told his people they had every right to take over the rest of what was once Yugoslavia; he gave them the promise of greatness. That he failed is almost incidental since, given that version of the world, the population that followed him was sure he was the victim of petty nationalists elsewhere in the country and, even more, of scheming outsiders who used the turmoil of Yugoslavia to feed their own greed.[9]

The case against Slobodan Milošević was an extraordinary development as it constituted the first time a former head of state had faced charges of genocide and crimes against humanity in an international court. His trial continued for nearly five years and was close to completion at the time of his death in March 2006. While his trial progressed, the divergence between the FBiH and Serbia increased. In the FBiH, the perception was that Milošević was "playing" with the international court and making a mockery of it; in Serbia, the perception was that he was being unfairly judged by foreigners who had little understanding of the situation in the former Yugoslavia. The different impacts of the ICTY on Bosnia and Hercegovina, and Serbia and Montenegro, are significant for our appreciation of the spread of Western legal proceedings in non-Western and peripherally Western societies.

My sense is that Serbs have a low level of trust of the ICTY, and many are unaware of prosecution cases against non-Serbs. My observations are similar to those of Mark Freeman (2004b, 3), human rights lawyer and manager of the International Centre for Transitional Justice in the former Yugoslavia, who observed: "Since the inception of its work, the ICTY has been viewed with distrust, even hostility, in Serbia and Montenegro, where most perceive it to be dominated by NATO states and inherently biased against Serbs." Freeman's conclusion is backed up by two surveys conducted in 2002, which showed only 6 percent of Serbs interviewed and 4 percent of Bosnian Serbs in RS "trusted" the ICTY.[10]

The trial itself, in any event, provided a great wealth of information on the sequence and nature of events during the war, especially regarding the guidance and financing of Serb aggression in Croatia and Bosnia. It provided evidence of the relationships between the government in Belgrade and Croatian and Bosnian Serbs. One UN official testified:

The [Serbs] relied almost entirely on the support they got from Serbia, from the officer corps, from the intelligence, from the pay, from the heavy weapons, from the anti-aircraft arrangements. Had Belgrade chosen even to significantly limit that support, I think that the siege of Sarajevo probably would have ended and a peace would have been arrived at somewhat earlier rather than having to force them militarily into that weaker position.[11]

That comment was made before the World Court concluded that it lacked sufficient evidence to judge the Serbian state with genocide, even though it agreed that genocide had occurred and that the leaders of Serbia had failed to prevent it.

Amnesty International Reports 2005[12] and 2006[13]

Amnesty's report for 2004 (reported in 2005) stated in summary that:

> Cooperation with the International Criminal Tribunal for the former Yugoslavia in The Hague deteriorated as the authorities failed to transfer almost all those indicted by the Tribunal believed to be in Serbia. There were allegations of extrajudicial executions, and trials continued of former officials accused of complicity in previous political crimes. Police torture and ill-treatment continued. Domestic violence and the trafficking of women and girls for forced prostitution remained widespread. Roma continued to be deprived of many basic rights. (Amnesty International 2005, 218)

Much the same narrative was provided in the 2006 report. While Serbia was congratulated for improved cooperation with the ICTY in the early 2005 period, "under intense international pressure," that cooperation had deteriorated as 2005 continued. Amnesty International discussed the opening of talks on the possibility of a stabilization and association agreement with the European Union, and it said that a revised criminal code and law pertaining to police had been introduced; but "legislative reform remained slow."

Domestic Violence and Trafficking for Forced Prostitution

Amnesty International reiterated its claim, made in previous reports (as well as those of 2005 and 2006), that domestic violence in Serbia and Montenegro was widespread. The trafficking of women and children in prostitution operations is also widespread. These claims support the argument that patriarchal attitudes in a society lead to crimes against women both at home and in illicit organizations. Amnesty International showed trafficking to be associated with corruption more generally and indicated that it involved off-duty police officers. It does not say, but we might infer from its report, that continued discrimination against minorities (especially Roma) appears to also be associated with the establishment and maintenance of a hierarchy that provides men of the dominant ethnicity with priority over others and that this hierarchy influences all other relationships in the society.

SEPARATION FOR MONTENEGRO: 2006 VOTE

The two states of Serbia and Montenegro shared a defence union but little else. They had their own currencies and economic policies, but tiny Montenegro (population about 650,000 and declining) was dwarfed by Serbia and, despite its poverty, persistently sought an exit route. In May 2006, a slim majority (56.5 percent, where 55 percent was the required level, and with a voter turnout of 86.3 percent) of Montenegrins voted to separate after eighty-eight years of union. European observers said the election was properly conducted, and the EU said it would accept the outcome. The implications of this for the two autonomous regions of Serbia who have indicated similar inclinations to separate are not lost on their inhabitants or observers.

The Montenegrin vote had repercussions in the Province of Kosovo, which was still administered by the United Nations and was still desperately seeking independence, probably as an Albanian state. UN peacekeepers in Kosovo followed the Montenegrin outcome with an announcement that the province should have autonomy in all but name. The "all but name" was a sop to Serbia. For a short interval the Serbian government was quiet in its reaction, giving rise to speculation that it had been given a carrot by the European Union, but within a few weeks Serbia warned that it would retaliate if Kosovo declared independence and other nations accepted the declaration.[14] What exactly Serbia could or would do at this stage, and whether Russia would provide support, are unknown.

ECONOMIC DEVELOPMENT AND
THE RURAL-URBAN CLEAVAGE: 2006 STUDIES

According to the IMF, unemployment in Serbia in 2006 hovered at around 20 percent, but corporate restructuring, including privatization and retrenchment, have led to new employment in the private sector.[15] The IMF applauded further privatization prospects and continued the reduction of state participation in managing the economy.[16] The World Bank noted that the Serbian economy grew, on average, 5.5 percent per annum from about 2000 onwards, peaking in 2004 with 9.3 percent GDP growth (one of the highest among what the Bank calls "transition" economies) and was measured at 6.3 percent in 2005. Serbia reduced its indebtedness by borrowing very little and reaching favourable agreements with main creditors for debt write-offs.[17]

These fairly optimistic reports are supplemented by current statistics on Serbia, such as that the adult literacy rate is still in the mid-ninety percentages, and it is over 99 percent for people aged fifteen to twenty-four (both sexes). University faculty with whom I spoke were not optimistic about educational reforms in the universities. Facilities were in disrepair, classrooms were noisy and dirty. That notwithstanding, Serbs are literate, and, if the government and economy were to use their capacities more beneficially, Serbia could emerge as a transformed society of about eight million, perhaps finally successful at becoming European if that is what they want. The distribution of income, however, is uneven, and World Bank's researchers noted the difference between the rural and urban populations.

Nearly half of Serbia's population still lives in rural areas that are markedly poor. According to one World Bank study (Ersado 2006), while some economic improvements have occurred in the urban centres, rural poverty has stagnated. Both the World Bank and the UNDP have undertaken needs and risk assessments of rural households (UNDP 2007; Ersado 2006). The economic and lifestyle differences between the rural and urban populations may be key to understanding the persistence of nationalist rhetoric and of governments' appealing to citizens in nationalist terms. Zala Volcić (2005, 639–58) at the University of Queensland conducted thirty interviews with Belgrade "intellectuals" aged twenty-three to thirty-five and concluded that these educated young people saw themselves as cosmopolitans who contrasted themselves to rural nationalists. Their urban lifestyles are in stark opposition to the impoverished lifestyles of their rural compatriots. My own impressions in Belgrade were consistent with those of Volcić, though I did not interpret the more cosmopolitan views of the young academics and lawyers as arrogant so much as fearful and despondent about what was happening to their country. One World Bank study had this to say:

> For a majority of Serbia's population, the living standard at present is much lower than it was at the beginning of the transition from planned to market economy in the early 1990s, a result of ten years of political and economic adversity, internal conflict and international isolation. While the economic downturn affected all segments of the society, it has made conditions more sharply worsen particularly for the rural population and other disadvantaged groups such as internally displaced people and refugees. (Ersado 2006, 2)

The researcher observed that poverty in rural Serbia was a relative as well as an absolute problem because rural populations compared their current situation with a past that was more prosperous and they were not sanguine about the future.

As noted in the last chapter, however, Serbs, like Bosnians, are voting with their feet. Their population growth rate is 0.13, insufficient for regeneration (UN 2006). Montenegro had a net loss of population, down to -0.27 during the period covered by the UN estimates and projections.[18] (UN 2006). Unlike Bosnia, Serbia has not had its territory cut in two, and even if it loses Montenegro and the province of Kosovo it would still have capacity to move forward as a viable society if it could develop a political agenda that enables the rural population to improve their lot. Perhaps if it actually did that it could negotiate better conditions within the European framework for its own legitimate businesses. Its long-term survival otherwise does not look positive.

PART THREE

Intervention and Justice

SFOR soldier feeding pigeons in Bosnia square

11

Breaching Borders

Wars are the historical means by which some populations dominate or eradicate others. They are as old as human populations (probably older, since humans are not unique in this respect). Domination has generally been linked to physical force, whether in numbers or technological skills. This has nothing to do with survival of the fittest since sheer numbers or technical strength do not translate into "fittest" except in the crudest interpretation. No doubt there have been many small intelligent populations rendered extinct by brutes with little to offer their progeny other than being part of a large number. Some human populations died because they failed to bow to the correct gods of the stronger groups.

The desire among decent folk to change the path of history by preventing or stopping the more numerous or technologically stronger from making wars against the weak, and obliging the predators to be accountable for their actions, is a step forward for humanity. Unfortunately, it is a step fraught with contradictions. In what follows, I briefly review arguments in favour of humanitarian intervention and against it. Then I ruminate on the actual cases of intervention in Yugoslavia and Cambodia before entertaining a proposal to create a new global institution dedicated to intervention. The models for the new institution would be the International Criminal Court and the International Court of Justice, or World Court.

Following this discussion, I propose to raise an issue not generally understood as an appropriate reason for continuing intervention – namely, that the chief civilian victims in these wars are women, often widowed and raped and then unable to gain property rights even while raising families and doing much of the work to reconstruct their respective societies in the aftermath of hostilities. All my studies found this: it was not an aberration. But while rape, if proven (and that is a big "if"), will be penalized in international courts, property rights of survivors are still domestic issues, and they are not now open to international scrutiny.

HUMANITARIAN INTERVENTION

Humanitarian intervention before, during, or following an internal war is justified by its supporters on grounds such as these:

- An innocent population is suffering and its basic human rights are being violated. These basic rights are set out in the Declaration on Human Rights and the Rome Statute, among other internationally accepted documents. Thus intervention when authorities are abusing people is not only justified, it is required.
- Intervention may prevent further hostilities by obliging both or all combatants to negotiate their differences. Peacekeeping has an honourable record in this respect.
- Other countries are threatened by the potential spread of hostilities or by the influx of refugees. They have the right to self-defence, and if they cannot exercise that right for themselves, the international community has an obligation to provide the aid they need.
- Other countries understand this to be a single planet with all people on it affected by wars in any one location.

Opposition to intervention on humanitarian grounds might include:

- Whoever "we" are when we propose to correct others, the implication is that we are morally superior to them. Our own human rights record has its blemishes too, so we should not be too quick to judge others' problems.
- State sovereignty is guaranteed in the UN Charter.
- The state system may be flawed but it does provide governments, and governments, for all their faults, are generally better than anarchy. So unless we are sure we can replace a bad government and are prepared to continue occupying a country until it can govern itself again, better not to intervene.

- Is intervention really another way of obliging other countries to abandon their distinctive cultures and behave as we wish they would?
- There is no institutional basis for "disinterested" humanitarian intervention. The ICC and ICJ are institutionally rooted in international law and backed up by national laws, but no such basis exists for intervention.
- Linked to the previous item is the ease with which the term "humanitarian" can be appropriated for what are actually invasions by interested parties.

No Institutional Framework

The most problematic of the objections is that there is no institutional framework for providing disinterested intervention on humanitarian grounds and, as a consequence, the term "humanitarian" can be easily abused or hijacked. The term "institutional" refers to rules and laws, properly agreed to and ratified by a quorum of states, regarding when and how interventions should take place, and a permanent organization for the conduct of these interventions, supported by military force on a continuing basis. Although the UN has voted in support of the "Responsibility to Protect" motion, it has yet to devise a set of principles for intervention that would gain the support of the Security Council members and all other states, and it has not devised a method of implementation. Since the UN is entirely dependent for military resources and financing on member states, it does not have the capacity to make independent decisions about when and where to intervene, even when the violations of human rights are evident to everyone. Further, even where all states agree that one state is committing genocide or its equivalent (an unusual circumstance), other states in the same region may not be willing to allow external states to intervene (e.g., East Africa, where those in control of the Sudanese government at Khartoum have established war by proxies against internal populations who do not share their priorities).

By way of example of abuses of the term "humanitarian," we might refer to the war launched by the United States and Britain against Iraq. President Bush and Prime Minister Blair claimed that their invasion was a humanitarian intervention (as a backup to the earlier claim that Iraq had weapons of mass destruction, a claim later shown to be unsupportable.) The invasion succeeded: Saddam Hussein was dethroned. But the country descended into the hell of internal war not only between one or two sects but between numerous sects, street warriors, criminal gangs, jumped-up warlords, police who joined the gangs, and ordinary citizens caught up in the battles. The only groups benefiting from the disintegration of this society were outsiders, the very ones that sought to wage an aggressive war against Iraq, including some of the America's largest corporations and numerous private armies and contractors. Whether or not the claim of humanitarian motives is believed, the problem was and still is this: once sovereignty has been breached, somebody has to move into the vacuum. States are not always well governed, but at least they are governed: power vacuums are open to the international mafia (as Bosnians and Serbs can tell us), to revolutionary thugs (as Cambodians can tell us), and to hyped-up kids terrified of the future (as Rwandans can tell us).

In short, if outsiders are interested in moving in, and if their motivations are genuinely humanitarian, they had better come prepared to take over, prevent the crime gangs from getting a foothold, have the courage (or foolhardiness) to tell everyone how to behave, and run the place dictatorially until it is able to get over its shock and start to govern itself. They have to rein in their own privateers and adventurers and act in the interests of the society they have invaded. Americans and Brits were unprepared to take over once they had made the mistake of going into an impoverished Iraq that had no weapons of mass destruction and, in fact, already lacked sufficient food for its population. In Cambodia, the massive UN force was not prepared to go into the jungles and flush out the remaining Khmer Rouge forces. So they left the country not much better off than it had been before their arrival, stuck with a continuing guerrilla war in the north and poverty and the influx of criminal activity everywhere.

As in all projects that are going to affect large numbers of people, interveners have to be conscious of their objectives and must devise realistic strategies for achieving them: otherwise they should not poke their thumbs in the dyke. Judging from the pretensions and failures of the belated Cambodian intervention, the United Nations should not be used as a vehicle for achieving the interests of its members if its actions are not going to be backed up by sufficient force to either eliminate the recalcitrant belligerents or force them to come to the negotiating table. More, it should not be involved at all unless its negotiators are well versed in the culture, language, and recent history of the locale to which they are assigned.

Intervention in Yugoslavia

As we have seen in the chapters on the wars and aftermath in Yugoslavia, interventions that fail may just prolong the agony and, in the end, result in an untenable solution. Our problem may not be our lack of humanitarian instincts but, rather, our deficient wisdom. In retrospect, some would say that NATO bombing should have begun much earlier. Or that negotiating with thugs and psychopaths is a waste of time. Or that the lack of knowledge about the region, its history and culture, and the individuals who were leading the diverse populations led to the flaws in strategy. All of these might be true, but the rest of the world probably did the best it could under the circumstances. Certainly Sarajevo's populace benefited from belated food supplies brought in by UN forces and UN threats against Serbian attempts to stop their entry. Elsewhere as well, Muslims and other Bosnians were saved by UN actions. But the mass killing at Srebrenica might not have taken place had the site not been declared UN-protected. The question at the end of the wars was: could the separate groups have reached settlements any better than those contained in the Dayton Agreement? It seems highly unlikely that the separate groups would ever have reached any agreements without being forced to the table by US negotiators backed by NATO military action. Without that, Serbia might have gained more, Croatia might have gained more, but the Muslims of Bosnia might well have been eradicated altogether.

These lessons might lead us to the conclusion – as they have Michael Howard, a political theorist who has considered the problem of wars – that managing conflict, as he terms intervention, is not necessarily a good thing. Some wars, he argues, "should and must be fought, and fought to a conclusion that may involve the total defeat of one party to the conflict; and ... the participants should be left to get on with it" (Howard 1996, 42–3). Further, he says, while there is a belief that civilian suffering is somehow avoidable in war, it may not be avoidable and it may not justify international intervention. At the other pole on this issue are the participants in the International Commission on Intervention and State Sovereignty (described in chapter 2), who argued for the "responsibility to protect" suffering populations who are under threat of extinction.

In the Yugoslav crisis, leaders of other states had to consider a range of conditions that did not lead to obvious conclusions. Following the argument by James Mayall (1996, 1–24), based on the study by Spyros Economides and Paul Taylor (1996, 59–93), the issues for the UN were whether to breach sovereign borders and whether such borders between former republics were, in fact, sovereign; the failure of the European Union to provide enforcement for its recognition of Croatia and Bosnia-Hercegovina; the fact that several wars overlapped and that none of the antagonists was prepared to settle for less than they thought they might gain through war; and the fact that resources were not provided by UN member states to enable UN peacekeepers to do their job. The most serious of these issues was the last. Says Mayall (1996, 20): "No amount of improvement in the defining and technical drafting of mandates will be sufficient, however, unless UN commanders in the field are given the resources to carry them out."

Economides and Taylor add several other dimensions to the question of whether and how the UN might have intervened. The lack of congruence between ethnicity and borders if the former republics became states was a central problem, and the UN had to determine whether, in view of that, it was to engage as peacekeepers, peace enforcers, or peace makers, and whether it should be primarily concerned with humanitarian assistance or with maintaining borders. Europeans were not eager to become involved, and Americans were ambivalent because they saw it as a European conflict. Russians were opposed to any action that threatened the Serb population, but they were unable to contribute to peace making because, in the early 1990s, their own situation was precarious.

The consequence of these divergent positions was that the UN was not prepared to take a strong line in the Balkans. The mandate kept changing. The initial objective was to preserve the frontiers of the Yugoslav state, and the embargo on the sale of arms together with the establishment of UNPROFOR were consistent with that objective. In early 1992, the UN saw its task as aiding a country with internal divisions to maintain itself, and it acted in response to requests from the Yugoslav state. A few months later, the mandate changed. The Yugoslav state had disappeared, and the Yugoslav army had become an aggressor against non-Serb republics that were in the process of becoming states themselves. UNPROFOR was expanded to deliver humanitarian assistance and was now empowered to take "all measures necessary" to protect the population of Sarajevo and the rest of the population throughout Bosnia and Hercegovina. The political objectives were never clear: while UN participants recognized that Serbs were the primary aggressors, Croatia's interest in sharing in the carving-up of Bosnian territory created, in the words of Economides and Taylor (1996, 72), "the sense that there should be a plague on all their houses." A few months further on, in January 1993, the UN was considering a plan to preserve the outer boundaries of Bosnia and Hercegovina but accepting the results of ethnic cleansing by creating internal borders between the ethnic groups – essentially the end result two years later at Dayton.

The central problems for interveners in the former Yugoslavia were that, at the beginning of the breakup, outsiders did not know that the various populations had different interpretations of their coexistence and their preferred destinies. The UN began with the idea that the right thing to do was to maintain the status quo. The departure of Slovenia was accepted, but when Germany led the European nations to accept the independence of Croatia and then, inevitably, the independence of Bosnia and Hercegovina, the possibility of maintaining the former borders evaporated. No one expected the viciousness of the internal wars, and nothing in UN manuals provided guidance for how to deal with it.

In retrospect, the intervention of the UN, the EC, and, ultimately, the US has to be questioned: did the interveners do as much, or even more, harm than would have occurred without their presence? It is impossible to answer that question in terms of how many lives were either saved or forgone, but it is possible to say that neither the UN nor any other external group knew what they were dealing with and that no one knew how to end the wars except, as finally happened, through NATO force.

Each Event Distinctive?

One of our hurdles in determining when or whether to intervene is that these wars are not all the same. We cannot learn from the Bosnian fiasco what we ought to do in another war that might resemble those in Cambodia or Rwanda. If the international community had gone into Rwanda before or during the conflict, it might have stopped the war – but only as long as UN forces were present and actively deflecting animosities. Eventually, the UN would have had to face the fact that the two groups – one an invading army and the other a defensive but also genocidal resident population – were incompatible. That would have meant prolonged occupation by UN forces. Would that have been a solution? Certainly it would have reduced the deaths, but it would not have solved the conflict nor would it have resulted in the current situation, which, though far from perfect, is peaceful, with inhabitants engaged in positive reconstruction.

As to Cambodia, since this was not genocide, on what legal grounds would genuine humanitarian intervention have been mounted? Or, forget the legality of it, at what point would humanitarian intervention have altered the outcome? Given the Cold War context, US bombing, China's interests, and Cambodia's relationship to Vietnam, it seems most unlikely that intervention would have solved the underlying problems, which were not ethnic and were, in fact, different from those in any other of the internal wars of the period apart from the cultural revolution in China.

Sorting Out Aggressors from Victims

A second problem with humanitarian intervention is that the differences between aggressors and the victims are not always obvious. It was not clear in Croatia or Bosnia at the time of the wars who instigated and who prolonged the agony; all parties were implicated in atrocities, so which of them should be held culpable? The ICTY has since then unearthed much evidence of Serb (or Croatian Serb and Bosnian Serb) actions that show them as primary aggressors, but the ICTY has also prosecuted many Croats and Muslims who committed human rights crimes.

In Rwanda, a similar problem occurred at the time: Hutus and Tutsis were unknown to most of the world, including the would-be interveners. And when, with the conclusion of the wars, Tutsis were going after Hutus in nearby countries and in refugee camps, the ambiguity became even greater. It took years before the dynamics of the conflict became clearer. It was evident to Roméo Dallaire, stationed in the midst of the conflict, that Hutus were preparing to kill and then did indeed kill resident Tutsis, but his vision of the horrors inflicted on Tutsis did not enable others to fully understand the role of the incoming Tutsi army.

State Borders and Histories

Intervention rests on the notion that there are insiders and outsiders: outsiders intervene in the wars between the insiders. But insiders are identified only because of state borders, and, as we've noted, state borders were established arbitrarily and often by outsiders in their historical time. A major reason for the internal wars occurring in the post-Cold War period is that countries stuck with arbitrary borders, or holding within them incompatible groups, are finally coming apart, no longer confined by Cold War security concerns. When a state implodes, its people might choose to identify themselves in terms of ethnicity, religion, language, or nationality, but whatever group they align themselves with, they are individually more vulnerable until some new political boundaries enclose them and are accepted by outsiders.

How many wars could be avoided if we established a court of variance, similar to municipal courts that determine whether general rules should always be maintained in particular circumstances, for determining where more appropriate property lines could be drawn? Nice idea in theory, but its application would not have stopped any of the wars I've discussed here. As long as people's identities are tied up with their version of their ancestral heritage and religion, and where they believe their collective existence is threatened, there will continue to be regions of the earth where no amount of border fiddling will satisfy existing appetites. Serbian leaders wanted it all, and Croatians still want a good deal more of Bosnia: there is no obvious, rational response to those demands. There is just no easy fix.

In the case of intervention in Yugoslavia, an observer aided by hindsight might say it was ill-advised, badly executed, and, for the UN, self-destructive. But in defence of both Europeans and Americans who tried diplomacy, strategic negotiations, and numerous peace-intended manoeuvres, they were not acting in their own particularistic state interests: this was one of the rare attempts to intervene on humanitarian grounds. The United States had less direct interest than Russia (with close ties to Serbia) or Germany (with close ties to Croatia) or Britain (which had historical ties to Tito's country). Its interest, and that of NATO under its direction though under the auspices of the UN, was to preserve peace in the region.

(NATO intervention in Kosovo might be otherwise argued, but our concern here is with the earlier wars.)

States

States, as I observed earlier, never really have the sacrosanct status that they pretend history has accorded them. However, the development of the state system, flawed and often ugly as it is, became an important beginning for the rule of law and for the control of dictatorial leaders. Once the borders were drawn and there was some expectation that neighbours would not breach them, there was a capacity to begin building a legal system, a policing system, a governing system, and an infrastructure that sometimes (not always) improved the lives of the territory's inhabitants.

If we propose to breach state borders, then we need a global system of laws – a system to which the world's populations have agreed – according the rights of intervention; and we need a military force to back up those rights and the decisions made under them. The United Nations as it is currently organized cannot do this, though its subsidiary units, the World Court and the International Criminal Court, are moving aggressively towards a new system.

ECONOMIC GLOBALIZATION: CONTEXT FOR POLITICAL CHANGE?

We live in a world that is undergoing considerable change. States remain the major global political organizations, but economic transactions and production have long moved across national borders. Globalization is not something new to our age, but it has intensified in the past three decades. The term came into general use in the 1970s (probably as a deliberate intervention into the ideological debates between the neoconservatives and others at the time). Not all countries are equally affected by global production chains and markets, not all products are produced globally, and some countries are virtually excluded from the production operations because of their geopolitical situation, small aggregate markets, or ongoing internal wars. In response to economic globalization, political entities have gradually expanded. States remain but many are now embedded in regional organizations: the EU, NAFTA, and ASEAN are leading examples. Military power is concentrated in the United States, but economic power is more dispersed between the United States, Europe, Japan, and, increasingly, China, India, and Brazil. Financial transactions cross all borders, as do the numerous organizations engaged in international criminal activities.

Of the 170 states in the world of the 1990s not more than 10 percent were ethnically homogeneous. Africa has numerous ethnic and linguistic groups throughout its many states, although some of these, like the Hutu/Tutsi combination, may be less ethnically different than their colonial masters taught them to believe. Joseph Nye argues that communal conflicts, especially those involving wars of secession, are not well handled by the United Nations because it was built to deal with interstate conflicts. He makes a useful point about identities in these situations: "In a world of identity crises on many levels of analysis, it is not clear which 'selves' deserve sovereignty: nationalities, ethnic groups, linguistic groups, or religious groups. Similarly, uses of force for deterrence, compellance [sic], and reassurance are much harder to carry out when both those using force and those on the receiving end are disparate coalitions of international organizations, states, and sub-national groups" (Nye 1996, 74).

New wine in old bottles is another way of seeing the problem of UN-led attempts to solve regional and communal or secessionist wars. The UN is simply not set up to deal with these, and too often the divergent economic and military interests of the big powers interfere with the demands that broken societies be helped. Further, it is not always evident that these demands are reasonable when the participants in the local wars are not themselves doing the beseeching. We have already seen that peacekeeping is possible only when the combatants want peace and are prepared to abide by agreements brokered by an external agent with the concurrence of all parties. These are the wars of yesterday, mostly between small states rather than between groups within them.

None of the alternatives is ideal, but there are alternatives that might be better than relying on the cumbersome process involved in UN deliberations. One is to shift the burden to regional groups such as the African Union, ASEAN, and the European Union, ensuring that they are adequately equipped and trained to deal with violent episodes in their member states. This would be a possibility if, during a lull between internal wars, all the states of a region were to agree to allow the others to enter and take up positions to conclude wars (should these arise). However, it is difficult to imagine that, for example, all the states of East Africa or Central Africa, most now engaged in battles of one kind or another, would ever agree to cede such rights to their neighbours; and, in their defence, it may be true that their neighbours could not be trusted to act with restraint if they were fully armed and well trained.

Instead of undertaking military interventions, an alternative that the UN might be able to instigate would involve holding meetings between states with ethnically, religiously, or linguistically divergent populations on a regional basis. If populations were invited to express their preferences for political organization, some, at least – never all, alas! – would find it possible to deal with differences in non-violent exchanges.

Two of our unnecessary stumbling blocks are the assumption that states need to be fairly large and the assumption among some ethnic or linguistic groups that all of their kin need to be under the same umbrella. It might have been possible during the 1980s to carve up Yugoslavia into Croatia without the Krajina, to turn regions with Serbian majorities into a separate Serbian state, and to add some part of what is now Republika Srpska to the Krajina fragment. This would have meant that there were two separate Serb states, but there are plenty of other states in the world that speak the same language and hold similar ethnic varieties and religions within their borders yet remain politically separate. However, no matter how rational a potential division of the former Yugoslavia might seem to outsiders, the isolation and plight of Bosnian Muslims would remain, and similar problems would arise elsewhere when neighbours or former compatriots are determined to get rid of a minority population. In any event, this would only have been a faint possibility before the implosion of Yugoslavia. Still, the slow and grudging acceptance of change in the RS, and the growth in confidence of leaders in the FBiH, suggest that maybe these populations can restart the economy and begin again as a united society. Maybe.

There are other situations in which preemptive negotiations and imaginative solutions have been successful in the past. The United Nations, despite its cumbersome and ill-adapted process for dealing with these internal wars, managed to enable Namibia to deal with decolonization, and in 1991 it worked with Salvadorians to cushion the transfer of power to an elected government. Although

the Cambodian elections did not lead to a phase of genuine reconstruction in Cambodia, the UNTAC process did contain the Khmer
Rouge in the northern region and enabled elections to take place.
Chester Crocker suggests that preemptive engagement sometimes
takes the form of face-saving exits engineered by incumbents themselves, who need only a little help from their friends. His examples
include Gorbachev in Afghanistan, de Gaulle in Algeria, and de
Klerk in South Africa. Crocker (1996, 80) suggests that external
powers should avoid insisting on elections in societies not yet prepared to hold them as escalation of warfare might be the result.
Iraq and Afghanistan provide current examples. Acknowledgment
of separation following provocative elections might have the same
result, as, indeed, was the case in Croatia and Bosnia.

One of the lessons we might learn from the examples discussed
in this book, or from many others "on stage" from the 1980s
through to the first decade of the twenty-first century, is that ethnicity is a much overrated aspect of identity. As soon as we try to look
at it squarely, we discover that it is frequently an artifact of demagogues, an excuse for getting rid of unwanted neighbours, or a rationale for moving in on territory occupied by others. Language
and religion, however, tend to matter to people without the en-
couragement of demagogues. If we are dealing with groups that
speak different languages, we may need to find polyglots who can
communicate in both or all of them. We need, as well, to find out
how much of what is happening is fuelled by demagogues, warlords, laundered money and criminal activity, the arms trade, or
other realities beyond claims of ethnic issues. Trade analysts inform
us that AK-47 Kalashnikov sales remain constant throughout developing countries, and US as well as former USSR arms suppliers are
still making a good living by enabling others to kill.[1]

Democracies are less eager to enter wars than are more authoritarian political entities. This is largely because their electorates are
less willing to submit to the rigours and risks of war unless they are
persuaded that the consequences of inaction will endanger their
dolce vita, and leaders generally do not want to attempt that unless
the reasons are very good indeed (or unless war for the sake of war
is how they package their administration). The United States, being the military power of the world, has to select which of many hot
spots can legitimately be "sold" to the American public as needing
American troops or other military intervention. Public opinion

testing in the US suggested that there was no support for military intervention in Bosnia, though there was full support in the first Gulf
War. Only about 10 percent of respondents supported humanitarian missions, and about the same percentage supported use of force
for missions that might protect oil supplies (Kohut and Toth 1996,
106). The distribution of responses is congruent with more general
public opinion data. In the mid-1990s, the American public, according to polls, was mildly supportive of the United Nations and much
less concerned with helping other countries or promoting democracy elsewhere than they were with international terrorism, the international drug trade, and illegal immigration. According to the
pollsters, "Within the American populace, there appears to be a
hard core of opponents to the UN, one that is growing rather than
shrinking" (113).

Conclusions Re: Intervention on the Present Model

Interventions will undoubtedly continue as long as the world is divided into states, each with its own material and ideological interests.
The issue is whether humanitarian intervention is a viable process
likely to improve the situation for beleaguered people in each specific situation. Among the cases I have reviewed here there is only
one instance in which interventions of any magnitude occurred during the events. The interventions in Rwanda were minimal,except
for the French contingent that arrived too late to stop the carnage
and, in any event, had its own political agenda. Vietnamese intervention in Cambodia was self-interested, and the UN intervention was
much too late and timid to stop the carnage. Unfortunately, the interventions in Yugoslavia are ambiguous: some were helpful for some
populations; but overall, they did not create a solution.

Since the Rwandan and Yugoslavian instances, there have been violent episodes elsewhere. The Democratic Republic of the Congo remains a hotbed of violence despite continuing and even heroic
efforts by UN diplomats to curtail illegal arms shipments and to prevent clashes in the North Kivu province.[2] Sudan became another one,
and the war against the Fur people of Darfur became front-page
news: even so, Western states were reluctant to commit troops to saving them from forced migration to refugee camps or death. The government at Khartoum managed to keep others at bay while it helped
a force of Arab herders to destroy the farming villages in their western

region, commit rape and murder, and disperse the population while arguing that the real problem was a rebellion in the region. The situation was ambiguous, as these incidents always are, because the farming and herding populations had a long-standing tense relationship, made all the more problematic as increasing desertification removed fertile land. Indeed, by 2007 even the Arab janjaweed were reported to be in conflict with one another.

Considering these events, I conclude that success for humanitarian interventionist strategies is dependent on knowing who the combatants are, knowing why they are in conflict, and having an articulated and publicly understood yet distinterested objective. Easier said than done. Without such knowledge, interventions under present world circumstances should be avoided unless both or all combatants request it.

CONDITIONAL AID AND
DEVELOPMENT POLICIES AS INTERVENTION

Another form of intervention involves making further international or bilateral aid conditional on the recipient's performance regarding human rights. Peter Uvin describes his own experience in Rwanda with an argument on this score. He was an aid worker in Rwanda prior to the genocide. At that time, Rwanda was considered a model developing country. Its macroeconomic growth, the presence of many NGOs and peasants' associations, health measures, and similar indices gave it a passing grade in the eyes of the international community. In Uvin's (2004, 2) words: "If our model pupils turn out to be serial killers ... what does it say about our understanding of what we are doing in the development world? Why are we so blind to local dynamics of power, politics, violence, and exclusion? From there, a second question emerged: what are the interactions between our presence – the resources, discourses, and practices of the development enterprise – and the dynamics that led to genocide?"

Political conditionality has had a short life since the conclusion of the Cold War, but for much of that time the condition attached to aid offers was that elections be undertaken, the implied assumption being that elections were the equivalent of democracy. But, as I've noted throughout this book, elections may have only the most superficial relationship to either democracy or human rights. The

European Union has insisted on elections and, thereby, on democracy for membership in the EU and for eligibility for membership in the European Bank for Reconstruction and Development. The Organization for the Security and Cooperation in Europe, discussed in chapter 7 on Bosnia and Serbia, likewise emphasizes democracy.[3] Peter Uvin marshals persuasive arguments against conditionality, and particularly against that form that equates elections with democracy, let alone human rights. These include doubts about the ethical standing of conditionality, its capacity to produce positive results and its potential for good, and inconsistency in its applications because of donor-state interests.

Joseph Stiglitz, former World Bank chief economist, argued that the imposition of conditionality on IMF loans reinforced traditional hierarchical relationships: "Rather than promoting the kind of open dialogue that is central to the democracy, it argues at best that such dialogue is unnecessary, at worst that it is counter-productive."[4] Other human rights activists, development aid workers, economists, and policy makers have arrived at the same conclusion: conditionality is ineffective and counterproductive.

Conditionality, if actually practised, is a punitive measure. The opposite strategy is to applaud and provide awards for countries with improving or good human rights records either before or after violent civil wars – before, to preempt war; and after, to help reconstruct. This strategy is unambiguously political, but it might be performed as a technical and economic action, as in working with countries to de-mine territory and demobilize troops, to reconstruct basic social and economic infrastructures, to promote accountability in government, and to encourage free elections and an independent media. This approach may be appealing to development workers who want to enable countries to become sensitive to human rights. As with conditionality, this carries with it some defects. Carlos Santiso (2001, 162), with the United Kingdom Department of International Development, captures some of them: "Democratic transitions often do not follow a natural, orderly or linear sequence. Democratization is an irregular, unpredictable and sometimes reversible process taking place in a highly fluid and volatile political environment."

As Uvin notes, that being so, it would be both difficult and presumptuous for aid workers to decide where the country is in the process of democratization and whether it is succeeding. What aid

workers can do is to provide help with forms such as construction
of courts or school buildings; training of judges, police, and teachers; and provision of basic necessities. In his view, and in that of
many others who have devoted themselves to development work or
the reconstruction of broken societies, the better approach – the
one more likely to have long-term positive outcomes – is to act on
the principle of local accountability, being available but not taking
control of projects or telling aid recipients how to behave, providing funds but never to the point of making people dependent. As
well, there is need for foreign governments to create trade policies
that are consonant with aid policies.[5]

A PERMANENT GLOBAL INTERVENTION ORGANIZATION

The United Nations was built in a very different time and under different circumstances from those we experience in the opening
years of the twenty-first century. Attempts to reform it, to make it
better fit changing times, have failed. Dominant states continue to
shield themselves from all incursions on their sovereignty; me-
dium-income states such as India, Pakistan, Brazil, and many others
have to shield themselves from the barracudas and from the poorer
states; poor and developing states have little to defend themselves
from others: they need help but they have learned to beware of aid
that comes with strings attached. And when overpopulation, desertification, crop failures, market changes (should they have markets
for any products), wars on their fringes that impinge on their internal relations, government paralysis, or any other conditions that
put them into jeopardy occurs, their lives are on the line and they
may move towards internal mutual hostilities.

In the next half century – nay, in the next two to three decades –
the number of states that reach that breaking point will increase
because of desertification and crop failures, possibly because of rising sea levels and loss of fresh water supplies, and loss also of fish
and other food staples. Aid agencies are already bracing for these
changes, trying to figure out how best to proceed on what will inevitably be insufficient supplies. But the United Nations and member
states are still not developing strategies to deal with countries that
stumble into internal wars, genocide, or crimes against humanity.
The world's totally inadequate response to the crises in East Africa

are indications of just how lacking in plans we are for these situations. We continue to act as if we are in the shoals of the Cold War.

Is it too much to propose that we create a new organization specifically designed to deal with human rights crises? I do not mean another bureaucracy on the lines of the United Nations. I mean something closer to a high-powered postdoctoral level institute, wherein one group consists of specialists in the cultures and languages of world regions who meet on a regular but not daily basis – several times per month for example – to build up their common understanding of what is occurring and work out ways of deflecting rivalries and conflicts. They would be supported by small bureaucratic staffs who would monitor internal conditions in each of a region's countries. When these staffs warn the cultural specialists that conditions are reaching a boiling point, the cultural specialists are immediately seconded by the institute and they, not bureaucrats or politicians, provide the intellectual direction for the operation. If they conclude that military force will be required, they must provide clear explanations of why, against whom, for what purposes, and what alternatives are being set aside. Military forces would continue to be under the aegis of the UN or NATO, but it would be the specialists who ask for military intervention. If military force is called in, those wielding it must be prepared to act quickly and without reserve. And all states would be always on notice that such an eventuality would be possible – thus, predictably, they would not choose to enter into an internal war if they could possibly find an alternative route to peace.

Meanwhile there would be another group of scientific specialists whose particular capacities would span the regional ecological conditions. If part of the region is or is becoming a desert, there would be scientists who specialize in survival modes in deserts or in how to regenerate fertile land. If the region is losing land to rising sea levels, the scientists and applied scientists would be there to anticipate the changes and to enable people to create safer havens before they meet disasters. The focus for scientists would be to predict and to offset ecological change.

And perhaps there needs to be yet a third set of specialists – this group engaged in understanding the impacts of changes in world economies, with a mandate to warn the well-established economies when their policies are causing serious harm to others. They would be free to make their opinions known worldwide and to encourage developed economies to make necessary changes so that others might survive.

I know that in none of these cases are all the specialists of the same mind. But at the present time, specialists rarely come together to deliberate on a given set of empirical data, especially with a view towards actually solving a political problem. Climate change has now, after many years of deliberations, finally reached consensus after hundreds of people with relevant scientific credentials and research backgrounds came together and shared their findings and conclusions. Perhaps the same would occur if economists, soil scientists, and anthropologists (for example) met together in a similar fashion. In short, this is not impossible; it is simply not yet the norm.

The new organization would be permanent yet with personnel who have other lives in universities and research institutes. Contracts with their university and institute home bases would provide for their secondment in the event that their particular expertise is required for a potential war in a particular region. Their tasks would be, first, to provide information and advice on how to prevent the war; then, if that fails, on how to intervene in a way that might halt the physical brutalities and bring the parties together for negotiation; and third, if that fails, on which parties should be hit – and hit hard – by military force. All of this should be known and publicized so that would-be perpetrators of wars would know the sequence.

Obviously this institute, unlike the United Nations, would have to have a full-time military force at its disposal. Perhaps this would be on loan, variously, from member countries, but it would not be negotiated situation by situation, time by time. The organization – and potential warriors in any region – would know that a certain number of well-trained soldiers and a certain amount of equipment would be available on a moment's notice at any time, and they would not be for decorative purposes. They would be prepared to fight and to kill, and they would have no personal or national vested interest in the outcome. But they would be properly paid.

All of this would be possible provided, at the inception of the new "Intervention Institute," member states of the UN guaranteed the funds for the ongoing bureaucracy and the secondment of experts as well as the military forces. But it is important that they not bargain over these expenditures or the personnel once they buy into the concept. There would not be any "oh, but it's not my turn" in any particular proposed intervention. If a Darfur came up, the bureaucracy would call in the experts right away. Those experts in East Africa would already have met on a regular basis and have discussed the ongoing events, and they would advise whether, in their opinion, negotiation would be possible, which groups to target as aggressors, and how best to deal with various other groups (because the situation is never simple). The intervention by such an institute would be widely advertised so that the participants would know immediately how much wriggle room they had before a military force sufficient to stop them would be sent in.

One might go on and on with details, but the overall objective is to make this the equivalent and the necessary adjunct to the International Criminal Court. The ICC is designed to judge and assign responsibility for criminal actions after events. The Global Intervention Institute (GII) that I am discussing would be designed to prevent aggression if possible, to enable negotiations if possible, and otherwise to stop aggressors by force. This GII could be put together by any group of countries in the same way as the ICC was put together, and it would simply ignore the notion of state sovereignty in the same way as the ICC ignores it.

The point is, if we, as the richest parts of the global economy, are going to talk about the "responsibility to protect," then we had better create the means to do so. The means must include a well-tested, durable, organized body of knowledge about the various regions of the earth where these eruptions are most likely to occur over a two- to three-decade period. We need to prepare to protect people who are most likely to be in need of protection. We need to use our language, cultural, economic, and scientific skills to prevent hostilities if at all possible. We need to consider all alternatives to military force but be absolutely prepared, and be known to be prepared, to enforce ceasefires and sharp stops to humanitarian crises when needed.

The United Nations, as presently structured, is not capable of doing this. It is hamstrung by the Security Council and the unwillingness of great powers to allow it to operate as a world government. It is they more than small powers who invoke the sovereignty clause, thereby allowing small powers like Sudan to follow suit. And it is their unwillingness to pay the price of world government, even while benefiting from economic globalization, that prevents us from stopping the wars in Darfur and Somalia. The world – the developed world, in particular – has a surfeit of talented, knowledgeable experts on every culture, language, regional economy, local ecology on the earth. For goodness' sake, let us put them to work!

PROPERTY RIGHTS IN POSTWAR SOCIETIES

In each of the societies we explored, women's fate was made the more difficult by property laws that left them without land on which to grow food or other capacities to sustain their dependents and themselves. Their societies were patriarchal; power and property were held by surviving men. One consequence of this was that, after the wars, even in Rwanda (where women were virtually running the everyday society), they could not count on the justice system to recognize their claims to property if their (dead) husband's kin still included male inheritors. Perhaps in Rwanda that will change as more women participate in the political system as designed, unusually for Africa, by the incoming army. In Cambodia there is no sign of change, nor yet in Bosnia and Serbia.

This is not a matter of unequal powers or rewards: it is the bedrock upon which seriously dysfunctional societies develop. A mindset that deems it acceptable to push widows off the only land on which they can create subsistence for their children; to beat up wives, daughters, and prostitutes; to traffic in kidnapped women and girls is a major impediment to the creation of a peaceful and more egalitarian society. In all of the societies we have examined here that mindset is still present, and until it is dealt with neither domestic nor international law will solve the problems of the broken pieces.

Our international justice institutions are prohibited from approaching this widespread impediment to justice because property is a domestic matter, and though our courts can deal with genocide they cannot deal with deprivation on the grounds of gender. This injustice is such that societies desperately in need of remediation and help are unable to move on as long as this property arrangement continues. If our objective is to enable societies to develop capacities for renewal, then we had best pay attention to this problem and make it into an international rather than a domestic issue.

12

Justice, Truth, Reconciliation, and Sobering Reality

In a ninety-four-page submission in March 2007, the International Criminal Court chief prosecutor, Luis Moreno-Ocampo (who learned his trade as an assistant prosecutor of the National Commission on the Disappearance of Persons in the 1984–85 trial of nine senior officers and heads of state during the 1976–83 military junta administration in Argentina) named a Sudanese government minister and a military commander as suspects to be tried for crimes against humanity in Darfur.[1] A few months earlier the same ICC prosecutor identified Joseph Kone, leader of the "Lord's Army" in northern Uganda, for crimes against humanity. These are new ways of intervening in domestic affairs of states. Instead of sending in armies and calling it war, the Court is sending in indictments and calling it justice. It may look like an improvement, but beware! These indictments have a certain similarity to bullets.

As the global economy expands and inevitably affects all territories of the earth, so, too, has the effort grown to bring political pressure to bear on states, their leaders, and those who transgress what much, but not all, of the world now understands as human rights. The ICC and the International Court of Justice (the World Court) are transformative agents in the world, obliging the locally powerful to accept constraints on their behaviour and providing a particular form of justice and protection for the powerless. The process is a version of justice developed and established in Western societies. There is little doubt that, when imposed on non-Western societies, this may be a means of obliging them to become more like "us," and some aspects of their cultures are diminished as a consequence.

We might argue that this Western justice system has served us well, and if we oblige others to live in a global economy then we should at least provide them, and ourselves, with something like global justice. If "we" enjoy the advantages of the rule of law, we should extend it to "them." The benefits we attribute to the rule of law are that it delivers accountability, deterrence, justice, truth, and reconciliation. It should also reduce the use of violence as the mode of conducting communal affairs. So, at least, do we believe when we encourage, nay pressure, survivors to agree to international criminal proceedings against the perpetrators of heinous crimes.

However, the actions of the ICC in these two indictments are controversial. In the Sudan case, the government firmly rejected the Court's right to issue indictments against its ministers and made it clear that it will not surrender them to external authorities. Despite international pressure, the violence against villagers in the Darfur region continues. As long as affluent states refuse to provide troops and funding to defeat the Khartoum government (thus rendering the UN ineffective), armed opposition is provided only by an ill-equipped force consisting of troops from poor neighbouring African countries.

In Uganda, meanwhile, Joseph Kone has declared that he will not surrender or abandon his criminal activities as long as the ICC holds an indictment over his head. Thus he uses it as an excuse for continuing to abduct children and turn them into armed soldiers or prostitutes. The Ugandan government, for its own reasons, has failed utterly to catch this man, and many observers argue that Ugandan tribal politics and President Musevini's own priorities are impediments to action. When Kone threatened to do more damage unless the ICC backed off, Musevini said his government would rather save the children than cooperate with the indictment. Affected villagers, and also concerned outsiders, are tempted to blame the ICC for prolongation of the terror instead of blaming the government for failing to end it.

The ICC prosecutor undoubtedly anticipated these objections. He can be sure that the indicted individuals are now less able to escape their countries than they might previously have been. They can be charged once they enter the foreign territory of countries that have signed relevant agreements and conventions. As well, issuing the indictments puts international pressure on reluctant or colluding governments to clean up their acts. Although neither the

ICC nor the United Nations has the authority or the military capacity to enter these countries and physically detain the indicted individuals themselves, the actions of the Court have an impact. Besides, in neither case was the local government prepared to act against identified perpetrators of criminal acts.

These two cases, still simmering as this is written, tell us where the ICC is going and what it considers as its priorities. It seeks out the leaders of genocides and crimes against humanity and will pursue them, prosecute them, and incarcerate them if the judges find them guilty as charged. Since it has no military capacity it has to use moral suasion, and serving indictments is its most powerful tool. When the International Criminal Tribunal for Yugoslavia indicted Milošević while he was still powerful in Serbia, the indictment supported the mobilization of the population in the street demonstrations that finally led to his downfall. The ICTY had less capacity to follow up than did the ICC since it was designed as a temporary tribunal with limited powers. So it may be that the world has entered a new and more aggressive phase of international peacekeeping with the establishment of the permanent criminal court.

Reduction of personal liberties is an effective threat when most countries participate in the agreements. When General Augusto Pinochet was detained in London for two years, and while the interested world deliberated on whether he should be handed over to a Spanish judge to be tried for crimes against Spanish citizens in Chile under his rule, many other leaders of countries that had violent human rights records must surely have had second thoughts about their personal freedom to travel. We noted previously that Henry Kissinger fled Italy when handed a subpoena related to crimes in which he was alleged to have had a role in Chile twenty years earlier. We have not yet seen a sitting president or prime minister subpoenaed while attending an international conference, but, in theory, that possibility now exists.

DOCUMENTING CRIME

Readers may recall from the discussion in chapter 3 that Bosnia claimed extensive reparations against Serbia for war crimes conducted by the State of Yugoslavia between 1992 and 1995. The case, heard by the ICJ, had many complexities, of which jurisdiction was one. Those concerns were overshadowed by the failure of the Court

.to insist on obtaining from Serbia or from the ICTY numerous documents from Yugoslavian military archives. On the basis of inadequate information, the Court acknowledged that what happened at Srebrenica was genocide (the ICTY had already deemed it such) but that there was no proof that the Serb state directed or controlled it. Serbia was merely scolded for failing to prevent a genocide. The story unfolds further, even as this chapter is being written.[2]

Those who agreed with the judgment (especially in Serbia) were relieved that the Serb state would not have to pay the large war crimes reparations claimed by Bosnia. Speculation about the reasons for the judgment referred to the potential for political fall-out. The ICJ may have feared it was intruding on state sovereignty or that Serbia might refuse to pay the reparations and that it would not be able to force the issue. Possibly it was concerned with the potential for further impoverishing Serbia and weakening its state. If these were the reasons, then one of the chief benefits claimed for the rule of law is damaged: courts are supposed to judge cases on their legal merits, not on whether the judgments will be politically awkward.

There was public speculation to the effect that, when the ICTY finally obtained the documents necessary for the prosecution of its case against Milošević, it promised to keep many that were marked "Defense. State Secret. Strictly Confidential" out of the public domain.[3] Judges and lawyers had access to these documents but they were not read into the tribunal records. Time was running out for the ICTY; and, besides, the defendant was unwell and the Court feared he might die before the judgment could be handed down (as it turned out, he did just that). The speculation was that Carla del Ponte, the chief prosecutor, agreed to seal the records as a condition for obtaining them. She could not authorize the transference of these records to the ICJ. Human rights groups have argued that the ICJ could have subpoenaed original documents directly from Serbia and did not have to depend on the ICTY. The Office of the Prosecutor at the ICTY issued a denial that it had been involved in any way with concealing documents, and it also stated that

the ICTY Office of the Prosecutor has no authority or involvement in proceedings before the International Court of Justice. The ICJ and the ICTY are two entirely separate legal institutions – the ICJ deals with disputes between states and the ICTY has jurisdiction to determine the criminal responsibility of individual perpetrators. When it comes to cases before the International Court of Justice, it is the responsibility of that institution to determine what evidence it will consider and to request documents it deems necessary. This is not and cannot be the responsibility of the ICTY or its Office of the Prosecutor. As can be read in the text of its judgment, the International Court of Justice chose not to request the documents in question.[4]

The failure to obtain documents known to be relevant to the case disturbed two dissenting judges and numerous legal experts around the world. Even without the documents, this decision was curious because details of Serbian state participation had already been unearthed in records of other trials at the ICTY. Among these records there was evidence that many officers and noncommissioned men from the Yugoslav army were serving with the Bosnian Serb army. *New York Times* correspondent Marlise Simons argues on the front page that, with reference to the ICJ's decision, lawyers whom she interviewed on a confidential basis said that there is substantial evidence that Serbian forces and secret police were involved in the preparations for the Srebrenica massacre. Some uncensored archives obtained by the *New York Times* include information on the military budget and minutes of the Yugoslavian Supreme Defence Council meetings during the war in Bosnia. Simons says that these provide strong evidence that "more than 4,000" men on Serbia's payroll were fighting in Bosnia. She also refers to Momir Bulatović, a former president of Montenegro who wrote that Ratko Mladić attended some council meetings in Belgrade.[5]

Those who disagree with the ICJ's decision, including the human rights community and, of course, Bosnians who demonstrated their anger in street marches, argue that this decision reduces deterrence potential and constitutes a lack of justice. One Serb at least was as shocked as were Bosnians. Natasha Kandić, director of the Humanitarian Law Centre in Belgrade, said the decision would add to the Serbs' lack of understanding of their own culpability. If, as seems to be the case, both Serb politicians and bureaucrats at the time of the 1995 massacre, as well as lawyers and judges who were permitted to read the documents, knew about the Serb state's involvement, then the fact that the ICJ failed to oblige them to speak is a blow to the notion that criminal law encourages the telling of truth.

As a historical note on a more famous case, Nazis in Germany kept careful records of their decisions and activities; those were vital forms of evidence that were used against them at the Nuremberg Trials. Of course, they could not destroy the evidence or bargain with the judges: they lost the war. The armed forces of Guatemala provide another example of record-keeping. They kept note of their activities during the 1950s and 1960s, when thousands of indigenous Guatemalans, human rights leaders, and liberals were killed. These files were recently discovered by accident, and though they are in poor condition, having been thrown into warehouses where rats and humidity destroyed many of them, those that are still legible are being made available to researchers and surviving members of families of the disappeared. Khmer Rouge leaders also left records, though it was many years before researchers discovered them and could piece together some of the activities that took place under KR leadership (this process is ongoing). As I noted in chapter 4, the US air force also kept meticulous records of its bombing forays over Cambodia, and from these we can now reconstruct the extent, timing, and impact of those destructive events. Considering the ICJ's action, then, potential génocidaires might well conclude that the destruction of files is one means of forestalling legal methods of justice.

SERBS STRUGGLING WITH JUSTICE

It is ironic that Serbs, who suffered relatively little physical damage during the wars of the 1990s and against whom the charge of genocide has been laid by both the ICTY and the ICJ, are the ultimate losers in the Yugoslavian conflict. They have been saved the cost of war crimes reparations, but they are less able to become flourishing members of the European Union than are any of the republics they attacked. Many Serbs express anger, frustration, and bitter recriminations when they are obliged to consider what is going on at The Hague. Despite repeated demands from the ICTY to give up the fugitives Radovan Karadžić and Ratko Mladić, Serbia and Republika Srpska failed to do so. The one leader who dared to surrender Slobodan Milošević to the ICTY was assassinated. European leaders have generally held firm that they would not let Serbia join their union until it conformed to their human rights agenda, though some human rights organizations fear a relaxation of that determination, as is indicated in these excerpts from a public letter to the European Union from Human Rights Watch in March 2007:[6]

> Human Rights Watch is extremely concerned about the indications from the EU in recent weeks that it may be prepared to resume negotiations with Serbia in the absence of full cooperation with the ICTY. In our assessment, such a move would undermine efforts to move Serbia towards a stable and democratic future based on respect for human rights and the rule of law, and significantly increase the risk that war crimes suspects in Serbia indicted by the ICTY will never face justice.
>
> As you know, in May 2006, the Commission, supported by the General Affairs and External Relations Council (GAERC) ... decided to suspend the negotiations of the Stabilization and Association Agreement (SAA) with Serbia in light of the successive governments' continuous failure to cooperate with the Tribunal ...
>
> Since that time Serbia has made no progress towards full cooperation, including transferring Mladić to the ICTY. The ICTY prosecutor continues to denounce forcefully Serbia's lack of cooperation ... Moreover, on February 26, 2007, the International Court of Justice (ICJ) ruled that Serbia's failure to transfer Ratko Mladić to the ICTY amounted to a violation of its obligations under the Convention on Genocide. The Court also ordered Serbia to transfer to the ICTY individuals indicted for genocide and to cooperate fully with the Tribunal.
>
> The ICJ decision underscores the fact that almost 12 years after the Srebrenica massacre, its indicted architects Ratko Mladić, and Bosnian Serb wartime President, Radovan Karadžić, remain at large. In addition to Mladić, four other war crimes suspects indicted by the ICTY are believed to be in Serbia. There is nothing to indicate progress towards full cooperation on Serbia's part. Yet there are signs that the EU may be prepared to water down its insistence on full cooperation as a precondition for resuming talks with Serbia.

One recent court case in Belgrade hints at possible change in Serbia. The national War Crimes Court convicted five of the Serb soldiers shown in a video of the paramilitary unit, the Scorpions, as they coolly executed six Muslim civilians. Readers may recall that these men filmed themselves taking the six prisoners from a truck and force marching them to a hillside, then machine-gunning them. Nearly a decade later, the film entered the public arena and was shown in Serbia as well as elsewhere. One or two of the soldiers, apparently suffering remorse, informed the Humanitarian Law Centre of the film's existence before they went into voluntary exile. With the formal support of the Serb president, the Serbian War Crimes Court charged the identified leader and five others. In April 2007, it judged five of them, including the leader, guilty in varying degrees, sentencing the leader to twenty years in prison and the others to lesser terms. This was the first national court ruling in Serbia to deal with the Srebrenica massacre.[7]

Television reports on this case included an interview with a local citizen in the small town in which the convicted men were living before the court case. She said she couldn't believe that the video was true because people in the town didn't do things like that.[8] Though the courts have declared that the video is genuine and one of the convicted participants has confessed, many Serbs maintain their belief in Serb innocence and the morality of what they did to "save Yugoslavia" when others – read Croatians and Muslims – were trying to destroy it. Lawyers at the Humanitarian Law Centre in Belgrade attribute this to a culture of impunity, racist beliefs about Muslims, patriarchal attitudes, and what we might call "groupthink" among the armed forces and a large portion of the civilian population.

Croatian War Crimes

A reviewer of this manuscript interrupts at this point and suggests that I ensure readers are aware that Croatia under Tudjman was also criminally responsible for war crimes. Were not the events at Gospić or Sisak, says she, also war crimes? One is reminded, of course, that Croatia was responsible for the concentration camps and crimes against Serbs, Muslims, Jews, and Roma during the 1940s, crimes for which no one took responsibility or was held accountable in a court of law, yet later historians have regarded those crimes as genocide. But her point is that Croatian forces also committed serious crimes during the 1990s, both in Croatia and in Bosnia, and this is manifestly the case. The public record informs us that Croatian prime minister Franjo Tudjman and Serbian president Slobodan Milošević were both responsible for encouraging war crimes.

The instances that have come before the ICTY (and for which individuals have been tried and convicted) involved murders in the
range of ten to 120 persons, and torture and rape as well. Many
Croatian Serbs were evicted from their homes or fled as the Croatian army or paramilitary forces destroyed their property and attempted to either kill enough Serbs to frighten the rest or otherwise
cause the entire Serb population to leave the territory However, the
Croatian domestic courts are reputed to be still dragging their feet
on war crimes committed by Croatians. In 2007, Amnesty International complained that the Croatian judicial system "failed to adequately address wartime human rights violations, regardless of the
ethnicity of the victims or of the perpetrators" (Amnesty International 2007, 95).

But we are left with a question: when do war crimes become
genocide? Is the killing of 100 persons equivalent to the killing of
7,000 to 8,000 persons? Do numbers matter? Or is the level of
planning more important? As in ordinary murder cases, premedita-
tion and planning of the acts are crucial. In the case of Srebrenica,
the evidence before the ICTY indicated that the large-scale planning, deployment of personnel, and carrying out of mass murders
was undertaken with the specific intent to eradicate in whole or in
part a population defined in terms of race, ethnicity, religion, or
nationality (as required by the UN Convention on the Prevention
and Punishment of the Crime of Genocide). The term "ethnic
cleansing" was used during the battles in Croatia and Bosnia, and it
could be a euphemism for "genocide on a small scale" if the acts
were premeditated, planned, and had as the actors' intention to
eradicate in whole or in part a specific population.

My own interpretation, subject to reconsideration should more
light be cast on the events, is that war crimes and crimes against humanity are not the same as genocide. The events at Srebrenica required a level of cold-blooded planning that went beyond "ordinary"
war crimes. Further, I am persuaded that Serbs and Bosnian Serbs,
armed and relatively well-organized, were the aggressors in Bosnia
and that Bosnian Croats, with external help, vacillated between supporting Muslims against Serbs and being in conflict with their Muslim neighbours during the wars in Bosnia. This does not ignore the
responsibility of the Government of Croatia for instigating the war
against Croatian Serbs nor the Government of Bosnia for inviting
conflict when it demanded independence, and it does not absolve

the many war crimes and crimes against humanity perpetrated by gangs and parmilitaries in the names of Croatia, Serbia, or Bosnia.

LOCAL WARS IN A GLOBAL CONTEXT

In all of the societies we have studied here – Cambodia, Rwanda, Bosnia, Serbia, and Croatia – observers, witnesses, judges, scholars and journalists have used the term "a culture of impunity" as if it explains what happened. Simon Gasiberege, the Rwandan professor who contributed to the creation of the gacaca courts spoke of the Hutu culture as one of impunity when it came to harming Tutsis. The Humanitarian Law Centre in Belgrade explained the actions of the "Scorpions" gang on such a culture. Croatian novelist and journalist Slavenka Drakulic used the same term to explain Serb and Croatian atrocities during the war (2004).[9] The term is in such common usage that it may have lost its meaning.

Those who used it appear to mean a culture in which responsibility is shirked, accountability is not taken seriously, guilt is foregone and opportunity trumps moral concerns. The government does not steward, the school does not teach, the police do not maintain safety, the media lie, the religious institutions seek power over truth, and the poor go to bed hungry. In many (not all) societies a prohibition against killing other humans is bedrock. Of course, like other moral directives, it is transgressed. The culture of impunity is one in which law is transgressed frequently and even without cause, where sheer hubris rules and neither morality nor law prevents or punishes the transgressors. People who have been immersed in such a culture need a great deal of time and disconfirming evidence, indeed large-scale cognitive dissonance, to oblige them to rethink who they are and where they are going.

Since we have established criminal courts for people who are said to be suffering from immersion in a culture of impunity, it seems to me that we have to dig a little deeper to explain why a society develops such a culture. It is certainly true that morality is a social invention, and we create and sustain it well or badly over generations. If we do this badly, then everyone suffers. Morality arises out of a sense of group cohesion and the need for cooperative interaction between groups. So if groups are ruptured and interaction has no meaningful context within group existence, then impunity for individual crimes is of no moral consequence.

The explanation provided by Gasiberege is that Hutus lost their sense of continuity with the past and with it, their identity. Masović, the director of the Missing Persons unit in Bosnia, identified it as past sins never accounted for. Although one explanation seems to be that the past was lost while the other is that it remained all too present, both are credible explanations. However, they seem to miss another dimension that is also present in all these cases: the culpability of the outside world whether through economic, political, military or other actions of the time.

The Cambodian case is the most obvious: even those who attribute the breakdown of the culture entirely to the Khmer Rouge, or those who go far back into history and blame it more generally on Buddhist culture or French incursions, are obliged to acknowledge that the US bombing was disastrous for much of the peasantry. We have discussed the role of Belgian colonial personnel, including religious leaders, on Rwanda. If the culture of impunity arose because, as Gasiberege argues, the Hutu were deprived of a cultural identity, then it must have had its origins in the Belgian period.

I might be off base here, but I doubt if the culture of impunity is a good explanation for what happened in the former Yugoslavia. Without doubt the events of the Second World War and then those following it were vicious. First, thousands of Serbs, Jews, and Muslims were killed, and then thousands of Croatians were killed in retribution, along with Chetnik soldiers who were competing for power with Tito's partisans. Germans trying to flee were not immune. The same things were occurring throughout the continent, yet not everywhere did this culture of impunity arise. In the western democracies there were no internal wars though every one of those countries had a record that might well have shamed them. I suggest that the lack of internal wars was contingent on the reconstruction of their economies, in good measure thanks to the US Marshall Plan. They rebuilt and have since then flourished in an increasingly global economy. Such relative tranquility may not continue indefinitely – Belgium is uttering threats of civil war as I write – but there can be little doubt that a functioning economy allows for the development of stable governments. And where stable governments are established, internal war is unlikely. The Eastern European countries have had a different history, and perhaps we need to do research to determine whether they are afflicted with this culture of impunity.

The economic globalization of the world has been mentioned along the way in this book. Its manifestations often include the erosion of local markets and business opportunities for small-scale entrepreneurs, and this process has accelerated throughout the period since the 1990s. But I have left this to one side in order to focus on intervention and accountability for criminals. More should probably have been said on the subject. Among other aspects of globalization, we have so much information about the internal wars elsewhere precisely because of globalized information services. The internet provides us with immediate news, both false and accurate, about any corner of the earth. The concern with intervention grows out of our greater global knowledge. International courts, likewise, were finally established precisely because people in many societies became concerned about the world's little wars.

Throughout the text we have noted the tendency of internal wars since the 1990s to involve substantial corruption in all sectors of society. This aspect may always have been part of wars, but it has become particularly characteristic of contemporary civil wars. Globalization provides easy routes for the sellers of war technology, so that populations, far from the manufacturing sites and not necessarily connected to governments, can access guns and missiles and more sophisticated killing machines, and they can pay for them by accessing what is now called "the international mafia" whose other products are everything from illegal booze and cigarettes to child as well as adult prostitutes, gems, and various luxury goods stolen elsewhere. The guns and other war materiel are often left over from previous inter-state wars, and are now surplus to state requirements. They are bought and sold on black markets, and fed into trouble spots.

We have noted that gangs, private armies, guerrillas, half-trained militias often consisting of teenagers, criminals, fanatics, and fragments of what were once national armies are often involved in these internal wars. Were they used by governments to "do the dirty work" or are these wars genuinely different from traditional wars? The evidence suggests that they are genuinely different, and that they occur where states are breaking down and economies are not working. In such situations the usual hierarchy of command linking soldiers to states is absent.

We are unsure of the hierarchical organization of the Khmer Rouge and whether the mass murders were actually ordered by the leaders or undertaken by the numerous young foot-soldiers and middle-ranking officers (as we noted in the chapter on Cambodia, this is still under debate). We do know that the KR army was not a state army and we have several witnesses who say that it was more organized at a regional level, but less effectively at a central level. That war occurred in the 1970s, while the world was still embedded in the Cold War. It was, of course, the Cold War that provided the context for the bombing that destroyed so much of the society and provided the soldiers for the Khmer Rouge. Whomever should be held accountable for the KR atrocities, the government since then has been no pillar of rectitude. Forest and land concessions have been part of a generalized corruption in that country.

The Rwandan war was planned and orchestrated at top levels (we know this because trials have demonstrated the truth of it), but the foot-soldiers were youngsters who were both pushed from behind and pulled by ideology and their peer groups to do the actual killing. The government today has not been charged with generalized corruption, so in this respect it may be an anomaly amongst the governments that came into being following internal wars. It is certainly an anomaly in that it is firmly in control of the country (at least for now) whereas in most other cases governments following the wars have been unstable.

The war in Bosnia and Hercegovina provides the (unfortunate) model of the process of what some writers now call "new wars." (Kaldor and Vashee, 1997). The new wars, in contrast to inter-state wars of the past, are internal conflicts often carried largely by gangs and militias, possibly backed by state governments but not organized by them and the line of authority and responsibility is blurred. Readers may recall that at a critical juncture in the war in Bosnia, international negotiators suddenly realized that Milosevic did not have control of the Bosnian Serb paramilitary forces.

This is how Kaldor (2001:90) describes the new type of war:

The new wars are "globalized" wars. They involve the fragmentation and decentralization of the state. Participation is low relative to the population both because of lack of pay and because of lack of legitimacy on the part of the warring parties. There is very little domestic production, so the war effort is heavily dependent on local predation and external support. Battles are rare, most violence is directed against civilians, and cooperation between warring factions is common.

The objective of the new wars is to literally cleanse an area of persons who do not fit the profiles of the warriors. Usually this means ethnic cleansing, but it may also be restricted to religious affiliation. The new notion of nationalism is the inclusion of only one racial, ethnic, or religious group and exclusion of all others either through killing or obliging them to go into exile. Homogeneity is what is wanted. Thus these wars are identity-based.

Possibly, but not necessarily, the gangs, criminals, and private armies who are often on the front lines of these wars, perpetrating the most brutal of the crimes, also have a political objective. They may intend to destabilize a region as well as evict its previous population, take it over and challenge existing state governments on a broader scale. The facts that the economies of these regions are generally in disarray before the wars, and that the governments are generally weak and unable to maintain control of their own armies – let alone gangs and paramilitaries – might allow such groups to infiltrate and push aside legitimate authorities. The defect of this argument is that such gangs rarely show much political acumen and their actions appear to be based on short-term and opportunistic plans. They appear to be more intrigued with criminal activity and accumulation of spoils than with larger political objectives.

The argument against the explanation in terms of cultures of impunity, then, is that those cultures, where they exist, are evident only or primarily during wars where the lines of battle are already established and the borders and sanctity of states are already in disarray. These wars involve child-soldiers and criminal gangs whose actions are not directed by a hierarchical authority embedded in the state. They gain power through military means and through access to international gun dealers and other criminal gangs. This all happens not because there is a culture of impunity in the society at large but because the society is breaking down and losing its capacity to maintain itself. The basic cause may be economic, or it could be because of persistent failures amongst the political elite to seek accommodation of divergent interests. And these failures, in turn, may be due to a global process that undermines local governments and local economies.

Identity Ideologies and Politics

Identity may be a necessary component of human development, but that it should emerge as a major concern during or preceding internal wars, yet be quiescent much of the rest of the time, has to be explained in terms other than its long-standing existence. In short, identity has to be threatened before it emerges as a cause of conflict. Again, the threat appears to come about when a society as a whole is under threat, and that occurs when the society is disintegrating. Those who stand to lose a great deal are, of course, the most threatened, and so it would not be surprising if, under stressful societal conditions, the group with the most clout is the most aggressive in trying to stop change that would undermine its dominance. Identity politics are those where the identity of threatened groups becomes an ideology initially expressing pain at loss or perceived threats, then, gradually an ever more aggressive stance blaming others whose existence is anathema to the group.

Identity concerns were involved in the Hutu actions, though the potential loss of land was at least as significant a cause of the genocide. Identity concerns were involved in the Balkan wars, but again, land was a prominent concern and I suggest that what happens is that "identity" becomes the ideological explanation (along with "a culture of impunity") in the absence of an understanding of the political economy of these regions. In the Cambodian case the issue of identity never came up: that was a war for survival with a sustained hatred for those who had destroyed the culture and society of the rural people.

OBJECTIVES IN THE POSTWAR PERIOD

Survivors and outsiders who attempt to deal with a war-torn society when the conflict is over have to make painful decisions about whether accountability for the crimes is the priority, whether accountability will lead to reconciliation, whether just getting enough food and shelter for the population is more important than accountability, and whether obliging criminals to be accountable might reignite the conflict. Let us begin with the issue of accountability.

Accountability

Given the global events that so often underlie internal wars, given the role of non-government actors in new wars, and given the breakdown of state governments prior to and during these wars, who should be held accountable for atrocities?

There is general assent to the culpability of leaders, whether as state officers or gang leaders. But it is not always easy to identify and capture them. In traditional inter-state wars there was a recognizable hierarchy, and it was reasonable for middle-ranking officers to claim that they merely followed orders of their superiors. In the new wars the hierarchy is not obvious, and whether members are obliged to follow orders or choose to do so is variable. The two infamous leaders of the Bosnian Serbs are known, but others are less easily identified and some are undoubtedly still acting freely within the Serb or RS populations. And as it turns out, the two major leaders must have a substantial social community protecting them all these years after they were identified and indicted by the ICTY.

Let us suppose we have found these leaders. How best should they be held accountable? Firing squads went out with cavalries: trials supplanted them. If we were still able to choose between these methods, we might want to consider whether getting rid of violent leaders is more important than proving their guilt in societies that are still trying to emerge from violent experiences. We might also want to consider whether the publicity of trials is beneficial or deleterious for the population: on the one hand, survivors may gain information about what happened; on the other, they may be subjected to defence and prosecutorial statements that might trigger still further violence. In any event, these considerations have now been precluded. Dangerous criminals are sometimes assassinated or killed during capture, but most societies today do not choose to eradicate them by firing squads. So if we want to hold them accountable, we do it through the international or national courts.

While leaders are culpable of persuading others, maybe even forcing others, to act on their orders, followers and even bystanders who did nothing to stop the madness are not innocent. Besides, as the protective envelope around the two Bosnian Serb leaders indicates, the culpability stretches far into the society. Where do we draw the line? How far down the hierarchy of crimes must survivors go to feel that justice has been achieved? Should the criteria focus on the nature of the crimes or on the status of the criminal? The crux of the problem is that so many people were not acting as individuals seeking personal goals; rather, they were acting, under unusual circumstances, as members of groups with group goals. The Scorpions were a paramilitary gang operating in Srebrenica (the White Eagles and Avengers were others); Hutu killers were organized within village or neighbourhood gangs if they were not in the Interahamwe and national armed forces. There is no universal method for determining whether all members of these groups are equally guilty, or, on the contrary, whether any of them should be held individually accountable for what the groups did.

Western criminal justice is designed to deal with individual crimes against other individuals. It can deal with leaders who had particular roles in criminal activity. But it is less well attuned to armies, militias, gangs, and other groups that act collectively. A large number of people, often a huge proportion of the total population, had to be mobilized to enact genocide or other serious crimes, as happened in Cambodia and Rwanda. If all who are guilty are caught and tried, the surviving community might well be drowned yet again in the horror of that time; and besides, the society would be deprived of much of its labour force. Recrimination would provide the basis for justice; reconciliation would not be served; and, because so many versions of events would be elicited, truth would remain amorphous. This, indeed, seems to be happening in Rwanda.

But if only a few leaders are prosecuted and survivors know there are others whose crimes were also serious, the sense that justice is being done, accountability fulfilled, and truth revealed will be much diminished. Reconciliation is unlikely in this case as well.

Before assuming that accountability is the primary task, survivors might want to consider the possibility that truth or reconciliation are more important. Truth is hard to come by either in a courtroom or by most other methods, but revelation may be more forthcoming if truth commissions are introduced initially, with court cases following them for those who are deemed to have withheld or lied about the truth – as in the South African Truth and Reconciliation Commission (Boraine,2000). If the objective is not accountability so much as truth, then it is possible that no court processes are ideal. Truth commissions – if well conducted and restricting the punitive measures for those who speak up (even when they were leaders and committed or ordered heinous crimes) – have the merit of ensuring that survivors and those who were complicit in the crimes learn what happened, when it happened, how it happened, and who was responsible for its happening. However, they are possible only if survivors and witnesses are unafraid to speak, and only if there is a police force capable of investigating the crimes to determine whether or not the survivors are telling the truth. In a society in which the perpetrators are still able to do harm, the conditions for truth commissions are not auspicious. If truth is to be elicited, then force must be met with force. Domestic courts may be hindered in the same fashion. When this occurs, international criminal courts have a greater capacity than do domestic courts to oblige perpetrators to account for their actions. But all such procedures require that their deliberations be publicized so that both survivors and followers of those leaders are informed.

In one of the chapters on Rwanda (chapter 7) I discuss a prisoner who referred to another man, a man who had committed suicide while in prison, as a gentle person who had been pulled into the vortex of the genocide even though he would never, had the choice been his, have harmed anyone. Many such stories have been elicited by researchers in Rwanda, where Hutus were sometimes forced by armed soldiers or otherwise persuaded that they had no choice but to kill their neighbours. These stories oblige judges to consider whether the charges against these killers are just.

The camaraderie of warriors, the ideologies of ethnic cleansing, the sheer hedonism of life on the frontlines of a civil war, the rush of adrenaline, and the provision of a job, uniforms, and illicit income encouraged many foot-soldiers in all of these wars to act in ways that would not have been possible during peacetime. They gained an identity and acceptance when they joined the gangs. And, when it was over, few gave themselves up or even seemed to comprehend that what they had done (and were still doing) was criminal. Forced to face a trial, they were astounded to be accused and sentenced in a foreign court.

At the risk of pointing out the obvious: individual humans need groups for their survival; and groups, not individuals, are the basic units of human society. We are born into families and our survival depends on their care; subsequently, most of us move through life as members of a succession of groups, encasing us in the collectivities of kin, village or larger region, school, work, religion, and play. Groups develop divisions of labour that enable their members to obtain food and shelter. Groups provide their members with a shared identity, and that identity is the basis of culture. But groups also oblige their members to conform. They offer approval and rewards to members in good standing; ostracism may be the penalty for dissent.

While the bloodbaths in Cambodia, Rwanda, Yugoslavia, and Nazi Germany cannot be explained simply with reference to peer group pressure, group pressure does provide an insight into why many ordinary people commit terrible crimes. Their identity becomes that of the group, and respect from the group is their reward. Those who disobey must have a reserve of self-awareness or a moral code that separates them from the group. Gaining others' respect is possibly less important to them than it is to those who accept the orders.[10] Individual differences are well embedded long before people are faced with awful choices, and, in fact, probably the choice to go with the herd is not experienced as a conscious decision. One is not excusing brutal action by considering the social context, but the consideration does raise questions about justice and punishment for herds of followers. The victors, after all, might also be herd-like in their groups or armies.

Collective Guilt?

Western law holds individuals responsible for their crimes. Individual responsibility is the vital soul of Western society, and it has proved itself to be a strong force for a healthy society. But we are addressing the conflicts of societies in which the cleavage is between groups, not individuals. The groups define themselves, and members have a group identity so powerful that they are prepared, as individuals, to both kill and die for it. To understand why individuals acted as they did may oblige external judges to recognize collectivities as actors. This is problematic because it immediately raises the spectre of collective guilt, and there are good reasons for eschewing that particular demon.

The argument against collective guilt usually refers to Germans who lived through the 1930s and 1940s: it is not acceptable to blame all of them for the murderous work of the Nazis. Many Germans were as appalled by what was happening as were the foreign enemies of Nazi Germany at that time. The same argument applies to Italians under Mussolini, French under the Vichy regime, and Croats under the Ustashe. But the difficulty is that many people did support fascism in these countries, and without those supporters – who must have been numerous – the leaders who led them into war and the establishment of concentration camps would not have emerged and survived. There are reasons for the support people gave these leaders, reasons that lie in the context of the period, and much of that context had to do with exterior influences and power. Thus does the circle widen: individuals did things because they were enmeshed in social networks that became packs or herds experiencing some kind of collective – or what some might call swarming – social psychology, and these groups or social networks did things because they were enmeshed in much larger networks of global power. They were global pieces, much like jigsaw fragments, part of a much larger puzzle over which they had little or no control. Some acted in fear. Others acted in jubilation, enjoying the freedom from constraints. Still others were silent bystanders, unwilling to intervene or to oppose actions that they knew were criminal or at least, within their own moral codes, immoral.

We cannot take an entire society to court, however, and charging its leaders with crimes is a means of charging the whole society with its responsibility for group crimes. However, this only works, in the sense of informing the society of its own past errors, if they accept responsibility for following those leaders. If, as in Serbia, Croatia, and Bosnia, and in Cambodia as well, a substantial proportion of the society is unaccountable, and treats The Hague trials or the special tribunal being established in Cambodia as foreign impositions, the trials fail to serve their fundamental purpose.

Although Bosnia's bid against Serbia failed, this case widened the definition of collective crimes. It obliges courts as well as citizens to consider whether statespersons and generals who act on our behalf are reasonably held accountable when their actions are deemed morally unacceptable by others. If we whom they represent deem them unacceptable, then the problem is how to rid ourselves of their leadership. It is possible, though not easy, to do this in a democratic society. It is much more difficult to do so in an autocratic or authoritarian society. If a population could rid itself of leaders only at the cost of violence and lives lost, is it reasonable to hold that population accountable?

But in the Bosnia v Serbia case the more problematic issue was whether the state in Serbia was responsible for what was done by Bosnian Serbs and other Serbs not directly under the hierarchical control of the Serb government. There lies the difference between traditional wars between state-organized armed forces and new wars between relatively unorganized gangs and paramilitaries. The court found a compromise: the Serb state was responsible for knowing but not stopping the genocide at Srebrenica.

Reconciliation

I have said little about reconciliation. This is because there is so little evidence of it in the societies I have been discussing. There is no agreed definition of the term, no obvious measure by which reconciliation might be achieved. It is a spiritual experience that affects former enemies, allowing them to forgive or at least to tolerate one another so that they may coexist. It is antithetical to the processes of justice in adversarial courts, which are more attuned to increasing the enmity between groups, to proving that this person or that one is guilty of the crimes that have so harmed others.

In the societies discussed in this book there is little evidence that international courts have brought about reconciliation. However, when the new states of the former Yugoslavia begin to prosecute their own cases, the reconciliation process might be encouraged. Identifying not merely others who were guilty but also "our own" guilty members might soften the hatred and allow a society to recognize that, even if it was the victim of many crimes, it, too, is culpable. Truth and a certain humility, then, are essential before reconciliation can thrive.

Vengeance can eradicate possibilities for genuine reconciliation. Consider the case of Rwanda. Reconciliation between Hutus and Tutsis is hard to imagine, though the government insists that all members of the population call themselves Rwandans and never again refer to the barriers between the two groups. This begins a symbolic process of recasting relationships, but the fact remains that Tutsis, ruling the country as victors, have undertaken a massive expression of vengeance against their fellow citizens. They are intent on punishing all who were or might have been génocidaires, not on gaining mutual trust. As well, the rulers are better educated and wealthier than Hutus. If one is an optimist, the election results described earlier imply that the whole population is satisfied with what amounts to Tutsi rule even if under the label "Rwandan." Certainly there is now peace, and the society does function. But given the repression of Hutu survivors, the incarceration of so many of their members, the continuing emigration of those who can escape, and the unforgiving stance of Tutsi leaders towards Hutus implicated in the genocides, this story does not seem to be finished. And only the most determined optimist would ignore the fact that Tutsis are still only a seventh or so of the total population and that they are ruling over the majority.

The creation of gacaca courts has pulled the population together by way of obliging them to listen and to judge their peers; it has also pushed them apart in unintended ways. An individual who testifies against another is afraid when the other is released from jail. Evidence is often hard to find, and oral testimony brings with it the danger of hyperbole and the temptation to avoid the truth if it might incriminate oneself or those one cares for. The lack of lawyers, the prevalence of illiteracy among community leaders and judges, the many hurdles that have been and are still encountered in establishing these courts attract criticism from human rights activists. However, there was no way that this little country could possibly have put all the persons charged with complicity through regular courts. A truth and reconciliation commission might have been more effective.

Victors, Losers, and Justice

I suggested in the introductory chapter that national willingness to engage in formal accountability and justice processes would be related to whether states were victors or losers. In Rwanda, the victors are eager to make every Hutu accountable for the genocide, even to the point of creating new grievances against their rule. In Serbia, whose leaders helped to ignite the civil war, Serbs were the greatest losers. They are reluctant to participate in the justice process at the ICTY and are only now, years after the end of the wars, beginning to process some of their own cases against native sons and daughters. In Bosnia and Hercegovina, the situation is more ambiguous, with no victors but with varying degrees of culpability for what happened. In spite of its severe losses of land, population, and community, FBiH is gradually developing its social institutions, including its own courts. It has retained some of its civic leaders, and they have provided social capital to begin the reconstruction process. Its other part, Republika Srpska, is lagging far behind and, like Serbia, is reluctant to undertake judicial proceedings against the leaders of its own population. According to Amnesty International 2007, as noted above, Croatia is having similar difficulties in dealing with its own culpability.

This pattern is not surprising: guilty people are rarely eager to punish themselves, and people who lose civil wars or who committed genocide while losing civil wars are not likely to be happy about taking responsibility for what happened. But the point needs to be made because it tells outsiders that each society that experiences these violent episodes has to be understood on its own terms. There is no solution that fits them all. Again, let it be said, there is no easy fix. This then raises the question of whether an international criminal court based on Western criminal law is appropriate to all cases. The fact that, in some cases, international lawyers have been willing to establish hybrid courts indicates an awareness that differences must be taken into consideration. But where is the appropriate line between the full Western criminal justice system and local systems such as that in Cambodia?

The answer, I suggest, lies not in abstract notions of justice but, in the Cambodian case, in the widespread culpability of too many people. No system that deprives current leaders of control over the outcomes will be accepted by them. Positive changes in Cambodia will have to come by way of political will and economic development. Let us review the situation there.

The Proposed Extraordinary Chambers for Cambodia

The proposed extraordinary chambers, as they are called, will, if they proceed, be a mixture of Cambodian and international criminal law. As well, they will include both Cambodian and international lawyers and judges, and they will occur on Cambodian soil. They will try only a handful of individuals believed to be the leaders of the Khmer Rouge. They will be paid for entirely by other countries, but the total amount so far pledged is only a fraction of what the ICTY and ICTR have cost. Some of the international judges and lawyers might provide their services on a pro bono basis, but that is unlikely to happen if, as the Cambodian lawyers demanded for a time, anyone defending one of the indicted leaders should pay a hefty price to Cambodia for the privilege. This would have left the defence up to Cambodian lawyers.

During much of 2007, the process was seriously stalled because the two groups of legal experts disagreed about many of the rules of procedure. Cambodians have complained that the international model does not embody the cultural norms of their society. It is based on a foreign understanding of the nature of justice. They have balked at rules designed to protect witnesses and rules for ensuring that judges are completely independent of political pressures. After much wrangling, a negotiated agreement was reached, though there remain areas of contention and the trial could be derailed at a later time.

Critics may read the difficulties of reaching consensus as implying fear of revelations about current leaders' histories. One notes that, if Cambodians had wanted national trials without international legal norms, they could have mounted them at any time in the past two dozen years. All that occurred was the Vietnamese "trial" of Ieng Sary and Pol Pot in absentia (and Sary's later rehabilitation). Some part of the lengthy delay can be attributed to the possibility of recurring large-scale violence, but that possibility decreased with the years, especially after Pol Pot's demise. However, small-scale violence has never ceased and has often determined political and social outcomes. The proposed extraordinary trials do not seem to be understood by current leaders as impediments to violence as a way of governing.

Although stalwart supporters of an international criminal trial – especially the Documentation Centre of Cambodia in Phnom Penh – want and demand justice, the majority of Cambodia's population is so insecure that the niceties of justice seem a long way off. A good part of the stumbling block here is that the government itself, as well as the local leadership at village levels, is implicated in the former regime. The links in some cases are significant; individuals who were undeniably involved in violent activities under the KR are still in leadership positions at village, district, or national levels. Other individuals were affiliated with the KR, but there is no evidence that they were in positions to impose violence on the population of their territories. An impoverished population, particularly in rural areas, see that neighbours, leading citizens, or government appointees, whom they know to have been among their former torturers, are still active and relatively powerful. The promise of trials for only a handful of surviving top KR leaders does not remove the threat of violence or provide the sense of justice that these people need. While undoubtedly the few old men who are targeted for trials should be tried, those who want a trial now may be settling for less than justice. The trials, if they actually occur, could become propaganda tools for powerful individuals in government and the economy.

Cambodia Missing Its Collectivities

When we consider what is now Cambodia, the implications of group membership become apparent by their absence. Cambodia lost its collective identities. The winners were not an ethnic group, a clan, a family, an elite, a class, or any other cohesive entity. They were simply the survivors of the Khmer Rouge. Some had fled to Vietnam to avoid the fratricide occurring within the ranks of the revolutionary movement; some had become refugees in the border areas of Thailand; and some had survived by hiding in the forests. They are not buddies, particularly; indeed, their enmities are well known and sometimes fatal. During the murderous regime families were split up and everyone, children included, was put through such terrifying experiences that many became incapable of caring for others – in some cases, even for themselves. Children were turned into warriors, spouses into informants. Trust dissolved. Neither surviving children nor their parents are sure of their identity in the aftermath. And when a society is not reconstructed, when institutions are not reinvented, when physical survival is about all that anyone can manage from day to day, identity has very little meaning.

If the assumption that society consists of collectivities and the relationships between them is correct, then Cambodia is not a living society. And we must ask a difficult question: will this tragic society have a better chance of revitalizing itself if the KR leaders are charged and imprisoned than it would if nothing happens? Would its chances of revival improve if, in addition to these few old men, the trials included village chiefs under the KR and others who held positions of responsibility? Would people benefit as much from these proposed trials as they might from, at long last, a truth telling? Or village-level sessions directed towards reconciliation? The problem is that alternatives might actually put everyone in more jeopardy because if people told the truths they know, the government and all the official institutional props would fall. The wizard would lose control. Insecurity, already pervasive, might engulf the survivors.

As a broken society without collectivities, without common purpose, with corruption at every pore and leadership that fails to support its followers, how is this society to find justice, truth, or reconciliation? I began this book with doubts about the possibility that the proposed extraordinary chambers would address the ills of a sick society. I end it with even greater doubts. This country desperately needs peace and truth, respite from endless violence but honesty about what happened. A trial of these old men – one was given an amnesty by the current rulers, the others (with the exception of one) have not been judged at all but, rather, have been allowed to gracefully and quite comfortably age – is not what it needs. Cambodia needs a police force that will seriously investigate the roles of village chiefs during the KR period, including those of the government's friends, many of whom are still in place. It needs a government that genuinely subjects itself to periodic elections instead of assassinating or jailing anyone who might oppose it. It needs to invest in the rural countryside so that people can live by sowing crops. It needs to rid itself of rapacious outsiders who are decimating the forests. It needs, to be sure, the rule of law; however, when this is used only for the purpose of ridding Cambodia of the bandits called the Khmer Rouge, it is insufficient. Cambodians need it every day for all of their activities.

GLOBAL AND LOCAL REALITIES AND ORIENTATIONS

Our focus on intervention and accountability has allowed less space for considering other conditions that affect the societies that have experienced these wars. One of these conditions is population changes. In Bosnia and Hercegovina, in Serbia and in Montenegro, the birth rates are so low that these societies cannot possibly replace themselves without substantial immigration. Yet immigration is not a probable development because there is very little to attract outsiders, and young people who can obtain employment elsewhere are leaving these countries. Displaced populations are hesitant to return because of identity politics. The Dayton solution in Bosnia is harsh in its obligatory divisions of school-children, and thus their parents are reluctant to return to homes in ethnically divided districts. Identity ideologies have so pervaded the countryside in Serbia and Montenegro that those who do not share in the ideologies are looking for exits.

Although the conflict in Rwanda was bitter, its people have not responded by limiting their birth rates. Indeed, the Rwandan birth rate of 40.37 per 1000 persons/yr, while lower than much of Africa today, is a great deal higher than in Eastern and Southern as well as Western European countries. Its nine million people are densely packed into 343 persons per km². (UN 2007 and World Fact Book 2007). Again Rwanda is faced with the problem of overpopulation relative to the carrying capacity of the land. As well, since Hutu are a majority of the population now, presumably it will be Hutu whose numbers increase fastest. Such population data, extreme in both directions, will have profound implications for succeeding generations in all of these countries. One might speculate that wars, whether of the new or more traditional varieties, are the likely outcome where too small a population tries to hold on to land that is scarce elsewhere.

Another aspect of post-war life is a growing divergence between urban and rural populations. In the case of Serbia we learned of a study that showed "intellectual" young people in Belgrade as being contemptuous of their country cousins. There was also a suggestion that much of the nationalism had a rural origin, and most of the critics and dissidents were urbanites. This may be related to the development of a global economy, global technologies of communication, global education systems, and other indices of contemporary globalization. The urban, educated young people are much freer to leave their birth countries and to become employed in a global marketplace. Identity for them, as a consequence, is not tied to their little region of the earth; for much less affluent rural people, fear of the global economy and its tendency to negatively change their lives, is not an irrational response.

In conclusion, then, we – the "international community" so often mentioned by writers on these subjects – might be a little less quick to talk about cultures of impunity and become a little more conscious of the inequalities and divisions within societies that often have a global context.

POSTSCRIPT

The foregoing refers to the organization and disintegration of small societies. While external powers attempt to influence broken societies by introducing Western legal systems and courts, the one thing still missing is their acknowledgment of their own culpability for some of these happenings. Cambodia's fate was much influenced by the self-interested actions of the United States, China, Thailand, and Vietnam. Rwanda's fate was and still is much influenced by its colonial experience and French commercial and cultural interests. Yugoslavia has always been buffeted between external empires, and its internal pieces are reflections of that history. As of the opening decade of the twenty-first century, we do not seem to have any means of insisting on accountability for those external forces. The World Court, in its judgment of Bosnia's case against Serbia, missed an opportunity to demonstrate that those who hold political and economic power can be held accountable for their role in planning and implementing genocide.

Cambodians, if they were able to come together and prepare a case, might also go to the World Court even at this late stage. The bombing of Cambodia was an illegal action. It destroyed a society and was the precursor to the subsequent civil war and the horrible crimes against humanity committed by the Khmer Rouge. But while the world is prepared to put on show trials against aged Khmer Rouge leaders, it has indicated no capacity or interest in trying the surviving leaders of China, Thailand, Vietnam, and the United States for their roles in the tragedy. And that, I suggest, is a major failure of the Western system of justice.

I write the above in a time when American jails situated outside the United States in Guantánamo Bay, Cuba; in Iraq; in Eastern Europe; and possibly elsewhere are operating in complete disregard of war crimes conventions that an earlier administration in the United States signed and ratified and that, for decades, have provided the benchmark rules for conduct of states regarding prisoners of war. In response to a unilateral declaration of war against all whom the US administration deems to be terrorists, the United States has abrogated agreements, conventions, and contracts with other countries and, since 11 September 2001, has fundamentally changed the relationship between its federal government and its own citizens. It has undertaken a war in Iraq even though no evidence of Iraqi participation in or support for the events of 9/11 was ever produced. It has created a culture of impunity for the torture of prisoners incarcerated throughout the globe, Abu Ghraib apparently being but one of many such infamous structures. The least powerful guards at that institution are the only ones to have paid a price for implementing practices ordered by higher authorities, who, with apparent impunity, implied that it was acceptable to torture those deemed to be "others."

Notes

1 Cambodian estimates vary enormously as shown by Bruce Sharp in
"Counting Hell" (http://www.mekong.net/cambodia/deaths/htm).
On Bosnia, this figure is half that frequently cited for war-related
deaths. See Tabeau and Bijak (2005). The Demographic Unit of the
ICTY numbers Bosnian deaths at 102,622. These sources and others
are cited in "War in Bosnia and Hercegovina" in *Wikipedia*
(30 January 2007). (I am indebted to an anonymous reviewer for
advising me of new population data.)

2 The term "social capital" was made popular by Robert Putnam in
several publications, including Putnam (1993 and 2000). Helliwell
(2000) adds to the discussion of this concept.

3 This is restated in new stories regarding the Canadian prime minister's
reference to the event as a genocide. See, for example, *Globe and Mail*,
11 May 2006.

4 See, for example, Oke (1988). Also, I quoted a contemporary journalist, Gunduz Aktan, in the *Turkish Daily News*, 21 May 2002, who wrote:
"The Armenian incidents do not amount to genocide because the
Armenians constituted a 'political group,' which is not covered by
the Genocide Convention" (Marchak 2003, 96).

5 Janis (1982) is a revised edition of a 1972 book on the same subject.
Social psychologists have since added substantially to the literature.
William H. Whyte is credited with the coining of the term in a 1952
article in *Fortune* magazine.

6 For examples of critical assessments, see Fuller and Aldag (1998) and
Kramer (1998).

7 Festinger himself wrote *A Theory of Cognitive Dissonance* in 1957. Since then, several experiments and arguments were published in the 1960s and 1970s. Among more recent publications are Burris, Harmon-Jones, and Tarpley (1997) and Harmon-Jones and Mills (1999).

8 According to Chesterman (2004, 157), "lustration" comes from Latin and refers to a purifying sacrifice following the quinquennial census in Rome.

9 Newspapers of the period provided much of this information, and Wikipedia provides an account of the history under "Talisman Energy" as of 2 March 2007.

10 On 13 January 2007, the *Globe and Mail* (Canada) reported that US Joint Chiefs Chairman General Peter Pace told Congress that the Pentagon had authorized a worldwide effort to hunt and kill terrorists, that the State Department and Pentagon had taken control of Somalia policy in order to use Ethiopian troops as a proxy force against Islamists, and that military officials intended to use the Somalia operation as a model for future actions.

CHAPTER TWO

1 German rule was actually more benign than Belgian rule as Germany never showed much interest in this tiny African territory.

2 On pages one and two, Bhatfia (2003) cites data from Collier (1993).

3 In Appendix C, this revised edition of Haass's book provides the text of Weinberger's 28 November 1984 speech to the US National Press Club.

4 From speech to the United Nations General Assembly, 27 September 1993, as quoted in Haass (1999, 17) and excerpted in Haass (1999, Appendix G).

5 Further discussion can be found in contributions to Stedman, Rothchild, and Cousens (2002), and Findlay (2002).

6 Bruce Jones, "The Limits of Peacekeeping: The UN Finds Itself Stretched Thin by Conflicts in Africa and Elsewhere," *Los Angeles Times*, 1 March 2006.

7 This narrative follows that of Findlay (2002, chap. 3).

8 As noted in an interview between Hans von (Graf) Sponeck and Milan Raivon at a conference in Manchester, December 2000, organized by Voices in the Wilderness UK (available at www.brusselstribunal.org/bios/Sponeck.htm).

9 H.C. Graf Sponeck, open letter to Britain's minister for Iraq, Peter Hain, *Guardian*, 3 January 2001.

10 Interview between Milan Raivon and Hans von Sponeck, 23 December 2001.

11 Ibid.

12 What follows is standard information on Iraq. My own sources include: Marr (2004), Cockburn and Cockburn (1999), Taylor (2003), Parker (2003), and Dodge and Simon (2003).

13 I have "sanitized" this paragraph by omitting reference to actions for which there is no widely accepted understanding. Some readers will wish I had included the more damning bits but they are invited to read the sources named in the previous footnote.

14 Arguments against the Iraq war are numerous, but the main three are as follows: (1) there were no weapons of mass destruction; (2) Iraq posed no threat to the United States or any other states not only because it lacked weapons and a well-trained army but also because its people were suffering from the blockade; and (3) Iraq was not the home of Wahabi Islamists – on the contrary, it was their targeted enemy because it retained a thoroughly secular state. Why the war was launched remains a matter of controversy.

CHAPTER THREE

1 Chile, Comisión Nacional de Verdad y Reconciliación (1991). Shorter version entitled *Síntesis del Informe de la Comisión de Verdad y Reconciliación "Para Creer en Chile."*

2 Reprinted in Kritz (1995, 203–06).

3 Blackwater U.S.A. is one of the private security contractors. It was accused in September 2007 by the Iraqi Prime Minister Nouri al-Maliki of being responsible for several shootings. Reported in *The Vancouver Sun* Sept 22, 2007 A12.

4 This is reported in Liam Lacey, "Older, But Is He Any Wiser?" *Globe and Mail,* 6 February 2004. It is attributed to Robert McNamara in a review of *In Retrospect: The Tragedy and Lessons of Vietnam* (McNamara and VanDeMark 1995).

5 The terms of these conventions and laws are widely available, including on Wikipedia, the free encyclopedia on the web.

6 The most revealing study of the ICTY is Bass (2000).

7 *International Justice Tribunal Online* touches on cost from time to time. See also Kimani (2002).

8 The Nixon government and Kissinger's role in Chile are discussed in Marchak (2003, chap. 11), which is based on *US Senate Select Committee*

on Intelligence Activities (United States 1975); Hersh (1983, 258–96); and Spooner (1994). See also Hitchens (2000).

9 The Convention against Torture and Other Cruel, Inhuman or Degrading Treatment or Punishment came into force in June 1987.

10 As reported in "British War Crimes Law Has Israel Furious," *National Post* (Canada), 28 February 2006, A10.

11 All quotations in this section, unless otherwise noted, are from the Rome Statute.

12 All major newspapers carried this story, and my understanding of the 171-page decision (not accessible at the time of writing) is based on the UN website, the *International Herald Tribune*, and several online newspapers dated 27 and 28 February 2007. Online sources prior to the decision include: UN website updates on information about current cases and International Court of Justice Press Release 2006/18, 9 May 2006, regarding the application by Bosnia and Herzegovina and the announcement of the conclusion of public hearings; Global Policy Forum, Institute for War and Peace Report (2006); Cobban, for Transitional Justice Forum (2006); and Wikipedia, "Bosnian Genocide Case at the International Court of Justice" (topic = Bosnia and ICJ). The case has been through several iterations due to the changes in the name and composition of Yugoslavia, problems of UN membership, and a counter-suit accusing Bosnia and Hercegovina of committing genocide against the Bosnian Serb population (later dropped). Republika Srpska as an entity and some Bosnia and Hercegovina citizens have objected to the case on the grounds of excessive cost. This has since been written up by a number of journalists. For an account of the deficiency of documents, see Simons (2007).

13 As stated in the International Court of Justice press release 2006/18, 9 May 2006. The ICJ website, at www.UN.icj-cij.org, provides the history of proceedings and full transcripts of hearings held between 27 February and 9 May 2006.

14 The quotation is cited by Kate Connolly in "Bosnia Sues Serbia for Genocide," *National Post* (Canada), 28 February 2006, A10.

15 Wikipedia, "Bosnian Genocide Case at the International Court of Justice" (topic = Bosnia and ICJ), calls this possibly the most important case since the Nuremberg Trials.

16 Among the many excellent studies of the period in Argentina are: Andersen (1993), Guest (1990), O'Donnell (1988), Nino (1996), and Smith (1991). In Marchak (1999), I describe the repression through the eyes of participants.

17 Malamud-Goti cites evidence in Argentina, Comisión Nacional sobre la Desaparición de Personas (1985).

18 For a survey of truth commissions see Hayner (2001).

19 A review of this literature is provided in excerpts in Kritz (1995, 2:71–125).

CHAPTER FOUR

1 This history is culled from existing scholarly sources, and readers should be warned that scholars are not all of the same mind. The range of interpretations on the Khmer Rouge is considerable: was it extremely centralized or did the district subleaders exercise discretion about killing populations under their control? How lethal and how organized were the Khmer Rouge forces in their retreat after 1979? How implicated were the defectors who ran the government in Phnom Penh from 1979 right through to the first decade of the next century? However, on the general contours of the UNTAC period, there is more agreement. I have attempted to take into account diverse interpretations where they are relevant to the concerns of this book: that is, regarding the global context, the interventions, and the subsequent social development or lack thereof.

2 Note that the air force data were released by the Clinton administration in 2000 primarily to enable identification of sites with unexploded ordnance. Until the publication of Owen's map based on these data, writers either did not know of this source or did not realize its importance. Thus, publications showing data beginning in 1969 and total bomb sites at a fifth of the total shown by the air force data are inconsistent with Owen and Kiernan's information.

3 For a discussion of American politics of the period, see Hersh (1983) and Shawcross (1984).

4 This is emphasized in Etcheson (2005, chap. 2). Many other writers have also recorded the similarity between the two regimes.

5 Gottesman (2003, chap. 3) is particularly helpful with regard to accounts of regional situations in this period.

6 This section follows the depiction of events in Berdal and Leifer (1996, 32–5).

7 Etcheson argues, contrary to many studies published earlier, that the KR remained a viable force capable of retaking the country after the withdrawal of the Vietnamese.

8 Agreement on a Comprehensive Political Settlement of the Cambodia Conflict (n. 3), pt. 1, sec. 3, art. 6, as cited in Findlay (2002, 125n5).

9 Berdal and Leifer (1996) provide somewhat lower estimates of costs at around US$1.79 billion, with twenty-two thousand military and civilian personnel deployed for the purpose.

10 Etcheson (2005, 40–1) argues that these benefits had to be measured against the failure to stop the war, to reintegrate soldiers and repatriated refugees, and to create a "neutral political environment."

11 As reprinted by the DCC, email newsletter, 26 May 2005.

12 As cited by Bill Bainbridge in *Phnom Penh Post* (no title) 12 September 2003.

13 Bainbridge, *Phnom Penh Post*, 12 September 2003, cites Heder's research and an independent visit to the area on 4 April 2003 by the *Cambodian Post* (names of visitors not reported).

14 Fieldnotes, September 2003. Note: the DCC is gradually compiling KR biographies through interviews with many country people who were involved. In addition, it is coordinating a large-scale project to help victims of the KR to deal with trauma.

15 For example, Sam Bith, a former commander of KR forces who had been in the KR for twenty-eight years and who defected in 1996 – long after the Vietnam invasion – was made a major-general in the Cambodian army and granted amnesty for his role in the previous organization.

16 Phelim Kyne, "Cambodia Fin Min May Testify at Genocide Trial," DCC, 15 May 2004.

17 Evan Osnos, "A Chilling Visit with Pol Pot's 'Brother': 27 Years after Cambodia's Genocide, Court Hopes Leaders Will Explain Terror," *Herald Tribune*, 17 February 2006. Reprinted by DCC, 17 February 2006.

18 Michelle Vachon, review of "A Moment in Time," *Cambodia Daily*, 23–4 April 2005.

19 Amnesty International, "Cambodia: Extraordinary Chambers Must Not Rush to Adopt Flawed Rules," public statement, 22 November 2006.

20 As quoted in the *Cambodia Daily*, 14 August 2003.

CHAPTER FIVE

1 Cambodia, National Assembly, news release by SRP members of Parliament, 28 February 2004.

2 This is quoted in the *Boston Globe Online* news by Rafael D. Frankel on 29 February 2004. It is consistent with my September 2003 interview with Sokha.

3 khmerintelligence@yahoogroups.com, digest number 534.

4 Samngat KI website, 17 April 2005 (available at www.khmerintelligence.org).

5 UNICEF funded the cartoon books project. The European Union gave a three-year grant in 1992, then USAID, the Asia Foundation, and USASIA funds arrived. Since then other democratic countries and private foundations have helped with LICADHO projects.

6 Médecins sans frontières has its own program in Cambodia.

7 Only white rice is provided to prisoners, even though brown rice is much better when it comes to providing vitamin B1, which is essential for warding off this life-crippling disease.

8 The sources for the data reported in the assessment are the 2004 Cambodia Socio-Economic Survey and a set of studies by the Cambodia Development Resource Institute and the Economic Institute of Cambodia as well as scholarly journal articles. The entire report is available online at www.worldbank.org/kh.

9 World Development Indicators developed by the UN Food and Agriculture Organization, as shown in World Bank (2006, viii-xi).

10 This is based on household surveys, but the World Bank warns that the two surveys (1994 and 2004) are not directly comparable.

11 According to the Centre for the Development of Cambodia in Phnom Penh, Chinese investment amounting to about $US217 million in 2004 is located in timber, textiles, mining, food processing and tourism (Pocha 2005).

12 Ker Munthit, Associated Press, in release dated 6 November 2003, distributed by Documentation Centre of Cambodia, 7 November 2003. See also World Bank (2004).

13 This report is labelled "confidential: not for citation or attribution" even though it is freely available on the World Bank's website.

14 English has supplanted French as the major non-indigenous language in Cambodia.

CHAPTER SIX

1 The following brief account is based on many sources, including Prunier (1995), Lemarchand (2003), and others cited in Marchak (2003).

2 Simon Gasiberege interview, taped fieldnotes, 2003.

3 Fictionalized accounts include the films *Hotel Rwanda* and *By the Pool in Kigali*. The second of these was based on the novel by Gil Courtemanche (2004) entitled *A Sunday at the Pool in Kigali.*

4 This section is based on the following sources: Human Rights Watch (2001a), Kleine-Ahlbrandt (2000), Global IDP Database online, Amnesty International (1998), and World Food Programme (1999).

5 Reported by Global IDP, May 2001 online.

6 Global IDP 2003, "Rwanda" online.
7 Statistics are taken from the World Bank Group, *Rwanda Data Profile*, 2000–2005 and are supplemented by the World Bank Group, *Gender-Stats database*, 1980–2004.
8 World Bank, Summary Education Profile: Rwanda, 1985–2004. Data incomplete.
9 *Reuters*, 16 August 2003.
10 *National Post*, 11 March 2004.
11 African Rights press release, 9 July 2004.
12 Fieldnotes, interview.
13 In 1998, I was scheduled to teach several summer courses at the University of Augsberg in the State of Bavaria. After arriving there, and with no advance warning, I was presented with a list of forty-eight organizations that the state said were dangerous to the society. And I, along with all who taught there, whether Germans or Auslanders like myself, had to sign the form saying that we did not support these groups. The order governed only persons employed by the state government, including teachers and university faculty. The organizations included a religious group, some extreme left or extreme right groups, and many apparently in-between but not acceptable to the Christian Democrats who were in power. I refused to do so and resigned.
14 Pan-Africa (PANA) online, 9 April 2001 (available at www.panafrican-movement.org).

CHAPTER SEVEN

1 These are excerpts from several interviews conducted in 2003. The interviewees were promised that no identifying information would be published.
2 Craig Timberg, "In Rwanda, Suicides Haunt Search for Justice and Closure," *Washington Post* (online), 17 February 2006.
3 Aimable Twahirwa, "Genocide Sentences 'Humiliate Survivors,'" *Mail and Guardian* (online), 10 January 2006.

CHAPTER EIGHT

1 In the 1981 Yugoslav census, in a population of 22,428 million, self-designated Serbs comprised 36.3 percent of the total population, Croats 19.8 percent, and Muslims 8 percent.
2 This is from Judah (2000, 155). It is consistent with other sources on the period.

3 Precisely when the term "Bosniak" became common is not clear. The
  Encyclopedia Britannica says it replaced "Muslim" by the mid-1990s.
  Others date it as following the internal war, but there are claims that it
  preceded the hostilities.
4 A voluminous literature has emerged regarding the influence of ethnicity on conflict. Best known is Bogdan Denitch, *Ethnic Nationalism*. 1994.
5 *Der Spiegel* online, "Slovenia Mass Grave Could Be Europe's Killing
  Fields," 21 August 2007.
6 Bose cites a total population of 4.4 million in 1992, slightly larger than
  what is cited in other sources.
7 See Shrader (2003) for a detailed account of this aspect of the war.
8 Many writers make this point. Findlay (2002, 228–41) does so in some detail.
9 The political manoeuvring around Goražde is described in detail in
  Silber and Little (1996, 324–34).
10 Wikipedia population estimate as of 2004. No census has been conducted, so this is an estimate taking into account the emigration and
  dislocations of populations.
11 Federation of Bosnia and Hercegovina, Wikipedia, accessed 25 January
  2007; also Republika Srpska, same access date.
12 Office of the High Representative, High Representative's Decisions
  by Topic, Removals and Suspensions. This is cited by Chesterman
  (2004, 131).
13 ICRC/Greenberg Research Report, *People on War: The Consultation in
  Bosnia and Herzegovina*, Sarajevo, October 1999, as cited by Bose (2002, 20).
14 Woodward (1995) estimates seventy thousand deaths, but most
  later texts use the higher figure of 300,000 dead. There is also
  some discrepancy in estimates of total population, Woodward
  estimating 4.3 million and several other texts estimating 4.4 million.
  See, for example, Cousens and Cater (2001, chap. 4). In 2007,
  Wikipedia estimates deaths at 100,000 to 110,000, with 1.8 million
  IDPs. I am using the lower figures, awaiting better evidence of
  accurate numbers.
15 The data on refugees cited here and following are from Cousens and
  Cater (2001, 72–86).
16 Fieldnotes, interview conducted in 2003.

CHAPTER NINE

1 Among them are graduates of an archaeological program at Simon
  Fraser University in Burnaby, Canada, that specializes in forensic identification of bodies in mass graves.

2 *Bosnia News* online, "Srebrenica Genocide Survivors Threaten a Mass Exodus Unless Srebrenica Is Granted Special Administrative Status," 8 March 2007. A follow-up on this appears in the 26 March 2007 edition, "Srebrenica Assembly Adopted Resolution for Special Administrative Status."

3 This is labelled "statement" and was given to me by one of the women who organized Women Victims of the War in 2004.

4 Christian Schwarz-Schilling, High Representative for BiH, "Police Reform Is about Making BiH a Safer Place to Live," weekly column online, 28 July 2006. Schwarz-Schilling took over briefly from Paddy Ashdown in January 2006 as the international community's High Representative and the European Union's Special Representative in BiH. See also *Guardian Weekly*, 2–8 February 2007, 2, for further commentary.

5 *Bosnia News*, 8 March 2007.

6 Divjak and Masović gave permission to identify them in this book.

7 ICG, "Courting Disaster: the Misrule of Law in Bosnia and Hercegovina," Balkans Report No. 127 (March 2002) (available at www.crisisweb.org).

8 "Prosecuting Gangsters in the Balkans," *Vancouver Sun*, 5 January 2004, B7.

9 Ibid.

10 Human Rights Watch, "A Chance for Justice? War Crime Prosecutions in Bosnia's Serb Republic." HRW Index No. 1803, 16 March 2006.

11 This public agenda survey, which was based on ten thousand face-to-face interviews conducted during January and February 2002, indicated that, while 51 percent of FBiH citizens approved of the ICTY, only 4 percent of RS citizens did so. Available on the International IDEA website (see Works Cited and General Bibliography), April.

12 See also the American Society of International Law, "International Law in Brief," 16 December 2003, for a review of the case online; and for discussion, see Kravetz (2004). ICTY case updated to 1 April 2006.

13 As reported 8 September 2007 in UN News Services (available at www.un.org).

CHAPTER TEN

1 See, for example, US Department of State, Bureau of European and Eurasian Affairs website at http://www.state.gov/p/eur/ (December 2004).

2 BBC News online, "Yugoslavia's Shattered Economy," 2 July 2001.

3 This section is based on the OSCE Mission to Serbia and Montenegro (2003) and interviews conducted in April 2004.

4 As a custom, black flowers are given when someone dies.

5 See, for example, socialistworld.net, the website of the Committee for a Workers' International.

6 See also website of the Internal Displacement Monitoring Centre of the Norwegian Refugee Council, Bosnia and Hercegovina, for discussion at http://www.internal-displacement.org/.

7 As cited by Nicolas Wood in the *New York Times Online*, 3 June 2005.

8 Website, the *Morning Star*, 28 July 2005, citing Jonathan Rooper, Srebrenica Research Group, www.srebrenica-report.com.

9 For a serious and sustained defence of Serbia and Milošević, see Johnstone (2002). Web biographies of Milošević written by admirers also provide a perspective on the standard view of him.

10 Surveys conducted throughout the former Yugoslavia in 2002 showed only 6 percent of Serbs trusted the ICTY while 83 percent trusted it in Kosovo, 51 percent in the Bosnian Federation, 21 percent in Croatia, and 24 percent in Montenegro. The survey was conducted by International IDEA "South East Europe Public Agenda Survey,"online at its website. Another, less systematic, survey published by the Belgrade Centre for Human Rights, showed similar results.

11 Human Rights Watch, citing David Harland testimony, Trial Transcript, 5 November 2003, p. 28706 (Executive Summary of the trial).

12 Amnesty International (2005, 58–60).

13 Amnesty International (2006, 71–3).

14 "Serbia Set to Retaliate against Kosovo's Declaration of Independence," *International Herald Tribune*, 31 August 2007.

15 Other estimates claimed an official 15 percent unemployment rate and an unofficial rate of double that.

16 IMF preliminary findings as of 27 June 2006 (updated 30 November 2006) are available on the IMF website at http://www.imf.org/external/country/scG/index.htm.

17 World Bank, *Country Brief 2006*, September 2006 (available on World Bank website at http://www. Worldbank.org).

18 UN *World Population Prospects* 2006 revision, was measured on a medium variant based on 2005 data with projections to 2010.

CHAPTER ELEVEN

1 See Sislin and Pearson (2001) for data on arms sales.

2 Daily news is provided on the UN website for the DRC (available at http://www.monuc.org/news.aspx?newsID=15321).

3 Uvin (2004, 56–9) discusses this development. See also Olsen (2002).

4 Stiglitz, World Bank.org 1998, as quoted in Uvin (2004, 68).

5 Uvin (2004, 110–21) summarizes arguments for and against conditionality and positive support.

CHAPTER TWELVE

1 "Court Seeks to Try Suspects for Atrocities in Darfur," *Globe and Mail*, 28 February 2007.

2 Much of this information is in articles written by Marlise Simons, *New York Times* correspondent at The Hague, dated 8 April and 9 April 2007. The headlines differ. As printed in the *International Herald Tribune*, the 8 April headline is "Genocide Court Ruled for Serbia without Seeing Full War Archive."

3 For example, Marlise Simons, 9 April 2007, "Genocide Court Ruled for Serbia without Seeing Full War Archive," *International Herald Tribune* online edition.

4 Statement of the Office of the Prosecutor, ICTY, The Hague, 16 April 2007, CdP/MOW/115e (avaliable at www.icty.org).

5 Marlise Simons, 8 April and 9 April 2007, reports in the *International Herald Tribune* and the *New York Times*. See also American Society of International Law, "ASIL insight: ICJ Rules Serbia Failed to Prevent Genocide," at www.asil.org/insights.htm.

6 Human Rights Watch letter to the EU on Relations with Serbia and ICTY Cooperation, Brussels, 26 March 2007, provided in full on the HRW website (HRW.org) (excerpts shown were visited 6 April 2007).

7 This was reported on 10 April 2007 in the *International Herald Tribune* (European edition).

8 As shown on CBC newscasts on 10 April 2007.

9 Croatian novelist and journalist Slavenka Drakuliæ witnessed several trials at the ICTY in The Hague. She discovered that some of the cruelest crimes, mass murders, gang rapes, and marketing of children into prostitution were committed by people who, as the title of her investigation says, "would never hurt a fly" (Drakulić 2004). Until the war, these people were seen by their compatriots as decent, trustworthy, ordinary human beings. Some committed their brutal deeds because they were terrified of being killed by superior officers or village bullies if they did not. But, for most, it wasn't fear that motivated them. It was the sense of belonging to the gangs or the armies and sharing in the excitement of war.

10 A related issue intrigued three Yale social scientists in the 1940s and
  1950s. They observed that Americans were becoming more "other-
  directed." They hypothesized that "inner-directed" people had inter-
  nalized authority in their childhood, while "other-directed" people
  took their cues from peers and contemporary society. Seeking explanations, they examined parental roles, schools, mass media, and other
  aspects of American life. See Riesman, Glazer, and Denney (1950).

Bibliography

African Rights. 1998 *Rwanda: The Insurgency in the Northwest*. Kigali: African Rights.

– 2000 (June). *Confessing to Genocide: Responses to Rwanda's Genocide Law*. Kigali: African Rights.

– 2001 (June). *The Heart of Education. Assessing Human Rights in Rwanda's Schools*. Kigali: African Rights.

– 2003a (January). *Gacaca Justice: A Shared Responsibility*. Kigali: African Rights.

– 2003b (January). *The History of the Genocide in Sector Gishamvu: A Collective Account*. Kigali: African Rights.

– 2004 (9 July). "A Step Backwards for Rwanda: Comment on the Parliamentary Recommendation to Ban Six NGOs." Press Release. Kigali.

Akhavan, Payam. 1997. "Justice and Reconciliation in the Great Lakes Region of Africa: The Contribution of the International Criminal Tribunal for Rwanda." *Duke Journal of Comparative International Law* 7: 325–49.

Amnesty International. 1998. "Rwanda, the Hidden Violence: Disappearances in the Context of the Armed Conflict in the Northwest." AI Index: AFR 47/023/1998, 23 June 1998.

– 2000–07. *Annual Reports*.

– 2005. *The State of the World's Human Rights*. London: Amnesty International.

– 2006. *The State of the World's Human Rights*. London: Amnesty International.

Andersen, Martin. 1993. *Dossier secreto: El mito de la guerra sucia*. Buenos Aires: Planeta.

Annan, Kofi A. 2002. *Prevention of Armed Conflict. Report of the Secretary-General*. New York: United Nations.

Argentina. Comisión Nacional sobre la Desaparición de Personas. 1985. *Nunca Más: Informe de la Comisión Nacional sobre la Desaparición de Personas*. Buenos Aires: Editorial Universitaria de Buenos Aires.

Aron, Robert. 1959. *Histoire de la Libération,* Paris: A Fayad.

Ashdown, Paddy. 2002. "What I Learned in Bosnia," *New York Times.* 28 October.

Aspen Institute. 1996. *Managing Conflict in the Post-Cold War World: The Role of Intervention* (report of Aspen Institute Conference, 2–6 August 1995). Aspen, CO: Aspen Institute.

Association of Citizens for Democracy et al. 2005. "An Appeal from Various NGOs in Belgrade," mimeo handout regarding Kosovo.

Bainbridge, Bill. 2002. *Phnom Penh Post,* "2003 Election a Democracy Barometer," 6–19 December, 13.

– 2003. "KR Tribunal's Nuremberg Model Criticized for Just Targeting Leaders." Documentation Centre of Cambodia online newsletter, 1–7.

Ballentine, Karen, and Heiko Nitzschke, eds. 2005. *Profiting from Peace: Managing the Resource Dimensions of Civil War.* Boulder, CO: Lynne Rienner.

Barbier, Edward, and Thomas Homer-Dixon. 1996. *Resource Scarcity, Institutional Adaptation, and Technical Innovation: Can Poor Countries Attain Endogenous Growth?* Toronto: The Project on Environment, Population and Scarcity.

Bass, Gary Jonathan. 2000. *Stay the Hand of Vengeance: The Politics of War Crimes Tribunals.* Princeton: Princeton University Press.

Bessinger, Mark R., and Crawford Young, eds. 2002 . *Beyond State Crisis?* Washington, DC: Woodrow Wilson Center Press.

Berdal, Mats, and Michael Leifer. 1996. "Cambodia." In *The New Interventionism, 1991–1994: United Nations Experience in Cambodia, former Yugoslavia and Somalia,* ed. James Mayall, 15–58. Cambridge: Cambridge University Press.

Berdal, Mats, and David Malone, eds. 2000. *Greed and Grievance: Economic Agendas in Civil Wars.* Boulder, CO: Lynne Rienner.

Berdal, Mats, and Monica Serrano. 2002. *Transnational Organized Crime and International Security: Business as Usual?* Boulder, CO: Lynne Rienner.

Bhatfia, Michael V. 2003. *War and Intervention. Issues for Contemporary Peace Operations.* Bloomfield, CT: Kumarian Press.

Boraine, Alex. 2000. *A Country Unmasked. Inside South Africa's Truth and Reconciliation Commission.* Cape Town, South Africa: Oxford University Press.

Bose, Sumantra. 2002. *Bosnia after Dayton: Nationalist Partition and International Intervention.* London: Hurst and Co.

– 2003. "Mostar: International Intervention in a Divided Bosnian Town, 1994–2001." In *International Intervention in the Balkans Since 1995,* ed. Peter Siani-Davies, 68–87. London: Routledge.

Bratt, Duane. 1996. "Assessing the Success of UN Peacekeeping Operation." *International Peacekeeping* 3, 4 (Winter):64–81.

British Broadcasting Corporation. 2001. "Yugoslavia's Shattered Economy." 2 July, as presented at 10:33 GMT (11:33 UK) http:/news.bbc.co.uk/1/low/business/1410623.stm.

Brown, Michael E., ed. 1996. *The International Dimensions of Internal Conflicts*. Cambridge, MA: MIT Press.

Brown, Michael E., and Richard N. Rosencrance, eds. 1999. *The Costs of Conflict: Prevention and Cure in the Global Arena*. Lanham, MD: Rowman and Littlefield.

Browning, Christopher R. 1998. *Ordinary Men: Reserve Policy Battalion 101 and the Final Solution in Poland*. New York: Harper Collins.

Burg, Steven L. 2004. "Intervention in Internal Conflict: The Case of Bosnia." In *Military Intervention: Cases in Context for the Twenty-First Century*, ed. William J. Lahneman, 47–65. Oxford: Rowman and Littlefield.

Burg, Steven L., and Paul S. Shoup. 1999. *The War in Bosnia-Herzegovina: Ethnic Conflict and International Intervention*. Armonk, NY, and London, UK: M.E. Sharpe.

Burris, C.T., E. Harmon-Jones, and W.R. Tarpley. 1997. "By Faith Alone": Religious Agitation and Cognitive Dissonance. *Basic and Applied Social Psychology* 19: 17–31.

Buruma, Ian. 2005. "The Indiscreet Charm of Tyranny," *New York Review of Books*. 12 May, 35–7.

Byers, Michael. 2006. *War Law: Understanding International Law and Armed Conflict*. New York: Grove.

Cambodia, Royal Government of. 2007. The Khmer Rouge Trial Task Force. "Chronology of Developments Relating to the KR Trial." Available online at http//www.cambodia.gov.kh/krt/English/chrono.htm.

Cambodian Centre for Human Rights. 2003a. Brochure. Phnom Penh: CCHR.

– 2003b. *Communities for Democracy: Report November 2002-May 2003*. Phnom Penh: CCHR.

– 2003c. *Report on the 2003 National Assembly Election*. Phnom Penh: CCHR.

Central Intelligence Agency (CIA). 2007.*World Factbook*. (available on line at www.cia.gov/library/publcations/the-world-factbook/)

Chandler, David. 1999. *Bosnia: Faking Democracy after Dayton*. London: Pluto Press.

– 2002a. *From Kosovo to Kabul: Human Rights and International Intervention*. London: Pluto Press.

– ed. 2002b. *Rethinking Human Rights: Critical Approaches to International Politics*. New York: Palgrave Macmillan.

Chandler, David P. 1993. *A History of Cambodia*. 2nd ed. Boulder, CO: Westview Press.

− 1999 *Voices from S-21: Terror and History in Pol Pot's Secret Prison.* Berkeley: University of California Press.

− 2000. *Brother Number One: A Political Biography of Pol Pot.* Rev. ed. Chiang Mai, Thailand: Silkworm Books. (Originally published by Westview Press in 1999.)

Chandler, David P., and Ben Kiernan, eds. 1983. *Revolution and Its Aftermath in Kampuchea: Eight Essays.* New Haven: Yale University Southeast Asia Studies. Monograph Series No. 25. Chesterman, Simon. 2004. *You, the People: The United Nations, Transitional Administration, and State-Building.* Oxford: Oxford University Press.

Chandler, David P., Ben Kierney, Chanthou Boua, eds. 1988. *Pol Pot Plans the Future: Confidential Leadership Documents from Democratic Kampuchea, 1976–1977.* New Haven, CO: Yale University Southeast Asia Studies.

Chesterman, Simon. 2004. *You the People. The United Nations, Transitional Administration, and State-Building.* Oxford: Oxford University Press.

Chile. Comisión Nacional de Verdad y Reconciliación (el Rettig Comisión). 1991. *Síntesis del Informe de la Comisión de Verdad y Reconciliación "Para Creer en Chile."* Santiago: Compaña Nacional de Educación por la verdad y los derechos humanos.

Cigar, Norman, and Paul Williams. 2002. *Indictment at the Hague: The Milosovic (sic) Regime and Crimes of the Balkan War.* New York: New York University Press.

Clarke, Richard A. 2004. *Against All Enemies: Inside America's War on Terror.* New York: Free Press.

Cobban, Helena, for Transitional Justice Forum (TJF). 2006. "Bosnia vs. Serbia/Montenegro." Available at tj-forum.org/archives/ (27 February 2006).

Cockburn, Andrew, and Patrick Cockburn. 1999. *Out of the Ashes: The Resurrection of Saddam Hussein.* New York: Harper and Collins.

Collier, Ellen C. 1993. *Instances of Use of United States Forces Abroad, 1798–1993.* Washington DC: Congressional Research Service, Issue Brief, Library of Congress.

Collier, Paul. 2000. "Doing Well out of War: An Economic Perspective." In *Greed and Grievance: Economic Agendas in Civil Wars,* ed. Mats Berdal and David Malone, 91–111. Boulder, CO: Lynne Rienner.

Combs, Nancy Armoury. 2003. "International Decision: *Prosecutor v. Plavsić.*" *American Journal of International Law* 97 (4): 929–37.

Connolly, Kate. 2006. "Bosnia Sues Serbia for Genocide," *National Post* (Canada), 28 February, 10.

Courtemanche, Gil. 2004. *A Sunday at the Pool in Kigali.* Trans. Patricia Claxton. Toronto: Vintage Canada.

Cousens, Elizabeth M., and Charles K. Cater. 2001. *Toward Peace in Bosnia: Implementing the Dayton Accords*. Boulder, CO: Lynne Reiner and International Peace Academy.

Crocker, Chester A. 1996. "Lessons on Intervention." In *Managing Conflict in the Post-Cold War World: The Role of Intervention*, ed. Aspen Institute, 77–88. Aspen, CO: Aspen Institute.

Cullum, Blanquita Walsh. "Cambodia's New Climate of Fear," *Washington Times Online*, 15 January 2006.

Dallaire, Roméo A. 2003. *Shake Hands with the Devil: The Failure of Humanity in Rwanda*. Toronto: Random House Canada.

Davis, Michael C., Wolfgang Dietrich, Bettina Scholdan, Dieter Sepp, eds. 2004. *International Intervention in the Post-Cold War World: Moral Responsibility and Power Politics*. Armonk, NY: M.E. Sharpe.

Denitch, Bogdan. 1994. *Ethnic Nationalism: The Tragic Death of Yugoslavia*. Rev. ed. Minneapolis: University of Minnesota Press.

De Soysa, Indra. 2000. "The Resource Curse: Are Civil Wars Driven by Rapacity or Paucity?" In *Greed and Grievance*, ed. Mats Berdal and David M. Malone, 113–36. Boulder, CO: Lynne Rienner.

Diamandouros, P. Nikiforos. 1986. "Regime Change and the Prospects for Democracy in Greece, 1974–1983." In *Transitions from Authoritarian Rule: Southern Europe*, ed. Guillermo O'Donnell, Philippe C. Schmitter, and Laurence Whitehead, 138–64. Baltimore: Johns Hopkins University Press.

Divjak, Jovan. 2001. "The First Phase, 1992–1993: Struggle for Survival and Genesis of the Army of Bosnia-Herzegovina." In *The War in Croatia and Bosnia-Herzegovina*, ed. Branka Magaš and Ivo Zanić, 152–75. London: Frank Cass.

– 2004. *Sarajevo, mon amour*. Paris: Buchet/Chastel.

Documentation Centre of Cambodia. 2002–03. *Searching for the Truth*. English edition magazine on DCC website (www.dccam.org).

Dodge, Toby, and Steven Simon, eds. 2003. *Iraq at the Crossroads: State and Society in the Shadow of Regime Change*. London: Oxford University Press for the International Institute for Strategic Studies.

Drakulić, Slavenka. 2004. *They Would Never Hurt a Fly: War Criminals on Trial in The Hague*. London: Abacus.

Drumbl, Mark A. 2000. "Punishment, Postgenocide: From Guilt to Shame to 'Globulitarianism Civis' in Rwanda." *New York University Law Review* 75: 1290.

Duffield, Mark. 1994. "The Political Economy of Internal War: Asset Transfer, Complex Emergencies and International Aid." In *War and Hunger: Rethinking International Responses*, ed. Joanna Macrae and Anthony Zwi, 50–69. London: Zed.

– 1999. *Internal Conflict: Adaptation and Reaction to Globalisation.*" Dorset, UK: The Corner House Briefing No. 121. (16 pp.)

Durch, W.J. 1996. *UN Peacekeeping, American Policy and the Uncivil Wars of the 1990s.* New York: St. Martin's Press.

Durch. W.J., and James A. Schear. 1996. "Faultlines: UN Operations in the Former Yugoslavia." In *UN Peacekeeping, American Policy and Uncivil Wars of the 1990s,* ed. W.J. Durch, 193–274. New York: St. Martin's Press.

Economides, Spyros, and Paul Taylor. 1996. "Former Yugoslavia." In *The New Interventionism, 1991–1994: United Nations Experience in Cambodia, former Yugoslavia, and Somalia,* ed. James Mayall, 59–93. Cambridge, UK: Cambridge University Press.

Edwards, Steven. 2004. "Trial of Milosevic Anything but Swift." *National Post* (Canada), 24 February.

Ersado, Lire. 2006. "Rural Vulnerability in Serbia." World Bank Policy Research Working Paper WPS4010 (September). Available in full at www.wds.worldbank.org.

Esser, J.K. 1998. "Alive and Well after 25 Years: A Review of Groupthink Research." *Organizational Behavior and Human Decision Processes* 73 (2–3): 116–41.

Etcheson, Craig. 1984. *Rise and Demise of Democratic Kampuchea.* Boulder, CO: Westview Press.

– 2003. "Beyond the Khmer Rouge Tribunal," published by the Documentation Centre of Cambodia, 27 October.

– 2005. *After the Killing Fields: Lessons from the Cambodian Genocide.* Westport, CO: Praeger.

Fawthrop, Tom, and Helen Jarvis. 2004. *Getting Away with Genocide? Elusive Justice and the Khmer Rouge Tribunal.* Ann Arbor: Pluto Press.

Fein, Helen, O. Brugnola, and L. Spirer. 1994. *The Prevention of Genocide: Rwanda and Yugoslavia Reconsidered.* New York: Institute for the Study of Genocide, John Jay College of Criminal Justice.

Festinger, Leon. 1963. *A Theory of Cognitive Dissonance.* Stanford, CA: Stanford University Press.

Festinger, Leon, Henry W. Riecken, and Stanley Schachter. 1956. *When Prophecy Fails: A Social and Psychological Study of a Modern Group That Predicted the Destruction of the World.* Minneapolis: Minnesota University Press.

Findlay, Trevor. 1996. "Turning the Corner in Southeast Asia." In *The International Dimensions of Internal Conflict,* ed. Michael E. Brown, chap. 5. Cambridge, MA: MIT Press.

– 1999. *The Blue Helmets' First War? Use of Force by the UN in the Congo, 1960–64.* Ottawa: The Lester B. Pearson Canadian International Peacekeeping Training Centre.

– 2002. *The Use of Force in UN Peace Operations.* Oxford University Press: Stockholm International Peace Research Institute.

Fleitz, Frederick H. Jr. 2002. *Peacekeeping Fiascoes of the 1990s.* Westport, CT: Praeger.

Freedman, Jim. 2003. "Disclosures of a Dark War in the DR Congo." On-line at www.humansecuritybulletin.info/editorial_2.htm.

Freeman, Mark. 2004a. "Bosnia and Hercegovina: Selected Developments in Transitional Justice." International Centre for Transitional Justice. Case Study Series. October. Available on ICTJ website (www.ictj.org).

– 2004b. "Serbia and Montenegro: Selected Developments in Transitional Justice." International Center for Transitional Justice. Case Study Series. October. Available on ICTJ website.

Frommer, Benjamin. 2005. *National Cleansing: Retribution against Nazi Collaborators in Postwar Czechoslovakia.* Cambridge: Cambridge University Press.

Fuller, S.R., and R.J. Aldag. 1998. "Organizational Tonypandy: Lessons from a Quarter Century of the Groupthink Phenomenon." *Organizational Behavior and Human Decision Processes* 73 (203): 163–84.

Gabiro, Gabriel. 2006. "Former Rwandan President's Acquittal Reversed." *Independent Online* at www.iol.co.za (18 February 2006).

Gallup International Association Public Opinion Poll. 2006. *Voice of the People 2006.* As reported in the *Globe and Mail,* 2 April.

Gasana, James K. 2002. "Natural Resource Scarcity and Violence in Rwanda." In *Conserving the Peace: Resources, Livelihoods and Security,* ed. Richard Matthew, Mark Halle, Jason Switzer, 201–45. Winnipeg: International Institute for Sustainable Development and the World Conservation Union.

Gentile, Carmen J. 2006. "Cambodia Oil, Blessing or Curse?" Distributed by Documentation Centre of Cambodia, Phnom Penh, 20 December.

Gerth, H., and C. Wright Mills. Trans and eds. 1958. *From Max Weber: Essays in Sociology.* New York: Oxford University Press.

Global Law Association, 1997. *Global War Crimes Tribunal Collection.* Nimegen, Netherlands.

Global Policy Forum, Institute for War and Peace Report. 2006. "Serbia and Montenegro on Trial for Genocide." Available on the Forum's website (www.globalpolicy.org).

Gottesman, Evan. 2003. *Cambodia after the Khmer Rouge: Inside the Politics of Nation Building.* New Haven: Yale University Press.

Guest, Iain. 1990. *Behind the Disappearances: Argentina's Dirty War against Human Rights and the United Nations.* Philadelphia: University of Pennsylvania Press.

Gurr, Ted Robert, and Monty G. Marshall. 2005. *Peace and Conflict 2005: A Global Survey of Armed Conflicts, Self-Determination Movements, and Democracy.* College Park, MD: Center for International Development and Conflict Management, University of Maryland.

Haas, Michael. 1991. *Genocide by Proxy: Cambodian Pawn on a Superpower Chessboard.* New York: Praeger.

Haass, Richard N. 1999. *Intervention: The Use of American Military Force in the Post-Cold War World.* Rev. ed. Washington, DC: Brookings Institution Press.

Harbeson, John W. 1987. "Military Rule and the Quest for a Post-Imperial Ethiopia." In *The Military in African Politics,* ed. J. Harberson, 156–86. New York: Published in cooperation with School of Advanced International Studies and Johns Hopkins University.

Harmon-Jones, E., and J. Mills. 1999. *Cognitive Dissonance: Progress on a Pivotal Theory in Social Psychology.* Washington, DC: American Psychological Association.

Hart, P. 1994. *Government: A Study of Small Groups and Policy Failure.* Baltimore: Johns Hopkins University Press.

Hayner, Priscilla B. 2001. *Unspeakable Truths: Confronting State Terror and Atrocity – How Truth Commissions around the World Are Challenging the Past and Shaping the Future.* New York: Routledge.

Heder, Steve. 1996. "The Resumption of Armed Struggle by the Party of Democratic Kampuchea: Evidence from National Army of Democratic Kampuchea 'Self-Demobilizers.'" In *Propaganda, Politics, and Violence in Cambodia: Democratic Transition under United Nations Peace-Keeping,* ed. Steve Heder and Judy Ledgerwood, 73–113. Armonk, New York and London, England: M.E. Sharpe.

Heder, Steve, and Judy Ledgerwood, eds. 1996. *Propaganda, Politics, and Violence in Cambodia: Democratic Transition under United Nations Peace-Keeping.* Armonk, New York, and London: M.E. Sharpe.

Helsinki Watch. 1992/93. *Crimes in Bosnia-Hercegovina.* 2 vols. New York: Human Rights Watch.

Helliwell, John F., ed. 2000. *The Contribution of Human and Social Capital to Sustained Economic Growth and Well-Being. International Symposium Report.* Ottawa: OECD.

Henderson, A.M., and Talcott Parsons, eds. and trans. 1966. *Max Weber: The Theory of Social and Economic Organization.* New York: The Free Press.

Henkin, Alice H., ed. 2002. *The Legacy of Abuse: Confronting the Past, Facing the Future.* New York: New York University School of Law and The Aspen Institute.

Hersh, Seymour M. 1983. *The Price of Power: Kissinger in the Nixon White House.* New York: Summit Books.

– 2004. "The Other War: Why Bush's Afghanistan Problem Won't Go Away." *New Yorker,* 12 April, 40–7.

Herz, John H., ed. 1982. *From Dictatorship to Democracy: Coping with the Legacies of Authoritarianism and Totalitarianism.* Westport, CT: Greenwood Press.

Hilditch, Tom. 2000. "Apocalypse, Still." *Post Magazine,* 24 September, 8–14.

Hitchens, Christopher. 2001. *The Trial of Henry Kissinger.* London/New York: Verso.

Hochschild, Adam. 1999. *King Leopold's Ghost: A Story of Greed, Terror, and Heroism in Colonial Africa.* Bolston: Houghton Mifflin.

Holloway, David, and Stephen John Stedman. 2001. "Civil Wars and State-Building in Africa and Eurasia." In *Beyond State Crisis? Post-Colonial Africa and Post-Soviet Eurasia in Comparative Perspective,* ed. Mark R. Beissinger and Crawford Young, 161–87, Washington, DC: Woodrow Wilson Center Press.

Homer-Dixon, Thomas. 1995. "The Ingenuity Gap: Can Poor Countries Adapt to Resource Scarcity?" *Population and Development Review* 21 (3): 587–612.

– 1999. *Environment, Scarcity and Violence.* Princeton: Princeton University Press.

Howard, Michael. 1996. "Managing Conflict – The Role of Intervention – Lessons from the Past." In *Managing Conflict in the Post-Cold War World,* ed. Aspen Institute, 35–43. Aspen, CO: Aspen Institute.

Human Rights Watch. 1996 (December). *Deterioration of Human Rights in Cambodia.* Vol. 8 (11C).

– 2000 (1 April). "Rwanda: The Search for Security and Human rights Abuses." HRW Index No. A1201.

– 2000–06. *Human Rights Watch World Report* (annual). Available on HRW website (www.hrw.org).

– 2001a (20 December). "Observing the Rules of War?" HRW Index No: A1308.

– 2001b (January). *Protectors or Pretenders? Government Human Rights Commissions in Africa.* New York: HRW.

– 2001c (May). *Uprooting the Rural Poor in Rwanda.* New York: HRW.

– 2002 (November). "The End of the Transition: A Necessary Liberalisation." *Africa Report* 53.

– 2003 (March). *Lasting Wounds: Consequences of Genocide and War on Rwanda's Children.* HRW Index No. 1506.

– 2004 (February). "Genocide, War Crimes and Crimes against Humanity: Topical Digests of the Case Law of the ICTY and the ICTR." Available at www.hrw.org.

– 2006a. (16 March). "A Chance for Justice? War Crime Prosecutions in Bosnia's Serb Republic." HR Index D1803.

– 2006b (8 February). *Looking for Justice: The War Crimes Chamber in Bosnia and Hercegovina.* HR Index D1801.

– 2006c (16 January). "Rwanda: Historic Ruling Expected for Former President and Seven Others." Available at www.hrw.org.

Human Security Centre, Lui Institute for Global Issues, University of British Columbia. 2005. *Human Security Report 2005: War and Peace in the 21st Century.* Oxford: Oxford University Press.

Huy, Vannak. 2003. *The Khmer Rouge Division 703: From Victory to Self-Destruction.* Phnom Penh. DCC.

Institute for Democracy and Electoral Assistance. 2003. *Reconciliation after Violent Conflict: A Handbook.* Stockholm: International IDEA.

Institute for the Study of Genocide. 2001. "Interview with Athanase Hagengimana, M.D." Available at http://www.isg-iags.org/newsletters/25/athanse.

International Centre for Criminal Law Reform and Criminal Justice Policy. 2001. *The Changing Face of International Criminal Law: Selected Papers.* Vancouver: Centre for Criminal Law Reform and Criminal Justice Policy.

International Commission on Intervention and State Sovereignty. 2001. *The Responsibility to Protect.* Ottawa: International Development Research Centre.

ICTY. 2001. *Prosecutor v. Delalić et al.* (Celebici). Appeals Chamber Judgment. 8 April. All cases available on ICTY website (www.ICTY.org).

– 2002. Case no. IT-95–5/18. 11 Oct. as updated to 6 March 2006.

– 2003a. *Prosecutor v. Galić* (Case No. IT-98-29-T). *Trial* Chamber Judgment. 5 December.

– 2003b. *Prosecutor v. Plavsić* (Case No. IT-00-39&40/1). Case Information Sheet.

– 2003c. *Prosecutor v. Plavsić* (Case No. IT-00-39&40/1). Sentencing Judgment.

– 2004. *Prosecutor v. Krstić* (Case No. IT-98-33-A). Appeals Chamber Judgment. 19 April.

International Crisis Group (ICG). 2000. "Bosnia's November Elections: Dayton Stumbles." Sarajevo/Brussels: ICG Balkans Report No. 104. 18 December. (Reports are all available on ICG website: www.crisisgroupweb.org.17.)

– 2002. "Courting Disaster: The Misrule of Law in Bosnia and Hercegovina." Balkans Report No. 127. March. Available at www.crisisgroupweb.org.

– 2003a. "Disarmament of Rwandan Hutu Rebels in the Congo: MONUC's Impotence a Liability." 23 May, media release.

– 2003b. "The International Criminal Tribunal for Rwanda: Time for Pragmatism." 26 September.

– 2003c. "Rwandan Hutu Rebels in the Congo: A New Approach to Disarmament and Reintegration: Executive Summary and Recommendations." Media release. Full report available at www.crisisweb.org.

– 2004. "Serbia's U-Turn: Executive Summary and Recommendations." ICG Europe Report No. 154. 26 March.

International Court of Justice (ICJ). 2003 (3 February). "Application for Revision of the Judgment of 11 July 1996 in the Case Concerning Application of the Convention on the Prevention and Punishment of the Crime of Genocide (*Bosnia and Herzegovina v. Yugoslavia*) (*Yugoslavia v. Bosnia and Herzegovina*)." General List no. 122. Available at ICJ website (www.icj-cij.org).

– 2006 (27 February). "Application of the Convention on the Prevention and Punishment of the Crime of Genocide (*Bosnia and Herzegovina v. Serbia and Montenegro*)." Press Release No 2006/9. Available at ICJ website (www.icj-cij.org).

– 2007 (26 February). "Application of the Convention on the Prevention and Punishment of the Crime of Genocide (*Bosnia and Herzegovina v. Serbia and Montenegro*)." Judgment. Available at ICJ website (www.icj-cij.org).

International Institute for Democracy and Electoral Assistance. (IDEA). 2001. "Key Findings. Balkan Public Agenda. Focus Group Study in Republic of Srpska." January.

– 2002. "South Eastern Europe and the Stability Pact. New Means for Regional Analysis. Federation of Bosnia and Hercegovina. Qualitative Analysis. Focus Group Study in Sarajevo." March. Full paper available on International Institution for Democracy and Electoral Assistance (IDEA) website (www.idea.int/).

Janis, Irving L. 1982. *Groupthink: A Psychological Study of Policy Decisions and Fiascos.* Boston: Houghton Mifflin.

Jett, Dennis C. 1999. *Why Peacekeeping Fails.* New York. St. Martin's Press.

Johnstone, Diana. 2002. *Fools' Crusade: Yugoslavia, NATO and Western Delusions.* New York: Monthly Review Press.

Jordens, Jay. 1996. "Persecution of Cambodia's Ethnic Vietnamese Communities during and since the UNTAC Period." In *Propaganda, Politics and Violence in Cambodia,* ed. Steve Heder and Judy Ledgerwood, 134–58. Armonk, NY: M.E. Sharpe.

Journal of Peace Research, 1998. Special issue on resources and conflict. Vol. 35, no. 3.

Judah, Tim. 2000. *Serbs: History, Myth and the Destruction of Yugoslavia.* 2nd ed. New Haven: Yale University Press.

Kaldor, Mary.2001. *New and Old Wars. Organized Violence in a Global Era.* Poliity Press: Cambridge.

Kaldor, Mary and Basker Vashee, eds. 1997. *New Wars. Restructuring the Global Military Sector.* Pinter: London and Washington.

Keen, David. 2000, "Incentives and Disincentives for Violence." In *Greed and Grievance: Economic Agendas in Civil Wars,* ed. Mats Berdal and David M. Malone, 19–42. Boulder, CO: Lynne Rienner.

Kiernan, Ben. 1996. *The Pol Pot Regime: Race, Power and Genocide in Cambodia under the Khmer Rouge, 1975–79.* New Haven: Yale University Press.

Kiernan, Ben, ed. 1993. *Genocide and Democracy in Cambodia: The Khmer Rouge, the United Nations and the International Community.* New Haven: Yale University Press.

Kiernan, Ben, and Chanthou Boua, eds. 1982. *Peasants and Politics in Kampuchea, 1942–1981.* London: Zed Press.

Kimani, Mary. 2002. "Expensive Justice: Cost of Running the Rwandan Tribunal." Arusha. 9 April. Available at www.ictr.org.

– 2003. "When Justice Takes Too Long," in Internews Arusha, 1 September. Available at www.ictr.org.

Kissinger, Henry. 2001. "The Pitfalls of Universal Jurisdiction." *Foreign Affairs,* July/August.

Klare, Michael T. 2001. *Resource Wars: The New Landscape of Global Conflict.* New York: Henry Holt.

Kleine-Ahlbrandt, Stephanie. 2000. "Rwanda." In *Internally Displaced People: A Global Survey.* London: Earthscan Publications.

Klinghoffer, Arthur Jay. 1993. *The International Dimension of Genocide in Rwanda.* New York: New York University Press.

Kohut, Andrew, and Robert C. Toth. 1996. "Intervention in the Post-Cold War World: A Public Perspective." In *Managing Conflict in the Post-Cold War World: The Role of Intervention,* ed. Aspen Institute, 105–17. Aspen CO: Aspen Institute.

Kramer, R.M. 1998. "Revisiting the Bay of Pigs and Vietnam Decisions 25 Years Later: How Well Has the Groupthink Hypothesis Stood the Test of Time?" *Organizational Behavior and Human Decision Processes* 73 (203): 236–71.

Krasner, Stephen. 1999. *Sovereignty: Organized Hypocrisy.* Princeton, NJ: Princeton University Press.

Kravetz, Daniela. 2004. "The Protection of Civilians in War: the ICTY's Galic Case." *Leiden Journal of International Law* (online) 17: 521–36. October.

Kritz, Neil J., ed. 1995. *Transitional Justice: How Emerging Democracies Reckon with Former Regimes.* 2 vols. Washington, DC: United States Institute of Peace Press.

Lahneman, William J., ed. 2004. *Military Intervention: Cases in Context for the Twenty-First Century.* Oxford: Rowman and Littlefield.

Lawson, Guy. 2005. "'Sorrows of a Hero': Review of Roméo Dallaire's *Shake Hands with the Devil.*" *New York Review of Books,* 26 May, 35–8.

Ledgerwood, Judy. 1996a. "Patterns of Political Repression and Violence during the UNTAC Period." In *Propaganda, Politics, and Violence in Cambodia,* ed. Steve Heder and Judy Ledgerwood, 114–33. Armonk, New York, and London: M.E. Sharpe.

– 1996b. "Politics of Violence: An Introduction." In *Propaganda, Politics, and Violence in Cambodia,* ed. Steve Heder and Judy Ledgerwood, 3–49. Armonk, New York, and London: M.E. Sharpe.

Lemarchand, René. 2003. "The Rwanda Genocide." In *Century of Genocide, Eyewitness Accounts and Critical Views,* ed. Samuel Totten, William S. Parsons, Israel W. Charny, 408–17. New York: Garland.

LICADHO. 1999. *Impunity in Cambodia: How Human Rights Offenders Escape Justice.* June, vol. 11(3)(C) (joint report with Cambodian Human Rights and Development Association (ADHOC) and Human Rights Watch). Phnom Penh: LICADHO.

– 2002. *Human Rights and Cambodia's Prisons: 2001 Health Report.* Phnom Penh: LICADHO.

– 2003a. *Briefing Paper: Threats to Human Rights Defenders in Cambodia.* Phnom Penh: LICADHO.

– 2003b. *2003 Briefing Report on Torture in Police Custody in Cambodia.* Phnom Penh: LICADHO.

Lizée, Pierre P. 2000. *Peace, Power and Resistance in Cambodia.* Houndmills, Basingstoke, Hampshire: Macmillan Press.

– 2004 "Needed: Monuments to Justice," *Globe and Mail,* 8 January.

Lobe, Jim. 2003. "Controversy over Rwanda Tribunal Has Geopolitical Undertones." Available at US@oneworld.net (11 August).

Loftus, Elizabeth. F., and Katherine Ketcham. 1994. *The Myth of Repressed Memory: False Memories and Allegations of Sexual Abuse.* New York: St. Martin's Press.

Macridis, Roy H. 1982. "France: From Vichy to the Fourth Republic." In *From Dictatorship to Democracy: Coping with the Legacies of Authoritarianism and Totalitarianism,* ed. John H. Herz, 161–78. Westport, CT: Greenwood Press.

Magaš, Branka, and Ivo Žaniæ, eds. 2001. *The War in Croatia and Bosnia-Herzegovina, 1991–1995.* London: Frank Cass.

Malamud-Goti, Jaime. 1990. "Transitional Governments in the Breach: Why Punish State Criminals?" *Human Rights Quarterly* 12, (1): 1–16.

– 1995. "Transitional Governments in the Breach: Why Punish State Criminals?" In *Transitional Justice: How Emerging Democracies Reckon with Former
Regimes*, vol. 1, ed. N. Kritz, 189–202. Washington, DC: United States Institute of Peace Press.

Marchak, Patricia. 1996. *The Integrated Circus: The "New Right" and the Globalization of Markets*. Montreal: McGill-Queen's University Press.

– 2003. *Reigns of Terror*. Montreal: McGill-Queen's University Press.

Marchak, Patricia, in collaboration with William Marchak. 1999. *God's Assassins: State Terrorism in Argentina in the 1970s*. Montreal: McGill-
Queen's University Press.

Marr, Phebe. 2004. *Modern History of Iraq*. Boulder, CO: Westview Press.

Martinez, Javier, and Alvaro Díaz. 1996. *Chile: The Great Transformation*.
Washington, DC: The Brookings Institution.

Matthew, Richard, Mark Halle, and Jason Switzer, eds. 2002. *Conserving the
Peace: Resources, Livelihood and Security*. Winnipeg: International Institute
for Sustainable Development and the World Conservation Union.

Mayall, James. 1996. "Introduction." In *The New Interventionism, 1991–94:
United Nations Experience in Cambodia, former Yugoslavia, and Somalia*, 1–24.
Cambridge: Cambridge University Press.

Mayall, James, ed. 1996. *The New Interventionism, 1991–94: United Nations
Experience in Cambodia, former Yugoslavia, and Somalia*. Cambridge: Cambridge University Press.

McAdams, A. James, ed. 1997. *Transitional Justice and the Rule of Law in New
Democracies*. Notre Dame and London: University of Notre Dame Press.

McCauley, Clark. 1987. "The Nature of Social Influence in Groupthink:
Compliance and Internalization." *Journal of Personality and Social Psychology* 57: 250–60.

McNamara, Robert S., and Brian VanDeMark, 1995. *In Retrospect: The Tragedy and Lessons of Vietnam*. New York: Times Books, Random House.

Mehta, Harish C., and July B. Mehta. 1999. *Hun Sen: Strongman of Cambodia*. Singapore: Graham Brash.

Meng-Try, Ea, and Sorya Sim. 2001. Victims and Perpetrators? Testimony
of Young Khmer Rouge Comrades. Documentation Series No. 1. Phnom
Penh: DCC.

Michnik, Adam, and Václav Havel, 1993. "Confronting the Past: Justice or
Revenge?" *Journal of Democracy* 4 (1): 20–7.

Migdal, Joel. 1988. *Strong Societies and Weak States*. Princeton: Princeton
University Press.

Mysliwiec, Eva. 1988. *Punishing the Poor: The International Isolation of Kampuchea*. Oxford: Oxfam.

Naylor, R. Thomas. 1993. "The Insurgent Economy: Black Market Operations of Guerrilla Organization." *Crime, Law, and Social Change* 20 (1): 23.

New York Review of Books. 2006. Vol. 53., no. 8, 11 May.

Nino, Carlos Santiago. 1996. *Radical Evil on Trial.* New Haven: Yale University Press.

Novick, Peter. 1968. *The Resistance versus Vichy: The Purge of Collaborators in Liberated France.* New York: Columbia University Press.

Nye, Joseph S., Jr. 1996. "International Conflicts after the Cold War." In *Managing Conflict in the Post-Cold War World: The Role of Intervention,* 63–76. Aspen, CO: Aspen Institute.

O'Ballance, Edgar.1995. *Civil War in Bosnia, 1992–94.* New York: St. Martin's Press.

O'Donnell, Guillermo. 1988. *Bureaucratic Authoritarianism: Argentina 1966–1973 in Comparative Perspective.* Berkeley, CA: University of California Press.

O'Donnell, Guillermo, Philippe C. Schmitter, and Laurence Whitehead, eds. 1986. *Transitions from Authoritarian Rule: Southern Europe.* Baltimore: Johns Hopkins University Press.

Ogata, Sadako. 2005. *The Turbulent Decade: Confronting the Refugee Crises of the 1990s.* New York: Norton.

Oke, Mim Kemal. 1988. *The Armenian Question, 1914–1923.* Nicosia: K. Rustem and Brothers.

Olsen, Gorm R. 2002. "The European Union: An Ad Hoc Policy with a Low Priority." In *Exporting Democracy: Rhetoric vs. Reality,* ed. Peter Schraeder, 11–45. Boulder, CO: Lynne Rienner.

Oppenheim, J., and W. van der Wolf, eds. 2001. *Global War Crimes Tribunal Collection.* Vol. 1: *The Rwanda Tribunal 1997.* Cited in *Global IDP Database on Rwanda, 2001.* Available at idpproject.org.

OSCE Mission to Serbia and Montenegro. 2003a. *Annual Report.*

– 2003b. *Environmental Legislation Guide for Everyone.*

Osiel, Mark. 1997. *Mass Atrocity, Collective Memory and the Law.* New Brunswick, US: Transaction Publishers.

Osnos, Evan. 2006. "A chilling visit with Pol Pot's 'brother' 27 years after Cambodia's Genocide, court hopes leaders will explain terror," in *Herald Tribune* 17 Feb, reprinted by Documentation Centre of Cambodia 17 Feb.

Ouellet, Julian. 2005. "Procedural Components of Peace Agreements." Online at beyondintractability.org/m/proceduralpeaceagree.jsp. Viewed 4 June.

Owen, Taylor, and Ben Kiernan. 2006. "Bombs Over Cambodia," *The Walrus,* October, 62–9.

Pan African News Agency. 2001. "Kagame Refuses to Withdraw Troops from DR Congo." Global IDP: www.idpproject.org online. 9 April.

Parker, George. 2003. *Assassins' Gate: America in Iraq.* New York: Farrar, Straus and Giroux.

Parsons, Talcott, ed. 1966. *Max Weber: The Theory of Social and Economic Organization.* Trans. from German by A.M. Henderson and Talcott Parsons. New York: The Free Press.

Peou, Sorpong. 2000. *Intervention and Change in Cambodia: Towards Democracy?* Thailand/Singapore: Silkworm Books/Institute of Southeast Asian Studies.

Pham, Phuong N., Harvey M. Weinstein, and Timothy Longman. 2003. "Trauma and PTSD Symptoms in Rwanda: Implications for Attitudes Toward Justice and Reconciliation." *Journal of American Medical Association* 292 (5): 602–12.

Philpott, Daniel. 2001. "Usurping the Sovereignty of Sovereignty?" *World Politics* 53 (2): 297–324.

Phnom Penh Post. 2002. "2003 Election a Democracy Barometer," 6–19 December, p. 13.

Pocha, Jehangir S. 2005. "Burying China's Complicity in the Killing Fields," 3 May, *International Herald Tribune,* 3 May (reprinted by Documentation Centre of Cambodia).

Polgreen, Lydia. "A Godsend for Darfur, or a Curse?" *New York Times Online,* 22 July 2007. Available at www.nytimes.com.

Ponchaud, Francois. 1977. *Cambodia: Year Zero.* Translated from French by Nancy Amphoux. New York: Holt, Rinehart and Winston.

Powell, Colin. 1992–93. "US Forces: Challenges Ahead." *Foreign Affairs* 72, 5: 32–4.

Powers, Samantha. 2001. "Bystanders to Genocide." *Atlantic Monthly,* September. Available at www.theatlantic.com/doc/print/200109/power-genocide.

– 2002. *A Problem from Hell: America and the Age of Genocide.* New York: Basic Books.

Program in Law and Public Affairs and Woodrow Wilson School of Public and International Affairs, Princeton University et al., 2001. *The Princeton Principles on Universal Jurisdiction.* New Jersey: Princeton University.

Prunier, Gérard. 1995. *The Rwanda Crisis: History of Genocide.* New York: Columbia University Press.

Psomiades, Harry J. 1982. "Greece: From the Colonels' Rule to Democracy." In *From Dictatorship to Democracy: Coping with the Legacies of Authoritarianism and Totalitarianism,* ed. John H. Herz, 251–65. Westport, CT: Greenwood Press.

Putnam, Robert D. 1993. *Making Democracy Work: Civic Traditions in Modern Italy*. New Jersey: Princeton University Press.

– 2000. *Bowling Alone: The Collapse and Revival of American Community*. New York: Simon and Schuster.

Regan, Patrick M. 2000. *Civil Wars and Foreign Powers: Outside Intervention in Intrastate Conflict*. Ann Arbor: University of Michigan Press.

Reno, William. 2000. "Shadow States and the Political Economy of Civil Wars." In *Greed and Grievance*, ed. Mats Berdal and David Malone, 43–68. Boulder, CO: Lynne Rienner.

Republika Srpska. 2004. *The Commission for Investigation of the Events in and around Srebrenica between 10th and 19th July, 1995*. Banja Luca. June The entire report can be visited at http://www.vladars.net/pdf/srebrenicajun 2004engl.pdf.

Riesman, David, Nathan Glazer, and Reuel Denny. 1950. *The Lonely Crowd: A Study of the Changing American Character*. Garden City, NY: Doubleday.

Roberts, David W. 2001. *Political Transition in Cambodia, 1991–99: Power, Elitism and Democracy*. Richmond, Surrey, UK: Curzon.

Robertson, Geoffrey. 2000. *Crimes Against Humanity: The Struggle for Global Justice*. London/New York: New Press.

Rodman, Peter W. 1994. *More Precious Than Peace: The Cold War and the Struggle for the Third World*. New York: Scribner's.

Ross, Michael L. 1999. "The Political Economy of the Resource Curse." *World Politics* 51: 297–322.

Rotberg, Robert I., and Dennis Thompson, eds. 2000. *Truth v. Justice: The Morality of Truth Commissions*. Princeton: Princeton University Press.

Ryan, Patrick, and George Rush, eds. 1997. *Understanding Organized Crime in Global Perspective*. London: Sage.

Rwanda, Ministry of Finance and Economic Planning. 2001. National Programme for Poverty Reduction. *Core Welfare Indicator Questionnaire (CWIQ) Survey. Main Report*. Kigali: Ministry of Finance and Economic Planning. August.

– 2002a. *A Profile of Poverty in Rwanda: An Analysis Based on the Results of the Household Living Condition Survey, 1999–2001*. Kigali: Ministry of Finance and Economic Planning. February.

– 2002b. *Rwanda: Poverty Reduction Strategy Paper* (National Poverty Reduction Program). Kigali: Ministry of Finance and Economic Planning. June.

Rwanda, National Human Rights Commission. 2001 (March). *Annual Report: 2000*. Kigali: National Human Rights Commission.

Rwanda, Government of. N.d. *Rwanda: Vision 2020*. Kigali: Government of Rwanda.

Sands, Philippe. 2006a. *Lawless World: The Whistle-Blowing Account of How Our Leaders Are Taking the Law into Their Own Hands*. New York: Penguin.

– 2006b. *Lawless World: America and the Making and Breaking of Global Rules from FDR's Atlantic Charter to George W. Bush's Illegal War*. New York: Viking.

Santiso, Carlos. 2001. "International Cooperation for Democracy and Good Governance: Moving Towards a Second Generation?" *European Journal of Development Research* 13, 1: 154–80.

Schear, J. 1996. "Riding the Tiger: the UN and Cambodia." In *UN Peacekeeping, American Policy and the Uncivil Wars of the 1990s*, ed. W.J. Durch, 143–5. New York: St. Martin's Press.

Schell, Jonathan. 2003. "No More unto the Breach." *Harper's* Part 1, vol. 306 (1834): 33–46 (March); Part 2, vol. 306 (1835): 41–55 (April).

Shrader, Charles R. 2003. *The Muslim-Croat Civil War in Central Bosnia: A Military History, 1992–1994*. Austin: Texas A&M University Press.

Schraeder, Peter, ed. 2002. *Exporting Democracy: Rhetoric vs. Reality*. Boulder, CO: Lynne Rienner.

Schwarz-Schilling, Christian. 2006. "Police Reform Is about Making BiH a Safer Place to Live." High Representative for BiH, weekly column, 28 July. Available at www.ohr.int/ohr-dept/pressa/default.asp?content_id=37719.

Shawcross, William. 1984. *The Quality of Mercy: Cambodia, Holocaust and Modern Conscience*. New York: Simon and Schuster.

Short, Philip. 2004. *Pol Pot: Anatomy of a Nightmare*. London: John Murray.

Siani-Davies, Peter, ed. 2003. *International Intervention in the Balkans since 1995*. London: Routledge.

Silber, Laura, and Allan Little. 1996. *The Death of Yugoslavia*. Rev. ed. London: Penguin Group and BBC Worldwide.

Simons, Marlise 2007 "Genocide Court ruled for Serbia without seeing full war archives," *New York Times* and *International Herald Tribune*, 9 April

Sislin, John, and Frederic S. Pearson. 2001. *Arms and Ethnic Conflict*. Lanham: Rowman and Littlefield.

Sivard, Ruth Leger. Annual Reports, 1976–96. *World Military and Social Expenditures*. Washington: World Priorities.

Smith, William C. 1991. *Authoritarianism and the Crisis of the Argentine Political Economy*. Stanford, CA: Stanford University Press.

South East Europe Democracy Support. 2002. South East Europe Public Agenda Survey. April. Synopsis available on International Institute for Democracy and Electoral Assistance (IDEA) website (www.idea.int/about).

Spooner, Mary Helen. 1994. *Soldiers in a Narrow Land: The Pinochet Regime in Chile*. Los Angeles: University of California Press.

Stedman, S., D. Rothchild, and E. Cousens, eds. 2002. *Ending Civil Wars: The Implementation of Peace Agreements*. Boulder, CO: Lynne Rienner.

Stiglitz, Joseph E. 2002. *Globalization and Its Discontents*. New York: Norton.

Tabeau, Ewim, and Jakub Bijak. 1995. "War-Related Deaths in the 1992–1995 Armed Conflicts in Bosnia and Herzegovina: A Critique of Previous Estimates and Recent Results." *European Journal of Population* 21, (2–3): 187–213.

Taylor, Scott. 2003. *Spinning on the Axis of Evil: America's War against Iraq*. Ottawa: Esprit de Corps Books.

Tilly, Charles. 1985. "War Making and State Making as Organized Crimes." In *Bringing the State Back*, ed. Peter Evans, Dietrich Rueschemeyer, and Theda Skocpol, 169–91. New York: Cambridge University Press.

– 1992. *Coercion, Capital, and European States, AD 900–1992*. Rev. ed. Oxford: Blackwell.

Tin-bor Hui, Victoria. 2004. "Problematizing Sovereignty." In *International Intervention in the Post-Cold War World: Moral Responsibility and Power Politics*, ed. Michael C. Davis, Wolfgang Dietrich, Bettina Scholdan, and Dieter Sepp, 83–103. Armonk, NY: M.E. Sharpe.

Todd, Emmanuel. 2002. *After the Empire: The Breakdown of the American Order*. Trans. from French by C. Jon Delogu. New York: Columbia University Press.

Totten, Samuel, William S. Parsons, and Israel W. Carny, eds., 1997. *Century of Genocide*. New York: Garland.

Ullman, Richard H., ed., 1996. *The World and Yugoslavia's Wars*. New York: Council on Foreign Relations.

United Nations. Department of Economic and Social Affairs. Population Division. 2007. *World Population Prospects 2006 revision*. (www.un.org/esa/population/publicatons/wpp 2006).

United Nations Development Program (UNDP) 2007. "Small Rural Households in Serbia and Rural Non-farm Economy." Full report available at www.undp.org.yu.

United Nations General Assembly. 2003. "Situation of Human Rights in Cambodia." Report of the Special Representative for Human Rights in Cambodia, Peter Leuprecht, pursuant to General Assembly resolution 57/225, 58th session, Item 119(b) of the provisional agenda. A/58/317, 22 August.

– 2004. "Report of the Secretary-General on Khmer Rouge trials." Item 105(b) A/59/432, 12 October.

United Nations News Centre. 2007. "Bosnian Muslim Army Chief Facing Trial at UN war crimes tribunal," on UN News site: www.un.org/apps/news/story.asp?/NewsID=23172&Cr=icty&Crl= (8 September).

United Nations. *World Investment Report* (annual).

– 1994. *Secretary General Report to the Security Council* S/1994/300, 16 March.

- 1999a. *Report of the Independent Inquiry into the Actions of the United Nations during the 1994 Genocide in Rwanda.* 15 December. Full report can be visited at http://www.un.org/News/ossg/rwanda_report.htm.
- 1999b. *Report of the Secretary General Pursuant to General Assembly Resolution 32/35, "The Fall of Srebrenica,"* UN. Document A/54/549/15 November.

United Nations. Department of Public Information. N.d. The United Nations and the Situation in the Former Yugoslavia. Reference Paper Revision 4. New York: United Nations.

United Nations Development Program. Komisiyo y'lgihugu y'Ubumwe n'Ubwiynge (National Unity and Reconciliation Commission) 2001. *Programme and Three-Year Plan of Action: Final Report of the International Consultant.* Pearl Eliadis, consultant (for Rwanda). N.p.: UNDP.

United Nations Institute for Disarmament Research. 1996. *Managing Arms in Peace Processes: Croatia and Bosnia-Herzegovina.* Paper by Barbara Ekwall-Uebelhart and Andrei Raevsky. New York and Geneva: United Nations.

United Nations Security Council. 2001. *Addendum to the Report of the Panel of Experts on the Illegal Exploitation of Natural Resources and Other Forms of Wealth of DR Congo,* 13 November. Available at www.un.org/docs/sc/.

United Nations Security Council. 2005. "Bosnia and Hercegovina Ready to Enter 'Post-Dayton' Era Just 10 Years after Brutal War, High Representative Tells Security Council." Final Briefing of Paddy Ashdown. Security Council, 5306th meeting. New York: Department of Public Information, UN, SC/8558.

Urquhart, Brian. 1994. "Who Can Police the World?" *New York Review of Books,* 12 May, 29–34.
- 1996 "The Making of a Scapegoat," *New York Review of Books,* 12 August, 320–25.
- 2000. "In the Name of Humanity," *New York Review of Books,* 27 April, 19–22.

Uvin, Peter. 2004. *Human Rights and Development.* Bloomfield: Kumarian Press.
- N.d. "The Introduction of a Modernized Gacaca for Judging Suspects of Participation in the Genocide and the Massacres of 1994 in Rwanda: A Discussion Paper." Prepared for the Belgian Secretary of State for Development Cooperation. unpublished.

Vachon, Michelle. 2005. "Review of 'A Moment in Time,'" *Cambodian Daily,* 23–4 April.

Van Zyl, Paul, and Mark Freeman. 2002. "Conference Report." In *The Legacy of Abuse,* ed. Alice Henkin, 3–20. New York: New York University and School of Law and the Aspen Institute.

Vaughan, Diane. 1996. *The Challenger Launch Decision: Risky Technology, Culture, and Deviance at NASA.* Chicago: University of Chicago Press.

Vlajki, Emil. 1999. *The New Totalitarian Society and the Destruction of Yugoslavia*. New York: Legas.

Volcić, Zaia. 2005. "Belgrade vs. Serbia: Spatial Re-Configurations of Belonging. *Journal of Ethnic and Migration Studies* 31 (4): 639–58.

Weiss, Thomas G. 1996. "Collective Spinelessness: UN Actions in the Former Yugoslavia." In *The World and Yugoslavia's Wars*, 59–95. New York: Council on Foreign Relations.

– 1999. *Military Civilian Interactions: Intervening in Humanitarian Crises.* Lanham: Rowman and Littlefield.

Williams, Philip, and John T. Picarelli, 2005. "Combating Organized Crime in Armed Conflict." In *Profiting from Peace: Managing the Resource Dimensions of Civil War*, ed. Karen Ballentine and Heiko Nitzhke, 123–52. Boulder, CO: Lynne Rienner.

Woodward, Susan L. 1995. *Balkan Tragedy: Chaos and Dissolution after the Cold War.* Washington, DC: Brookings Institution.

World Bank. 2004. *Cambodia at the Crossroads.* (Report on the Government of Cambodia's "Rectangular Strategy for Growth, Employment, Equity and Efficiency in Cambodia" in preparation for Consultative Group Meeting 6–7 December). Available online at: www.worldbank.org/kh.

– 2006. *Cambodia Data Profile 2000–2005.* Available online at www.world bank.org/kh.

– 2007. *Cambodia: Halving Poverty by 2015? Poverty Assessment 2006.* Available online at: www.worldbank.org/kh.

World Fact Book 2007, published by Central Intelligence Agency on web (www.cia.gov/library/publications/the-world-factbook).

World Food Programme (June). 1999. *Rwanda: Displacement in the North-West (Ruhengeri and Gisenyi).* Rome. Available at www.wfp.org.

Zalaquett, José. 1992. "Balancing Ethical Imperatives and Political Constraints: The Dilemma of New Democracies Confronting Past Human Rights Abusers." *Hastings Law Journal* 43 (68): 1426–32.

– 2002. "The Pinochet Case: International and Domestic Repercussions." In *The Legacy of Abuse*, ed. Alice Henken, 47–70. New York: New York University and School of Law and the Aspen Institute.

PERIODICALS, MAGAZINES, AND NEWSPAPERS

Cambodia Daily
Globe and Mail (Canada)
Harpers
International Herald Tribune
Phnom Penh Post

Post Magazine (Hong Kong)
National Post (Canada)
New York Review of Books
New Yorker
New York Times
Walrus (Canada)

ONLINE NEWSLETTERS AND WEBSITES

Avocats san frontières
BostonGlobe
Documentation Center of Cambodia
Global IDP DataBase
Human Rights Watch
Integrated Regional Information Networks
International Center for Transitional Justice
International Court of Justice/World Court
International Crisis Group
International Criminal Tribunal for Yugoslavia
International Criminal Tribunal for Rwanda
Institute for the Study of Genocide
Office of the High Representative, Bosnia-Hercegovina
Royal Government of Cambodia, Khmer Rouge Trial Task Force, Chronology
Samngat KI (Khmer Intelligence)
PANA (Pan Africa)
United Nations, Investment Report

FILMS AND VIDEOS

Gacaca: Living Together in Rwanda
Hotel Rwanda
By the Pool in Kigali
No Man's Land
Welcome to Sarajevo

Index